THE
HISTORY
OF OUR

CUSTOMS,	NATIONAL
AIDS,	DEBTS,
SUBSIDIES,	And TAXES;

FROM

WILLIAM the CONQUEROR,

TO THE

PRESENT YEAR M,DCC,LXXIII.

By T. CUNNINGHAM, Esq.

The SECOND EDITION Corrected,

WITH

Several IMPROVEMENTS suggested by Sir CHARLES WHITWORTH, Chairman of the Committee of SUPPLY and WAYS and MEANS.

THE LAWBOOK EXCHANGE, LTD.
Clark, New Jersey
2006

ISBN-13: 978-1-58477-649-9
ISBN-10: 1-58477-649-8

Second printing 2007

Printed in the United States of America on acid-free paper

THE LAWBOOK EXCHANGE, LTD.
33 Terminal Avenue
Clark, New Jersey 07066-1321

Please see our website for a selection of our other publications and fine facsimile reprints of classic works of legal history:
www.lawbookexchange.com

Library of Congress Cataloging-in-Publication Data

Cunningham, Timothy, d. 1789.
The history of our customs aids subsidies national debts and taxes from William the Conqueror to the present year MDCCLXXIII / Timothy Cunningham.
p. cm.
Originally pub.: The history of the customs, aids, subsidies, national debts, and taxes, of England, from William the Conqueror to the present year, 1778. London, Printed for J. Johnson, 1778.
"Corrected with several improvements suggested by Sir Charles Whitworth, chairman of the Committee of Supply and Ways and Means."
Includes bibliographical references and index.
ISBN 1-58477-649-8 (alk. paper)
1. Taxation--Great Britain--Early works to 1800. 2. Finance--Great Britain--Early works to 1800. I. Cunningham, Timothy, d. 1789. History of the customs, aids, subsidies, national debts, and taxes, of England, from William the Conqueror to the present year, 1778. II. Title.
HJ2603.C9 2005
336.41'09'02--dc22

2005020374

THE HISTORY OF OUR

CUSTOMS,	NATIONAL
AIDS,	DEBTS,
SUBSIDIES,	And TAXES;

FROM

WILLIAM the CONQUEROR,

TO THE

PRESENT YEAR M,DCC,LXXIII.

By T. CUNNINGHAM, Esq.

The SECOND EDITION Corrected,

WITH

Several IMPROVEMENTS suggested by Sir CHARLES WHITWORTH, Chairman of the Committee of SUPPLY and WAYS and MEANS.

LONDON:
Printed for W. GRIFFIN, in Catharine-Street, Strand.
M,DCC,LXXIII.

THE

HISTORY

OF

TAXES, &c.

THE HISTORY OF

Taxes, Subsidies, National Debts, &c.

THOUGH by the Law of Nature all things were common, and all persons equal, there being neither *meum* nor *tuum*, king nor subject; yet, when this law came to be limited by the law of nations, and property came to be claimed, it naturally caused trade and commerce; whereupon sovereign princes became absolutely necessary to maintain and defend such property and commerce: and, in order to support them in their administrations of government, and to defray the expences which they must necessarily incur, in maintaining ambassadors at foreign courts, principally to procure justice to be done to merchants; their charges of procuring treaties with foreign princes for the advancement of trade, and of maintaining a navy for the defence of the merchants, by protecting them at sea from enemies and pirates, and also their charges in supporting a court of admiralty for the deciding of maritime causes; they seem originally to have taken subsidies, tributes, or customs, by virtue of the prerogative inherent to their crowns, as given to them by the law of nations, *quasi ministeriorum suorum stipendia*: which having been customary to have been paid time out of mind, were accounted as an estate of inheritance annexed to their crowns.

In England, whatever was given to the king by parliament, to assist him on extraordinary occasions, was called a *subsidy*. The money so given was *in* *subsid'um regis, an aid to the king*, the better to provide for the dignity of the crown, or the safety of the nation, in cases where the standing revenue was not sufficient. In the very early times of the constitution, there was no room for the demand of any subsidy; for, if we may believe Ordericus Vitalis *, fol. 523, the revenue of the Conqueror, arising from his demesnes and quit-rents, besides fines and other casual profits, amounted to 1061 pounds a day, paid in sterling money. But, though he may be mistaken as to the fact, that such large payments were made in ready money, yet it is certain, from Domes-day Book, that a multitude of rents were reserved, and paid to the king in money, notwithstanding the assertion of Gervase of Tilbury, in his Dialogue of the Exchequer, Book I, chap. 7, that the king's rents were paid in cattle and provisions till Henry the Second's time. But be this matter as it will, the income of the Crown was undoubtedly very great; because there were appropriated for the use of it, 1422 manors, besides other lands and quit-rents; and these lands, so registered in Domes-day Book, Sir Robert Cotton says, were such as the Confessor had been in possession of. If so, the lands accruing to the Crown from the forfeitures of those who had joined with Harold, must still have made a considerable addition to the Conqueror's power and revenue; and, we may imagine, the provisions he made for his dignity and necessary support, must have been exceedingly great; since it is somewhere said, that Hugh de Grant Maisnell, one of his great officers, had near eighty thousand pounds a year in those days.

As a great part of the lands in England was subject to knight-service †, the profits incident to this

* Ordericus Vitalis, Mon. Utic. Vix. an. 1141, edit. in Normanicis Duchesnii. Du Fresne.

† As all these old tenures are taken away by 12 Car. II, cap. 24, and the hereditary excise substituted in lieu of them, we thought it unnecessary to take up the reader's time with a full explanation of the nature of them.

tenure were very great; and the common aids to make the eldest son a knight, and to marry the eldest daughter, brought in a vast revenue. Besides these, if the tenure was *in capite*, that is, immediately from the king, the heir, after his full age, was to sue livery, that is, to pray to be admitted into possession of his lands, upon payment of half a year's profit of them; and, if he was of age at his father's death, then he was to pay *primier seisin*, which was one whole year's value of the land.

And, not only the knight-service lands paid the aids before-mentioned, but those held in socage paid them likewise, of common right, according to Lord Coke, 1 Inst. 91.

Here we see a vast income, and great dependences upon land. But, besides the regular profits arising from these tenures, the king, in cases of necessity, and for defence of the realm, could tax and tallage in a very extraordinary manner, all his towns and boroughs of antient demesne; for the tenure was considered to be of a base nature, and not much superior to that of villenage, with this difference only, that our old books call these tenants *villanos privilegiatos*. As to the fact, that great profit was made by such tallages, the reader is referred to Maddox's History of the Exchequer, where he will find abundant satisfaction.

Besides these, there were other prerogative profits; as strays, treasure-trove, wreck, waifs, amercements, tolls, forfeitures, and escheats; besides a multitude of fines of various sorts, for offences, for franchises, and for law proceedings; but we cannot think that our kings could formerly, as seems to be hinted by Mr. Maddox, arbitrarily refuse to grant the subject the benefit of their process, or deny or delay the execution of justice. And we think clearly, that the law in *Magna Charta* of *nulli negabimus*, *nulli vendemus*, *nec differemus justitiam*, was only declarative of, and to enforce the common law and the right of the subject. For, besides the antient coronation oath taken by our kings, by which they ſwore to do juſtice; it appears plainly, from the ſecond political law of King Edgar*, that if the party could not have juſtice in the lord's court, the hundred, or the county courts, (where all the property of the nation was formerly determined) he might then appeal to the king, who would do him juſtice. Indeed, he was to be fined for a falſe appeal, and to pay the king a ſum of money for his writ, which remains to this day for original writs; but ſtill he had a right to appeal; and to have that appeal received, and determined in a judicial way: though there was afterwards, in troubleſome times, much oppreſſion of the ſubject, on account of the money exacted for thoſe remedial writs. But a reaſonable fine might well have been authorized by parliament, (as moſt of the prerogatives of the crown were firſt given by conſent of parliament, if we may believe the Mirror of Juſtices, p. 3) not only to defray the expence the king was obliged to be at, for the maintenance of his court of juſtice, but perhaps to deter men from the proſecution of groundleſs and vexatious ſuits.

Another conſiderable article of the crown revenue, was the profits ariſing from the Jews. Our hiſtories are every where full of the great and extraordinary taxes and impoſitions laid on them: they were a conſtant fund for a neceſſitous court. Mr. Maddox has produced a multitude of the Exchequer records to evince this truth; but, as he has not given any reaſon for the exerciſe of this arbitrary power, but only taken notice of the fact that they were ſo taxed; and, as this conduct of our antient kings ſeems to have perplexed Lord Coke in ſome parts of his works; we ſhall beg leave to enquire into the grounds and reaſon of this behaviour; becauſe ſuch arbitrary and extraordinary methods are contrary to the analogy of our conſtitution in other reſpects.

Some think our kings had a right to uſe the Jews in what manner they pleaſed, and that their fortunes

* Wilk. Leg. Angl. 77.

and eſtates were abſolutely at the king's diſpoſal, and this by a grant from the legiſlature. For, it appears by the twenty-ninth law of the Confeſſor*, that the Jews were the abſolute property of the king. The words are *Judæi et omnia ſua ſunt regis; quod ſi quiſpiam detinuerit eos, vel pecuniam eorum, perquirat rex, ſi vult, tanquam ſuum proprium:* and the reader may ſee this law enforced among the ordinances of Henry the Second, and Richard the Firſt, concerning the Jews. He may likewiſe find a very memorable record in the firſt volume of Rymer's Collections, where Henry the Third mortgages, for five thouſand pounds, to his brother the earl of Cornwal, *omnes Judæos Regni Angliæ*, with a power of diſtraining the bodies of all or any of them, if the money was not paid at the times prefixed. The Jews were univerſally odious, not only from the difference of religion, but likewiſe from their exceſſive and imprudent uſury. Another reaſon of this univerſal deteſtation of them may be drawn from a paſſage in Mezeray's Hiſtory, who ſays, that the Jews invited the Caliph of the Saracens in the year 1009, to beſiege Jeruſalem and the Holy Sepulchre, which he accordingly did, and took it: and this fact falls in very well with the time of the Confeſſor's law before-mentioned.

We ſhall ſay little of the tax or tribute called Danegelt; becauſe the nature of it is very uncertain; and about which learned men have greatly differed. We refer the reader to Mr. Selden's Treatiſe *De Mari Clauſo*, where he will find it was of two ſorts; one, the money raiſed to bribe the Danes to leave England; and the other, for hiring a fleet from the Danes to defend the ſeas againſt the pirates. Both theſe were omitted to be raiſed by the Confeſſor: but the Conqueror, under the pretext of foreign invaſions, levied a moſt arbitrary and extravagant one of ſix ſhillings on every hide of land, by virtue of the ſuppoſed prerogative to collect Danegelt; which, in the firſt grant of it, in Ethelbert's time, was by par-

* Wilk. Leg. Angl. 203.

liament, according to Mr. Selden. But this method of raiſing money was entirely at an end in the time of Henry the Second; and ſo that branch of the revenue wholly cut off.

As to the firſt-fruits and tenths of eccleſiaſtical preferments, which are of modern date, being given by 26 Hen. VIII, cap. 3, to the crown, we ſhall likewiſe ſay but little of them. We ſhall only obſerve, that Clement the Fifth, or, as ſome ſay, Pope John the Twenty-ſecond, firſt reſerved the firſt-fruits of livings to himſelf; and that Gregory the Ninth, in the year 1229, was the firſt who demanded and received the tenths of the clergy; which we mention to correct a miſtake that is in the firſt volume of Roll's Reports, p. 473; where it is ſaid, that the Pope never had any tenths here till Edward the Firſt's time*; and that a regular taxation of all the benefices here, was then made upon that account. This was not any certain eſtabliſhed revenue to the popes, but was aſked by them according to the real or pretended exigencies of the church. And this tax was frequently levied on the clergy for the king's uſe, and ſometimes for the king's and the pope's jointly, that there might be leſs oppoſition to the grant or collection of it. The firſt grant by the pope of the tenths of the clergy to any of our kings, was that to Richard the Firſt, according to Sir Henry Spelman. And this tax, according to Matthew Paris, was only on the moveables, and differs from the preſent revenue, which affects the lands of the clergy. Theſe tenths and firſt-fruits, by the ſtatute of Hen. VIII. were to be collected by the biſhops; but they were diſcharged of this burden by 3 Geo. I, cap. 10; and the biſhops and archbiſhops were chargeable formerly with the

* "En temps Edw. I. le Pape eſcrie un letter al roy (que eſt "recorded en l'Exchequer en Fanſh. Office per que il requeſt le "roy, que puiſſoit eſtre un taxation de touts benefices (car devant "ceo le pape navoit icy aſcun diſmes) et que le roy averoit un "moitié ove lui, mes puis en proces de temps le pape, priſt tout "a luy meſme, et exclude le roy et ſes ſucceſſors."

collection of the subsidies granted by convocation, and were answerable for them in the Exchequer.

Prisage is an antient duty, payable at common law to the king, of two tons of wine of every ship laden with twenty tons, or more; one to be taken before, and the other behind the mast. Such wine may be tasted, and the fullest vessels may be taken for prisage; and so it was decreed in the Exchequer, in the year 1679, on a bill brought by the attorney-general, against Hart and Sir William Waller, defendants. If a ship has but ten tons, then only one ton is to be taken; and none, if there be but nine tons, unless there be evidence of fraud: but if there be nine and a half tons, that is fraud apparent to cheat the king, and then prisage of one ton shall be taken; and so it has been held in the Exchequer, as may be seen in Hardress's Reports, 477. Merchant strangers, the cinque-ports, and the citizens of London, are discharged from prisage; but then such citizens must be freemen and house-keepers, paying scot and lot, else they will not be entitled to this exemption, as appears from Hanger's case, reported by Moore 833, by Calthrope 24, and more fully in the third volume of Bulstrode's Reports, fol. 1. It may be further observed, that full prisage shall be paid on breaking of bulk; because prisage is not within the statutes of 28 Edw. III, cap. 13, and 20 Rich. II, cap. 4, as the customs are, which shall be paid only for what is entered. See Yelverton's Reports 200, and Hardress 362.

Butlerage is a duty of two shillings for every ton of wines imported by merchant-strangers only. It is called Butlerage, because it is paid to the king's chief butler. And, by 1 Hen. VIII, cap. 5, whoever makes false entries of wines to defraud the king of prisage and butlerage, is to forfeit double the value; which, by 2 and 3 Edw. VI, cap. 22, is enforced by the loss and forfeiture of all the offender's goods and chattels, provided the prosecution be within three years. A moiety of the forfeiture is to go to the king, and the other to the informer.

The customs are likewise said to be part of the inheritance of the crown at common law; that is, before any act of parliament was made concerning them. See Dyer's Reports 43, Davis's Reports 8. The same is said in Dyer 165, and in Coke's 12 Rep. 33, of the six shillings and eight-pence for every sack of wool *, and the like sum for every three hundred woolfels, and thirteen shillings and four-pence for every last of hides; a last containing twelve dozen, according to Sir Henry Spelman. This indeed is a mistake; for these particular sums were given to the king and his heirs by act of parliament †, 3 Edw. I. as appears from 2 Inst. 58, 59, and Vaughan's Reports 162. But, though the judges might be mistaken as to the fact, that those particular duties were the right of the crown at common law; yet they were right in asserting, that the customs, time out of mind, belonged to the crown; for that some duty was paid for wools and leather before that statute is evident; since it appears from the Red Book in the Exchequer, if we believe Lord Chief Justice Hale, that something was paid, though not that precise sum. If so, then Lord Vaughan might well have spared that unnecessary reflection upon the learning of the judges ‡,

* A sack contained twenty-six stone, and every stone fourteen pounds.

† The letters patent of Edw. I. recite, "Cum prælati, magnates, et tota communitas quandam novam consuetudinem nobis et hæredibus nostris de lanis, pellibus, et coriis, viz. de sacco lanæ dimid. marc. de 300 pellibus dimid. marc. et de lasto corii, 13s. 4d. &c."

‡ Upon a question, says Lord Vaughan, raised upon occasion of a new imposition laid by Queen Mary upon cloths; the judges being consulted about it, 1 Eliz. were of opinion (he cites Dyer, 165) that English merchants do not pay at common law any custom for any wares or merchandizes, but three; that is, wools, woolfells, and leather; that is to say, "Pro quolibet sacco lanæ continent. 26 pierres, et chescun pierres 14 pound, un demy marke; and for 300 woolfells, half a mark; and for a last of leather 13s. 4d. and that was equal to strangers and English

if his meaning be that no custom at all was paid before that statute. And besides, it appears from the 30th chapter of *Magna Charta*, that merchants were to come into this kingdom to buy and sell *per antiquas consuetudines*; which proves that some custom was paid: and, though Lord Vaughan lays great stress upon the statute of 3 Edw. I, that this grant on wools, woolfells, and leather, is called *quædam nova custuma*, and so wholly the creature of that act, we think the only inference to be justly drawn from it, is, that only the *quantum* of those customs was new: and that some duty was paid before, which was the old custom, in opposition to the new one then granted.

That this is no forced construction, will appear from the duties granted by the alien merchants, 31 Edw. I, called, *custuma nova*; not as if nothing had been ever paid by them; but only relatively, in opposition to the duty granted in the third of Edw. I; and so it was new in comparison of that. It is probable, that the customs, as well as prisage, were antiently given to the king, by act of parliament, for the support of the houshold*, and defraying the king's expence of providing proper accommodations for

"merchants. This was, continues Lord Vaughan, the opinion "of all the judges of the times: whence we may learn how fallible even the opinion of all the judges is, when the matter to be "solved must be cleared by searchers not common, and depends "not upon cases vulgarly known by readers of the Year-"books."

* By Stat. 25 Edw. I, cap. 6 (which is intitled, "The King "or his heirs will take no aid or prices, but by the consent of "the realm, and for the common profit thereof.") It is enacted as follows: Moreover, we have granted, for us and our heirs, as well to archbishops, bishops, abbots, priors, and other folk of holy church, as also to earls, barons, and to all the communalty of the land, that for no business from henceforth, we shall take such manner of aids, tasks, nor prices, but by the common assent of the realm, and for the common profit thereof, saving the antient aids and prices due and accustomed.—And, by 34 Ed. I, cap. 1, it is ordained, that the king, or his heirs, shall have no tallage or aid without the consent of parliament.

the merchants. And this ſuppoſition of the cuſtoms being granted by parliament, is agreeable to all the other parts of the conſtitution. Beſides, it is expreſsly declared, by 45 Edw. III, cap. 1, and 11 Rich. II, cap. 9, that no impoſitions ſhall be ſet on wools, woolfells, and leather, without conſent of parliament.

It is true our kings have, in fact, exerciſed this power of laying impoſts on merchandize; and ſome eminent lawyers have written in defence of this prerogative, as ſome learned judges have judicially maintained it: which the reader may ſee in Sir John Davis's Treatiſe of Impoſitions, and in Lane's Reports, fol. 22. But ſtill the commons have conſtantly proteſted againſt it, as appears from a multitude of the rolls of parliament; and ſuch practice hath been condemned by other judges of the greateſt authority and learning. Indeed Queen Mary, Queen Elizabeth, and King James the Firſt, did it; but as to the legality of it, we refer the reader to Lord Coke's ſecond Inſt. fol. 63, and 12 Rep. 33, and the ſtatute of tonnage and poundage, 12 Car. II, where this power ſo to charge merchandize, is altogether denied.

We are now come to the *cuſtuma nova*, or *cuſtuma parva*, petty cuſtom, or duty payable by merchant-ſtrangers, and begun in the time of K. Edw. I. (A. D. 1304.) when they granted him, that they would pay him and his heirs three-pence in the pound for all merchandizes exported and imported by them. And becauſe the charter, containing the above grant, is mentioned and referred to in the 12th rule, annexed to the book of rates in the ſtatute of tonnage and poundage (12 Car. II, cap. 4) and the curious reader may be deſirous to be acquainted with it, we ſhall here inſert a tranſlation of the Latin copy, tranſcribed by Mr. Prin, from the original record in the Tower.

For Merchant-ſtrangers concerning liberties granted to them.

THE king to his archbiſhops, *&c.* ſendeth greeting, concerning the good condition of all the merchants of the kingdoms, lands, and provinces underwritten; that is to ſay, Germany, France, Spain, Portugal, Navarre, Lombardy, Tuſcany, Provence, Catalonia, our dukedoms of Aquitain, Tholouſe, Turin, Flanders, Brabant, and all other lands and foreign places, by what name ſoever called, coming into our kingdom of England, and there remaining.

We being very ſolicitous out of our ſpecial care, that under our dominion, a freedom of tranquility and full ſecurity for the ſaid merchants may be provided for the future, ſo as they may the more readily apply themſelves to the ſervice of us, and of our kingdom, we graciouſly anſwering their petitions, and ordaining more amply for ſecuring their condition, in form following underwritten, are pleaſed to grant to the ſaid merchants for us, and our heirs for ever.

Imprimis, That is to ſay, that all merchants of the ſaid kingdoms and lands, may come from any other place ſafe and ſecure under our tuition and protection into our ſaid kingdom of England, and every where within our dominion, with their merchandizes of what ſort ſoever; and be unmoleſted and quiet concerning murage*, pontage†, and pavage‡: and that within our ſaid kingdom and dominion, they may traffic in the cities, boroughs, and market-towns, only in groſs, as well with natives, or inhabitants of this our kingdom and dominion aforeſaid, as with ſtrangers, foreign and domeſtic. But ſo as their wares, vulgarly called mercery, or the ſpecies thereof, they may ſell by retail, as formerly

* Repairing public walls. † Bridges. ‡ Pavements.

hath been accustomed: and, that all the said merchants may carry, or cause to be carried, whither they please, their merchandize, which they have brought into our said kingdom and dominion, or otherwise acquired, except to the lands of the manifest and notorious enemies of our kingdom, paying the customs which shall be due, wines only excepted, which shall not be exported out of our said kingdom or dominion, after they have been imported into our said kingdom or dominion, without our pleasure and especial licence, by any way or means whatsoever.

Item, That the said merchants may lodge in the cities, boroughs, and towns aforesaid, at their own pleasure, and there stay with their goods, to the content of them who entertain them.

Item, That every contract made by the said merchants, with what persons soever, and from what places soever, for what kind of merchandizes soever, shall be firm and stable; so that neither of the merchants shall depart from, or go back from, his bargain, after a God's penny is given and received between the principal persons contracting*; and, if it happen that a contention arise on the said contract, there shall be a trial, or inquisition, according to the usages and customs of the fairs and towns where such contract shall be made or begun.

Item, We promise to the aforesaid merchants and, for us and our heirs for ever, grant, that we, by no means whatsoever, will make, nor suffer to be made, any prize, or arrest, or detention, by occasion of prize, for the future, upon their said wares, merchandizes, or other their goods, by us, or by any other, or others, in any case and necessity whatsoever,

* *Denarius dei*, God's penny, or earnest money, given and received by the parties who contract. The earnest-money is called *denarius Dei*, or *God's penny*, because, in former times, the piece of money so given to bind the contract, was given to God; that is, to the church, or the poor.

againſt the will of the ſaid merchants, without the price preſently paid, for which the ſaid merchants might ſell to others, wares of the like ſort; or otherwiſe to ſatisfy them, ſo as they ſhall repute themſelves contented; and, that no appraiſement, or value ſhall be put upon the ſaid merchant's wares, merchandizes, or goods, by us or our miniſters.

Item, We will, that all bailiffs, and officers of fairs, cities, boroughs and market-towns, ſhall do ſpeedy juſtice to the ſaid merchants, complaining to them, from day to day, without delay, according to the merchant's law, concerning all and every thing which, by the ſaid law, may be determined. And, if any defect ſhall happen to be found in any of our bailiffs or miniſters, aforeſaid, whereby the ſaid merchants, or any of their factors, ſhall ſuffer loſs, although the merchant recover his loſſes againſt the party in the whole, yet nevertheleſs, the bailiff, or other miniſters, as the fault requires, ſhall be puniſhed at our ſuit; and, we grant the ſaid puniſhment in favour of the merchants aforeſaid, for compleating their right.

Item, That in all kinds of pleas, ſaving in the caſe of crime for which the pain of death is liable to be inflicted, where the merchant ſhall be impleaded, or he implead another, of whatſoever condition he that is impleaded be of, whether a foreigner or a domeſtic, in the ſaid fairs, cities, or boroughs, where there is a ſufficient plenty of merchants of the lands aforeſaid, and inquiſition there ought to be made; half of the inquiſition ſhall be of the ſaid foreign merchants, and the other half of honeſt and lawful men, where the plea happens to be: and, if a ſufficient number of the merchants of the ſaid lands ſhall not be found, let thoſe be put in the inquiſition who ſhall be found fit in that place, and let the reſidue be of other good and fit men, in the places in which that plaint ſhall be.

Item, We will, ordain and appoint, that in every market-town and fair of our ſaid kingdom, and elſewhere, within our dominion, our weight is to be put in a certain place; and before weighing thereof, the ſcale to be empty in the preſence of buyer and ſeller, and the arms thereof to be equal; and, when he hath ſet the ſcale equal, he is forthwith to take off his hands, ſo that it may remain equal; and that throughout our whole kingdom and dominion, there be one weight and meaſure, both of them ſealed with the ſign of our ſtandard; and that every one may have a ſcale of one quartern and under, where, contrary to the governor of the ſaid place, or liberty by us, or our anceſtors, it was not granted, or, contrary to the cuſtom of the villages and fairs hitherto obſerved.

Item, We will and grant, that ſome certain faithful, and diſcreet perſon, reſiding in London, may be appointed a juſtice in behalf of the before-mentioned merchants, before whom they may plead ſpecially, and more ſpeedily recover their debts, if the ſheriffs and mayors diſtribute not to them, day by day, compleat and ſpeedy juſtice, that then a commiſſion be granted to the aforeſaid merchants, beſides this preſent charter, viz. concerning thoſe (goods) which are to be conveyed between merchants and merchants, according to the merchants' law.

Item, We ordain and appoint, and our will and pleaſure is, for us and our heirs, that this ordinance and ſtatute be firmly kept for ever; notwithſtanding any liberty whatſoever, which we or our heirs for the future ſhall grant, the ſaid merchants ought not to loſe their above-written liberties, or any of them: and for and in conſideration of their obtaining the ſaid liberties and free uſages, and our priſes to be remitted to them*, all and ſingular the ſaid merchants'

* Tolls or duties.

for themſelves, and all others on their part, have heartily and unanimouſly granted to us, that for every hogſhead of wine which they ſhall bring in, or cauſe to be brought in, within our kingdom or dominion thereof, and from whence they are obliged to pay freight to the mariners, to pay to us and to our heirs, by the name of cuſtom, two ſhillings over and above the antient cuſtoms due, and accuſtomed to be paid in money, within forty days after the ſaid wines are put in ſtore out of the ſhips.

Item, For every ſack of wool, which the ſaid merchants, or others, in their names, do buy, and out of this kingdom, tranſport, or buy to tranſport, ſhall pay forty-pence over and above the antient cuſtom of half a mark, which formerly was paid. And, for a laſt of hides carried out of this our kingdom and dominion thereof, to be ſold, half a mark over and above that, which, according to antient cuſtom, was formerly paid; and likewiſe for three hundred wool-fells to be carried out of this kingdom, forty-pence, beſides that certain ſum, which, according to antient cuſtom, was formerly given.

Item, Two ſhillings for every ſcarlet, and cloth dyed in grain.

Item, Eighteen-pence for every cloth, in which part of a grain colour is intermixed.

Item, Twelve-pence for every other cloth without grain.

Item, Twelve-pence for every quintal of wax: and whereas ſome of the ſaid merchants deal in other commodities, as goods weighed with averdupois weights, and in other fine goods, as cloth of *tarſe*, of ſilk, of *candatis* *, of hair, and in divers other merchandizes, in horſes alſo, and other animals, corn, and other wares and merchandizes of different ſorts, which cannot eaſily be put to a certain rate of cuſtom; the ſaid merchants have conſented to

* It is probable it ſhould be *ſindonibus*, lawn, cambrick, or other fine linen.

give us and our heirs for every twenty ſhillings eſtimation and value of thoſe wares and merchandizes, by whatſoever name they be called, three-pence in the pound, upon the entrance of their ware and merchandizes, into our kingdom and dominion aforeſaid, within twenty days after ſuch wares and merchandizes ſhall be brought into our kingdom and dominion aforeſaid, and there ſhall be unladen or ſold; and likewiſe, three-pence for every twenty ſhillings, at the exporting of what kind ſoever of wares or merchandizes brought into our kingdom and dominion aforeſaid, beſides the antient cuſtoms formerly given to us, or to others.

And, over and above the value and eſtimation of the ſaid wares and merchandizes, for which three-pence for every twenty ſhillings, as aforeſaid, are to be paid, they are to have credit by letters, by them to be produced from their principals or partners; and, if they have none, let it be determined in this caſe, by the oaths of the ſaid merchants or, in their abſence, of their ſervants.

Moreover, it may be lawful for the ſociety of the merchants aforeſaid, to ſell wool to the fellows of the ſaid ſociety, and likewiſe to buy the ſame one of another within our kingdom and dominion, without payment of cuſtom: provided that the ſaid wool come not to ſuch hands, whereby we may be defrauded of our cuſtoms.

And furthermore be it known, that after the ſaid merchants have once, in any one place within our kingdom and dominion, paid our cuſtoms granted, as aforeſaid, to us, for their merchandizes, in form aforeſaid, and thereupon they have their warrant, they ſhall be free and unmoleſted in all other places within our kingdom and dominion, from payment of the ſaid cuſtom for the ſame commodities or merchandizes by the ſaid warrant, whether ſuch merchandizes remain within our kingdom and dominion, or are carried out, except wines, which, without our leave, or licence, as aforesaid, are by no means to be exported out of our kingdom.

We will also, and for us, and our heirs, grant, that no exaction, prize, or loan, or any other burden, shall be imposed in any part or measure, on the persons of the said merchants, their merchandizes or goods, contrary to the form before expressed and granted.

Witnesses hereto, the reverend fathers, Robert archbishop of Canterbury, primate of all England; Walter, bishop of Coventry and Litchfield; Henry de Lacy, earl of Lincoln; Humphrey de Bohun, earl of Hereford and Essex, and constable of England; Adomarus of Valentia, Galfrid of Geynvil; Hugh de le Spencer; Walter de Bello Campo, steward of our house; Robert of Bures, and others. Given by our hand at Westminster, the first day of February.

The funds before mentioned, were the principal sources of the income of our antient kings, and which had been more than sufficient to have answered all their expences, ordinary and extraordinary, if it had not been for the extravagance and superstition of some, and the unhappy arbitrary conduct of others, which occasioned those bloody and expensive civil-wars that make a considerable part of our history. There are few instances of taxes or subsidies till Richard the First's time. There were some *scutages*, or *escuages* raised in Henry the Second's time, as appears from the Red Book in the Exchequer; for, in the twelfth year of his reign, two-pence in the pound was given for the first year, and a penny in the pound for four years after, out of all rents and moveables, for defending the Holy Land: and, in the last year of his reign, there was a tenth of all moveables given for an expedition into the Holy Land.

When Richard the First came to the crown, there was in the Treasury nine hundred thousand pounds; and, in two years time, he raised eleven millions of marks; which may be computed at near eight millions ſterling: but notwithſtanding theſe vaſt ſums, and others ariſing by fines and compoſitions, he ſold a great part of his demeſnes.

He had ten ſhillings eſcuage for every knight's fee in his firſt year; and for his ranſom he had twenty ſhillings for every knight's fee, the fourth part of the rents of all huſbandmen; a fourth of the rents of ſome clerks, and a tenth of others; all the gold and ſilver which the churches had, and all the wool of the Ciſtertian monks.

For his expedition into Normandy, he had two ſhillings of every plough-land, and of the occupiers of every knight's fee a third part; though Henry the Firſt, by his charter, which is extant in the Red Book in the Exchequer, diſcharged the demeſnes of his tenants by knight's ſervice, that they might the better attend their duty in the wars: and in the year 1198, he had five ſhillings of every plough land.

Theſe taxes were ſo extraordinary, that they rouzed the jealouſy of the people in the ſucceeding reigns, as their patience and acquieſcence might probably put King John and Henry the Third upon making experiments of the like nature. But thoſe arbitrary taxes occaſioned the civil wars in thoſe kings reigns; and put the people upon aſſerting their rights and antient liberties; and probably alarmed the towns and boroughs to inſiſt upon their members being regularly ſummoned to parliament, the better to defend themſelves, and guard againſt all attempts upon their property. For, in King John's charter at Runnymead, it is enacted, that the boroughs ſhall have their antient liberties, and that a common council ſhould be ſummoned for the future to aſſeſs aids: which clauſe, though it be not in Henry the Third's Magna Charta, yet is in force, having been confirmed ſeveral times in Henry the Third's time, as appears from Matthew Paris's Hiſtory; who expreſsly ſays, Henry the Third's charter was the ſame with King John's; and therefore this clause must be necessarily implied to be within the law of *omnis civitas habeat libertates suas*, of which this of sending burgesses was one. And that the boroughs had such right to send their representatives, is evident even from the first writ of summons extant of the forty-ninth of Henry III, (*i. e. A. D.* 1265) published by Sir William Dugdale, which, by many learned men is reckoned to be the foundation and pretence of the commons' parliamentary right.

Those who assert the commons were then first summoned to parliament, ground themselves on this writ; because it is the first we have of this kind. But, considering the civil wars, the accidents, from time to time, and the wilful embezzling and destroying our old records, this is a very uncertain and fallacious way of reasoning. Besides, they differ among themselves in the reason and policy of this change in the constitution; some saying it was the act of the king to weaken the great lords, by bringing in an over-balance from the commons; and others assert it was the lords design to get a united interest, as a counterpoize against the encroachments and power of the crown. And the reasons given by both, may rather serve to shew neither are in the right, than to confirm the opinion advanced by each of them. For, not to insist upon the great likeness of our constitution to the old German, where the people always had a share in all consultations of great importance, and the same names and expressions used and applied by our records and historians to the commons, after they were confessedly a part of the legislature, as are given them in times wherein this right is disputed; that irresistible argument of the silence of our historians, in respect to so memorable a change in the constitution; the silence of Bracton, and all our old lawyers; which would be a very reprehensible negligence, if this alteration were then made; the prescriptive right of some boroughs to send members, and the prescriptive discharge of those of antient demesne, which were in being long before the Conqueror's time; we say, not to insist upon all these arguments, which singly ought to have great weight with every man who is a lover of liberty, we think it appears very plainly from the writ itself, that the commons had a right to be summoned to parliament. For the record says, "Writs shall be directed to London, York, &c. "and to the other boroughs." Does not this prove, that the boroughs were well known which should send burgesses, and that this practice had been long settled and established, and the method known and antient? Else how could the writ be executed? The instructions are general, that the proper boroughs make their returns; which plainly proves a clear, known, and established usage; and in which there could be no mistake, or disobedience to the writ. This seems a very clear argument of the commons old and undoubted right to be summoned to parliament.

The demesne lands of the crown, which, in antient times, as Sir Robert Cotton says, it was held impious to alienate, were from time to time much lessened and reduced; so that, in the twentieth of Edw. III, the revenue of the crown was but one hundred and fifty-four thousand, one hundred and thirty-nine pounds, seventeen shillings and five-pence, as appears from a pell of that king's reign; and this, by wars, and other ill management, was brought down, in 12 Hen. IV, to amount to no more than forty-eight thousand pounds, including the subsidy of wool, and the tenths of the clergy then granted.

When Henry the Fifth first designed and attempted the conquest of France, his income was but fifty-six thousand, nine hundred and sixty-six pounds, according to Sir Robert Cotton; and, in Henry the Sixth's time, it was sunk to five thousand pounds a year, till that notable resumption by parliament of all the crown lands made 28 Hen. VI, Rot. 53.

These ſeveral gradual deficiencies in the crown-revenue gave riſe to ſubſidies to aſſiſt the king on his various emergencies; and they were of different kinds.

In the 13th of Edw. III, Rot. 8, the lords gave to the king the tenth ſheaf of all the corn of their demeſnes, the tenth fleece of wool, and the tenth lamb; but the commons would only grant upon condition of redreſſing their grievances.

By 17 Edw. III, Rot. 17, the king was to have a ſubſidy of forty ſhillings for every ſack of wool over and above the old cuſtoms.

By 45 Edw. III, Rot. 10, the ſum of two and twenty ſhillings and three-pence was granted on every pariſh, to make up the ſum of fifty thouſand pounds. But that being found to be greatly deficient, they laid five pounds ſixteen on every pariſh, including the twenty-two ſhillings and three-pence.

In the 51ſt of Edw. III. Rot. 19, the lords and commons granted a ſubſidy by way of poll-tax of four-pence on every man and woman above the age of fourteen.

In the 21ſt of Rich. II, Rot. 75, a ſubſidy on the ſtaple commodities was granted to the king for life.

In the 9th of Hen. VI, Rot. 15, twenty ſhillings of every knight's fee is granted, and twenty ſhillings of every pound value in land.

By 14 Hen. VI, Rot. 12, two ſhillings and ſix-pence in the pound is granted to be paid by every one, who has above five pounds a year in lands, annuities, or offices.

By 18 Hen. VI, Rot. 14, a ſubſidy, by way of poll-tax, is granted on aliens only; ſixteen-pence on every houſe-keeper, and ſix-pence on others.

In the 32d of Hen. VIII, ch. 50, (*Raſtal*) there were four fifteenths and tenths granted, and two ſubſidies of twelve-pence in the pound on lands; and by aliens who had lands in truſt, two ſhillings were to be paid for every pound: this of aliens is mentioned to shew how the land was held formerly; it being since resolved, in favour of the crown, that the king may have the benefit of such trust, by the decree of a court of equity, as appears from Allen's Reports, fol. 14.

In the year 1641, monthly assessments on lands were introduced; and in 2 Will. and Mar. the pound-rate on lands came in. But of late, this tax on lands is called *an aid*, and is so distinguished.

The principal and chief way of supplying the king, was by the grant of fifteenths, of which Lord Coke, in his 2d Inst. page 77, gives the following account: *viz.* "For this gift and grant by the king, "of the liberties contained in this great charter, "(*Magna Charta*, chap. 38,) and of others con-"tained in the king's charter of liberties of the "forest, the archbishops, bishops, abbots, priors, "earls, barons, knights, freeholders, and other the "king's subjects, citizens, and burgesses, assembled "in parliament, gave unto the king one fifteenth; "which proveth, that, as the fifteenth was granted "by parliament, so was this great charter also "granted by authority of the same; but since this "time, the manner of the fifteenth is altered; for, "now the fifteenth, which is also called the *task*, "is not originally set upon the polls, as at this "time it was, but now the fifteenth is certainly rated "upon every town. And this was by virtue of the "king's commissions into every county of England. "In 8 Edw. III *, taxations were made of all the "cities, boroughs, and towns in England, and re-"corded in the Exchequer, and that rate was at "that time the fifteenth part of the value of every "town, and therefore retaineth the name of the "fifteenth still. And, after the fifteenth is granted "by parliament, then the inhabitants rate them-"selves for payment thereof; and, if one town be

*Rot. pat. 6 Edw. III, 2 part, nu. 26.

"joined with another in the rate of the total, and "subdivided on each a certain rate in that com- "mission, and the one is rated too low, and the "other too high, there lieth a writ called, *ad æqua- "liter taxand.* to be taken out of the Exchequer to "rate the towns equally. The subsidy is uncertain, "because it is set upon the person, in respect of his "lands or goods, which commonly do ebb and "flow."

The fifteenth, Lord Coke, in his 4th Inst. p. 33, says amounted to twenty nine thousand pounds, and the subsidy to seventy thousand pounds. But, for the greater part of Queen Elizabeth's time, the subsidy came to one hundred thousand pounds, by the diligence and care of the commissioners appointed by her.

The method of collecting these fifteenths and subsidies was, by commission from the king to two persons who had power to nominate *clericum unum*, to act with them; and these chief taxors were in each county to call before them a sufficient number of the best men of every city and town, out of whom they were to choose four or six at their discretion, and to swear them to make true enquiry what goods each person was possessed of, and to make indentures of the same; one to be delivered to the chief taxors, and the other was to be kept by themselves. And the taxors were to take care to make a true return: and the taxing of the taxors themselves was reserved to the treasurer and the barons of the Exchequer. And the earls, barons, and knights of the shire, with the freeholders in each county, were by writ directed to them to be assistant to the taxors.

This was the form observed, as appears from the records of the Lord-treasurer's Remembrancer, in the 34th of Edw. I, Rot. 47; 7 Edw. II, Pat. Rot. Mem. 3. So Pat. Rot. 3 Edw. III, part 3, Mem. 18; and from the Pat. Rot. 6 Edw. III, part 3, Mem. 19.

Lord Coke indeed, in his 4th Inſt. 34, and in 2 Inſt. 77, (ſee page 22) ſays, that there was a more exact taxation made in 8 Edw. III, which being returned into the Exchequer, was made the rule and ſtandard ever after. He does not cite any authority, but refers in the margin to the 6th Edw. III, part 2, num. 26. But there was no ſuch taxation that we can find in the 8th of Edw. III, among the records of the Lord-treaſurer's Remembrancer; nor indeed can we find from Sir Robert Cotton's Abridgment of the Rolls of Parliament of that Year, (for the rolls themſelves have been ſince deſtroyed or loſt) that any aid was granted that year; though there is a writ of ſummons in Rymer and Sir William Dugdale for that purpoſe. But we think Lord Coke grounded himſelf on the Year-Book of 11 Hen. IV, 35, where it is ſaid, that the fifteenth granted 6 Edw. III, being tortiouſly levied, a commiſſion iſſued, 8 Edw. III, (probably the writ, *ad æqualiter taxand.* mentioned by Lord Coke, 2 Inſt. 77, ſee p. 23) for the county of Somerſet, where the cauſe of action aroſe, to make a juſter aſſeſſment. Nothing is ſaid in that book, but that this might, and did, extend only to Somerſetſhire: and that this taxation was made all over England, we take to be Lord Coke's own inference; for there is nothing of it in the book; nor is there any record of that year among Mr. Petyt's Collections, which are in the Inner Temple library; as there are likewiſe many of the forms of taxations in the time of Edw. II, and Edw. III, particularly that of 6 Edw. III, referred to by him in the margin. So that we think Lord Coke was miſtaken; and his miſtake hath miſled ſome other judges of great abilities and learning.

The clergy too uſed to ſupply the king, by granting him a tenth, which Brooke ſays in his Abridgement, title Quinzime 9, was to be levied of their lands. Sometimes the clergy of themſelves would give the king money; and what the archbishops proposed was generally assented to by the lower clergy; and the abbots and bishops voluntarily gave what they thought fit. But the most usual way was for the pope to tax them, till Edward the first, in the twenty-third year of his reign, summoned them to parliament by the *præmunientes* clause; which course, with some interruptions, continued till the middle of Henry the Sixth's time; and then that method of meeting in a parliamentary convention was omitted, and they were afterwards summoned only as a convocation, where they granted their money. The sum agreed on by the lower clergy was presented to the prelates, and they carried it to the archbishop, and being confirmed by him, the parliament, since the 32d of Hen. VIII. have interposed, and given their grants a full and more authoritative sanction. Each bishop was, as before mentioned, liable to the collection of the money so granted; and this method continued till the year 1664.

Indeed, Mr Petyt, in his Treatise of the Commons Right, page 145, says the bishops were discharged of this trouble in Queen Elizabeth's time; but there is nothing of it in the acts of parliament of the first and thirteenth of her reign, for that purpose.

It is said, in Lane's Reports, p. 51, that the successor of a bishop shall not be charged for the deficiencies and arrears of a subsidy incurred in the predecessor's life-time; but only his heir or executor. See Moor's Reports, p. 17. For the antient method of granting and collecting these tenths, see Clau. Rot. Dorso, 7 Edw. II, Mem. 3, among the Records of the Lord-Treasurer's Remembrancer, and 32 Hen. VIII, chap. 22, 23, in Rastal's Statutes.

Another way of supplying the crown, was by granting the subsidies of tonnage and poundage; the foundation of which was the guarding of the seas, that merchants might trade hither with safety; and this has been constantly made the consideration of granting such subsidies. The Saxon laws put a merchant, who had crossed the seas thrice at his own expence, upon the foot and degree of a Thane; that is, a baron, or nobleman.

The old fund, or tax, to secure the seas from pirates, was that called Danegelt, mentioned before. But, in 21 Edw. III, the merchants having been robbed and murdered, there was an ordinance made by the king and peers, that two shillings should be taken of every ton of wine, and six pence of all goods imported. But this was complained of by the commons as a violation of the law, Rot. 11; and this, it seems, was the beginning of tonnage and poundage.

In 46 Edw. III, Rot. 15, we find the citizens and burgesses, after the knights of the shire were gone home, granted the like sum on the application of the prince to them. But the first legal grant of it that we can find, was in 47 Edw. III, Rot. 12, when two shillings a ton was granted on wine, and six-pence in the pound on all merchandize coming into the realm, or going out; as was the old parliamentary stile. This serves to correct a passage in Sir John Davis's Reports, p. 11, where he says, tonnage was first granted in the 5th of Richard the Second.

The next grant was that of poundage only, in 2 Rich. II, Rot. 29 and 30, part 1; being six-pence in the pound on all merchandize. At the same time the parliament granted a subsidy on the staple commodities.

In 5 Rich. II, chap. 3, two shillings tonnage, and six-pence poundage, were granted.

In 7 Rich. II, Rot. 13, there were two shillings tonnage, and six-pence in the pound granted.

In 13 Rich. II, Rot. 20, three shillings tonnage, and six-pence poundage.

In 17 Rich. II, Rot. 12, there were three shillings tonnage, and twelve-pence poundage.

In 2 Hen. IV, Rot. 9, there was only seven-pence poundage, and two shillings tonnage.

In 4 Hen. IV, Rot. 28, there was twelve-pence poundage, and three shillings tonnage.

The like sum was granted, 6 Hen. IV, Rot 9; and the same sum was given, 1 Hen. V, Rot. 17.

Lord Coke says, that in 3 Hen. V, tonnage and poundage was first granted to Hen. V, for life; and he refers to the 50th Roll of that year. This he takes notice of in three different places in his works; and particularly observes, that this was the first leading grant of this kind; as the reader may see in 12 Rep. 34, 2 Inst. 61, and 4 Inst. 32. But the number of the Roll is mistaken, or misprinted: for there are but sixteen Rolls in the first part of that year, and but forty-nine in the second; but it is in the first part of the Rolls of that year, Rot. 5. This will serve to correct a mistake of Sir John Davis, and some others of our eminent lawyers, who affirm, that tonnage and poundage was first granted to Hen. VI, for life, in 31 Hen. VI, Rot. 8. And this became a precedent for the demands of all our succeeding princes.

Edward the Fourth, in the fourth year of his reign, had it for his life, Rot. 24; so had Henry the Seventh, Henry the Eighth, Edward the Sixth, Queen Mary, Queen Elizabeth, and King James the first. But Charles the First, unhappily relying on his prerogative, as if tonnage and poundage were the right of the crown, ordered these duties to be collected without a previous grant from the legislature: and this, among other things, created great jealousies and uneasiness between him and his parliaments; so that he had only occasional and temporary grants of tonnage and poundage. It would be unnecessary to set forth every minute difference, that appears in the grants of these duties by parliament. In many of them there is an exception for the king's prisage wines, that they shall not pay the tonnage duty. But this was unnecessary (unless it were for the benefit of the king's patentee) because the king cannot pay duty to himself. For, though the king has paid custom for his wine ever ſince King William's time, yet that is only curteſy, and he is no ways obliged to do it; as was reſolved in the Exchequer, in the caſe of one Robinſon, upon a ſeizure made on purpoſe to conteſt that matter. Some of theſe old acts have a great affinity with the 12th of Charles II; as 9 Hen. VI, Rot. 15, and 4 Edw. IV, Rot. 24.

We are now come to the great ſtatute of 12 Car. II, chap 4, called, *the ſubſidy of tonnage and poundage*; which is the foundation of the preſent cuſtoms. Theſe duties have been conſiderably increaſed by later ſtatutes, and are diſtinguiſhed by different names; to denote either the quantity or quality of them, or the time when they were granted. The duties granted on merchandize by the twelfth of Charles the Second, are by ſome called, in a more reſtrained ſenſe, *the old ſubſidy*, or *cuſtoms*. Others are known by the name of the *new ſubſidy*, one third ſubſidy, two-third ſubſidy, petty cuſtoms, or alien's duty, old and new impoſts, new duties, and additional duties. But they all ſignify only certain charges on goods imported.

The ſubſidy of tonnage and poundage, which is divided into ſubſidy inwards, and ſubſidy outwards, was granted to Charles the Second for his life; and afterwards to King James for his life. At the Revolution, it was granted to King William only for years; and ſo continued till the 6th of Queen Anne, when half of the cuſtoms inwards was granted to the year 1808; and, by 1 Geo. I, ch. 12, was granted to the king and his heirs for ever. And the other half, by 7 Ann. ch. 7, ſect. 28, was likewiſe granted to the queen, and her heirs for ever. The ſubſidy outwards, by 9 Ann. chap. 6, was granted for thirty-two years; and, by 3 Geo. I, ch. 7, was made perpetual. By an account delivered into parliament, the firſt ſeſſion after the Revolution, this tax brought in, on a medium of four years, 577, 507l. 12 s. 10 d. ½; but, according to Dr. Davenant, it brought in 600,000l. free of all charges and deductions.

The excise called *the temporary excise*, was granted to King Charles the Second during his life; from whose death it has been continued, by several acts of parliament, and now (by 1 Geo. III, cap. 1) stands continued to his present majesty for his life.

The excise called *the hereditary excise*, was granted to King Charles the Second, his heirs and successors for ever, in recompence for the profits of the court of wards, purveyance, and the tenures by knight-service, &c. then abolished by act of parliament. These two excises, according to the above-mentioned account, produced at a medium of four years, 610,486 *l.* 10 *s.* 9 *d*; but according to Dr. Davennant, they were computed at 666,383 *l.* clear. A tax of two shillings upon every fire-hearth, &c. and therefore called *the hearth money*, was granted to King Charles the Second, his heirs and successors for ever; which, according to the said account, produced about 200,000l. but, according to the Doctor, 245,000 *l.*

The revenue of the Post-Office, or tax upon letters sent by the post, was granted to King Charles the Second, his heirs and successors for ever; which, by the above account, produced fifty-five thousand pounds; but, according to the Doctor, sixty-five thousand pounds; and this revenue hath been since increased, by an additional tax upon letters, as well as by a more regular and strict collection.

An imposition upon wines and vinegar was granted to King James the Second, from the 24th of June, 1685, the 24th of June, 1693, towards repairing the Navy, which, by both the above accounts, produced 172,900*l.* 11 *s.* 8 *d.*½; and which, having been made good by new duties, hath been suffered to expire. An imposition upon tobacco and sugar was granted for the same time; which, by the said accounts, produced 184,861 *l.* 8 *s.* but it hath been suffered to expire.

An imposition on French linens, brandies, &c. was granted from July 1, 1685, to July 1, 1690;

which, according to the ſaid accounts, produced 93,710*l.* 8*s.* 1*d.* and was likewiſe ſuffered to expire.

Theſe, with ſeveral other ſmall branches, not worth particularizing, were all the taxes we were ſubject to at the time of the Revolution; which, at the higheſt computaion, produced but 2,061,856*l.* 7 *s.* 9 *d.* ½: and yet, with this revenue, King James the Second ſupported his civil liſt, kept a formidable navy ready to put to ſea, an army of near thirty thouſand men at land, and ſaved money yearly, if we can credit an account of the iſſues of his revenue given into parliament, which amounted to no more at a medium, than 1,609,365 *l.* 2 *s.* 9 *d.*

At the time of the Revolution, there were no national debts, properly ſo called. There was indeed a debt of ſixty thouſand pounds due to the ſervants of King Charles the Second, which his ſucceſſor neglected to pay; and the payment of it was provided for by an act of the firſt ſeſſion after the Revolution. As to the debt called *the banker's debt*, though charged by letters patent from King Charles the Second upon the hereditary exciſe, no proviſion was made by parliament for its payment, until the 12th of King William, when it was enacted by parliament, that, in diſcharge of certain annual perpetual payments and arrears thereof, granted by King Charles the Second to ſeveral patentees, out of the hereditary exciſe, the ſame exciſe ſhould, from the 26th of December, 1705, ſtand charged for ever with the payment of three pounds *per annum*, for the principal ſums of the owners, their heirs and aſſigns for ever, nevertheleſs redeemable upon payment of a moiety of the principal ſums; by which means the nation became charged with a debt of 664,268 *l.* being the moiety of 1,328,526 *l.* which theſe principal ſums amounted to; and which is the only debt we are now charged with, that had any part of its riſe before the Revolution.

Thus our national affairs, as to *debts* and *taxes*, stood at the time of the Revolution, the 5th of November 1688; and the convention, which declared the prince and princess of Orange, king and queen of this kingdom, made no alteration: but soon after that Convention had created a parliament (that is to say, had declared themselves the parliament *) they passed the following acts, relating to the public revenue.

AN act for granting a present aid to their majesties, for the extraordinary occasions which oblige them to a great and present expence. 1 Will. & Mary, sess. 1. chap. 1.

By this act there was to be raised, within six months, from the 25th of March 1689, the sum of 412,925*l.* 14*s.* 6*d.* by a monthly assessment of 68,820*l.* 19*s.* 1*d.* to be paid quarterly by the several counties, according to the proportions in the act mentioned †.

* In the quarto edition of the Statutes, this parliament is said to have begun the 13th of February, 1688: in the former editions, it is the 23d. It appears, from the Journals of the House of Commons, that the house met the 22d of January, and chose a Speaker, &c. and that on the 13th of February, the prince and princess of Orange were proclaimed king and queen.

† The proportions were as follow:

	l.	*s.*	*d.*
For the county of Bedford	896	17	9
Berks	1132	6	7
Bucks	1315	6	5
Cambridge	1020	0	0
The isle of Ely	349	17	11
The county of Chester	747	17	2
The city and county of the city of Chester	53	8	4
The county of Cornwall	1540	18	3
Cumberland	168	6	1
Derby	862	8	4
Devon	3229	19	2
The city and county of the city of Exon	116	7	4

1 Will. & Mary, seff. 1. 1688. chap. 3.

The commiffioners appointed by this act fhall have, and execute the like powers and authorities, rules and directions, touching the better

	l.	s.	d.
Dorfet	1344	10	5
The town and county of Poole	10	19	8
The county of Durham	323	16	9
The county of York; with the city and county of the city of York, and town and county of Kingfton upon Hull	3469	5	2
The county of Effex	3098	8	10
The county of Gloucefter	1808	10	3
The city and county of the city of Gloucefter	39	8	0
The county of Hereford	1131	13	4
Hertford	1345	16	3
Huntingdon	633	14	2
Kent, with the city and county of the city of Canterbury	3326	18	8
Lancafter	1006	13	6
Leicefter	1084	14	3
Lincoln, with the city and county of the city of Lincoln	2570	2	0
London, with the liberty of St. Martin's le-grand	4291	11	4
Middlefex, with the city and liberty of Weftminfter	3040	10	0
Monmouth	390	0	0
Northampton	1413	18	2
Nottingham, with the town and county of the town of Nottingham	873	8	0
Norfolk	3373	12	0
City and county of the city of Norwich	180	0	0
Northumberland, with the towns of Newcaftle and Berwick upon Tweed	372	15	8
The county of Oxon	1135	10	8
Rutland	240	8	11
Salop	1203	14	2
Stafford	852	11	8
The city and county of the city of Litchfield	13	0	0
The county of Somerfet	2771	10	0
The city and county of the city of Briftol	199	8	4

affeffing, diftributing, collecting, levying, receiving, and paying the faid feveral fums of 68,820*l.* 19*s.* 1*d.* as are limited, enacted, directed, and appointed, to the commiffioners in 29 Car. II, intitled, An act for raifing the fum of five hundred *, eighty-four thoufand, nine hundred and feventy-eight pounds, two fhillings, and two-pence halfpenny, for the fpeedy building thirty fhips of war.

1 Will. & Mary, feff. 1, 1688, chap. 3.

The county of Southampton, and the Ifle of Wight	2189	8	8
Suffolk	3298	10	8
Surry, with the borough of Southwark	1597	0	2
Suffex	1821	7	9
Warwick, with the city and county of the city of Coventry	1192	8	9
Worcefter	1053	19	0
City and county of the city of Worcefter	55	9	6
County of Wilts	1966	17	7
Weftmoreland	116	0	0
County of Anglefea	125	13	8
Brecknock	282	10	5
Cardigan	105	15	0
Carmarthen	272	6	8
Carnarvon	146	12	2
Denbigh	223	10	7
Flint	118	17	4
Glamorgan	378	17	10
Merioneth	100	16	1
Montgomery	276	12	2
Pembroke	326	10	0
Radnor	174	6	8
The town and county of Haverford-weft	15	3	5

* The fum charged on each county, by 29 Car. II, is exactly one half of what is laid thereon by the prefent act; and was affeffed by a pound rate, upon all lands, tenements, hereditaments, annuities, rents, parks, warrens, goods, chattels, ftock, merchandizes, offices (other than military offices, and offices relating to the navy, and offices within his majefty's houfhold) tolls, profits, and all other eftates, both real and perfonal.—Receiver-general to have two-pence, collectors four-pence, and commiffioners' clerks one penny in the pound.—Collectors to levy the fum affeffed by dif-

1 Will. & Mary, seff. 1, 1688, chap. 3. The fum borrowed upon the credit of this act, as appears from fect. 20, thereof, was 370,000*l.* at 6 *per cent. per ann.* until the principal fhould be paid; but the real produce, according to an account delivered into the Houfe of Commons, by the commiffioners of accounts in the year 1697, and publifhed by the Houfe of Lords in 1702, was 400,875*l.* 11*s.*

chap. 10. *An act for taking away the revenue arifing by hearth-money.*

This was a tax of two fhillings upon every fire-hearth, &c. and therefore called hearth-money, firft granted to King Charles the Second, his heirs and fucceffors for ever; which, according to an account delivered into parliament the firft feffion after the Revolution, produced about 200,000*l.* but, according to Dr. Davenant, 245,000*l.* But, as this tax had been confidered as a grievance in that and the following reign, it was taken away by the above act; the preamble to which is in the following words:

"WHEREAS his majefty having been informed, that the revenue of the hearth-money was grievous to the people, was pleafed by his gracious meffage fent to the Commons affembled in parliament, to fignify his pleafure, either to agree to a regulation of it, or to the taking it wholly away, as fhould be thought

trefs, and to break open any cheft, trunk, box, or other things, &c.—Tenants bound to pay, and landlord obliged to allow fuch payment.—All fee-farm rents, and all other manner of rents, payments, fums of money, annuities, iffuing out of any land within city or county, fhall be liable, &c. Woodlands affeffed, may be cut down for payment; tithes, tolls, profits of markets, fairs, or fifhery, or other annual profits, not diftrainable, may be fold, &c.—Two or three inhabitants to afcertain, and rate the yearly value and profits of all offices belonging to the courts at Weftminfter.

convenient by the said Commons: AND 1 Will.
WHEREAS, upon mature deliberation, the said & Mary,
Commons do find, that the said revenue cannot sess. 1,
be regulated, but that it will occasion many 1688,
difficulties and questions; and that it is, in itself, chap. 10.
not only a great oppression to the poorer sort, but a badge of slavery upon the whole people; exposing every man's house to be entered into, and searched at pleasure, by persons unknown to him: We, your majesties most dutiful and loyal subjects the Commons, being filled with a most humble and grateful sense of your majesties unparallelled grace and favour to your people, not only by restoring their rights and liberties, which have been invaded contrary to law, but in desiring to make them happy and at ease, by taking away such burdens as by law were fixed upon them, by which your majesty will erect a lasting monument of your goodness in every house in the kingdom, &c."

*An act for raising money by a poll towards the reducing of Ireland**. chap. 13.

The sum borrowed upon this act, as appears from sect. 25, thereof, was 300,000 *l.* at

* All persons, bodies politic and corporate, guilds, or fraternities, for every hundred pounds in debts and ready money were to pay ten shillings.

Every person having any office, place, or public employment, to pay three shillings in the pound.

All judges, serjeants at law, barristers, attorneys, sollicitors and scriveners, advocates, proctors, and public notaries, and all persons practising physic, to pay three shillings in the pound.

Servants, having above three pounds a year, to pay one shilling in the pound; and having three pounds, or under, to pay six-pence in the pound.

A duke to pay fifty pounds; a marquis, forty pounds; an earl, thirty pounds, a viscount, twenty-five pounds; a baron, twenty pounds; the eldest son of a duke, to pay thirty pounds; the younger son, twenty-five pounds; the eldest son of a marquis, twenty-five pounds; the younger, twenty pounds; the eldest son of an earl, twenty pounds;

1 Will. & Mary, seff. 1, 1688, 7 *per cent*; but, by the account above referred to, it appeared that the real produce was 287,904*l*. 1*s*. 11*d*. ½.

chap. 14. *An act for preventing doubts and questions concerning the collecting the public revenue.*

BY this act, all revenues whatsoever, except the duties arising by fire-hearths and stoves [taken away by chap. 10. above.] other than such as are, or shall be incurred, at or before the 25th of March, 1689, granted to either King Charles the Second, or King James the Second; which had continuance on the 5th of

the younger, fifteen pounds; the eldest son of a viscount, 17 s. 10 d. the younger son, 13 l. 6 s. 8 d. the eldest son of a baron, fifteen pounds; the younger son, twelve pounds; a baronet to pay fifteen pounds; a knight of the Bath, fifteen pounds; knight batchellor, ten pounds; every king's serjeant at law, twenty pounds; and every other serjeant, fifteen pounds; every person of the degree of an esquire, or so reputed, or owning or writing himself such, five pounds; every gentleman, or reputed gentleman, or owning, or writing himself such, twenty shillings; every widow shall pay the third part rated by this act, on that degree, of which the husband of such wife was in his life-time.

An archbishop was to pay fifty pounds; a bishop twenty pounds; a dean of any cathedral, or collegiate church, shall pay ten pounds; an archdeacon fifty pounds; a canon or prebendary fifty pounds; a doctor of divinity, law, or physic, five pounds; every person holding two or more benefices, worth one hundred and twenty pounds yearly, five pounds.

Every merchant, trading in the port of London, was to pay ten pounds; and every merchant, or other person using any trade, or manual occupation, and holding a house of thirty pounds *per annum*, in London, or within twenty miles of it, ten shillings; every member of the East-India company was to pay forty shillings for every hundred pounds stock; every member of the Guinea company, the like sum; and every member of the Hudson's bay company, the same; every merchant-stranger and Jew, to pay ten pounds; every person having a share in the New River, to pay two shillings for every twenty shillings.

November, 1688; and all arrears of the same shall be paid to their majesties, until the 25th of December, 1689. 1 Will. & Mary, seff. 1689, chap. 14.

These revenues, according to the account before referred to, produced, from the 5th of November, 1688, to the 30th of June, 1690, the sum of * 1,437,646 *l.* 1 *s*; the proportional part of which, from the 5th of November, 1688, until the 25th of December, 1689, or until the next session of parliament, may, without entering minutely into fractions, be computed at about 900,000 *l.*

An act for a grant to their majesties of an aid of twelve pence in the pound for one year for the necessary defence of their realms. Chap. 20.

THIS aid was raised on all personal estates (which, as appears from sect. 2, of the act, paid

* The particulars of this sum are as follow:

				l.	*s.*	*d.*
The customs, to wit, the subsidy of tonnage and poundage	422,837	0	4½			
Loans thereupon, over and above 500,000 l. credit, by 2 Will. and Mary, seff. 1, chap. 4.	47,223	13	4½	470,060	13	9
The hereditary and temporary excise	541,191	11	4½			
Loans thereupon, over and above 250,000 l. credit, by 2 Will. and Mary. seff. 1. c. 3	301,633	7	3	842,824	18	7½
The letter-money	—	—		56,279	3	5
The small branches and casualties	67,181	5	2½			
Loans thereupon, to wit on the revenue of Cornwall —	1,300	0	0	68,481	5	2½
				1,437,646	1	0

1 Will. & Mary, sess. 1, 1689. chap. 20. only six shillings for every hundred pounds, public offices, lands, tenements, hereditaments, annuities, issuing out of lands, &c, to be raised within the year, from the first of March, 1688-9.

The sum to be borrowed upon this act is not ascertained in it, but the interest was seven pounds *per cent*; and, by an account delivered into the House of Commons, in pursuance of a clause in it, it appeared that the real produce was 496,007*l.* 3*s.* 3*d.*

Chap. 24. *An act for an additional duty of excise upon beer, ale, and other liquors.*

THIS duty was given for three years from the 24th of July, 1689, and was in part appropriated by chap. 28, of this session, to the payment of 600,000*l.* to the States-general, and the residue by 2 W. and M. session 2, chap. 10, to other uses. See the next chapter.

Chap. 28. *An act for appropriating certain duties for paying the States-general of the United Provinces their charges for his majesty's expedition into this kingdom, and other uses.*

§ 1. FOR satisfying and defraying the debts and charges, and for the purposes hereinafter mentioned, be it enacted, &c. that part of the money, payable by 1 James II, chap. 4*, not exceeding 60,000*l.* shall be appropriated and applied to the payment of the wages due to the servants of the late King Charles II, who were his servants at the time of his decease, to be paid to them, their executors, administrators, and assigns, in three years from the 24th of December, 1689; and that the residue of the mo-

* This was an impost or duty on tobacco and sugar, granted from the 24th of June, 1685, until the 24th of June, 1693.

ney, arifing and payable by the faid act, and the revenue arifing by two other acts, 1 Jam. II, chap. 3 *, and chap. 5 †, and by another act of this prefent parliament, intitled, ' An act for an additional duty of excife upon beer, ale, and other liquors' [fee chap. 24, above] fhall be appropriated and applied from the 29th of September, 1689, during the continuance of the faid acts; in the firft place, towards payment of 600,000*l.* to the States of, the United Provinces, for their affiftance to his majefty at his coming into this nation; which fum of 600,000 *l.* is meant and intended in full fatisfaction of their faid affiftance, and the charges thereof: and, after the faid 600,000 *l.* fhall be paid, the refidue fhall be for, and towards the fubduing of the rebellion of Ireland, and other charges of the war againft France. 1 Will. & Mary, feff. 1, 1688, chap. 28.

It appears, from accounts at the Excife-Office, that the net produce of the above additional excife, from the 24th of July, 1689, to the 24th of July, 1692, was 499,709 *l.* 1 *s.* 8 *d.* after deducting 47,394 *l.* for charges of management.

This feffion was ended on the 20th of Auguft, 1689.

The next feffion was begun October 23, 1689; and, on the 2d of November, the following refolution was agreed to: *viz.* " that for the reducing of Ireland, and joining with their majefties allies abroad, in a vigorous profecution of the war againft France, a fupply of *two millions* fhould be granted to their majefties." And for raifing this fupply were paffed the following acts:

* This was an impoft on wines and vinegar, granted from the 24th of June 1685, to the 24th of June 1693.

† This was an impoft on all French linens, and all Eaft-India linens, and feveral other manufactures of India; and on all French-wrought filks and ftuffs; and on all other wrought filks; and on all brandies imported: granted from the firft of July, 1685, until the firft of July, 1690.

1 Will. & Mary, seff. 2, 1689, chap. 1. *An act for granting to their majesties an aid of two shillings in the pound for one year.*

THIS aid was to be raised on lands, tenements, hereditaments, offices, and personal estates, within the year, from the 25th of December, 1689, at 7 *per cent.* no sum was ascertained; but, by an account delivered into the House of Commons, it appeared that the real produce was 1,015,395 *l.* 4 *s.* 10 *d.* $\frac{1}{2}$.

By this act the sum of 400,000 *l.* was appropriated to the payment of seamen; and for stores, provisions, victuals, &c.

Chap. 3. *An act for preventing all doubts and questions concerning the collecting the public revenue.*

BY this act all revenues whatsoever were continued to their majesties from the 25th of November, 1689, until the 25th of December, 1690. See page 36. chap. 14.

The remainder, after deducting 900,000 *l.* (see page 37) from 1,437,646 *l.* 1 *s.* which is 537,000 *l.* 1 *s.* we shall consider as the money granted by this act; though, in fact, it is only the produce of these revenues, from the 25th of November, 1689, to the 30th of June, 1690.

Chap. 5. *An act for a grant to their majesties of an aid of twelve pence in the pound for one year.*

THIS aid was charged on lands, tenements, hereditaments, offices, and personal estate, to be raised with the above two shillings aid, at 7 *per cent. per annum*, to be paid quarterly. The sum is not ascertained; but, by an account delivered into the House of Commons, it appeared that the real produce was 507,697*l.* 11*s.* 9*d.* $\frac{1}{2}$.

An act for the review of the late poll granted to their majesties, and for an additional poll towards the reducing of Ireland. 1 Will. & Mary, seff. 2, 1689, chap. 7.

THE fum to be raifed is not afcertained in the act: but the real produce was 23,059 *l.* 7 *s.* 1 *d.*

This parliament was prorogued January the 7th, foon after diffolved, and a new parliament fummoned to meet at Weftminfter, on the 26th of March following.

According to the quarto edition of the Statutes at Large, this parliament was held the 20th of March, 1689. The former editions of the Statutes have it the 20th of May, 1690: but the Journals of the Houfe of Commons make it the 20th of March, 1689. On the 1ft of April the Houfe voted, that a fupply of 1,200,000 *l.* fhould be given to their majefties for the public occafions, in profecuting the war with France, and reducing Ireland: And for raifing this fum, they paffed the following acts: 2 Will. & Mary, feff. 1, 1689.

An act for raifing money by a poll and otherwife, towards the reducing Ireland, and profecuting the war againft France. Chap. 2.

THE produce of this poll-tax, (which was to be paid into the Exchequer by the 20th of Auguft, 1690,) was 239,299 *l.* 17 *s.* 5 *d.* ½.

An act for granting to their majefties for their lives, and the life of the furvivor of them, certain impofitions upon beer, ale, and other liquors. Chap. 3.

§ 2. THE rates upon beer, *&c.* given by 12 Charles II, chap. 23, are now given to the king and queen for their lives. [These duties were further continued by 1 Ann. ftat. 1. chap.

2 Will. and Mar. seff. 1, 1689, chap. 3. 7, and 1 Geo. I, ftat. 1, chap. 1, and perpetuated by 1 Geo. I, ftat. 2, chap. 12, fect. 8.]

§ 4. It fhall be lawful for natives, or foreigners, to advance and lend upon the credit of this act, any fum not exceeding 250,000 *l*. and to have, for the forbearance of all fuch monies, as fhall be lent before the 10th of June, 1690, intereft at 8 *per cent*; and for what fhall be lent after the faid tenth of June, 7 *per cent.*

Chap. 4. *An act for granting to their majefties a fubfidy of tonnage and poundage, and other fums of money, payable upon merchandizes imported and exported.*

§ 2. Tonnage and poundage, granted by 12 Charles II, chap. 4, are given to their majefties, from the 24th of December, 1690, for four years.

§ 5. And whereas their majefties are contented and pleafed, that the fubfidy of tonnage and poundage fhould be made a fund of credit, in confidence that their good fubjects will, in due time, make provifion for taking off the anticipation thereof; therefore, *&c.* it fhall be lawful for natives or foreigners to lend and advance unto their majefties, any fum not exceeding 500,000 *l*. in the whole; and have and receive, for the forbearance of fuch monies as fhall be lent before the tenth of June, 1690, intereft not exceeding 8 *per cent per annum*; and for what fhall be lent after the faid tenth of June, 7 *per cent.*

This feffion was adjourned on the 23d of May to the 7th of July following; and on the 12th of September, it was prorogued until the 2d of October, as appears by the Journals of the Houfe of Commons.

2 Will. and Mar. In the fecond feffion, which began October 2, 1690, and ended the 5th of January follow-

ing, they granted for the navy, and for building a great number of ſhips of war, and a dock at Plymouth, 2,361,695 *l.* and for maintaining an army of 69,636 men, with every thing relating to it, they granted 2,294,560 *l.* being in the whole, 4,656,255 *l.* and for raiſing this extraordinary ſupply, the following acts were paſſed. ſeſſ. 2, 1690.

An act for granting an aid to their majeſties of the ſum of 1,651,702 *l.* 18 *s.* Chap. 1.

This was to be raiſed within the year, from the 26th of December, 1690, by a monthly aſſeſſment of 137,641 *l.* 18 *s.* 2 *d.* to be paid by the ſeveral counties, according to the proportions in the act of 1 Will. and Mar. 1 ſeſſ. 1, chap. 3, (ſee p. 31) mentioned *. The ſum to be borrowed is not aſcertained in the act, but the intereſt is expreſſed to be 7 *per cent*; and, by the account in 1702, before referred to, it appears, that the real produce was 1,613,747 *l.* 9 *s.* 1 *d.*

An act for doubliug the duty of exciſe upon beer, ale, and other liquors, during the ſpace of one year. Chap. 3.

No ſum appears in this act to have been borrowed upon it; but the produce, according to the account before referred to, was 611,349 *l.* 0 *s.* 4 *d.* $\frac{2}{1}$.

An act for granting to their majeſties certain impoſitions upon all Eaſt-India goods and manufactures, and upon all wrought ſilk, and ſeveral other goods and merchandizes, to be imported after the 25th of December, 1690. Chap. 4.

§ 57. It ſhall be lawful for any perſon and perſons to advance and lend unto their majeſties,

* The county of Bedford was to pay 1793 *l.* 15 *s.* 6 *d.* and, by the former act, no more than 896 *l.* 17 *s.* 9 *d.* and the ſums on all the reſt were doubled in like manner.

2 Will. and Mar. seff. 2, 1690. chap. 4. upon the security of this act, any sum, or sums of money; and to have and receive for the forbearance thereof 8 *per cent. per annum*, and no more.—The sum borrowed upon this act appears, from the said account, to be 300,550 *l.* 9 *s.* 10 *d.*

Chap. 5. *An act for the continuance of several former acts therein mentioned* [viz. 1 *Jac.* II, chap. 3, *and* 1 *Jac.* II, chap. 4,] *for the laying several duties upon wines, vinegar, and tobacco.*

§ 5. It shall be lawful to advance and lend unto their majesties, as well upon the credit of this act, as upon the security of the said two former acts of King James (from and after the sum of 600,000 *l.* mentioned in act 1 W. and M. chap. 24, for his majesty's expedition into this kingdom, shall be fully satisfied and paid to the States-General) any sum, or sums of money; and to have for the forbearance thereof 8 *per cent.* for one year and no more.—The sum borrowed upon this act, according to the said account, was 700,100 *l.*

Chap. 10. *An act for granting to their majesties several additional duties of excise upon beer, ale, and other liquors, for four years, from the time that an act for doubling the duty of excise, upon beer, ale, and other liquors, during the space of one year doth expire.* See p. 43, chap. 3.

§ 6. The sum of 500,000 *l.* part of the duties granted by this act, and the said act 1 W. and M. chap. 24, after the said 600,000 *l.* shall be paid to the States-General, is appropriated for the building, and for the guns, rigging, and other furnishing of twenty-seven ships of war; whereof seventeen to be of the third rate, and to contain and measure one thousand one hundred tons, or thereabouts, and carry eighty guns a-piece; and ten to be of the fourth rate, and to contain of meaſure nine hundred tons, or thereabouts, and to carry ſixty guns a-piece. 2 Will. and Mar. ſeſſ. 2. 1690. chap. 10.

§ 8. The reſidue of the ſaid former exciſe, after payment of the ſaid 600,000 *l.* ſhall be kept apart, and paid weekly into the Exchequer.

§ 9. A ſeparate account ſhall be kept in the Exchequer of all the monies paid by virtue of this or the ſaid former act.

§ 10. One third part thereof to be paid the treaſurer of the navy for building the ſaid twenty-ſeven ſhips of war, &c. This one-third, from the 17th of November, 1691, to the 18th of November, 1695, amounted, according to the ſaid account, to 482,617 *l.* 11 *s.* 1 *d* ½.

§ 14. Any perſons, natives or foreigners, may advance upon the credit of two third parts of the money to ariſe from this act, any ſum not exceeding the ſum of 1,000,000 *l.* in the whole; and have, for the forbearance thereof, intereſt not exceeding 7 *per cent.*—The money really borrowed upon theſe two-thirds, as appears from the ſaid accounts, was 999,815*l.* 0*s.* 8*d.* ½.

§ 21. Appropriation of the remaining two-thirds of the money: *viz.* for the payment of ſeamen, that ſhall ſerve in the royal navy for the year 1691; and for building of three ſhips to be of the third rate, to contain and meaſure each 1050 tons, and providing guns, rigging, and other furniture for the ſaid ſhips; and to and for the paying for ſtores, proviſions, and victuals, to be ſupplied for the ſaid navy; and to and for the expence of the Office of Ordnance in reſpect to naval affairs; and for the other neceſſary uſes and ſervices to be performed for the ſaid navy, in the time aforeſaid, the ſum of 700,000 *l.*

And out of the money in the Exchequer, ariſing by this or any other act of this ſeſſion, ſhall be appropriated for the payment of their majeſties land-forces and armies, that have

2 Will. & Mary, seff. 2, 1690. chap. 10. ferved, or fhall ferve in England or Ireland, or elfewhere, and the paying for arms, ammunition, carriages, and all other incident charges neceffary to the fame, the fum of 1,500,000 *l.*

§ 23. Their majefties may difpofe of 500,000*l.* not appropriated; fo as the fame may be applied to the carrying on the prefent war.

This feffions ended January 5, 1690, as before mentioned.

3 Will. & Mar. 1691. In this feffion, which began October 22, 1691, and ended February 24 following, the following fupplies were granted:

1. A fum not exceeding 1,575,890 *l.* for the charge of the navy to be fet out for the year 1692, including the ordnance, and the charge of building one dry dock, and two wet docks at Portfmouth.

2. A fum not exceeding 1,935,787 *l.* 16 *s.* 3 *d.* (together with the fum of 165,000 *l.* to be anfwered out of the revenue of Ireland) for the land forces for 1692, in order to the carrying on a vigorous war againft France.

The ways and means for raifing thefe fupplies were as follow.

Chap. 1. *An act for granting to their majefties certain impofitions upon beer, ale, and other liquors for one year.*

No fum appears in this act to have been borrowed upon it; but the real produce of the money arifing from it, from the 17th of November 1691, to the 18th of November 1692, amounted to 381,080 *l.* 5 *s.* 9 *d.* $\frac{3}{4}$

Chap. 5. *An act for granting an aid to their majefties of the fum of* 1,651,702 *l.* 18 *s.* *towards carrying on a vigorous war againft France.*

This was to be raifed by a monthly affeffment of 137,641 *l.* 18 *s.* 2 *d.* to be paid by the feveral counties, according to the proportions of the 1 Will. and Mar. seff. 1, chap. 3, (see p. 31) The sum to be borrowed is not ascertained; but by the said account of 1702, it appears that the produce was 1,613,873 *l.* 2*s.* 3*d.* 3 Will. & Mar. 1691. Chap. 5.

An act for raising money by poll, payable quarterly for one year, for the carrying on a vigorous war against France. Chap. 6.

This act was founded upon resolutions so singular, that it seems necessary to give them at large, as follow: *viz* January 23, resolved,

1. That towards the said poll all persons do pay 12 *s.* quarterly, except the poor receiving alms, and their children under sixteen years of age; as also the children under sixteen of all persons exempted from contributing to church and poor; and of all day-labourers and servants in husbandry; and of such as have four children or more, and are not worth 50 *l.*

2. That every gentleman, or reputed gentleman, worth 300 *l.* and every person above that quality, and under the degree of a peer, do pay 20 *s.* quarterly.

3. That tradesmen, shopkeepers, and artificers, worth 300 *l.* or upwards, do pay 10 *s.* quarterly.

4. That every person charged, or chargeable to the militia, with finding a horse or mare, to pay 20 *s.* quarterly, for every horse over and above what he is charged with on any other head.

5. That every person not contributing a horse to the militia, who keeps a coach and horses, do pay 20 *s.* quarterly, over and above what he is charged with on any other head, except such as keep stage, or hackney coaches.

6. That every person keeping an hackney or stage coach, or coaches, do for every coach pay 1 *l.* 5 *s.* quarterly.

3 Will. & Mar. 1691. chap. 6.

7. That every lord of parliament, ſpiritual or temporal, do pay 10 *s.* quarterly.

8. That nonjurors do in every caſe pay double.

9. That all attornies, proctors, and other officers of all courts, eccleſiaſtical and civil, be charged as gentlemen. And

10. That all clergymen, preachers, and teachers, in any congregation whatſoever, who have by benefices, contribution, or otherwiſe, 80 *l.* or upwards, be charged as gentlemen.

The ſum to be borrowed upon this act is not mentioned; but the produce, according to the ſaid account, was 606,308 *l.* 1 *s.* 6 *d.* ½

4 Will. & Mar. 1692.

In this ſeſſion, which began November 4, 1692, and ended March 14, the following ſupplies were granted: *viz.*

1. A ſum not exceeding 1,926,516 *l.* 10 *s.* for the charge of the navy for the year 1693, including the charge of ordnance, and finiſhing the naval yard at Hamore near Portſmouth, and the building four bomb veſſels, and eight new ſhips of the fourth rate.

2. A ſum not exceeding 750,000 *l.* for making good the ſum of 1,341,700 *l.* intended to be raiſed by the act for a quarterly poll.

3. A ſum not exceeding 2,090,563 *l.* 19 *s.* 6 *d.* for the charge of the land forces for the year 1693, including the extraordinary charge of the office of ordnance in relation to the land ſervice, and the charge of the tranſports, hoſpitals, contingencies, and other extraordinary charges of the war.

The ways and means for raiſing theſe ſupplies were as follow:

An act for granting to their majesties an aid of 4 s. in the pound for one year for carrying on a vigorous war against France. 4 Will. & Mar. 1692. Chap. 1.

§ 2. All persons, bodies politic and corporate, guilds, and fraternities, having any estate in ready money or debts, or having any estate in goods, wares, or other personal estate whatsoever, shall pay 24 s. for every 100 l.

§ 3. Persons having any office or employment of profit, to pay 4 s. in the pound for their salaries or profits.

§ 4. All manors, lands, tenements, yearly profits and hereditaments, are charged with 4 s. in the pound of the yearly value.

All sums of money, which, in pursuance of 3 Will. and Mar. chap. 6, have been lent to their majesties, not exceeding 735,391 l. 18 s. 5 d ½, shall be transferred to the register of this act.

The sum of 700,000 l. shall be appropriated to the payment of officers and seamen that have and shall serve in the royal navy, and for the paying for stores, provisions, and victuals for the said navy, and for the office of ordnance; and the residue of the money to be raised by this act, shall be appropriated for the payment of the land forces, and the paying for arms, ammunition, and other charges incident to the war, and not otherwise.

The sum borrowed is not mentioned in the act; but from the said account, it appears to be 1,161,482 l. 16 s. 1 d.

An act for granting to their majesties certain rates and duties of excise, upon beer, ale, and other liquors, for securing certain recompences and advantages in the said act mentioned, to such persons as shall voluntarily advance the sum of 1,000,000 *towards carrying on the war against France.* Chap. 3.

3 Will. & Mar. 1691. chap. 6.

§ 2. From the 20th of January 1692, an additional excise upon beer, ale, and other liquors, is imposed for 99 years. [Continued for ever by 1 Geo. I, stat. 2, chap. 12, sect. 8]

§ 8. Natives and foreigners may contribute 1,000,000 *l.* before May 1693, upon the terms following: viz. 100,000 *l.* out of the monies arising by this act, to be yearly distributed among the contributors from the 24th of June 1693, until the 24th of June 1700, and afterwards 70,000 *l.* to be divided as follows: viz. a contributor of 100 *l.* to receive a share thereof during the life which he names.—Any person may contribute as may hundreds as he pleases, for which he is to name lives, during which he shall be entitled to receive as many shares or dividends of the said yearly fund, as there are hundred pounds by him advanced.———Survivors to have the advantage of the deaths of the nominees, till only seven be left, and the king to have the dead man's share—if the whole sum be not advanced, the contributors shall be paid such part of the annual funds as is proportionable to the advance.—There was only 881,493 *l.* 14 *s.* 2 *d.* advanced upon this act: [See 5 W. and M. chap. 5.]

§ 10. Contributor may assign or devise his interest. — If no assignment, interest goes to executors.

§. 19. A clause of loan, to make up the sum of 1,000,000 *l.* in case the whole should not be advanced.

§ 20. Seven pounds per cent. allowed to the lender, and the charge of the principal and interest transferred to the next parliament aid, and, if no aid, to next revenue.

§ 21. If 500,000 *l.* only be advanced before May, the king may borrow 500,000 l. to be paid out of money raised by this act, betwixt that time and September; and, if that fall short, next aid chargeable.

§ 22. If the whole sum be not raised before May, persons contributing shall have the advantage of 14 per cent. for the life of the nominee. 4 Will. & Mar. 1692. chap. 6.

§ 23. Persons contributing upon survivorship, may change it into the advantage of 14 l. per cent. for life.

An act for granting to their majesties certain additional impositions upon several goods and merchandizes for the prosecuting the present war against France. [*Made perpetual by* 9 Ann. *chap.* 21, *sect.* 1; *but repealed as to the provisions for rating goods* ad valorem, *by* 11 Geo. I, *chap.* 7, *sect.* 1.] Chap. 14

§ 17. Clause of credit for any sum not exceeding 510,000 l. upon the credit of this act at 8 per cent. interest.

§ 23. The sum of 1,226,516 l. appropriated out of this year's tax to the payment of officers and seamen that have served, and shall serve, in their majestie's navy royal, and for the paying for stores, provisions, and victuals, supplied and to be supplied, for the said navy, &c.

An act for the review of the quarterly poll granted to their majesties in the last session of this present parliament [3 W. and M. chap. 6.] Chap. 16

The loan upon this review was 6,307 l. 2*s*. 2*d*.

The supplies granted in this session, which began *Nov.* 1693, and ended by prorogation, *April* 25, 1694, were as follows: *viz.*

1. For maintenance of the fleet for the year 1604, in the whole, 2,400,000 l.

2. For seamen's wages then in arrear, 500,000 l.

3. For a deficiency upon the 2d act of the preceding session, 118,506 *l*. 5 *s*. 10 *d*. And

4. For raising a great many new regiments of horse, dragoons and foot, and maintaining an army of 83,121 men for the service of the year 1694.

5 Will. & Mar. 1692, chap. 5. The ways and means for raising these supplies were as follow, *viz.*

An act for granting to their majesties an aid of 4 s. in the pound for carrying on a vigorous war against France.

This was to be raised within the year, from the 25th of December 1693, by an assessment on the several counties to be paid quarterly. There is no sum ascertained; but, by the account before referred to, there was raised the sum of 1,000,000 *l.*

Chap. 5. *An act to supply the deficiency of the money raised by a former act, intituled "An Act", &c.* [4 and 5 W. and M. chap. 3. See p. 49.]

Whereas by 4 and 5 W. and M. chap. 3, it was enacted, that it should be lawful for any persons, natives, or foreigners, to contribute towards the advancing the sum of ten hundred thousand pounds for the purposes therein mentioned, by paying into their majesties receipt of Exchequer, such sum or sums of money, at such time, and upon such terms respectively, as in the said act are particularly mentioned and expressed: And whereas the several sums paid in upon the said act, by the several contributors, did and do in the whole amount to but the sum of 881,493 *l.* 14 *s.* 2 *d.* We, &c.

§ 2. It shall be lawful for any persons, natives or foreigners, to contribute towards the advancing the sum of 118,506 *l.* 5 *s.* 10 *d.* to make up the whole sum of 1,000,000 *l.* upon the terms following: viz. that every such person, out of the rates and duties of excise granted by the said recited act, shall have and receive for every sum of 100 *l.* by them advanced, a yearly annuity of 14 *l.* and proportionably for a greater sum, for the life of the person so advancing the same, or during any other life to be nominated by the person so advancing such sum, &c.

An act for granting to their majesties certain rates and duties upon salt, and upon beer, ale, and other liquors, for securing certain recompences and advantages in the said act mentioned, to such persons as shall voluntarily advance the sum of ten hundred thousand pounds towards carrying on the war against France. 5 Will. & Mar. 1693. chap. 7.

§ 2. Rates upon salt granted for three years: [—Made perpetual by 7 and 8 *W.* III, ch. 31.]

31. § 2. for the application of the money granted by this act, see 9 and 10 *W.* III, chap. 34.

§ 27. Additional excise upon beer, &c. for sixteen years.

§ 33. The sum of 140,000 *l.* out of the said duties, shall be a yearly fund for answering or paying the annuities herein after mentioned.

§ 34. Natives or aliens may advance 1,000,000 l. by paying the sum of ten pounds, or diverse entire sums of ten pounds upon this act, and for the raising the said sum of 1,000,000 l. any person who will become an adventurer, shall and may advance the sum of 10 l. for which sum so advanced, he, she, or they, for sixteen years, shall be entitled to receive a share or dividend of the said yearly fund *.

§ 49. Money lent on this act to be tax free.

§ 53. Borrowing clause if 1,000,000 *l.* be not advanced before the 24th of June 1694.

§ 54. 8 per cent, interest to be allowed, and this fund, &c. chargeable for the payment of principal and interest.

§ 55. Surplus, after all the annuities directed by this act, shall be lawfully satisfied, to be disposed of according to 2 W. and M. sess. 2, chap. 10. See p.

* Every adventurer was to have 14 l. *per cent.* for sixteen years; for 1,000,000 : 140,000 : 100 : 14, that is, if the million produces 140,000 *l.* in one year, 100 *l.* will produce 14 *l.*

5 Will. & Mary. 1693. Chap. 14.

An act for raising money by a poll, payable quarterly for one year, for carrying on a vigorous war against France.

The loan upon this act (interest at 6 per cent. per annum) was 569,203 *l.* 19 *s.* 7 *d.*

Chap. 20. Origin of the Bank of England.

An act for granting to their majesties several rates and duties upon tonnage of ships and vessels, and upon beer, ale, and other liquors, for securing certain recompences and advantages in the said act mentioned, to such persons as shall voluntarily advance the sum of 1,500,000 *l. towards carrying on the war against France.*

§ 2. Tonnage upon ships given for four years. [For the continuance hereof, see 7 and 8 *Will.* III, chap. 31.]

§ 10. One half part of the duties of excise, granted by 2 W. and M. sess. 2, chap. 10, given to their majesties, their heirs and successors. For the appropriation of these duties, see 1 *Geo.* I, stat. 2, chap. 12, and sect. 12; and 6 *Geo.* I, chap. 4.

§ 17. The sum of 140,000 *l.* out of the said duties of tonnage and excise, shall be a yearly fund for answering the annuities herein after mentioned.

§ 18. The said 140,000 *l.* to be kept apart in the Exchequer.

§ 19. Their majesties may make commissioners take subscriptions for 1,200,000 *l.* —— The sum of 100,000 *l.* annually appropriated to the subscribers *. ——— The auditor of the Exchequer shall divide the monies arising out of the said duties into five several parts, and two several parts (which is according to the proportion of the said yearly sum of 100,000 *l.* to the said yearly sum of 140,000 *l.*) which five several parts are appropriated for paying the said 100,000 l.

* Surplus how applied, See 1 *Geo.* I, stat. 2, chap. 12, sect. 12.

§ 20. Their majesties may appoint rules for transferring, and make the subscribers a corporation, by the name of *the governor and company of the Bank of England*, &c. 5 Will. & Mar. 1693. chap. 20.

§ 34. Any persons may contribute towards the raising 300,000 *l.* and receive yearly sums for one, two, or three lives; that is, every contributor, who shall advance 100 *l.* upon one life only, shall have and receive yearly an annuity, rent, or payment of 14 *l.* and so proportionably for a greater sum, for and during the life of such person so advancing and paying the same, or during any other life, to be nominated by the person paying any such sum; and, in case such contributor shall think fit, upon payment of his money, to have an annuity for two lives, then he shall have a yearly annuity, rent, or payment, of 12 *l.* for every 100 *l.* and so proportionably for a greater sum, advanced for and during two lives, and the life of the survivor of them; and, in case such contributor shall think fit, upon payment of his money, to have an annuity for three lives, then he shall have an annuity of 10 *l.* for every 100 *l.* for the term of three lives, and the life of the survivor of them. See farther provisions relating hereto, 9 and 10 *W.* III, chap. 34, sect. 5.

§ 39, 40. If 1,500,000 *l.* be not raised before October on this act, deficiency to be supplied by loan, at 8 per cent.—— If the duties fall short, next subsidy given by parliament charged.

§ 41. Out of the money to be raised by this act, 1,500,000 *l.* shall be appropriated to the navy and ordnance.—All other money unappropriated shall be applied to the army.

§ 43. Out of 1,500,000 *l.* hereby appropriated, and out of the sum of 1,000,000 *l.* by 5 and 6 Will. and Mary, chap. 1, appropriated for the use of the navy, the sum of 1,156,994 *l.* shall be applied to pay the wages

5 Will. & Mary, 1693. of officers and ſeamen, and other ſervices belonging, according to the courſe of the navy, to the head of wages performed, and to be performed; and alſo to pay the officers and ſoldiers of the two marine regiments. And that the ſum of 1,257,266 *l.* be applied for and towards the paying for victuals and neceſſary proviſions and ſtores, and other extraordinary ſervices of the navy and ordnance.——And that the ſum of 85,740 *l.* be applied for and towards paying the wages of the yards, and other ordinary ſervices of the ſaid navy.

Chap. 21. Orig. of ſtamp-office. *An act for granting to their majeſties ſeveral duties upon vellum, parchment, and paper, for four years, towards carrying on the war againſt France.*

The loan upon this act was 330,000 *l.* at 8 *per cent.* intereſt.

§ 17. Natives or foreigners may advance, and lend upon the credit of this act, any ſum not exceeding 330,000 *l.* at 8 *per cent.*

Chap. 22. *An act for the licenſing and regulating Hackney coaches and ſtage coaches.*

§ 3. Hackney coaches in London, &c. not to exceed 700.—Charge of licence 50 *l.* together with an annual rent of 4 *l.* to be paid quarterly. The licence was to continue but for 21 years.

§ 18. One hundred and ſeventy-five coaches to drive upon the Lord's-day.—The ſum hereby raiſed was 39,137 *l.*

6 Will. & Mar. 1694. The ſupplies granted in this ſeſſion, which began Nov. 12, 1694, and ended not till the 3d of May, 1695, were as follow:

1. For the navy, 2,382,712 *l.*
2. For the army, 2,500,000 *l.*

3. For paying what remained due to those whose ships were employed in reducing Ireland, 330,769 *l.* 10 *s.* 7 *d.* 6 Will. & Mary, 1694.

The ways and means for raising these supplies were as follow:

An act for granting to their majesties a subsidy of tonnage and poundage [for five years] and other sums of money payable upon merchandizes exported and imported. Chap. 1.

The loan upon this act (for securing of which an annuity of 300,000 *l.* was given by the next chapter,) amounted to 1,250,000 *l.*

An act for granting to his majesty an aid of 4 s. *in the pound for one year; and for applying the yearly sum of* 300,000 *l. for five years out of the duties of tonnage and poundage [granted by the preceding act] and other sums of money, payable upon merchandizes exported and imported, for carrying on the war against France with vigour.* Chap. 3. [1695.]

The sum to be borrowed upon the above aid of 4 *s.* is not ascertained; but the interest is expressed to be 5 *per cent.* and the loan thereon, according to the account so often referred to, was 1,177,903 *l.* 7 *s.*

An act for enabling such persons as have estates for life in annuities, payable by several former acts therein mentioned, to purchase and obtain further and more certain interests in such annuities; and, in default thereof, for admitting other persons to purchase or obtain the same, for raising monies for carrying on the war against France. Chap. 5. [6 and 7 W. III. 1695.]

§ 1. Recites 4 and 5 W. and M. chap. 3. See p. 51.

§ 2. Recites 5 and 6 W. and M. chap. 20. See p. 56.

6 and 7 Will. III, 1695, § 3. Recites 4 and 5 W. and M. chap. 3, 5 and 6 W. and M. chap. 5. See p. 56.

§ 4. And whereas the perſons, who are or may be intitled to ſuch eſtates for ſingle lives in the ſaid annuities, or ſome of them, are or may be willing and deſirous (for a reaſonable price or conſideration) to have ſuch their reſpective eſtates for ſingle lives, changed or converted into certain term or terms for 96 years, to be computed from the 25th of January 1695, of and in ſuch or the like annuities as they have for ſingle lives, as aforeſaid:

§ 5. Any perſon having 14 *l. per cent.* for life, upon the former acts, may convert it into an eſtate of 96 years for 63 *l.* that is, four years and a half's purchaſe.

§ 6. Any perſon having an eſtate for life, not taking advantage before July; any other paying 70 *l.* ſhall have a term of 96 years, charged with, and ſubject to the former eſtate for life.

§ 12. One moiety of the money advanced, appropriated to the navy and ordnance; and the other moiety to the land forces.

§ 14. Clauſe of loan at 5 *per cent.* if 618,420 *l.* 6 *d.* be not advanced *.

Chap. 6. *An act for granting to his majeſty by certain rates and duties, upon marriages, births, and burials, and upon batchelors and widowers, for the term of five years, for carrying on the war againſt France with vigour.* — The loan upon this act (intereſt at 8 *per cent. per annum*) was 650,000 *l.*

Chap. 7. *An act for granting to his majeſty ſeveral additional duties on coffee, tea, chocolate, and ſpices, towards ſatisfaction of the debts due for tranſport ſervice for the reduction of Ireland.*

* There was only the ſum of 235,951 *l.* 6 *d.* advanced.

The ſum due for tranſport ſervice, as appears from the preamble to this act, was 330,769 *l.* 10 *s.* 7 *d.* 6 and 7 Will. III, 1695.

An act for granting to his majeſty certain duties upon glaſs wares, ſtone, and earthen bottles, coals and culm, for carrying on the war againſt France.—[Continued by ſtat 7 and 8 W. III, chap. 31; but half the duties on glaſs and glaſs wares, and the whole duties on ſtone and earthen wares, were taken away *per* ſtat. 9 and 10 W. III, chap. 45; and afterwards the remaining half duty on glaſs and glaſs wares, was taken away by ſtat. 10 and 11 W. III, chap. 18.] Chap. 18.

§ 21. A clauſe of loan for 564,700 *l.* upon this act, at 7 *per cent.*

§ 25. Appropriation of the monies ariſing by this and the marriage act, 6 and 7 W. III, chap. 6, *viz.* for the ſervices of the navy and ordnance, for ſea ſervice, and for pay of the officers and ſoldiers of the two marine regiments, the ſum of 448,712 *l.* that is to ſay, out of this preſent act 200,000 *l.* and out of the marriage act the ſum of 248,712 *l.*

The ſupplies granted this ſeſſion, which began November 22, 1695, and ended April 27, 1696, were as follow: *viz.* 7 W. III, 1695.

1. For the navy for the year 1696, 2,500,000*l.*

2. For the officers of two marine regiments, 16,972 *l.*

3. For maintaining 87,440 land-forces, 2,007,881 *l.* 19 *s.* 11 *d.*

4. For the extraordinary ſervice of the ordnance, general officers, tranſports, hoſpitals, &c. 500,000 *l.*

5. For the expence of the civil-liſt for the year 1696, 500,000 *l.*

7 W. III, 1695. 6. For the relief of the poor French Protestants, 15,000 *l.*

The ways and means for raising these supplies were as follow: *viz.*

Chap. 2. *An act for enlarging the times to come in and purchase certain annuities therein-mentioned, and for continuing the duties formerly charged on low wines, or spirits of the first extraction, for carrying on the war against France.*

§ 1. Recites 6 and 7 Will. III, chap. 5, and the powers thereby granted. See p. 57.

§ 2. And whereas diverse persons, in pursuance of the said recited act, did, within the said respective times thereby limited, contribute to pay into the said receipt of Exchequer, several sums of money, amounting in the whole to 235,951 *l.* 6 *d.* for purchasing further or more certain estates in some of the annuities beforementioned:

§ 3. And whereas the persons, who are, or may be intitled to such of the said annuities, as do still depend upon single lives, and wherein further estates are not already purchased by the said former act, are, or may be willing and desirous, or (in case of their, or any of their neglect or refusal) other persons may yet be willing and desirous to purchase and obtain a term of years, as aforesaid, in the annuities last mentioned, or some of them, at the like rates, or for such considerations, as were prescribed by the said former act, so as further times be allowed them for the doing thereof: now, for the better encouragement of such persons, who shall so contribute monies, with as much ease as may be, for the carrying on the war against France,

§ 4, Persons intitled to annuities of 14 *l. per annum* for one life, on the acts 4 and 5 W. and M. chap. 3, and 5 and 6 W. and M. chap. 20, may, for 63 *l.* more, purchase such annuities for the residue of the term of 96 years, to take effect after the estate for life. — The amount of this contribution was 15,847 *l.* 13 *s.* 11 *d.* 7 W. III, 1695.

An act for granting to his majesty an aid of 4 *s. in the pound for one year, for carrying on the war against France.* Chap. 5. [7 and 8 W. III, 1696.]

This was to be raised by assessment on the several counties within the year, from the 25th of December, 1695. The interest upon this loan was 6 *per cent.* and the sum borrowed 1,417,513 *l.*

An act for continuing several duties granted by former acts upon wine and vinegar, and upon tobacco, and East-India goods, and other merchandize imported, for carrying on the war against France. Chap. 10.

§ 7. Persons may lend 1,500,000 *l.* on this act, &c. and have tallies and orders for repayment, with interest, at 5 *per cent. per annum* for the first 400,000 *l*; 6 *per cent. per annum* for the second 400,000 *l*; 7 *per cent. per annum* for the third 400,000 *l*; and 8 *per cent. per annum* for the remaining 300,000 *l.*

An act for granting to his majesty several rates or duties upon houses for making good the deficiency of the clipped money. Chap. 18.

§ 2. From the 25th of March, 1696, for seven years, every dwelling-house inhabited to pay 2 *s.*—House with ten windows to pay 4 *s. per annum* above the 2 *s*; twenty windows, 8 *s. per annum.*

For the increase and continuance of these duties, see 9 and 10 W. III, chap. 20, 1 Ann. stat. 1, chap. 13. 5 Ann. chap. 13. 7 Ann. chap. 7. 8 Ann. chap. 4. 3 Geo. I, chap. 8,

7 and 8 W. III. 1695. sect. 18; 5 Geo. I, chap. 3, sect. 22; and chap. 19. 6 Geo. I, chap. 21, sect. 61, &c.

§ 31. Any person, &c. may lend 1,200,000 *l.* on this act at 7 *l. per cent.* for 600,000 *l*; and for the remainder 8 *per cent.*

Chap. 20. *An act for granting to his majesty an additional duty upon all French goods and merchandize.*

§ 31. The sum of 1,200,000 *l.* may be lent on the credit of this act for 7 *per cent.* interest for the first 600,000 *l*; and for the remainder 8 *per cent.*

Chap. 30. *An act for laying several duties upon low wines, or spirits of the first extraction, and for preventing the frauds and abuses of brewers, distillers, and other persons chargeable with the duties of excise.*

§ 31. To the end that the rates and duties herein after-mentioned, as also the weekly sum of 6000 *l.* be taken out of the hereditary branch of excise, and that part of the excise granted to his majesty for life; and 600 *l.* a week out of the Post-Office, may be made funds or securities for raising any sum or sums of money, not exceeding 515,000 *l*; that is to say, 500,000 *l.* for defraying the expences of his majesty's houshold and family, and other his majesty's necessary occasions; 15,000 *l.* for the relief of the poor French Protestants; the king may borrow 70,000 *l.* on the credit of the duties hereby granted, at 6 *l. per cent.* for the first 40,000 *l*; and 7 *per cent.* for the remaining 30,000 *l.*

§ 38. The sum of 600 *l.* a week shall be separated from the hereditary and temporary excise, for payment of tallies remaining unsatisfied, and the interest thereof at 6 *per cent.* until the same shall be paid off; and afterwards the like weekly sum shall be separated and appropriated for the payment and satisfaction of such further sum and sums of money not exceeding, in the whole, the ſum of 400,000 *l*; (part of the ſaid 515,000 *l*.) and the intereſt thereof, at 7 *per cent. per annum*; and 8 *per cent. per annum* for the remaining 115,000 *l*. 7 and 8 W. III. 1695.

§ 43. The ſum of 600 *l*. a week to be paid out of the Poſt Office for ſatisfying tallies; and, after ſatisfaction thereof, to be applied to the repayment and ſatisfaction of the further ſum of 45,000 *l*. borrowed upon the credit of this act.

An act for continuing to his majeſty certain duties upon ſalt, glaſs wares, ſtone and earthen wares, for carrying on the war againſt France, and for eſtabliſhing a national land bank; and for taking off the duties upon tonnage of ſhips and upon coals. Chap. 31.

§ 11. Voluntary ſubſcriptions may be made by any perſon or perſons, (other than the governor and company of the Bank of England) for raiſing 2,564,000 *l*; and the yearly ſum of * 179,480 *l*. ariſing out of the ſaid duties, ſhall be applied, iſſued, and directed to the ſubſcribers, their executors, and aſſigns for ever, proportionable to the ſubſcription of each perſon.

§ 13. Contributors to be incorporated by the name of the governor and company of the national land bank.

§ 27. Duties granted by 5 and 6 W. and M. chap. 20, and 6 and 7 W. III, chap. 18, (ſee p. 53, 58) further continued for five years.

§ 28. The ſum of 560,000 *l*. to be applied for paying the remainder of 564,700 *l*. and intereſt advanced on the ſecurity of the foreſaid act of 6 and 7 Will. III, chap. 18; and the ſum of 140,000 *l*. for making good the rates of tonnage of ſhips, granted by 5 and 6 W. and

* Which is 7 *l*. *per cent.*

7 and 8 W. III. 1696. M. chap. 20.—A like ſum for making good the duties on ſalt.

§ 30. And whereas the intent of incorporating the ſubſcribers, is in order to enable them to lend monies on ſecurities of lands at low intereſt, the ſaid governor and company ſhall lend out the ſum of 500,000 *l.* at 3 *l.* 10 *s. per cent. per annum*, to be paid quarterly, at 4 *per cent.* payable half yearly.

§ 74. Clauſe of loan on orders regiſtered at 7 *per cent.* or on bills at 3 *l. per cent. per diem*, for 2,564,000 *l.*

§ 89. Over and above 700,000 *l.* granted by 7 W. III, chap. 5, for the navy, the further ſum of 1,816,972 *l.* is hereby appropriated to the ſame ſervice.

This project did not take place.

8 and 9 W. III. 1696. This ſeſſion began October 20, 1696; and as all the public funds hitherto eſtabliſhed had proved deficient, and all ſorts of public ſecurities were at a great diſcount, the Houſe of Commons, the very firſt day of their ſitting, reſolved, *nem. con.* "That they would make "good all parliamentary funds, ſince his ma"jeſty's acceſſion to the crown, that had been "made credits of loan from the *ſubject*;" which was tantamount to a grant of 6,000,459*l.* 14 *s.* 9 *d.* ¼; for ſuch was the amount of the deficiencies by the ſtate thereof laid before the Houſe, according to order, by the commiſſioners for taking and ſtating the public accounts.

The ſupplies afterwards granted this ſeſſion were the following: *viz.*

1. For maintaining 40,000 ſeamen for 1697, and other expences relating to the navy, 2,372,197*l.*

2. For maintaining 87,440 land-forces for

1697, and other expences relating to the army, 2,507,881 *l.* 19 *s.* 11 *d.*

3. A supply for making good the deficiencies of parliamentary funds.

4 For making good the deficiency in recoining hammered money; and the recompence to be given for bringing plate into the Mint to be coined. This was afterwards computed and restricted to 125,000 *l.*

5. For the support of the civil list, 515,000 *l.*

The ways and means for raising these supplies were as follow, *viz.*

An act for granting an aid to his majesty, as well by a land-tax as by several subsidies, and other duties, payable for one year. 8 and 9 W. III, 1697. chap. 6.

By this act, besides 3 *s.* in the pound upon land, a tax, called the *capitation tax*, of one penny *per* week for one year, was laid upon all persons not receiving alms; and over and above this penny, several additional farthings, half-pence, and pence *per* week, according to people's circumstances. These two funds were computed to produce 3,000,000 *l*; and therefore his majesty was enabled, upon the first, to borrow the sum of 1,500,000 *l.* at 8 *per cent.* including the debts transferred to that fund; and upon the other, he was enabled to issue bills at the Exchequer for another 1,500,000 *l.* at 5 *per cent. per* day interest.

An act for granting to his majesty several duties upon paper, vellum, and parchment, to encourage the buying of plate and hammered money into the Mint to be coined. [See 1 Ann. stat. 1, chap. 13, sect. 17.] Chap. 7.

By this act, an additional duty of 20 *per cent.* of the true value, was laid upon all home-made paper, &c. and 25 *per cent.* upon foreign;

8 and 9 W. III, 1697. and upon this fund his majesty was enabled to borrow 125,000 *l.* at 8 *per cent.*

Chap. 20. *An act for making good the deficiencies of several sums therein mentioned; and for enlarging the capital stock of the Bank of England, and for raising the public credit.*

Whereas several persons, as well natives as foreigners, bodies politic and corporate, did advance and lend, at the receipt of his majesty's Exchequer, very considerable sums of money, upon the security of the several and respective aids, revenues, or funds, herein after mentioned; that is to say, upon the first aid of 4 *s.* in the pound, payable out of lands, and other things, for one year, by virtue of 4 W. and M. chap. 1, (see p. 49,) and upon the third aid of 4 *s.* in the pound, payable by virtue of 6 W. III, chap. 3, (see p. 57,) and upon the fourth aid of 4 *s.* in the pound, payable by virtue of 7 W. III, chap. 5, (see p. 61,) and upon the monies which were to arise by 5 and 6 W. and M. chap. 14—And whereas the greatest part of the monies so lent upon the aids, revenues, or funds before-mentioned, hath been actually satisfied and paid off; but the several terms, for which the said respective aids of 4 *s.* in the pound, and the said poll-money were granted, being determined, and expired, and 300,000 *l. per annum*, out of the revenue of customs, being appropriated, by act of parliament, to the satisfaction of other loans, it doth plainly appear, that the several aids and funds herein before-mentioned are deficient, and could not fully satisfy all the monies which were charged thereupon, and the interest thereof; and for so much as remains unsatisfied, the respective lenders, their executors, administrators, and assigns, have, or are entitled to have, in their hands, tallies, and orders of repayment, levyed and drawn according to the forms used in the Exchequer: And whereas by 7 and 8 W. III, chap. 31, &c. (see p. 63) the several sums of 560,000*l.* and 140,000*l.* and 140,000*l.* mentioned in the said last recited act, amounting in the whole to 840,000*l.* being taken or subducted from the sum 2,564,000*l.* in the said last act likewise mentioned, the remainder thereof will amount to 1,724,000*l* which is, or may be borrowed for the service of the war against France: And the person, or persons, who have advanced, or shall advance the same, have, or may have, in their hands, tallies and orders of repayment, or bills for the sums so advanced, which cannot, in any reasonable time, be satisfied out of the said duties, chargeable therewith, by the act last mentioned. And whereas several persons did advance and lend several other sums of money upon 2 W. and M. sess. 2, chap. 10. (see p. 46) And whereas several persons have also advanced and lent very considerable sums of money upon the security of other aids granted by 4 and 5 W. and M. chap. 5, (see p. 52,) and upon certain duties granted upon vellum, &c. by 5 and 6 W. and M. c. 21, (see p. 56.) and upon the credit of a certain yearly sum of 300,000*l.* payable for 5 years, by 6 W. and M. chap. 1, and 6 and 7 W. III, chap. 3, and upon credit of 6 and 7 W. III, chap. 6, and upon credit of several impositions, payable for wines, by virtue of 7 and 8 W. III. ch. 10. And whereas a great part of the monies so lent upon the said several duties mentioned in the said several acts, hath been actually repaid and satisfied with interest; but, by computing the product of these duties, for the time past, and considering the terms yet to come unexpired in them respectively, it is supposed and feared, that the same duties respectively at the end of the several terms for which they are granted, will be more or less deficient, to answer, pay off, and clear

8 and 9 W. III, 1697.

8 and 9 W. III, 1697. all the principal and intereſt of the monies, which were authorized to be borrowed thereupon; and the perſons intitled to the monies not paid off upon the duties laſt mentioned, have, or may have, in their hands, tallies and orders of repayment for the ſame: And whereas ſeveral perſons, or corporations, did advance and lend other conſiderable ſums upon the credit 4 and 5 W. and M. chap. 15, part of which monies doth ſtill remain unſatisfied, and the perſons intitled thereunto have likewiſe tallies and orders of repayment for the ſame; and, purſuant to 7 W. III, chap. 30. (ſee p. 62.) ſeveral other ſums of money have been lent on the credit of the duties granted by the ſaid laſt act; and, by virtue of the ſame act, and 8 W. III, chap. 3, the ſeveral weekly ſums therein mentioned, do ſeverally ſtand charged to pay off and ſatisfy, in courſe, ſeveral tallies in thoſe acts mentioned, for the payment whereof proviſion is thereby made, together with ſuch ſeveral and reſpective rates of intereſt for the ſame, as are thereby allowed: And whereas by reaſon of the deficiencies of ſeveral of the aids, &c. above mentioned, which have not, or will not be ſufficient to anſwer the principal and intereſt charged thereupon, and by reaſon of the remoteneſs of the courſe of payment of the tallies and orders charged upon ſome of them, and upon other duties in this act before-mentioned, the owners of the ſaid tallies, or orders, are frequently neceſſitated to ſell and diſpoſe thereof at great loſs, or at an exceſſive diſcount, whereby the public credit is very much prejudiced and impaired, and the trade, and the other public and private affairs within the realm do exceedingly ſuffer: And whereas it is computed or eſtimated, that the deficiencies, or ſums, which are, or will be wanting to ſatisfy and pay off all principal and intereſt due, or to be due, on the deficient aids, duties, or funds,

before-mentioned (over and above all the arrears 8 and 9 W. III, 1697.
ſtanding out upon any of them, which are determined over and above all monies to be raiſed by ſuch of them as are yet unexpired) do or may amount to the ſums following; that is to ſay, upon the ſaid firſt aid of 4 *s.* in the pound [4 W. and M. chap. 1.] 55,622 *l.* 10 *s.* 5 *d.* upon the ſaid third aid of 4 *s.* in the pound [6 W. III, chap. 3.] 470,372 *l.* 3 *d.* upon the ſaid fourth aid of 4 *s.* in the pound [7 W. III, chap. 5.] 917,101 *l.* 13 *s.* 2 *d* ½; upon the ſaid quarterly poll [5 and 6 W. and M. chap. 14.] 89,275 *l.* 13 *s.* 4 *d.* upon the ſaid three fourth parts of the cuſtoms [2 W. and M. ſeſſ. 1, chap. 4.] 213,447 *l.* 15 *s.* 9 *d.* upon the ſaid act, charging ſalt and other things therein mentioned [7 and 8 W. III, chap. 31.] 1,711,500 *l.* upon the ſaid two thirds of the additional exciſe [2 W. and M. ſeſſ. 2, chap. 10, and 5 and 6 W. and M. ch. 7.] 160,000 *l.* upon the ſaid additional impoſitions, payable for goods and merchandizes [4 and 5 W. and M. ch. 5.] 445,177 *l.* 7 *s.* 4 *d.* upon the ſaid duties payable upon vellum, &c. [5 and 6 W. and M. chap. 21.] 224,114 *l.* 7 *s.* 8 *d* ½; upon the ſaid duties charged upon marriages, &c. [6 and 7 W. III, ch. 6.] 648,000 *l.* and upon the ſaid continued impoſitions payable for wines, vinegar, &c. [7 and 8 W. III, chap. 10.] 146,181 *l.* 19 *s.* 5 *d.* ½; and on the ſaid yearly ſum of 300,000 *l.* out of the ſubſidy of tonnage and poundage [6 W. and M. chap. 1.] 142,666 *l.* 7 *s.* 3 *d.* ¾; amounting in the whole to the ſum of 5,160,459 *l.* 14 *s.* 9 *d.* ¼. We the Commons of Great Britain, in parliament aſſembled, having duly weighed and conſidered the premiſſes, and being deſirous to raiſe ſuch aids and ſupplies, and to uſe ſuch proper methods, as may make good the ſaid deficiencies, and raiſe the public credit, have chearfully and unanimouſly given and granted unto your ma-

8 and 9 W. III, 1697.

jesty, the supplies, impositions, and other duties, herein after mentioned. — Tonnage and poundage continued till the first of August, 1706.

§ 4. Duties on wines and vinegar, continued until 1706.

§ 6. Duties on tobacco to be paid according to the act of 7 and 8 W. III, chap. 10.

§ 7. Additional duties on goods and merchandizes, by 2 W. and M. sess. 2, chap. 4, continued until 1706.

§ 8. Additional impositions on goods and merchandizes, by 4 and 5 W. and M. chap. 5, continued until 1706.

§ 12. Duties on vellum, parchments, &c. by 5 and 6 W. and M. chap. 21, continued until 1706.

§ 14. Duties on marriages, births, and burials, by 6 and 7 W. III, chap. 6, continued until 1706.

§ 15. Duties on houses, by 7 and 8 W. III, chap. 18, continued until 1706.

§ 20. And for the better restoring of the credit of the nation, and advancing the credit of the corporation of the governors and company of the Bank of England, the common, capital, and principal stock of the said governor and company, shall be augmented and enlarged by the voluntary new subscriptions of all such person and persons, who shall be willing to subscribe any sum or sums of money.

§ 21. And for the better settling and adjusting the right and property of each member of the present corporation of the governor and company of the Bank of England, old and new members are impowered to settle the capital stock, or else the lord-keeper may adjust the same; and, in case the value of the said capital stock, upon such adjustment shall exceed 1,200,000 *l.* the overplus shall be divided amongſt the old members of the ſaid corporation, in proportion to their reſpective intereſts at that time. 8 and 9 W. III, 1697.

§ 23. Any perſon may ſubſcribe money for enlarging the capital ſtock; which ſubſcription ſhall be anſwered and made good in manner and proportion following; that is to ſay, four-fifths of each ſubſcription, ſhall be anſwered and made good to the ſaid capital and principal ſtock, by aſſigning to them the principal and intereſt whereunto ſuch ſubſcribers ſhall be really intitled by tallies of loan, and orders of repayment, or by tallies of *pro*, or aſſignment for monies lent or advanced, or are, or ſhall be charged, upon ſome of the aids, ſupplies, revenues, impoſitions, or other funds herein after mentioned; and, by delivering up at the ſame time, the tallies ſo aſſigned; that is to ſay, upon the ſaid firſt aid of 4 *s.* in the pound, the ſaid third aid of 4 *s.* in the pound, &c. and the other fifth ſhall be made good by Bank notes.

§ 24. Bank to allow 8 *per cent.* on tallies brought in, until the principal be paid off.

§ 26. Subſcribers to the capital ſtock, incorporated with the preſent governor and company, &c.

§ 38. All the monies brought into the Exchequer for the ſubſidy of tonnage and poundage, wines, vinegar, tobacco, &c. additional impoſitions, vellum, parchment and paper, marriages, births and burials, rates on houſes; all the monies brought into the Exchequer, borrowed upon the credit of 7 and 8 W. III, ch. 10, after the payments of the ſums in that act mentioned; (ſee p 61.) the monies ariſing upon the credit of 7 and 8 W. III, ch. 18, after the payments therein mentioned, (ſee p. 61.) ſhall be and are hereby declared to be the general fund, for making good the particular funds before in this act, expreſſed or computed to be deficient,

8 and 9 W. III, 1679. and are and ſhall be appropriated towards making good the ſaid deficient funds, by the payment and ſatisfaction of the principal and intereſt due, and to grow due thereupon.

§ 50. If at the end of one year, the duties hereby appropriated, be not ſufficient to pay off the intereſt due for that year, the deficiency to be ſupplied out of the next aids.—In caſe, upon the firſt of Auguſt, 1706, the fund hereby granted, be not ſufficient to pay off the principal and intereſt due on the foreſaid tallies and orders, the deficiency to be ſupplied out of ſuch aids, to be granted after the ſaid firſt of Auguſt, 1706.

§ 53. Additional duties on ſalt for one year.

§ 56. The ſaid duties on ſalt ſhall be applied for the payment of the intereſt due upon the ſaid tallies and orders charged upon the deficient funds before-mentioned.

Chap. 21. *An act for laying a duty upon leather for the term of three years, and making other proviſion for anſwering the deficiencies, as well of the like duties upon coals and culm, as for paying the annuities upon the lottery, and for lives charged on the tonnage of ſhips and the duties upon ſalt.* [The money ariſing by this act being deficient, is ſupplied by 1 Ann. ſtat. 1, cap. 13.]

By this act a duty of 15 *l. per cent.* of the true value, was laid upon all leather, tanned, tawed, dreſſed, or made in this kingdom, or imported for three years, from April the 20th, 1697: And for boots, ſhoes, or other made leather wares exported, the exporter was to have 5 *per cent. ad valorem.*

By the ſame act, the annuities for ſingle lives, granted by 4 W. and M. chap. 3, and 5 W. and M. chap. 5 and 20, were allowed to the 24th of June, 1697, to purchaſe a certain term for the residue of ninety-six years, from January 25, 1695, at four years purchase; and if they did not so purchase before that day, other persons were allowed to the 29th of September, to purchase the remaining term after the life in being, at the same rate. 8 and 9 W. III, 1697.

The money arising by the duty upon leather was appropriated to the payment of 564,700 *l.* with interest remaining due of the money lent upon the 6th of W. III, chap. 18, (see p. 59.) with a proviso, that, if there should be a deficiency at the end of three years, it should be made good out of the first aids to be afterwards granted by parliament.

The money arising by the sale of annuities was, in the first place, to be applied to the payment of the arrears of the annuities, upon the tonnage and salt duties, incurred between May 17, 1696, and May 17, 1697; next to the payment of 280,000 *l.* remaining due, of the money lent upon those acts; and the deficiency, if any, to be made good out of the first aids, to be granted by parliament, after the said 29th of September, 1697.

An act for granting to his majesty certain duties upon malt, mum, sweets, cyder and perry, as well towards carrying on the war against France, as for the necessary expence of his majesty's houshold, and other occasions. [The money arising by this act being deficient, is supplyed by 1 Ann. stat. 1. chap. 13.] Chap. 22. Malt-tax first imposed.

By this act 6*d* per bushel was laid upon all malt then made for sale, that from the 20th of April, 1697, to the 20th of July 1699, should be made for sale, or not for sale; and over and above former duties, 10*s.* a barrel for mum, 12*s.* for sweets, and for cyder and perry 4*s.* per hogshead. The importation of malt was prohibited, and the duty to be repaid upon ex-

8 and 9 W. III, 1697. portation; and, upon the credit of this act, 1,400,000 *l.* was to be raised by way of lottery, at a farthing a day interest for every 10 *l.* advanced, except the fortunate tickets, which were to bear no interest.

Chap. 24. *An act for granting to his majesty a further subsidy of tonnage and poundage upon merchandizes imported for the term of two years and three quarters; and an additional land-tax for one year, for carrying on the war against France.*

By this act an additional subsidy of tonnage and poundage was imposed, and was to continue from the first of May 1697, to the first of February, 1699. And an additional land-tax of 1 *s.* in the pound was laid upon lands, *&c.* and upon these two funds his majesty was enabled to borrow 1,200,000 *l.* or circulate Exchequer bills to that amount, at 5 *d.* *per cent.* per day interest.

Chap. 25. *An act for licensing hawkers and pedlars, for a further provision for payment of the interest of the transport debt for reducing Ireland.*

By this act a duty of 4 *l.* was laid upon every hawker and pedlar, travelling on foot, and 4 *l.* more on every one that travelled with any beast of burden, for every such beast he travelled with, from the 24th of June, 1697, to June the 24th, 1698.

Chap. 34. *An act for the lessening the duty upon tin and pewter exported, and granting an equivalent for the same, by a duty on drugs.* [Duties on drugs are continued by 6 Ann. chap. 22. for four years, and made perpetual by 7 Ann. chap. 7. sect. 26.]

By this act it was enacted, that after May 10, 1697, untill the first of August 1700, drugs imported from the place of their growth, in

English built ships, should pay the subsidy of tonnage according to their full value in the book of rates, whereas they before paid but according to one third; and drugs otherwise imported, to pay treble such value; but drugs used in dying were excepted.

This session began Dec. 3, 1697, and ended July 5, 1698; and the first thing done by the committee of supply was to direct their chairman to move, that the states, estimates and accounts to them referred, might be referred to a select committee to examine, which was agreed to, and ordered accordingly. And their first resolution, as to money-matters, was, that, in a just sense and acknowledgment of what great things his majesty hath done for these kingdoms, the sum of 700,000 *l.* *per annum* should be granted him during his life, for the support of the civil list; which was, after debate, agreed to by the house. 9 W. III, 1697.

The other supplies resolved and agreed were as follow:

1. For maintaining 10,000 men, at 4 *l.* per man, for 13 months (including the charge of ordnance for sea service), 520,000 *l.*

2. For maintaining guards and garrisons, 350,000 *l.*

3. For cancelling Exchequer-bills, 2,700,000*l.*

4. A supply for the speedy paying and disbanding the army.

After this, the committee entered into an examination of what arrears or debts were due to the army, the navy, &c. and to foreign princes for subsidies. They likewise found that there was a great deficiency in the three-shillings aid and subsidies granted with it, as also in the one-shilling aid of last session, and that it would be impossible to raise sufficient for clearing all the demands within the ensuing year; therefore they made only the following grants, to be raised for the year 1698, *viz.*

1. For making good the said deficiencies, 1,476,000 *l.*

2. For part of the arrears due to the army, 981,288 *l.* 13 *s.* 9 *d.*

3. For part of the arrears due to the navy, and for services belonging to it, 981,288 *l.* 13 *s.* 9 *d.* $\frac{1}{2}$

The ways and means for raising these supplies were as follow:

9 and 10 W. III, 1698. chap. 5.

An act for satisfying and discharging the arrears of several annuities which incurred between the 17th of May 1696, and the 17th of May 1697.

§ 1. For raising and discharging the sum of 255,663 *l.* 5 *s.* 8 *d.* which remains due and unpaid, to satisfy, clear, and pay off the several annuities, or sums of money, which, between the 17th of May, 1696, and the 17th of May, 1697, incurred and became due, and ought to have been paid, as well out of the five-seventh parts of the late duties of tonnage of ships, and other vessels, and out of two-seventh parts of the same duties, as also out of certain duties charged upon salt; persons entitled to annuities for life at 4 *per cent. per annum*, upon the several acts of parliament mentioned in 6 and 7 W. III, chap. 5, (see p. 57,) may, for every 100 *l.* paid for a single life, advance 56 *l.* more, for converting the same into a term certain for the residue then to come of 96 years, to be reckoned from the 25th of January, 1695, to take effect after the said estate for life, and in the same proportion for higher or larger annuities.

An act for granting to his majesty the sum of 1,484,015 l. 1 s. 11 d. ¾ *for disbanding forces, paying seamen, and other uses therein mentioned.* 9 and 10 W. III, 1698. chap. 10.

This money was raised by assessments on the several counties, according to the proportions in the act mentioned. Upon this fund was charged 850,000 *l.* lent between October 8, 1697, and April 4, 1698, with interest at 8 *per cent.* and also what should remain unsatisfied of the said annuity arrear upon the 11th of April, 1698; and his majesty was enabled to borrow upon it 1,400,000 *l.* at 8 *per cent.* including the two sums transferred to it, as aforesaid.

An act for granting several duties upon coals and culm. Chap. 13.

This act laid an additional duty of 5 *s. per ton*, and 7 *s.* 6 *d. per chalder*, upon all coals imported from Scotland, or any part beyond sea; and a duty of 5 *s. per chalder*, and 3 *s.* 4 *d. per ton*, upon all coals carried by sea, from any port of this kingdom, to any other port thereof; and for all culm water-born, 1 *s. per chalder.* This tax was imposed for five years, from May 1698; and the loan upon it was 500,000 *l.*

An act for continuing the duties [in 6 and 7 W. III, chap. 7,] *upon coffee, tea, chocolate, and spices, towards satisfaction of the debt due for transport-service for the reduction of Ireland.* Chap. 14.

These duties were continued to the first of May, 1701, and continued further by 12 and 13 W. III, chap. 11, until 1706.

9 and 10 W. III, 1698. chap. 23. *An act for granting to his majesty a further subsidy of tonnage and poundage, towards raising the yearly sum of 700,000 l for the service of his majesty's houshold, and other uses therein mentioned, during his majesty's life.*

§ 14. If the said revenue produce more than 700,000*l. per annum*, the overplus not to be disposed of but by parliament. [Repealed by 12 and 13 W. III, chap. 12, sect. 4.]

Chap. 24. *An act for enlarging the time for purchasing certain estates, or interests in several annuities, therein mentioned.*

§ 1. Persons having, or not having annuities for life, at 14 *l. per cent. per annum*, upon the several acts mentioned in 6 and 7 W. III, chap. 5, may, before December 1698, advance for every 100 *l.* &c. 56 *l.* for changing the same into a certain term for the residue of 96 years, to take effect after the said estate for life, &c. The sum raised upon this act was 221,724 *l.* 10 *s.*

Chap. 25. *An act for granting to his majesty, his heirs and successors, further duties upon stampt vellum, parchment, and paper.*

These duties were to commence August 1, 1698, and to continue for ever.

Chap. 27. *An act for licensing hawkers and pedlars, for a further provision of interest for the transport debt for reducing of Ireland.* See 8 and 9 W. III, chap. 25, p. 74.

Chap. 30. *An act for encreasing his majesty's duties upon lustrings and alamodes.*

By this act, lustrings and alamodes, which were before valued, in the book of rates, at 40 *s.*

per pound weight, were, from June 24, 1698, to be valued at 4 *l.* and to pay all duties upon importation according to that rate. 9 and 10 W. III, 1698.

An act for granting to his majesty an aid by a quarterly poll for one year. Chap. 38.

This act granted a poll-tax of 1 *s. per* quarter on all persons, not exempted on account of poverty, from paying to church and poor, with several exceptions as to children under sixteen years old; and all gentlemen and persons of rank to pay the several larger sums therein mentioned. Upon this fund his majesty was enabled to borrow 500,000 *l.* the first moiety advanced at 7 *l.* the other at 8 *l. per cent.* interest; and, by the same act, he was enabled to borrow 500,000 *l.* on the coal duty, at 7 *l. per cent.* interest for the first 100,000 *l.* and at 8 *l. per cent.* for the remaining 400,000 *l.*

An act for raising a sum not exceeding two millions upon a fund for payment of annuities, after the rate of 8 l per cent. per annum, and for settling the trade to the East-Indies. Chap. 44. Origin of the East-India Company.

§ 46. From the 29th of September, 1698, the sum of 160,000 *l.* out of the duties upon salt, and the additional stamp duties granted by this act, shall be the yearly fund for answering annuities of 8 *per cent.* to the subscribers of 2,000,000*l.* [See 10 Ann. chap. 28.] Who were to be incorporated, and to have the sole privilege of trading to the East-Indies, till the 29th of September, 1711; after which, upon three years notice, and repayment of their principal money advanced, and all arrears of interest, the duties, annuities, and things granted by this act were to cease.

This act laid an additional duty of 5 *d. per* gallon on all salt imported, from the 1st of July,

9 and 10 W. III, 1698. 1698, to the 25th of December, 1699, and from thence for ever, 7 *d. per* gallon; and on all home-made salt, 2 *d.* ½ a gallon, during the time aforesaid, and from thence for ever, 3 *d.* ½ a gallon, with proper additional allowances on several sorts of salted fish exported.

Upon this act was founded our present East-India Company; but the East-India Company then subsisting, were allowed to continue their trade to the East-Indies, until the 29th of Sept. 1701.

10 Will. III, 1698. The supplies granted in this session, which began Dec. 6, 1698, and ended May 4, 1699, were as follow:

1. For paying and disbanding the army intended to be disbanded, and other necessary occasions, 800,000 *l.*

2. For maintaining 15,000 sea men, 980,000 *l.*

3. For the ordinary of the navy, 220,000 *l.*

4. For maintaining guards and garrisons, 300,000 *l.*

5. For the office of ordnance, 50,000 *l.*

For answering the supplies these following acts were passed.

Chap. 1. *An act for granting an aid to his majesty, for disbanding the army, and other necessary occasions.*

On January the 12th, the House of Commons resolved, that a supply of 800,000 *l.* should be granted for the speedy paying and disbanding the army intended to be disbanded, and for other necessary occasions; and that, whoever should advance, or lend a sum of money, not exceeding 800,000 *l.* for disbanding the army, and for other necessary occasions, should be repaid out of the first aids to be granted that session of parliament.

An act for granting to his majesty the sum of 1,484,015 l. 11 d. ¼ for disbanding the army, providing for the Navy, and for other necessary occasions. 10 and 11 W. III, 1699. Chap. 9.

By this act, which was a land-tax of 3 s. in the pound, his majesty was enabled to borrow 1,400,000 *l.* including the 800,000 *l.* above-mentioned, at 7 *per cent.* and out of the first of the produce, the said 800,000 *l.* was to be repaid. And, as there were malt tickets, and tallies upon several funds, then remaining in the hands of the treasurer of the Navy, amounting to 287,727 *l.* 13 *s.* 11 *d.* the commissioners of the Treasury were, by this act, allowed to issue the same, at a discount not exceeding 10 *l.* *per cent.* to be applied to the victualling and course of the Navy. And farther, they were by the same act impowered to allow, out of the monies arising, by 6 W. and M. chap. 1, (see p. 57) after payment of what had been borrowed upon it, the sum of 40,000 *l.* by way of premiums to contractors for circulating Exchequer bills, And lastly, by a clause in this act, seven commissioners, who had been chosen by ballot, but none of them to be members, were appointed for six months, to take an account of the real and personal estates, forfeited in Ireland, since February 13, 1688, and the grants, dispositions, and reversals of outlawries thereupon, and for what considerations; and to give an account of their proceedings, when required, to the king and parliament in England.

An act for laying further duties upon sweets, and for lessening the duties, as well upon vinegar, as upon certain low wines and whale fins, and the duties upon brandy imported, and for the more easy raising the duties upon leather, and for Chap. 21

charging cinders, and for permitting the importation of pearl ashes, and for preventing abuses in the brewing of beer and ale, and frauds in importation of tobacco.

The duties imposed by this act were as follow: for all sweets made for sale between May 10, 1699, and July 10 following, 12 *s.* per barrel; from thence to March 25, 1701, 24 *s.* per barrel; and from thence to March 25, 1706, 36 *s.* per barrel. And it imposed for four years, from the 15th of May, 1699, a duty of 5 *s.* per chaldron on cinders imported, or carried coast-ways.

11 Will. III, 1699. For answering the supplies granted in this session, which began 10 Nov. 1699, the following acts were passed.

11 and 12 W. III, 1700, Chap. 2. *An act for granting an aid to his majesty, by sale of the forfeited, and other estates and interests in Ireland; and by a land-tax [of 2 s. in the pound] in England, for the several purposes therein mentioned.* The sum borrowed upon this act was 613,000 *l.* 6 *s.* 8 *d.*

Chap. 3. *An act for laying further duties upon wrought silks, muslins, and some other commodities, of the East-Indies; and for enlarging the time for purchasing certain reversionary annuities therein mentioned.*

By this act an additional duty of 15 *l. per cent.* of the true value, was laid upon silks and Bengals, and stuffs, made in Persia, China, or the East-Indies, of silk or herba; and all calicoes, painted, dyed, printed, or stained there; and all muslins, imported between the 25th of March, 1700, and the 30th of September, 1701. This duty produced, from the 25th of March, 1700, to the 29th of September, 1701, 132,638 *l.* 12 *s.* 3 *d.* By the latter part of this act, the time for purchasing the reversion of the annuities, so often mentioned, was enlarged to the second of November, 1700, and now advanced to five years purchase. The contribution raised hereon was 59,580 *l.*

This session ended April 12, 1700; soon after which the parliament was dissolved, and writs issued for chusing a new one.

The ways and means for raising the supplies granted in this session, (which began February 10, 1700, and ended June 4, 1701) were as follow: 12 and 13 W. III, 1700,

An act for granting an aid to his majesty for defraying the expence of his Navy, guards and garrisons for one year, and for other necessary occasions. Chap. 10.

This was an aid of 3 *s.* in the pound upon lands, tenements, hereditaments, offices, pensions, and personal estates. The sum of 1,484,948 *l.* 19 *s.* 3 *d.* was to be raised within the year, from the 25th of March, 1701.

An act for granting to his majesty several duties upon low wines, or spirits of the first extraction, and continuing several additional duties upon coffee, tea, chocolate, spices, and pictures, and certain impositions upon hawkers, pedlars, and petty chapmen, and the duty of 15 per cent. upon muslins, and for improving the duties upon japanned and lacquered goods, and for continuing the coinage duty, for the several terms and purposes therein mentioned. Chap. 11.

Upon this act his majesty was enabled to borrow 300,000 *l.* at 6 *l.* *per cent.* for the first 150,000 *l.* and 7 *per cent.* for the residue.

§ 26. Monies lent on this and the other acts herein mentioned, shall be applied as follows, *viz.* for the sea service 200,000 *l.* ordinary of

12 and 13 W. III, 1700. the Navy (excluding the charge of the regiſter for ſeamen) 190,000 *l.* towards extraordinary repairs of the fleet, 90,000 *l.* and for the ſervice of the Navy and the victualling thereof, and for the ſea ſervice of the office of ordnance, the ſum of 900,000 *l.* for land ſervice by the office of ordnance, 25,000 *l.* ſubſiſtence to guards and garriſons, 300,000 *l.* clothiers debts on account of the extraordinary expence of guards and garriſons, 40,000 *l.* for pay of twelve batallions intended for the aſſiſtance of the States-General, and for levy-money for the ſaid batallions, 181,033 *l.* 2 *s.* 6 *d* for payment of ſeven quarters intereſt due at Lady-Day, 1699, upon the malt tickets remaining unſatisfied, a ſum not exceeding 37,780 *l.* 1 *s.* and for payment of one years intereſt of the loans remaining due upon the firſt aid of 3 *s.* in the pound, a ſum not exceeding 33,847 *l.* 18 *s.* 5 *d.* and for payment of one year's intereſt, for the monies remaining unſatisfied, which were advanced upon the credit of the late duties upon vellum, &c. 1232 *l.* and, for paying one year's intereſt of the money remaining due upon the third quarterly poll-tax, 18,381 *l.* 12 *s.* and for paying one year's intereſt of the loans remaining unpaid upon the third aid of 3 *s.* in the pound, 1738 *l.* 7 *d.* and for 18 months intereſt of the principal money remaining due upon the regiſter for the late duties charged upon leather, 52,966 *l.* and for and towards half-pay now due, and which ſhall grow due, to diſbanded officers and ſoldiers, 41,000 *l.* and for completing the 66th payment upon the malt-tickets, ſo much as together with what remains in the Exchequer, ſhall be ſufficient to complete the ſum of 10,000 *l.* for the 66th payment, and the intereſt thereof; and for the ſalaries of five commiſſioners for ſtating the accounts of the army, tranſport debts, and prizes, and for incident charges in the execution of their truſts.

An act for appropriating 3700 l. weekly, out of certain branches of excise for public uses, and for making a provision for the service of his majesty's houshold and family, and other his necessary occasions. 12 and 13 W. III, 1700. Chap. 12.

§ 1. From the 25th of December, 1700, for five years 3700 *l.* per week, out of the excise duties shall be paid into the Exchequer [pertuated by 1 Geo. I stat. 1. chap. 1 sect. 1.]

§ 3. Residue of the branches of excise, *&c.* chargeable, with the yearly sum of 700,000 *l.* to be for the use of the king's houshold and family, *&c.*

§ 9. Any person or persons, may lend 820,000 *l.* upon credit of the said weekly payments; and that tallies of loan shall be levied for all and every sum and sums of money so lent, and that orders, according to the course of the Exchequer, shall be drawn, signed, and issued for the repayment of the same, and for the interest thereof, at 6 *l. per cent. per annum*, for the first 400,000 *l.* and 7 *l. per cent. per annum* for the remaining 420,000 *l.*

TAXES

SUBSISTING AT THE END OF

KING WILLIAM's REIGN.

AS our taxes were now become very numerous, it ſeems neceſſary to divide them into cuſtoms, exciſes, and inland duties.

By cuſtoms, are meant thoſe duties that are payable at the Cuſtom-houſe upon the importation of goods, and which conſiſt of five ſeveral parts, or branches, called, I. The old ſubſidy, or ſubſidy inwards. II. The petty cuſtom, or aliens duty. III. The additional duty. IV. The one *per cent.* inwards. And V. The compoſition on petty ſeizures.

The branch of cuſtoms was firſt granted by 12 Car. II, chap. 4, from the 24th of June, 1660, during the king's life; and was ſubſiſting at the end of King William's reign, under the title of *Cuſtoms*, having been continued till 1706, by ſtat. 8 and 9 W. III, chap. 20, (ſee page 66.) By 6 Ann, chap. 11, the one half of it was continued to the firſt of Auguſt 1808; and from thence for ever, by ſtat. 1 Geo. I, chap. 12, and was appropriated for the payment of annuities, amounting to 80,000 *l. per annum*, for ninety-nine years, from the 24th of June, 1708. The other half, by 6 Ann, chap. 19, was continued to the firſt of Auguſt, 1714; and from thence for ever, by 7 Ann, chap. 7, ſect. 28; and by 1 Geo. I, chap. 12, ſect. 1, 2, 15. This moiety, as alſo the ſurplus of the firſt moiety, after payment of the ſaid annuities, and the whole thereof, after the laſt day of June, 1808, are made part of the AGGREGATE FUND, by that act eſtabliſhed.

I. Subſidy inwards, or old ſubſidy. This duty conſiſts of two diſtinct parts, TONNAGE and POUNDAGE; which names ariſe from the different regulations whereby it is impoſed and levied. By the act of 12 Car. II, chap. 4, it is called, a *tonnage duty on wines imported*; being a certain ſum of money, payable out of, and charged upon, every ton of wine imported. And it is called a *poundage duty* on other goods and merchandize imported; becauſe it is regulated by a certain ſum, to be paid for the value of every pound, or twenty ſhillings of goods imported.

II. Petty cuſtoms, or aliens duty. This duty is payable by merchant ſtrangers, that is, aliens born, or denizens, on all goods imported, liable to the ſubſidy of poundage; but goods liable to the ſubſidy of tonnage, are not liable to this duty; becauſe an equivalent is included in the advanced ſum of the ſeveral ſubſidies laid on thoſe goods, when imported by aliens, or in foreign ſhips.

III. Additional duty. This duty, as well as the old ſubſidy, is compoſed of a *tonnage* and *poundage*.

IV. One *per cent.* inwards. This duty, as well as the old ſubſidy, and additional duty, conſiſts of a *tonnage* and *poundage*; being payable in ready money upon all goods and merchandizes liable to thoſe duties, and imported from any port, or place of the Mediterranean Sea, beyond the port of Malaga, into any part of Great Britain, in any ſhip or veſſel that hath not two decks, and doth not carry leſs than 16 pieces of ordnance mounted, together with two men for each gun, and other ammunition proportionable. But by ſtat. 9 Geo. II, chap. 33, ſect. 3, Britiſh ſhips exporting from any of his Majeſty's dominions, fiſh taken and cured by his Majeſty's ſubjects only (ſo that one moiety of their full lading be fiſh only) are not liable to this duty.

V. Compoſition on petty ſeizures. Though all goods, ſeized by the officers of the cuſtoms for non-payment of duties, are to be proſecuted to condemnation, either in the court of Exchequer, or before the juſtices of the peace, &c. and the King's moiety, or ſhare, paid unto the proper officers, before any writ, or order of delivery may be granted, except in the caſe of periſhable goods; yet when the ſeizure is ſo ſmall, that the cuſtom thereof does not exceed forty ſhillings, the commiſſioners of the cuſtoms, have, by their patent, a power to compound for it; and, in that caſe, the King's part is to be paid to the collector of the port of ſeizure, who is to account for it by the name of *compoſition on petty ſeizures*, which he is to comprehend under the general head of Cuſtoms.

Theſe five branches were eſtabliſhed during the reign of King Charles the Second, under the the title of *tonnage and poundage*; and were ſubſiſting at the end of King William's reign, under the title of *Cuſtoms*, having been continued till 1706, by 8 and 9 Will. III, (ſee p. 72) This, therefore, may be called the *firſt* branch of the public revenue, ranked under the head of CUSTOMS.

The ſecond branch of the public revenue is called, *the one per cent. outwards*, and was firſt granted by 12 Charles II, chap. 4, sect. 2, as a part of the subsidy of poundage, and continued therewith to August 1, 1710. By 9 Ann. chap. 6, it was continued to the 8th of March, 1742, and by 3 Geo. I, chap. 7, made perpetual.

The third branch is called *the new subsidy*, and consists of a *tonnage and poundage*. It was first granted by 8 and 9 W. III, chap. 23, sect 1, 4, from May 1, 1697, to Feb. 1, 1699. It was afterwards, by 9 and 10 W. III, chap. 23. sect. 1, continued from 31 Jan. 1699, during the king's life. By 1 Ann. chap. 7, sect 2, 1 Geo. I, chap. 1, sect. 2, 1 Geo. II, chap. 1, sect. 2, it was granted during the respective lives of Queen Anne and King George the First and Second; and, by 1 Geo. III, chap. 1, to his present Majesty for life; and is, with several other duties in the last mentioned act, to be applied towards the raising of 800,000*l. per annum* for the support of his Majesty's household, and of the honour and dignity of the crown.

The 4th is that called, *the impost on wines and vinegar*, first granted to King James the Second, from the 24th of June, 1685, to June 24, 1693. It was afterwards continued, for short terms, by several acts, and made perpetual by 3 Geo. I, chap. 9, sect. 10. By the 9th of Ann. chap. 21. and 1 Geo. I, chap. 21, this branch, with others in the said 9 Ann. mentioned, was made part of the South-Sea Company's original fund, for the payment of their annuity on their capital stock, increased by the said 1 Geo. I, from 9,177,967 *l.* 15 *s.* 4 *d.* to 10,000,000 *l.* and for the payment of 8,000 *l* *per ann.* allowed the said company, by the said acts, for charges of management.

The 5th, is that called, *the impost on tobacco*, first granted by King James the Second, from the 24th of June, 1685, to the 24th of June, 1693. It was continued afterwards by several acts, and made perpetual by 3 Geo. I, chap. 9, This branch makes part of the South-Sea Company's original fund.

The 6th is *the impost* 1690, first granted upon fifty-five several sorts of goods, by 2 W. and M. seff. 2, ch. 4, sect. 3, (see p. 43) from the 25th of December, 1690, to Nov. 10, 1695. It was afterwards continued by several acts, and made perpetual by 3 Geo. I, chap. 9, sect. 2, 3, 10. It makes part of the South-Sea Company's original fund.

The 7th is that called *the impost* 1692-3, first imposed (upon seventy-two several sorts of goods particularly named, consisting of different duties almost upon every sort; and upon all other goods not particularly rated in the first book of Rates, except mum, and goods particularly charged with the former impost, one shilling in the pound) by 4 and 5 W. and M. chap. 5, sect. 2. (see p. 52.) from March 1, 1693, to March 1, 1696. It was made perpetual by 3 Geo. I, chap. 9, sect. 2, 3, 10; and part of the South-Sea Company's original fund.

The 8th is called *the coinage*, first granted by 18 Car. II, chap. 5, sect. 11, from the 20th of December, 1666, for five years. It was afterwards continued by 25 Car. II, chap. 8, sect. 1, 1 Jam. II, chap. 24, 4 and 5 W. and M. ch. 24, 12 and 13 W. III, chap. 11, 7 Ann. chap. 24, 1 Geo. I, chap. 43, 9 Geo. I, ch. 19, 4 Geo. II, chap. 12, 12 Geo. II, chap. 5, 19 Geo. II, chap. 27, 7 Geo. II, ch. 27, and by 1 Geo. III, chap. 16, for seven years, from the first of March, 1761; and by 9 Geo. III, chap. 25, made perpetual.

The 9th is that called *the excise on salt*; because it was put under the management of the commissioners of excise; but, as it is paid upon the importation of foreign salt, it is placed under the head of customs. It is a duty of 3 *d per* gallon, first imposed by 5 and 6 W. and M. chap. 7, sect. 3, and by 7 and 8 W. III, ch. 31, sect. 2, continued for ever. By 9 and 10 W. III, chap. 44, (see p. 79.) there was granted a farther duty of 7 *d. per* gallon, from December 24, 1699, for ever; which by 3 Geo. II, chap. 20, was repealed, after December 25, 1730. But, by 5 Geo. II, chap. 6, it was revived from the 25th of March, 1732, for three years. It was afterwards continued by several acts, and by 26 Geo. II, chap. 3, made perpetual.

The 10th is that called, *the new duty on spice and pictures*, first granted by 6 and 7 W. III, chap. 7 (see p. 58.) from May 1, 1695, to May 2, 1698. It was afterwards continued by several acts, and by 11 Geo. I. chap. 9. made perpetual.

The 11th is that called, *the second 25 per cent. on French goods*, granted by 7 and 8 W. III, chap. 20, (see Part 1st. p. 62.) from Feb. 28, 1696, to Feb. 28, 1717. It was afterwards continued by several acts; and by 11 Geo. I, made perpetual. By 1 Geo. I, chap. 12, this branch makes part of the AGGREGATE FUND.

The 12th is that called, *the new duty on whale-fins*, granted by 9 and 10 W. III, chap. 45, sect. 2, from the 10th of July, 1698, to July 10, 1706. It was afterwards continued by several acts, and by 3 Geo. I, chap. 9, made perpetual. It makes part of the South-Sea Company's original fund.

The 13th is that called, *the new duty on coals, culm, and cinders*, first granted by 9 and 10 W. III, chap. 13, from May 15, 1698, to May 15, 1703. It was continued, as usual, and by 5 Geo. I, chap. 19, made perpetual. By 8 Ann. chap. 4, this branch was appropriated for the payment of annuities, amounting to 135,000l. for thirty-two years, from the 29th of September, 1710, and for the charges of paying the ſaid annuities. But, upon the ſubſcription into the South-Sea capital of part of the ſaid annuities, in purſuance of the 5th of Geo. I, chap. 19, and of other part, in purſuance of the 6th of Geo. I, chap. 4, the ſaid branch is now part of the South-Sea Company's additional funds.

The 14th, is that called *the* 15 *per cent. on muſlins*, firſt granted by 11 and 12 W. III, chap. 3, from March 25, 1700, to September 29, 1701. It was afterwards continued by ſeveral acts, and made perpetual by 11 Geo. I, chap. 9. By 1 Geo. I, this branch makes part of the AGGREGATE FUND.

The 15th, is that called *the exciſe on liquors imported*, firſt granted by 12 Car. II, chap. 23, from the 25th of December, 1660, during the king's life. It was afterwards continued by ſeveral acts, during the reſpective lives of King James II, King William, Queen Anne, King George the Firſt and Second; and by 1 Geo. III, chap. 1, it is granted to his preſent majeſty for life. This duty, both in England and Scotland, is under the management of the commiſſioners of the exciſe, who generally impower the collectors of the cuſtoms at the ſeveral ports to levy it for them; and therefore it is here put under the head of cuſtoms.

Theſe, except the duties of priſage and butlerage, (for on account of which ſee p. 7.) were the ſeveral branches of the cuſtoms ſubſiſting at the Revolution. We ſhall next give the exciſes ſubſiſting at the end of King William's reign; which were as follow, *viz.*

The two firſt, were the *temporary* and *hereditary* exciſes; for which ſee p. 29.

The 3d, was a new exciſe granted to King William and Queen Mary, their heirs and ſucceſſors, for ninety-nine years, from Jan. 25,

1692-3, by 4 W. and M. chap. 3. See p. 49. It was made perpetual by 1 Geo. I, chap. 12.

The 4th was a ſecond new exciſe granted to them, their heirs and ſucceſſors, for ſixteen years, from May 17, 1697, by 5 W. and M. chap. 7. See p. 53.

The 5th was a third new exciſe, granted to them, their heirs and ſucceſſors, from the ſame day, without limitation of time, by 5 W. and M. chap. 20. See p. 54.

The 6th was *an exciſe upon ſalt*, firſt granted to them from March 25, 1694, to May 17, 1697, by 5 W. and M. chap. 7, and continued to his majeſty, his heirs and ſucceſſors, for ever, by 7 and 8 W. III, chap. 31.

The 7th, was *a ſecond exciſe upon ſalt*, granted to King William, his heirs and ſucceſſors, for ever, by 9 and 10 W. III, chap. 44. See p. 78.

The 8th, was *an exciſe upon malt*, &c. now commonly called the *malt-tax*, firſt granted to King William, by 8 and 9 W. III, chap. 22. See p. 73.

The 9th, was *an exciſe on ſweets*, granted to King William, until the 25th of March, 1706, by 10 and 11 W. III, chap. 21. See p. 81.

The 10th, was *an exciſe on ſpirits, or low wines*, granted by 12 and 13 W. III, chap. 11, to commence the 25th of March, 1701, and to continue until the 25th of March, 1706.

All theſe are called *exciſes*; becauſe they were managed, and collected by the commiſſioners, and regulated by the laws of exciſe.

We come laſtly to thoſe branches of the public revenue, ſubſiſting at the acceſſion of Queen Anne, which we have ranked under the head of *inland duties*, and were as follow, *viz.*

1. The *Poſt-Office Revenue*, or duty upon letters ſent by the poſt, which having been granted to King Charles the Second, his heirs and ſuc-

cessors for ever, belonged to King William in right of his crown, and received no addition during his reign.

2. The several small branches and casual profits arising to the the crown by *wine licences*, *seizures*, *&c.*

3. *The first stamp duty*, granted to King William and Queen Mary, for four years, from June 28, 1694, by 5 W. and M. chap. 21; (See p. 56.) and continued to August 1, 1706, by 8 and 6 W. III, chap. 20.

4. *The duty upon hackney coaches*, granted to King William and Queen Mary, without limitation of time, by 5 W. and M. chap. 22.

5. *The duty on marriages, births, and burials, &c.* first granted to King William, for five years, from May 2, 1695, by 6 and 7 W. III, chap. 6, and continued to the first of August, 1706, by 8 and 9 W. III, chap. 20.

6. *The duty on houses and windows*, granted to King William for seven years, ftom March 25, 1696, by 7 and 8 W. III, chap. 18, and continued to the first of August, 1706, by 8 and 9 W. III, chap. 20.

7. *The duty on hawkers and pedlars*, first granted to King William for one year, by 8 and 9 W. III, chap. 25. It was the next session continued to June 24, 1701; and afterwards continued to June 24, 1706, by 12 and 13 W. III, chap. 11. See p. 83.

8. *The second stamp duty*, granted to King William, his heirs and successors for ever, by 9 and 10 W. III, chap. 25.

Of these eight branches of inland duties, six were introduced since the Revolution; and, when we consider that many of these customs, excises, and inland duties, affect the necessaries of life, or at least, the indispensable conveniences of life, as well as some of the materials necessary for working up our manufactures; and that, when a tax is laid upon any commodity, the dealers in that commodity always do, and indeed must raise the price a great deal more than the tax laid upon it, in order to make good the interest of the money they advance for paying that tax, and the risk they run of losing it by bad debts; we cannot be at a loss to find the true cause of the increase of wages, and the advanced price of all manufactures in this country; without maliciously imputing it to the idleness or extravagance of our people: for the labourer must live by his wages; and he that employs him by his profits: and if by taxes you increase the necessary expence of both, the former must have higher wages, and the latter greater profits; otherwise the one must starve, and the other become bankrupt.

The ways and means for raising the supplies granted this session, (which began December 30, 1701, in the thirteenth year of King William, and first of Queen Anne) were as follow: 9 W. and 1 Ann. 1701.

An act for granting an aid to his majesty, by laying duties upon malt, mum, cyder and perry. [Regranted by 1 Ann. stat. 2. chap. 3.] Chap. 5.

By this act a duty of 6*d.* per bushel, was laid upon malt; 10*s.* per barrel upon mum; and 4*s.* per hogshead on cyder and perry, to continue from the 9th of March, 1701, until the 24th of June, 1703. The sum borrowed upon this act (interest at 6 *per cent.*) was 600,000*l.* and the net produce of the duty for the time above-mentioned, as appears per account in the Excise-office, was 945,150*l.* 5*s.* 4*d.* ½. A composition may be made with any person for the said duties on malt not made for sale, at the rate of 5 s. *per annum*, for every head in the family.

Chap. 7. *An act for the better support of her majesty's houshold, and of the honour and dignity of the crown.*

By this act was established, what has been since called *the civil list revenue*; and, as it has been, and probably will be, repeated at the beginning of every reign, it seems proper to give a particular account of it. It was enacted by the first section, that from the 9th of March 1701-2, during the life of Queen Anne, the *excises* subsisting at the Revolution, (See p. 8.) should be continued to her majesty, in manner and form, and under the forfeitures mentioned in the acts therein recited, or by any other law in force relating to the excise.

By the 2d, it was enacted, that the tonnage and poundage granted by 9 W. III, chap. 23, should, from the 9th of March, 1701-2, be continued to her majesty during her life.

By the 3d, that the said two branches, together with the hereditary excise, the revenue of the Post-Office, first-fruits, fines of the Alienation Office, post-fines, wine-licences, sheriffs profers, compositions in the Exchequer, and seizures of uncustomed and prohibited goods, the revenue of the Dutchy of Cornwal, and any other revenue arising by the rents of lands in England or Wales, or for fines, for leases of the same, should be for raising 700,000 l. yearly for the support of her majesty's houshold, and of the honour and dignity of the crown; with a proviso, nevertheless, that the said hereditary and temporary excise, should be subject to the weekly payment of 38,700 l. according to 12 and 13 W. III, chap. 12. (See p. 85.) during the term of five years.

By the 4th, it was provided, that after the said term of five years, so much money as, together with the 3 *per cent. per annum*, (then to commence payable to patentees, by letters patent of K. Charles the Second*,) should make up the sum of 3700*l.* *per week* during her majesty's life, should be taken out of the hereditary excise, and the excise thereby granted, and the said 3 *per cent. per annum*, being deducted out of the hereditary part, the rest of the 3,700*l.* *per week*, should be disposed of to the public use and service.

The remaining sections of this act contain several very proper and necessary regulations for preventing the alienation of any of the crown revenues.

As by this act a revenue was established during her majesty's life, for the support of what is now called *the civil list*; as soon as her majesty had given the royal assent to this and the other acts then ready (March 30, 1702) she made a speech to both houses, in which, after returning thanks for this settlement, (which was no more than what had been settled upon her predecessor in time of peace) she told them, "That "she would take great care that it should be ma-"naged to the best advantage; and, while her "subjects remained under the burthen of such "great taxes, she would straiten herself in her "own expences, rather than not contribute all "she could to their ease and relief, with a just "regard to the support of the honour and dig-"nity of the crown: that it was probable, the "revenue might fall very short of what it had "formerly produced: however, she would give "directions, that 100,000*l.* should be applied "to the public service in that year, out of the "revenue they had so unanimously given her." From hence we may conclude, that Queen Ann, for the first year of her reign (and for the following years during the war, as this contribu-

* See p. 30.

tion was annually made by her majesty) had not 600,000 *l.* for defraying the whole expence of her civil list; whereas that expence, from the Revolution to the beginning of her reign, had amounted to about 660,000 *l.* yearly, one year with another.

Chap. 10. *An act for taking, examining, and stating the public accounts of the kingdom.*

Whereas many and great aids and provisions have been given, raised, and assigned, for the necessary defence of the crown and these kingdoms, and for the support of the government; to the end therefore, that both your majesty and the whole kingdom may be satisfied, and truly informed therein, may it please, *&c.*

Chap. 12. *An act for granting an aid to her majesty, by divers subsidies, and a land-tax.*

By this act the sum of 1,979,931 *l.* 19 *s.* 1 *d.* was to be raised within the year, from March 25, 1702, by a land-tax of 4 *s* in the pound. The sum borrowed upon it was 1,800,000 *l.* at 6 *per cent. per annum* interest. And the further sum of 800,000 *l.* (to be raised within the year from the 25th of March, 1702) was borrowed at 6 *per cent. per annum*, upon the following subsidies.

Upon stock in trade 6 *d.* in the pound, or 50*s.* *per cent.*

On securities for money at interest, 3 *d.* in the pound.

On annuities, pensions, stipends, or yearly payments, not charged upon land, or not exempted by parliament, 4 *s.* in the pound.

On all fees, salaries, wages, perquisites, allowances, poundage, gratuities, rewards, emoluments, income, and profits arising from, or belonging to, offices of state, or law, or offices ecclesiastical, civil, or military, 1 *s.* in the pound over and above the 4 *s.* in the pound charged in the land-tax.

On the income of all practisers in the law, preachers, and teachers in separate congregations, brokers, factors, practisers in physic or surgery, and apothecaries, and all other professions whatsoever, 4 *s.* in the pound.

And 4 *s.* to be paid by *every* person (over and above all the other rates) except persons receiving alms, and their children under sixteen years, and poor house-keepers, not paying to church or poor, and their children under sixteen years; and the children of day-labourers. and servants in husbandry under sixteen years, of such as have four or more, and are not worth 50 *l.* These subsidies produced only 300,524 *l.* 9 *s.*

An act for making good deficiencies, and preserving the public credit. Chap. 13.

This act recites, that several bills of credit, commonly called Exchequer bills, were made forth, and issued by divers acts of parliament, which were made, and passed in the reign of King William; and that the several branches of the public revenue mentioned in the said acts, were deficient in the whole to the amount of 2,338,628 *l.* 15 *s.* 5 *d.* $\frac{3}{4}$, besides interest due, and to grow due; therefore the tonnage and poundage granted by 12 Car. II, chap. 4, (See p. 87.) the duties on wines, *&c.* granted by 1 James II, ch. 3, (See p. 89.) the duties on tobacco, granted by 1 James II, ch. 4, (See p. 89.) the additional impositions on goods, *&c.* granted by 2 W. and M. sess. 2, ch. 4, (See page 90.) the additional impositions on goods, *&c.* granted by 4 W. and M. chap. 5, (See page 90.) the duties on vellum, *&c.* granted by 5 and 6 W. and M. chap. 21, and continued by 8 W. III, chap. 20; the duties on houses, granted by 7 W. III, chap. 18, and the duties on whale fins, granted by 9

W. III, chap. 45, were continued from July 31, 1706, to August 1, 1710.

By sect. 16 of this act, the overplus of the several duties granted by the 8th of W. III, ch. 20, 7 W. III, chap. 10, 31, 9 W. III, ch. 45, after satisfaction of principal and interest, then standing charged upon them, should be appropriated and applied to make good the said deficient sum of 2,338,628 *l.* 15 *s.* 5 *d.* $\frac{3}{4}$, and interest due, and to grow due, according to the respective acts: And, by sect. 16, it was enacted, that the produce of the several branches by this act continued, meaning the produce from August 1, 1710, together with the said overplus (if any should be) should be appropriated to make good the said deficiency, amounting to 2,338,628 *l.* 15 *s.* 5 *d.* $\frac{3}{4}$, and interest due, and to grow due thereon.

1 Ann. sess. 2, 1702. The ways and means for raising the supplies granted this session, which began Oct. 20, 1702, were as follow:

Chap. 1. *An act for granting to her majesty a land-tax for carrying on the war against France and Spain.*

By this act the tax upon lands was to be 4 *s.* in the pound, proportioned as formerly upon the several counties, *&c.* and the commissioners were named in the act, being all land-holders, as usual, though it was then well known, that very few land estates were assessed at near the full value, and most of them at less then half; so that, according to computation, it was reckoned at less than two millions; whereas, if that opportunity had been laid hold of to introduce a new assessment, the crown impowered to appoint commissioners, and those commissioners armed with sufficient powers, the tax would probably have produced double that sum — By this act the sum of 1,976,931 *l.* 19 *s.* 1 *d.* was to be raised within the year, from the 25th of March 1703, to be paid quarterly. The sum borrowed was 1,800,000 *l.* at 5 *per cent.*

An act for granting a supply to her majesty by several duties imposed upon malt, mum, cyder, and perry. Chap. 3.

The loan upon this act (at 5 *per cent.* interest) was 600,000 *l.*

An act for continuing the duties upon coals, culm, and cinders. Chap. 4.

The loan upon this act was 500,000 *l.* at 5 *per cent.*

An act for granting an aid to her majesty, by sale of several annuities at the Exchequer, for carrying on the war against France and Spain. Chap. 5.

This act recites, that by 4 W. and M. chap. 3, (See p. 49.) certain rates, or duties of excise upon beer, ale, and other liquors, were imposed during the term of 99 years, from the 20th of January, 1692, and made liable to the payment of several annuities, which were to be purchased in the form thereby prescribed; and that by an act 5 W. and M. chap. 20, (See p. 54.) two seventh parts of other duties of excise upon beer, ale, and other liquors, thereby granted to their majesties, their heirs and successors, are made liable to the payment of other annuities, which were to be purchased in the manner and form thereby prescribed: and that, by virtue, or in pursuance of the said several acts, and another act, 5 W. and M. chap. 5, (Se p. 52.) for supplying the deficiency of the money raised by the act first above-mentioned, several annuities were purchased at divers rates, for one, two, or three lives: and that several of the said annuities so purchased (and whereupon no reversion, or further estate, or interest, hath been purchased, and which have not been changed into a certain term of years, in pursuance of any subsequent act, or acts of parliament, in that behalf) were determined by the deaths of such contributors, or their nominees respectively; for whose life, or lives, the same were to continue respectively, which annuities, so determined, did amount, at least, to the sum of 5277 *l. per annum*, which was payable out of the duties of excise, imposed by the said first mentioned act of parliament, and to the sum of 565 *l. per annum*, which was payable out of the said two seventh parts of the other duties of excise before-mentioned. Now the Commons grant a further aid to arise by contributions for annuities to be purchased, *&c.* and enact, that any persons (being her majesty's natural born subjects) may pay into the Exchequer any sum of money not exceeding 79,155 *l.* [that is, at 15 years purchase] for purchasing annuities, *&c.* out of the excise, granted by 4 W. and M. chap. 3, and 8475 *l.* [at 15 years purchase] for purchasing annuities, *&c.* out of the two seventh parts of the excise granted by 5 W. and M. chap. 5.

Chap. 15. *An act for granting to her majesty several subsidies for carrying on the war against France and Spain.*

§ 1. All stock in trade was to pay 6 *d.* in the pound, or 50 *s. per cent.*

§ 3. Securities for money at interest, 3 *d.* in the pound, or 25 *s. per cent.*

§ 4. Annuities, pensions, stipends, or yearly payments, not charged upon land, or not exempted by parliament, 4 *s.* in the pound.

§ 5. On all fees, salaries, wages, perquisites, allowances, poundage, gratuities, rewards, emoluments, income, and profits accruing from offices of state, or law, or offices ecclesiastical, civil, or military, one shilling in the pound, over and above the 4 *s.* in the pound charged in the land-tax.

§ 6. The income of all practisers in the law, preachers and teachers in separate congregations, brokers, factors, practisers in physic and surgery, and of all other professions whatsoever, 4 *s.* in the pound.

If the sums assessed in London and Westminster, did not amount, the one to 78,642 *l.* 15 *s.* 7 *d.* ½, and the other to 31,096 *l.* 7 *s.* 3 *d.* the deficiencies in both places were to be re-assessed. ——The sum borrowed upon this act was 600,000 *l.* but these subsidies proved deficient by 17,384 *l.* 9 *s.* and 7 *d.*——The commissioners of the land-tax were again appointed to be the commissioners for carrying this act into execution.

An act for taking, examining, and stating the public accounts of the kingdom. Chap. 19.

Whereas many and great aids, and provisions, have been given, raised, and assigned for the necessary defence of the crown, and these kingdoms, and for the support of the government: to the end therefore, that both your majesty, *and the whole kingdom*, may be satisfied, and truly informed therein, be it enacted, *&c.* that William Bromley, Esq. Thomas Coke, Esq. Sir Godfrey Copley, Bart. Robert Byerley, Esq. Henry St. John, Esq. Francis Scobell, Esq. and Sir William Drake, Bart. shall be constituted commissioners for taking the accounts of all money of the public revenue of the crown, *&c.*

In this session the commissioners of accounts' appointed by an act of the former, presented to the house a representation, narrative, and observations upon the public accounts, whereupon an address, or rather remonstrance to her majesty, was agreed to, and presented by the whole house, Feb. 12, 1702-3: which is a piece that ought to be studied carefully by every man in the kingdom, but is too long to be inserted here; and therefore we shall only observe, that in this remonstrance, they complain (amongst other things) against the Earl of Halifax, then auditor of the Exchequer, for not transmitting regularly the imprest rolls to the Remembrancer of the Exchequer, by which the latter was prevented from suing such accomptants as were in arrear; against the Earl of Ranelagh, late paymaster, for not accounting for upwards of twenty-one millions sterling; and against Jacob Vanderesche, Esq. paymaster to his then late majesty's Dutch forces, they complain in these words:

"That he hath received 3,025,753 *l.* 9 *s.* " 6 *d.* which, by computation, is 52,907 *l.* 6 *s.* " 9 *d.* ¼ more than the pay of those troops " could have amounted to, if they had been " always compleat, no deductions made from " them, and upon an English establishment, " which all of them were not; and yet the " said Vanderesche hath passed no account at " all; and, though often summoned, hath never " appeared before the said commissioners of " public accounts, but stands indebted to the " said troops, in 112,229 *l.* 9 *s.* 8 *d.* which is " now demanded as an arrear due to them from " your majesty and the public."

From these and the like complaints they observed, that the great debt which lay upon the nation, and all the arrears which were owing to her majesty's forces, did not arise so much from the deficiencies of the funds, as for want of care in the management, and fidelity in the application of them.

The House of Lords likewise entered into an enquiry into the public accounts, and desired that the commissioners, who were members of the House of Commons, might have leave to be examined before their committee, but the commons, *after searching precedents*, did not think fit to consent to it. However, their lordships ordered the report of their proceedings to be printed at the end of the session; and even from their own report it appears, that the design of their enquiry was to justify the Lord Halifax; and to shew that there had been as great neglects in the public offices before the Revolution as afterwards; but, at this distance of time, it is impossible to judge the truth of the facts contested between the two houses; only we must observe, that the Earl of Ranelagh, who had been expelled the House of Commons, and 'Squire Vanderesche, do not seem to have had one friend in the house of Lords; for there is not one word in their report about either of them.

This session began 9th of November, 1703, and ended the 3d of April, 1704; and the ways and means for raising the supplies, were as follow: 2 and 3 Ann, 1703.

An act for granting an aid to her majesty by a land-tax, to be raised in 1704. Chap. 1.

By this act (which passed in the House of Commons, *nemine contradicente*) a tax of 4 *s.* in the pound was continued for one year more, upon all lands, tenements, and hereditaments, personal estates, annuities, pensions, and offices. The loan upon it was 1,850,000 *l.* at 5 *per cent*,

Chap. 2. *An act for granting an aid to her majesty, by continuing the duties upon malt, mum, cyder, and perry, for one year.*

The loan upon this act was 650,000 *l.* at 5 *per cent. per annum.*

Chap. 3. *An act for granting an aid to her majesty, for carrying on the war, and other her majesty's occasions, by selling annuities at several rates, and for such respective terms, or estates, as are therein mentioned.*

By this act, the 3700 *l.* per week, payable out of the hereditary excise, by 12 W. III, chap. 12. (See p. 85.) and 1 Ann, seff. 1, chap. 7, for five years, was mortgaged for 99 years, from March 25, 1704, in order to raise 1,018,867 *l.* 18 *s.* 6 *d.* by the sale of annuities for ninety-nine years, at fifteen years purchase, 900,000 *l.* of which was to be applied to the use of the war, and 118,867 *l.* 18 *s.* 6 *d.* to pay the annuities, until the 25th of December, 1705, inclusive; and also to raise 300,000 *l.* more for the use of the war, together with what should be necessary to discharge the annuities till the said 25th of December, 1705, inclusive.

§ 9, 10, 11. Persons may advance 1,018,867 *l.* 18 *s.* 6 *d.* for purchasing annuities for ninety-nine years, at fifteen years purchase; and for raising a further sum of 300,000 *l.* persons may purchase annuities for one life at nine years purchase, for two lives at eleven years purchase, three lives at twelve years purchase, or for ninety years, at fifteen years purchase; to commence from March 25, 1704.

An act for granting to her majesty an additional subsidy of tonnage and poundage for three years; and for laying a further duty upon French wines condemned as lawful prize, and for ascertaining the value of unrated goods imported from the East-Indies. Chap. 9.

This is commonly called *the one third subsidy*, and was granted for three years, from March 8, 1703-4; and together with an additional duty of 15 *l.* per ton, for all French wines condemned as prize, was made a fund for borrowing 300,000 *l.* at 5 *per cent.* interest.

These were all the provisions made by this session; but the Committee of ways and means resolved on, and the house agreed to, several other provisions, which the parties interested had weight enough to prevent being carried into execution: for December 12, it was resolved, that a duty of 12 *d.* a gallon, over and above all other duties, shuld be laid upon all wines, in the hands of the retailer, for three years, and to extend to such wines as retailers had then in their hands; and January 3, it was resolved, 1st, That all grants of lands, tenements, hereditaments, and pensions, from the 6th of February 1684, (the day King Charles the Second died) should be resumed. 2dly, That all serjeants at law, barristers, attornies, solicitors, and all public notaries and scriveners, or persons practising as such; and every chancellor, commissary, official, and register; and every advocate, proctor, apparitor, and persons practising as such; all preachers and teachers in separate congregations; all brokers to merchants, and all factors, and other persons acting by commissions from merchants, or others; and all and every person or persons, practising the art of physic, or surgery; and all and every person, and persons, exercising any other professions whatsoever, not being such professions as were chargeable to the land-tax, under the head of offices, should pay a tax of 4 *s.* for every 20 *s.* which, he, she, or they, should or might, by estimation, receive, perceive, or take, for, or by reason of such, his, her, or their, practices, or professions, for one year. And 3dly, That a further tax should be laid upon offices, pensions, and salaries.

Upon these resolutions, bills were, as usual, ordered to be brought in, but none of them had the good fortune to be passed into a law: even the said second resolution of January 3, though such a regulation had formerly been inserted in the land tax act, yet now could not obtain a place in that bill, the same having been before passed into a law, or in any other bill that was passed into a law; the reason of which probably was, because it had never produced any thing worth while; and indeed it never can, whilst the commissioners are named by parliament, and the assessors publicly known; which will always be the case, unless our landed gentlemen should, at last, for the sake of their country and their posterity, agree to a new assessment, and a strict scrutiny being frequently made into the yearly value of their own estates. We say for the sake of their posterity; for, should our commerce and manufactures be lost, by the burdens, dangers, and difficulties they are now exposed to, our lands will not only be greatly lessened in value, but will, by our losing our superiority at sea, become an easy prey to some foreign invader.

An act for the better and more regular paying and assigning the annuities, after the rate of three pounds per cent. per annum, payable to several bankers, and other patentees, or those claiming under them. Chap. 15.

Whereas by 12 W. III, chap. 12, it was enacted, that in lieu and discharge of certain perpetual annual payments, and of all arrears thereof, granted by King Charles the Second, to the respective patentees therein named, the hereditary revenue of excise, in the said act mentioned, should, from and after December 26, 1705, be and stand charged for ever with the payment of annual sums after the rate of three pounds *per cent. per annum*, for the principal sums mentioned in the said respective letters-patent, to be issued and paid out of the said revenue, by quarterly payments, out of the receipt of the Exchequer, by the officers of the same, unto the respective owners and proprietors of the several annual sums, and to their heirs and assigns for ever, without any further or other warrant, to be sued for, had, and obtained in that behalf; the said annual payments, after the rate of three pounds *per cent.* to be subject nevertheless to be redeemed, on payment of a moiety of the principal * sums mentioned in the said respective letters-patent. And whereas, by 1 Ann, stat. 1, chap. 7, it is enacted, That from and after the expiration of the term of five years therein mentioned, so much money as, together with the said payments, after the rate of 3 *l. per cent. per annum*, should make up the sum of 3700 *l.* for every week, during her majesty's life, should and might be taken out of the said hereditary duties of excise, and out of the duties of excise thereby granted for her majesty's life, and either or any of them; and

* See. p. 30.

the said payments, after the rate of 3 *l.* *per cent. per annum*, being deducted out of the hereditary part thereof, the residue of the said 3700 *l.* *a week*, should be applied and disposed of to, and for the public use and service. And whereas, by 2 and 3 Ann. chap. 3, it is enacted, That from and after the 25th of December, 1705, the said full, clear, and entire weekly sum of 3700 *l.* out of all the monies arising by the said hereditary duties of excise, and by the said duties of excise payable, during her majesty's life, and by every and any of them, according to the tenor and direction of the act of parliament above recited in that behalf; and from and after her majesty's disease, then the like full, clear, entire, and weekly sum of 3700 *l.* out of all the monies to arise by the said hereditary duties of excise; and every, or any of them, from time to time for ever, shall be brought and paid into the Exchequer; and that out of the monies of the said hereditary duties of excise, the said annual sums, after the rate of 3 *l. per cent. per ann.* prescribed by the said act of 12 W. III, chap. 12, shall be satisfied and paid, according to the directions therein contained, and subject to the power of redemption therein mentioned; now, for the better and more regular paying and assigning the said annuities, after the rate of 3 *l.* *per cent. per annum*, be it enacted, *&c.* that the auditor of the Exchequer, shall, with all convenient speed, certify to the lord-treasurer, the names of persons intitled to annuities, at 3 *l. per cent. per annum*, *&c.*

§ 2. Every person to have a warrant for payment, paying 1 d. in the pound fees.

§ 4. The annuities to be free from taxes, and to be as a personal estate, and not descendable to the heir.

§ 6. Persons entitled to annuities in right of their wives, not to dispose of such annuities, unless the wife be a party to the assignment.

The supplies granted this session, which began October the 24th, 1704, were as follow: 3 and 4 Ann. 1704.

An act for granting an aid to her majesty by a land-tax, to be raised in the year 1705. Chap. 1.

This tax was 4 *s.* in the pound, upon which was borrowed 1,150,000 *l.* at 5 *per cent.*

Before this year, the palaces of Whitehall and St. James were charged to a 4 *s.* aid in the sum of 10,686 *l.* 5 *s.* 4 *d.* But, by this act, the charge thereon, amounted to the sum of 30,754 *l.* 6 *s.* 3 *d.* which proportion hath been ever since observed in the assessments of the land-taxes: but, by a clause in 1 Geo. I, chap. 31, the deficiency on the said palaces, for the years 1706, 7, 8, 9, 10, amounting to 45,908 *l.* 12 *s.* 6 *d.* ¾ was discharged.

In the committee of ways and means, 5 *s.* in the pound was voted upon all pensions, offices, annuities, and yearly stipends: but, upon the report of the bill, that part which laid the additional shilling thereon, was struck out. The bill passed in the House of Commons, *nem. con.*

An act for raising money by sale of several annuities, for carrying on the present war. Chap. 2.

This act recites, that by 2 and 3 Ann. chap. 3, provision is made, that from and after the 25th of December, 1705, the sum of 3700 *l.* out of the monies therein mentioned, payable during her majesty's life, and from and after her majesty's decease; then the like sum of 3700 *l.* out of the said monies, from time to time for ever, ſhould be brought and paid into the Exchequer every week, in the manner and form, and under ſuch penalties, as are thereby preſcribed: that out of the ſaid weekly payments, certain annual ſums, after the rate of 3 *l. per cent. per annum*, therein mentioned, ſhould be ſatisfied and paid, and that out of the monies of the ſaid ſeveral branches of exciſe, ariſing in or by the ſaid weekly payments, the ſeveral annuities to be purchaſed in purſuance to the ſaid act, 2 and 3 Ann. ſhould alſo be paid and ſatisfied; and that all the reſt and reſidue of the monies ariſing by the ſaid weekly payments, and which, at the end of every year, the firſt year to begin the 25th day of December, 1705, ſhould remain, after ſatisfying, or reſerving ſufficient to ſatisfy all the payments which ſhould be then incurred, or grown due, as well for and upon the ſaid annual ſums, at 3 *l. per cent. per annum*, as alſo for and upon all the ſaid annuities, to be purchaſed upon the ſaid act, ſhould be applied and diſpoſed of, to and for the public uſe and ſervice, and not otherwiſe: that the ſaid annual ſums, after the rate of 3 *l. per cent. per annum*, do amount in the whole to the yearly ſum of 39,855 *l.* 16 *s.* ½; and the annuities purchaſed on the ſaid act of 2 and 3 Ann. for the ſaid term of 99 years, do amount in the whole to 67,924 *l.* 10 *s.* 6 *d.* ½; and the annuities purchaſed ſeverally on the ſame act for ſingle lives, do amount in the whole to 22,313 *l.* 6 *s.* 8 *d.* and the annuities ſeverally purchaſed on the ſame act for the lives of two perſons, and the ſurvivor of them, do amount in the whole to 10,528 *l.* and the ſeveral annuities purchaſed on the ſame act for the lives of three perſons, and the ſurvivors, and ſurvivor of them, do amount in the whole to 3979 *l.* 13 *s.* 4 *d.* and the charges of paying the ſaid annuities do amount to the yearly ſum of 1200 *l.* ſo that there doth remain at this time undiſpoſed of the money of the ſaid weekly payments, to be applied to the public uſe and ſervice, the yearly ſum of 46,598 *l.* 13 *s.* 5 *d.* or thereabouts, beſides the expectancies after the determination of the ſaid reſpective eſtates, for one, two, or three lives: therefore, *&c.* it ſhall be lawful for any perſons to advance and pay into the Exchequer any ſum or ſums of money, not exceeding, in the whole, the ſum of 877,930*l.* 19 *s.* 3 *d.* ½, for purchaſing ſuch ſeveral and reſpective annuities, as are herein mentioned, that is to ſay, any ſum, and ſums of money, not exceeding, in the whole, the ſum of 877,930*l.* 18 *s.* 3 *d.* ½ for any annuity, or annuities, to be paid during the full term of 99 years, from the 25th of December 1705, at the rate of fifteen years purchaſe; which rate doth amount to the ſum of 150*l.* for every ſuch annuity of ten pounds *per annum*, and proportionably for any greater annuity: which annuities ſhall not exceed, in the whole, the ſum of 46,000 *l* *per annum.*

§ 2. And whereas the perſons, who are, or may be intitled to the reſpective eſtates for life, or lives, purchaſed upon the ſaid act of 2 and 3 Ann. or ſome of them, are, or may be willing, or deſirous, for ſuch reſpective prices, or conſiderations, as are herein after mentioned, to have ſuch their reſpective eſtates, for life or lives, changed or converted into a certain term, or terms, for 99 years, to be computed from the ſaid 25th of March, 1704, of and in ſuch, or the like annuities, as they have for life, or lives, as aforeſaid, or that they, or ſuch as they ſhall nominate, ſhall or may be intitled to have, receive, and enjoy the like annuity, from and after the determination of his eſtate, for life or lives, for and during the reſidue, which ſhall be then to come, and unexpired, of the ſaid term of 99 years; and in caſes where the preſent owner of any ſuch annuity for life, or lives, is or may be unwilling, to purchaſe a further, or more certain eſtate, or intereſt therein, it is likely that ſome other perſon, or perſons, is, or may be deſirous to be admitted to purchaſe a future eſtate, or intereſt in, ſuch or the like annuity or annuities, to take effect from and after the determination of the reſpective eſtate, for one, two, or three lives, in being, and to continue for and during the then reſidue and the remainder of the ſaid term of 99 years, to be reckoned from the 25th of March, 1704, which ſhall be then to come and unexpired: Now, for the raiſing any further ſum and ſums of money, not exceeding 187,930 *l.* 19 *s.* 3 *d.* ½, other part of the ſaid ſum, not exceeding 877,930 *l.* 19 *s.* 3 *d.* ½; it is enacted, *&c.* that it ſhall and may be lawful for any perſon or perſons, natives or foreigners, being as original contributors, or by meſne aſſignments, or by other lawful ways and means, intitled to any eſtate, for one life in being, of or in any annuity, purchaſed upon the ſaid act of 2 and 3 Ann. to advance and pay into the Exchequer, ſo much money, as every or any ſuch annuity, being computed for ſix years, doth, or ſhall amount to, either for changing, or converting the ſaid eſtate for a ſingle life, into a certain term for the ſaid 99 years, to be computed from the ſaid March 25th, 1704; and that any perſon, intitled to any eſtate for two lives in any annuity, purchaſed, or obtained upon the ſaid act of 2 and 3 Ann. may advance and pay into the Exchequer, ſo much money as every ſuch annuity, being computed for four years, ſhall amount unto, either for changing, or converting the ſame eſtate for two lives, into a certain term for the ſaid 99 years, to be reckoned from March 25, 1704, or for the like annuity, to be paid to him, his executors, adminiſtrators, and aſſigns, immediately after the determination of the ſaid eſtate for two lives, during the then reſidue of the term of 99 years laſt mentioned, at the election of the purchaſers reſpectively; and that any perſon or perſons, intitled to any eſtate for three lives, of or in any annuity, purchaſed or obtained upon the ſaid act of 2 and 3 Ann. may advance and pay into the Exchequer, ſo much money as any ſuch annuity, being computed for three years, ſhall amount unto, either for changing or converting the ſame eſtate for three lives into a certain term for 99 years, or for the like annuity to be paid to him, his executors, adminiſtrators, and aſſigns, immediately after the determination of the ſaid eſtate for three lives, during the then reſidue of the term of 99 years laſt mentioned, at the election of the purchaſers reſpectively, *&c.*

An act for continuing the duties upon malt, mum, cyder, and perry, for one year. Chap. 3.

The ſum borrowed upon this act was 650,000 *l.* at 5 *per cent. per annum.*

An act for continuing duties upon low wines, and upon coffee, tea, chocolate, ſpices, and pictures, and upon hawkers, pedlars, and petty chapmen, and upon muſlins; and for granting new duties upon ſeveral of the ſaid commodities, and alſo upon callicoes, China ware, and drugs. Chap. 4.

By this act, the duties upon the ſeveral goods mentioned in the title, were continued from 1706, (to which time they had been continued by 12 and 13 W. III, chap. 11.) to the 24th of June 1710; and the additional duties upon the goods mentioned in the act, were to commence from the 1st of February, 1704-5, and to continue to the said 24th of June, 1710; which continued and additional duties were, by the act, made a fund for borrowing 700,000 *l.* at 6 *per cent.*

Chap. 5. *An act for granting to her majesty a further subsidy on wines and merchandizes imported.*

This is two thirds of the new subsidy, granted and continued by 9 W. III, chap. 23, upon all goods liable to the said new subsidy, except tobacco, and such currants, as shall be imported in English-built shipping, legally navigated, and sugar from the English plantations, and goods exempted from the new, and one third subsidies.

4 Ann. 1705. This session began the 25th of October, 1705, and the ways and means for raising the supplies granted in it, were as follow:

Chap. 2. *An act for granting an aid to her majesty by a land-tax, to be raised in the year* 1706.

By this act a tax of 4 *s.* in the pound was laid upon all lands, tenements, hereditaments, pensions, offices, and personal estates, for one year, in the same manner as in the former land-tax act. The sum borrowed upon this act was 1,850,000 *l.* at 5 *per cent.*

Chap. 5. *An act for continuing the duties upon malt, mum, cyder, and perry, for the service of the year* 1706.

The sum borrowed upon this act was 650,000 *l.* at 5 *per cent.*

An act for continuing an additional subsidy of tonnage and poundage, and certain duties upon coals, culm and cinders, and additional duties of excise, and for settling and establishing a fund thereby, and by other ways and means, for payment of annuities, to be sold for raising a further supply to her majesty, for the service of the year 1706, *and other uses therein mentioned.* Chap. 6.

The Commons, duly considering her majesty's great occasions for money to carry on the present war, and having regard, as well to the great burden of taxes now lying upon her majesty's subjects, as to the present condition of the public funds, and the present incumbrances thereupon, are therefore desirous, by such easy and effectual ways and means, as in this act are expressed and intended, to raise a sum of money, not exceeding, in the whole, 2,575,761 *l.* 16 *s.* 2 *d.* and such further sum of money, as will be sufficient, during the first two years of the term herein after mentioned, to compleat the payment of the annuities to be purchased upon this act, &c.

By this act, one third part of such, or the like several and respective duties, as by the act, 9 and 10 W. III, chap. 23, were granted to him during his life, and which, by 1 Ann. stat. 1, chap. 7, are continued to her during her majesty's life, for and upon any kind of wine or wines, and for and upon all manner of goods and merchandizes, which, after the 8th of March 1706, at any time during the term of 98 years, shall be imported, or brought into this realm, shall be continued to her majesty, her heirs, and successors.

§ 4. All such duties, as by 9 and 10 W. III, chap. 13, (see p. 77.) were charged upon the ſeveral ſorts of coal and culm therein mentioned, and the duty upon cinders, impoſed by 10 and 11 W. III, chap. 21, (ſee p. 81.) which duties upon coals, culm, and cinders, were continued by 1 Ann. ſtat. 2, chap. 4, from May 14, 1700, until May 15, 1708, ſhall be continued until the 30th of September, 1710.

§ 6. The exciſe on beer, granted by 5 and 6 W. and M. chap. 7, (ſee p. 53.) ſhall be continued from May 17, 1713, during 95 years. [Made perpetual by 1 Geo. 1, ſtat. 2, chap. 12, ſect. 8.]

§ 20. All the monies ariſing for the ſaid ſeveral ſubſidies of tonnage and poundage, coals, culm, and cinders, and the ſaid ſeveral rates and duties of exciſe, together with the ſum of 280,000 *l.* after mentioned, or ſo much of the ſaid ſubſidies, *&c.* as ſhall be ſufficient for anſwering the full and due payment of all the annuities to be purchaſed upon this act, ſhall be the general fund for payment of the ſame, and ſhall be charged therewith, and liable thereunto, and ſhall not be diverted to any other uſe, intent, or purpoſe whatſoever.

§ 21. And for the raiſing any ſum, or ſums of money, not exceeding, in the whole, the ſum of 2,855,761 *l.* 16 *s.* 2 *d.* that is, 2,575,761 *l.* 16 *s.* 2 *d.* thereof, for carrying on the preſent war, and 280,000 *l.* reſidue thereof, to be applied, with the produce of the ſaid ſubſidy of tonnage and poundage, for making good, or compleating the quarterly payments herein after mentioned, *&c.* it is enacted, *&c.* that any perſon may advance the ſaid ſum, for purchaſing annuities for 99 years, from March 25, 1706, at fifteen years and a half purchaſe, or 255 *l.* for 10 *l.* *per annum*; which annuities ſhall not exceed, in the whole, the ſum of 184,242 *l.* 14 *s.* *per annum.*

To find the frugality of this way of raising money, let us consider what the world would say of a landed gentleman, who should mortgage his estate, not only for the sum he then wanted, but for an additional sum for enabling him to pay the interest to grow due yearly, without being obliged to contract his yearly expence, in order to save money for the payment of that interest. Would not every one think such a gentleman in the high road to ruin?

An act for laying further duties on low wines, and for preventing the damage to her Majesty's revenue by importation of foreign cut whalebone, and for making some provisions as to the stamp-duties, and the duties on births, burials, and marriages, and the salt duties, and touching million lottery tickets, and for enabling her majesty to dispose of the effects of William Kidd, a notorious pirate, to the use of Greenwich Hospital, and for appropriating the public monies granted in this session of parliament. Chap. 12.

This act recites, that certain excise duties were granted by 12 and 13 W. III, chap. 11, (see p. 83,) and continued by 3 and 4 Ann. chap. 4, from the 24th of March 1706, until the 24th of June 1710, and grants further duties on low wines, &c. over and above the former. [Farther continued for 96 years, by 5 Ann. chap. 19, and made perpetual by 1 Geo. I, stat. 2, chap. 12, sect. 8.]

As her majesty was not enabled to borrow any money upon this act, it is probable, that the duty had not answered the money formerly borrowed upon it, and therefore the duty was continued for another year, to make good the deficiency, so that this act cannot properly be reckoned to have granted any money, unless what relates to Kidd's forfeiture, which amounted to 6472 *l.* 1 *s.*

On January the 8th, the House approved of two resolutions of the Committee of ways and means, for laying a tax upon all lands, tenements, hereditaments, and pensions, granted by the crown since the 6th of February 1684; and that this tax should be a *fifth* part of the value of the grant at the time it was made, and ordered that a bill should be brought in for this purpose; but the minister, as well as others, were too much interested to allow such a bill to be passed into a law.

5 Ann. 1706. This session began the 3d of December 1706, and the ways and means for raising the supplies granted in it, were as follow:

Chap. 1. *An act for granting an aid to her majesty by a land-tax to be raised in the year* 1707.

This land-tax was 4 *s.* in the pound; and upon it was borrowed the sum of 1,850,000 *l.* at 5 *per cent. per annum.*

Chap. 2. *An act for continuing the duties upon malt, mum, cyder, and perry, for the service of the year* 1707.

The loan upon this act was 650,000 *l.* at 5 *per cent.*

Chap. 13. *An act for continuing the duties upon houses, to secure a yearly fund for circulating Exchequer bills, whereby a sum not exceeding* 1,500,000 l. *is intended to be raised for carrying on the war, and other her majesty's occasions.*

By this act, the duties on houses, granted by 7 and 8 W. III, chap. 18, and continued by 1 Ann. stat. 1, chap. 13, are made perpetual; and, after the last day of July 1710, are made a fund for paying to the Bank 4 *l.* 10 *s.* *per cent per annum*, upon Exchequer bills, which were to be circulated by them, to the amount of 1,500,000 *l.* and which the Treasury was empowered to issue for the use of the war, and other her majesty's occasions; but, as to what might grow due for the said 4 *l.* 10 *s.* *per cent. per annum*, before the said 1st of August 1710, no other provision was made for it, except the surplus of these duties on houses, if any should be, after satisfying what was charged by the said act of 7 and 8 W. III, chap. 18; for, if no surplus, the Treasury was to issue Exchequer bills for the payment of this interest, or allowance to the Bank. All these Exchequer bills were to carry what interest the Bank should please to indorse upon them; and the Bank was to remain a corporation, till the said principal sum, and all arrears of the said allowance should be paid off, which it might be upon one year's notice, and then these duties were to be applied to what use the parliament should direct; or, in the mean time, if the duties should, at the end of any quarter, produce more than was sufficient for paying this allowance, such surplus was to be disposed of by parliament.

An act for continuing the duties on low wines and spirits of the first extraction, and the duties payable by hawkers, pedlars, and petty chapmen, and part of the duties on stampt vellum, parchment, and paper, and the late duties on sweets, and the one-third subsidy of tonnage and poundage, and for settling and establishing a fund thereby, and by the application of certain overplus monies, and otherwise, for payment of annuities, to be sold for raising a further supply to her majesty, for the service of the year 1707, and other uses therein expressed. Chap. 19.

§ 1. The duties on low wines, which were continued, or granted, until the 24th of June, 1710, by 3 and 4 Ann. chap. 4, are further continued for ninety-six years *; the duties on hawkers and pedlars, granted by 9 and 10 W. III, chap. 27, and continued by 3 and 4 Ann. chap. 4, shall be further continued from the 23d of June 1710, for the term of 9 years. *Made perpetual by* 1 Geo. I, *stat.* 2, *chap.* 12, *sect.* 8

§ 3. The duties on vellum, parchment, and paper, granted by 5 and 6 W. and M. chap. 21, and by 1 Ann. stat. 1, chap. 13, continued to the 1st of August 1710, shall be further continued for 96 years. *Made perpetual by* 1 Geo. I, *stat.* 2, *chap.* 12, *sect.* 8.

§ 5. Sweets to pay 36*s.* per barrel, for 99 years. *Made perpetual by* 1 Geo. I, *stat.* 2, *chap.* 12, *sect.* 8.

§ 8. The additional subsidies of tonnage and poundage, and other duties, which were granted, and continued by 4 Ann. chap. 6, from the 8th of March 170 , during the term of 98 years, shall be further continued, from the expiration of the said term of 98 years, for the term of one year.

§ 9. Lord Treasurer to make good the quarterly payments.

§ 10. And for the better securing the quarterly payments, which shall grow due on or before Michaelmas 1710, upon the annuities to be purchased in pursuance of this act, the sum of 35,000 *l.* part of the contribution-monies to be raised by sale of annuities upon this act, shall be towards discharging the said quarterly payments.

§ 11. And whereas the rates and duties of excise granted by 4 and 5 W. and M. chap. 3,

* Made perpetual, by 1 Geo. I, stat. 2, chap. 12, sect. 8.

do annually produce more than sufficient to discharge the annuities charged thereupon; the overplus of which rates and duties hath been, and is to be computed, on the 24th of June yearly: the rates and duties of excise granted by 5 W. and M. chap. 20, the overplus whereof hath been, and is to be computed as followeth; that is to say, as to five seventh parts thereof (being appropriated to make good the fund of the governor and company of the Bank of England) the same have been, and are to be computed on the first of June yearly; and as to the other two seventh parts thereof, being for payment of several other annuities, the same have been, and are to be computed on the 25th of March yearly. The rates and duties of excise granted 5 and 6 W. and M. chap. 7, for the term of sixteen years, for payment of the lottery annuities therein mentioned; the overplus whereof, when the same shall arise, is to be computed on the 25th of March yearly; and the particular rates and duties upon salt, and the particular duties upon stampt vellum, parchment, and paper, granted by 9 and 10 W. III, chap. 25, and 9 and 10 W. III, chap. 44, and are charged with several annuities, amounting to 160,000 *l. per annum*, to the companies, or persons intitled to the trade to the East-Indies; the overplus of which several rates and duties last mentioned, hath been, and is to be computed on the 29th of September yearly. Now it is enacted, *&c.* that the Lord Treasurer, *&c.* shall apply the said overplus monies of the said several rates, duties, and funds, to make good the quarterly payments on this act.

§ 14. The monies arising from the said several rates and duties upon low wines and spirits of the first extraction; the duties payable by hawkers, *&c.* and the duties upon sweets, and the ſaid duties upon ſtampt vellum, parchment, and paper; the ſaid additional ſubſidy, and the ſaid ſum of 35,000 *l.* and the ſaid reſpective overplus monies of the ſaid former annuity funds, ſhall be a general fund for the payment of all the annuities to be purchaſed on this act.

§ 15. For the purchaſe of annuities for 99 years, perſons may advance 1,155,000 *l.* at 16 years purchaſe, from March 25, 1707.—Annuities not to exceed 72,187 *l.* 10 *s.* *per annum*, payable quarterly.

Chap. 27. *An act for continuing ſeveral ſubſidies, impoſitions, and duties, and for making proviſions therein mentioned, to raiſe money by way of loan for the ſervice of the war, and other her majeſty's neceſſary and important occaſions, and for aſcertaining the wine meaſure.*

§ 1. The duties of tonnage and poundage, granted by 12 Car. II, chap. 4, which, by ſubſequent acts, were continued until the 1ſt of Auguſt 1706, and by 1 Ann. ſtat. 1, chap. 13, were granted to continue until Auguſt 1, 1710, are continued to Auguſt 1, 1712.

§ 4. The duties on wines and vinegar, granted 1 James II, chap. 3, and continued by 1 Ann. ſtat. 1, chap. 13, until Auguſt 1, 1710, ſhall be further continued until Auguſt 1, 1712.

§ 5. Duties on tobacco, granted by 1 James II, chap. 4, and continued by 1 Ann. ſtat. 1, chap. 13, until Auguſt 1, 1710, are further continued to the 1ſt of Auguſt 1712.

§ 7. Duties on Eaſt-India goods, *&c.* granted by 2 W. and M. ſeſſ. 2, chap. 4, and continued by 1 Ann. ſtat. 1, chap. 13, are further continued to the 1ſt of Auguſt, 1712.

§ 8. Duties on goods and merchandizes granted by 4 and 5 W. and M. chap. 5, and continued by 1 Ann. ſtat. 1, chap. 13, are continued to Auguſt 1, 1712.

§ 10. Duties on whale-fins, *&c.* granted by 9 and 10 W. III, chap. 45, continued to Auguſt 1, 1712.

§ 12. Clauſe of loan for borrowing at 6 *per cent.* intereſt, the ſum of 822,381 *l.* 15 *s.* 6 *d.* $\frac{1}{4}$, and ſuch farther ſum as ſhould be found neceſſary, for paying the intereſt quarterly, till the duties ariſing by this act, or the ſaid act of 1 Ann. ſtat. 1, chap. 13, ſhould be ſufficient for that purpoſe; ſo that to borrow a ſum of money, and then to borrow a further ſum to pay the intereſt thereof, was now become a common practice.

This ſeſſion began the 23d of October, 1707, and the ways and means for raiſing the ſupplies granted in it, were as follow: 6 Ann, 1707.

An act for granting an aid to her majeſty to be raiſed by a land-tax in Great Britain, for the ſervice of the year 1708. Chap. 1.

By this act was to be raiſed the ſum of 2,043,836 *l.* 16 *s.* 5 *d.* $\frac{1}{2}$, *viz.* on England, Wales, and Berwick upon Tweed, 1,995,882 *l.* 5 *d.* $\frac{1}{2}$; and on Scotland, to be paid at Edinburgh, free of all charges, 47,954 *l.* 16 *s.*

The loan upon this act was 1,880,000 *l.*

An act for charging and continuing the duties upon malt, &c. for the ſervice of the year 1708. Chap. 4.

The loan upon this act was 650,000 *l.*

An act for raiſing a further ſupply to her majeſty for the ſervice of the year 1708, *and other uſes, by ſale of annuities charged on a fund not exceeding* 40,000 l. *per annum, to ariſe by appropriating ſeveral ſurpluſſes, and by granting fur-* Chap. 5.

ther terms in the duties on low wines, and on hawkers, pedlars, and petty chapmen, the ſtamp duties, the one third ſubſidy, the duty on ſweets, and one of the branches of exciſe, and by making other proviſion in this act mentioned.

The preamble to this act, recites, 5 and 6 W. and M. chap. 7, 4 Ann. chap. 6, 5 Ann. chap. 19, 4 and 5 W. and M. chap. 3, and then it is enacted, that from and after the 25th of March, 1708, for the term of 99 years, the ſum of 40,000 *l.* ſhall be ſet apart, and appropriated for the payment of the annuities to be purchaſed on this act.

§ 2. And for the better raiſing, ſecuring, and eſtabliſhing of the ſaid fund, the ſaid ſum of 40,000 *l.* ſhall be charged upon, and payable out of all the overplus, or ſurplus monies of the ſaid rates, duties, ſubſidies, and other funds, ſettled for payment of the annuities purchaſed upon the ſaid acts of 4 Ann. chap. 6, and 5 Ann. chap. 19, and the overplus of the exciſe acts, 4 and 5 W. and M. chap. 3.

§ 3. And for the better ſecuring the quarterly payments, which ſhall grow due before Michaelmas, 1710, upon the annuities to be purchaſed in purſuance of this act, the ſum of 100,000 *l.* part of the contribution-monies to be raiſed by ſale of annuities upon this act, or ſo much thereof, as ſhall be ſufficient to make good the ſaid yearly fund of 40,000 *l.* for the firſt two years and a half of the ſaid term of 99 years, ſhall be reſerved and applied towards diſcharging the quarterly payments, to grow due before the 30th of September, 1710.

§ 4. The duties upon low wines, by 5 Ann. chap. 19, granted for the term of 96 years, ſhall be continued in Great Britain, after the ſaid 96 years for one year; and the duties upon hawkers and pedlars, and powers for granting licences, which, by 5 Ann. chap. 19, are to continue for 96 years, from the 24th of June, 1710, ſhall be paid in Great Britain after the ſaid 96 years for one year; and ſuch duties upon vellum, *&c.* as by 5 Ann. chap. 19, were continued for 96 years, from the laſt of July 1710, ſhall be continued in Great Britain, after the ſaid 96 years for one year; and the tonnage and poundage, *&c.* called *the one-third ſubſidy*, which, by 5 Ann. chap. 19, are continued for one year, after 96 years, commencing the 8th of March, 1706, ſhall be continued throughout Great Britain, from the expiration of the ſaid one year, for one whole year from thence.

§ 5. The exciſe upon beer, *&c.* which, by 4 W. and M. chap. 3, was granted for 96 years, from the 25th of January, 1692, ſhall be continued throughout Great Britain, after the ſaid 96 years, for fifteen years.

§ 8. Natives or foreigners may pay into the Exchequer, ſums not exceeding 640,000 *l.* for purchaſing annuities payable for 99 years, from the 25th of March, 1708, at 16 years purchaſe, *viz.* 160 *l.* for every annuity of 10 *l.* the conſideration to be paid on or before the 25th of September, 1708, all the annuities not to exceed 40,000 *l.* *per annum*, payable at the four moſt uſual feaſt-days.

An act for continuing one half part of the ſubſidies of tonnage and poundage, and other duties upon wines, goods and merchandizes imported, which were granted to the crown in the twelfth year of King Charles the Second, and for ſettling a fund thereby, and by other ways and means, for payment of annuities not exceeding 80,000 l. *per annum, to be ſold for raiſing a further ſupply to her majeſty, for the ſervice of the year* 1708, *and other uſes therein expreſſed.* Chap. 11.

§ 1. For raising the sum of 1,280,000 *l.* *viz.* 1,000,000 *l.* for the charges of the war, *&c.* and 260,000 *l.* to make good the payments of the annuities to be purchased on this act, as herein after mentioned; there shall be paid to her majesty, *&c.* from the last day of July 1712, for 96 years, one half part of the subsidies granted by 5 Ann. chap. 27, *viz. one half of the old subsidy.*

§ 5. The said 260,000 *l.* part of the contribution-money, to be raised by sale of annuities on this act, shall be reserved for the payment of the said annuities quarterly, before the said duties can take place for payment thereof.

§ 7. For raising the said 1,280,000 *l.* all persons may pay into the Exchequer sums not exceeding 1,280,000 *l.* for purchasing annuities payable during 29 years, from the 24th of June 1708, at 16 years purchase, *viz.* 160 *l.* for every annuity of 10 *l.*——All the annuities not to exceed 80,000 *l.* *per annum*, and payable at the four usual feasts.

Chap. 17. *An act for assuring to the English company trading to the East-Indies, on account of the united stock, a longer time in the fund and trade therein mentioned, and for raising thereby the sum of* 1,200,000 l. *for carrying on the war, and other her majesty's occasions.*

§ 1. In this act is the following recital, among others; *viz.* And whereas an indenture tripartite, bearing date July 22, 1702, made between her majesty of the first part, the governor and company of the merchants of London trading to the East-Indies, of the 2d part, and the English company trading to the East-Indies of the 3d part, it was, among other things, agreed, with her majesty's approbation, that the said governor and company of merchants of London, trading to the East-Indies, should purchase from the members of the ſaid Engliſh company, ſo much of their capital ſtock, as would make the property of the ſaid governor and company of merchants of London, trading into the Eaſt-Indies, equal to the property which would then remain to the other members of the ſaid Engliſh company trading to the Eaſt-Indies; and that the whole trade, which might, or ſhould be carried on during the term of ſeven years, to be reckoned from the date of that indenture, to and from the Eaſt-Indies, and the other parts within the limits aforeſaid, for, or in reſpect of their ſeveral ſtocks and funds thereby agreed to be united, ſhould be for the benefit and behoof of all the members of the ſaid Engliſh company trading to the Eaſt-Indies, proportionable to their ſhares in the capital or principal ſtock thereof; and, that the ſaid governor and company of merchants of London, trading to the Eaſt-Indies, ſhould have a right and power equal to the reſt of the members of the ſaid company, in the direction, management, and carrying on of the ſaid trade, during the ſaid term of ſeven years; and that, after the end, or expiration of the ſaid term of ſeven years, the whole trade to the Eaſt-Indies, and other the parts within the limits aforeſaid, for, or in reſpect of their united ſtock and fund, ſhould for ever (ſubject to the redemption of the ſaid fund by parliament) be wholly managed and carried on by the ſaid Engliſh company trading to the Eaſt-Indies, by whatſoever name the ſame ſhould then be called.—And to that end and purpoſe, many covenants, conditions, and agreements, were contained in the ſaid indenture, as by the ſame may more fully appear. And whereas the united ſtock of the ſaid governor, and company of merchants of London trading to the Eaſt-Indies, in their own names, or in the names of others in truſt for them, doth at this time amount to 1,992,800 *l.* part of the ſum of 2,000,000 *l.* mentioned in 9 and 10 W. III, chap. 44, and their united fund doth amount to 159,420 *l.* *per annum*, part of the ſum of 160,000 *l.* mentioned in 9 and 10 W. III, chap. 44. And, as well the ſaid governor and company of merchants of London trading into the Eaſt-Indies, as the reſt of the members of the ſaid Engliſh company trading into the Eaſt-Indies, are willing to advance your majeſty a further ſum of 1,200,000 *l.* upon the terms herein after expreſſed, &c. therefore the ſaid Engliſh company trading to the Eaſt-Indies, as well for and on behalf of the ſaid governor and company of merchants of London trading into the Eaſt-Indies, as for, and on behalf of all other the members of the ſaid Engliſh company, ſhall pay into the Exchequer, * 1,200,000 *l.* &c.

Chap. 19. *An act for continuing the half ſubſidies therein mentioned, with ſeveral impoſitions, and other duties, to raiſe money by way of loan, for the ſervice of the war, and other her majeſty's neceſſary and important occaſions, and for charging of prize goods and ſeizures, and for taking off the draw-backs of foreign cordage, and to obviate the clandeſtine importation of wrought ſilks.*

By this act the half-ſubſidies, granted by 5 Ann. chap. 27, were continued from July 31, 1712, to Auguſt 2, 1714. *Made perpetual by* 7 Ann. *chap.* 7, *ſect.* 29.

* For this they were to have no intereſt, upon condition that they ſhould continue a company, and enjoy their ſole privilege of trading, together with their annuity of 160,000 *l.* until March 1726.

Prize wines were made liable to a duty of 25 *l.* per ton, and all prize goods were made liable to other duties; and upon the credit of the duties, or subsidies granted, or continued by this act, or by the said act of 5 Ann, chap. 27, after satisfaction of what had been charged upon them, her majesty was enabled to borrow 729,067 *l.* 15 *s.* 6 *d.* ¾, together with such sums as should be sufficient to pay the interest of the said sum at 6 *per cent.* quarterly, till the duties should become sufficient for that purpose.

An act for continuing several duties therein mentioned, upon coffee, chocolate, spices, pictures, and muslins, and additional duties upon several of the said commodities, and certain duties upon callicoes, china wares, and drugs; and for continuing the duties called the two-third subsidies of tonnage and poundage, for preserving the public credit; and for ascertaining the duties of coals exported for foreign parts; and for securing the credit of the Bank of England; and for passing several accounts of taxes raised in the county of Monmouth; and for promoting the consumption of such tobacco, as shall have paid her majesty's duties. Chap. 22.

The duties mentioned in the title of this act, which had been continued by 3 and 4 Ann. chap. 4, were continued from the 23d of June, 1710, for four years next ensuing; and the said two-thirds subsidy, imposed by 3 and 4 Ann. chap. 5, was continued from the 7th of March, 1708-9, for three years next ensuing. These duties were continued, not for raising any supply for the ensuing year, but for what was called preserving public credit; because it then appeared, that the produce of them, in the time for which they had been before granted, would not satisfy the principal and interest of the sums borrowed upon them; therefore regularly a state of their produce should have been laid before the committee of supply, the deficiency from thence calculated, and a sum granted for making good that deficiency, which sum should have been provided for in the committee of ways and means, by continuing those duties.

7 Ann. 1708. This session began the 16th of November, 1708, and the ways and means for raising the supplies granted in it, were as follow:

Chap. 1. *An act for granting an aid to her majesty, to be raised by a land-tax in Great-Britain, for the service of the year* 1709.

This land-tax was 4 *s.* in the pound, and the loan upon it was 1,880,000 *l.* at 5 *l. per cent.*

Chap. 3. *An act for charging and continuing the duties upon malt, &c. for the service of the year* 1709.

The loan upon this act was 650,000 *l.* at 6 *l. per cent.*

Chap. 7. *An act for enlarging the capital stock of the Bank of England, and for raising a farther supply to her majesty, for the service of the year* 1709.

By this act a new agreement was established with the Bank; which was conditionally made before, or soon after the meeting of the parliament; and, being laid before the parliament, by way of a proposal from the Bank, the same was approved of, first, by the committee of ways and means, and on the 10th of February by the house, whereupon an address was resolved on, that her majesty would issue a commission under the great seal, for taking subscriptions for enlarging the capital stock of the

Bank, to enable them to comply with the proposal they had made, and the House had accepted. But, that the reader may the more easily understand the terms of this proposal, it seems proper to give him a short state of the affairs of the Bank, as they then stood.

By the 5th of W. and M. chap. 20, the capital stock of the Bank consisted of 1,200,000 *l.* being the sum then lent by them to the government, for which they were to have an annuity of 100,000 *l.* till repaid, and till then they were to continue a corporation; but the corporation was to cease upon twelve months notice after the 1st of August 1705, and repayment of the said sum, and all arrears of the said annuity. By 8 and 9 W. III, chap. 20, the Bank was empowered to encrease their capital, in order to enable them to pay off tallies, or orders upon several deficient funds, and they were to have an annuity at the rate of 8 *l. per cent.* upon all such as they did pay off, in proportion to which their capital was to be increased, which was not to be redeemed till after the 1st of August, 1710, upon twelve months notice, when, upon repayment of all that was due to them, the corporation was to cease; and by this act it was provided, that during their continuance, no other Bank was to be erected, or permitted by act of parliament; but this was the only exclusive privilege as yet granted. Thus the affairs of the Bank stood until 5 Ann. chap. 13, when the Bank undertook to circulate 1,500,000 *l.* in Exchequer Bills, in consideration of which they were to have an annuity of 4 *l.* 10 *s. per cent.* till paid off; and to enable them to circulate those bills, they were empowered to make what call they pleased for money from their proprietors, and were to continue a corporation till those bills ſhould be paid off and cancelled; after which, that is to ſay, by an act of the very next ſeſſion, the money paid in upon this call was converted into capital ſtock, ſo as that the whole addition made to the original capital, by the laſt mentioned act of King William, or by this act, ſhould not exceed 1,001,171 *l.* 10 *s.* —But in this laſt act there was a proviſo, that it ſhould not reſtrain the corporation from calling in from their members, any further ſum, or ſums of money.

Thus we may ſee, that at the beginning of this ſeſſion, the capital ſtock of the Bank amounted to 2,201,171 *l.* 10 *s.* for 1,200,000 *l.* of which they had from the govenment, an annuity of 100,000 *l.* and as to the reſidue, they had an intereſt at the rate of 8 *l. per cent. per annum*, for all the tallies, or orders which they had paid off, by virtue of the ſaid act of 8 and 9 W. III, chap. 20, and which were ſtill remaining in their hands unredeemed; and beſides, they had an intereſt of 4 *l.* 10 *s. per cent. per annum*, for all the Exchequer bills iſſued by virtue of the ſaid act of 5 Ann. chap. 13; none of which, as will preſently appear, had yet been diſcharged, or cancelled; but, on the contrary, a great addition made to them, by the new bills iſſued quarterly, for paying the intereſt, or premium, as it became due.

This was the ſtate of their affairs at the beginning of this ſeſſion, and now they offered to pay off, and deliver up to be cancelled, all the Exchequer bills iſſued by virtue of the ſaid act of 5 Ann. chap. 13, amounting with intereſt to 1,775,027 *l.* 17 *s.* 10 *d.* ½. 2dly, To advance and lend to the government 400,000 *l.* without any intereſt after the 1ſt of Auguſt, 1711, but were to deduct at the rate of 6 *l. per cent.* intereſt from the day the money was advanced until the ſaid 1ſt of Auguſt, ſo that for this 400,000 *l.* they were to have intereſt for the firſt two years, but none afterwards. And 3dly, They offered to circulate new Exchequer bills to the amount of 2,500,000 *l.* In conſideration of all this, they were to have liberty to double their capital by new ſubſcriptions, at ſuch rate as they thought fit. 2dly, They were to have annuity of 106,501 *l.* 13 *s.* 5 *d.* being at the rate of 6 *l.* *per cent. per annum*, for the 1,775,027 *l.* 17 *s.* 10 *d.* $\frac{1}{2}$, which they were to advance for cancelling the ſaid old Exchequer bills; the 4 *l.* 10 *s.* *per cent. per annum*, formerly allowed them for circulating thoſe bills being now to ceaſe. 3dly, The new Exchequer bills were to carry an intereſt 2 *d.* *per cent. per diem*; and over and above, they were to have 3 *per cent. per annum*, from the time they ſhould be iſſued till the day they ſhould be diſcharged. 4thly, They were to continue a corporation, and enjoy their firſt fund of 100,000 *l.* *per annum*, until the 1ſt of Auguſt, 1732; but, upon twelve months notice after that day, and payment of all then due to them, their corporation and annuity were to ceaſe. 5thly, No new Exchequer bills, were, without their conſent, to be iſſued, until all now iſſued, ſhould be diſcharged. And, 6thly, No company in partnerſhip, exceeding the number of ſix perſons, were, during their continuance, to be allowed to circulate bills, or notes payable on demand, or at any time leſs than ſix months.

Theſe terms being accepted by the Houſe, and her majeſty's commiſſion iſſued in purſuance of their addreſs, ſubſcription-books were opened for adding 2,201,171 *l.* 10 *s.* to their capital, at the rate of 115 *l.* for every 100 *l.* capital ſtock, which was near the price their ſtock then ſold for, and the ſubſcription was instantly filled; so that from henceforth their capital amounted to 4,402,343 *l.* and from what is above we may see, that they had now a very large revenue coming into them weekly from the government, besides the profits they made by banking.

Now, as to the fund settled by this act, for raising this additional revenue to the Bank, for paying the interest to grow due upon these new Exchequer bills, and for discharging and cancelling them by degrees, the duty on houses, which had been continued for ever by the 5th of Ann. chap. 13, was appropriated to the payment of the said annuity of * 106,501 *l.* 13 *s.* 5 *d.* and as a fund for the new Exchequer bills, the subsidies of tonnage and poundage, called the two-third subsidies, and the duties upon coffee, cocoa-nuts, chocolate, cocoa-paste, tea, nutmegs, cinnamon, cloves, mace, and pictures, mentioned in stat. 6 Ann. chap. 22, *viz.* those granted by 3 Ann. chap. 4, and the further rates imposed upon white callicoes, porcelane, called china wares, and drugs, which are hereby made perpetual, and the half subsidies granted by 5 Ann. chap. 27, and 6 Ann. chap. 19, and hereby made perpetual, *viz.* half the *old subsidy*; and all monies, which shall arise of the other half subsidies, continued by 6 Ann. chap. 11. over and above the annuities charged thereon, shall be a fund, as well for paying all such monies as shall be due for interest on the Exchequer bills, and for the premium of 3 *l.* *per cent.* *per annum*, and for raising the yearly sum of 200,000 *l.* for paying off the

* An annuity of 71,001 *l.* 4 *s.* 3 *d.* ¾, was established in lieu hereof, by 11 Geo. I, chap. 9, sect. 1. And farther provision is made relating hereto, by 1 Geo. II, stat. 2, chap. 8.

ſaid bills *. But, as theſe duties were then under mortgage, and could not be applied to this uſe, till the ſums formerly charged upon them were paid off, therefore the Treaſury was by this act impowered to iſſue new Exchequer bills every quarter, for the payment of the intereſt and premium, to grow due quarterly, until the funds thus appropriated ſhould be free and ſufficient to anſwer the ſame; and theſe new bills thus to be iſſued quarterly, the Bank likewiſe undertook to circulate, at the ſame intereſt and premium with the principal bills. Thus for *four* or *five* years, we were to borrow money quarterly, to pay the intereſt growing due upon the principal ſum now borrowed, and that intereſt to be quarterly converted into principal, bearing an intereſt at the rate of 6 *l. per cent.* the intereſt of which intereſt was again, at the end of next quarter, to be converted into principal bearing intereſt; and ſo from quarter to quarter, until the appropriated fund ſhould become ſufficient to anſwer the ſame. A moſt frugal way of raiſing money for the public ſervice, and worthy *the wiſdom of the nation!* But any thing rather than put the people out of conceit with the war, by loading them with new taxes; and all the uſurers, both public and private, were fond of this method of carrying it on.

An act for continuing ſeveral impoſitions and duties, to raiſe money by way of loan; and for exporting Britiſh copper and braſs wire duty free; and for circulating a further ſum in Exchequer bills, in caſe a new contract be made in that behalf, &c. Chap. 8.

* A moiety of the inland duty on coffee, and all the duty on chocolate, is appropriated to this fund by 10 Geo. I, chap. 10,—for the further application of this fund, which is now part of the AGGREGATE FUND, ſee 1 Geo. I, chap. 12. 3 Geo. I, chap. 8.

By this act, the duties continued by 6 Ann. chap. 17, to August 1, 1714, were further continued to August 1, 1716; and, after payment of what had before been borrowed upon them, were made a fund for issuing new Exchequer bills to the amount of * 612,739 *l.* in case the Bank should agree to circulate the same upon the like terms as in the former act, in which case, the general fund, established by the former act, was likewise to be a collateral security for these new bills. And the duties thus continued by this act, were also to be a fund for borrowing 645,000 *l.* at 6 *per cent.* together with such sums as should be necessary to borrow, for paying the interest to grow due quarterly, till these duties should become free, and sufficient to satisfy the same.

The said bills carry an interest of two pence *per cent. per diem*, and the Bank was allowed a premium of 3 *l. per cent. per annum*, for circulating and exchanging for ready money the said bills, after they have had a currency in the revenue or taxes, and shall have been re-issued at the Exchequer.

Chap. 24. *An act for continuing the former acts for the encouragement of the coinage, &c.*

By this act the duties, continued by 4 Ann. chap. 22, were further continued, from March 1, 1708-9, for seven years, and to the end of next session; and the Treasury was empowered to issue the following sums out of the coinage duty, besides the 3500 *l.* formerly allowed, *viz.* 6000 *l.* to pay a reward of two-pence half-

* But by indenture between the Earl of Godolphin, Lord High Treasurer, and the Bank of England, bearing date the 28th of September, 1709, the Bank agreed, in pursuance of a resolution of a general court, to circulate but to the amount of 400,000 *l.*

penny per ounce for plate, or foreign coin, brought to the Mint to be coined; and the yearly sums of 12,000 *l.* for the Mint in Scotland, and 400 *l.* for prosecuting false coiners, *&c.* in Great-Britain.

The ways and means for raising the supplies granted in this session (which began November 15, 1709,) were as follow: 8 Ann. 1709.

An act for granting an aid to her majesty, to be raised by a land-tax, in Great-Britain, for the service of the year 1710. Chap. 1.

This tax was 4 *s.* in the pound, and the loan upon it was 1,880,000 *l.*

An act for charging and continuing the duties upon malt, &c. for the service of the year 1710. Chap. 3.

The loan upon this act was 650,000 *l.*

An act for continuing part of the duties upon coals, culm, and cinders, and granting new duties upon houses, having 20 *windows, or more, to raise the sum of* 1,500,000 *l. by way of lottery.* Chap. 4.

By this act, the duties on coals, culm, and cinders (being three fifth parts only of the said duties continued by 4 Ann. chap. 6, until the 30th of September 1710,) are continued until September 30, 1742. These duties were made perpetual, by 5 Geo. I, chap. 19, sect. 1.

§ 4. New duties are granted on houses, from the 29th of September 1710, until September 30, 1742, *viz.* for every dwelling-house, inhabited within Great-Britain, having 20 windows or more, and under 30, the yearly sum of 10 *s.* and for every such dwelling-house, having 30 windows or more, the yearly sum of 20 *s.* which several and respective duties, as to such houses in England, Wales and Berwick, is over and above the ſeveral duties amounting to 10*s. per annum*, chargeable upon houſes there, by former acts made in England. Theſe two duties were granted for raiſing an annual fund of 135,000*l.* and, if deficient in any one year, that deficiency to be made good out of the next aid to be granted by parliament; and upon this fund, the ſum of 1,500,000*l.* was to be raiſed for carrying on the war, by a lottery, at 10*l.* a ticket, and the adventurers were to be intitled to annuities for 32 years, the blanks at 14*s. per annum*, and the benefit tickets to ſeveral greater annuities, from 5*l.* to 1000*l.* yearly.

The prizes (No. 3752, in the act 3750) to be paid half yearly, at Lady-day, and Michaelmas, amounted to 32,625*l.* yearly. The blanks (No. 140,248 in the act 146,250) at 14*s.* per blank, to be paid at Michaelmas yearly, amounted to 102,373*l.* 12*s. per annum*.

The contribution-money was to be paid into the Exchequer on or before the 1ſt of September 1710; and an intereſt of 8*l. per cent. per annum*, to be allowed the contributors from the time of actual payment, until the 29th of September 1710: and the receivers to be allowed by the Treaſury, not exceeding one penny in the pound, for what paid by them of the ſaid contribution-money into the Exchequer.—The books for receiving ſubſcriptions to this lottery, were opened on the 20th of January, 1709, at Mercer's Chapel, and above 600,000*l* were ſubſcribed that day, and the remainder about the end of March following.

Chap. 7. *An act for granting to her majeſty new duties of exciſe, and upon ſeveral imported commodities, and for eſtabliſhing a yearly fund thereby, and by other ways and means, to raiſe* 900,000*l. by* *sale of annuities, and (in default thereof) by another lottery, for the service of* 1710.

By this act, a new excise was laid upon beer, ale, and other liquors, and an additional duty over and above all former duties, upon spice, raisins, and snuff, for establishing an annual fund of 81,000 *l.* on which was to be raised 900,000 *l.* by the sale of annuities for 32 years at the rate of 9 *l. per cent.* and if this whole sum should not be subscribed before the 1st of May, 1710, then the residue to be raised by such another annuity lottery as that just mentioned. Consequently this excise and duty was to continue from Lady-day 1710, for thirty-two years.

An act for laying certain duties upon candles, and certain rates upon monies to be given with clerks and apprentices, towards raising her majesty's supply, for the year 1710. Chap. 9.

By this act, a new duty, over and above all former duties, was laid upon all candles imported, and an excise upon all candles made in Great-Britain, by which a new and very numerous body of people were made subject to the laws of excise, and a most heavy burden was laid upon all our manufactures. This duty and excise commenced May 1, 1710, and were by this act to continue for five years; and, by the same act, a tax was laid upon all sums received with clerks or apprentices to commence at, and to continue for the same time. And upon all these together, her majesty was enabled to borrow 500,000 *l.* at 6 *l. per cent.* Thus we find, that in this session, our ministers and members found themselves under a necessity to impose some new taxes; but they took care that these new taxes were such as fell more heavy upon the poor or middling sort of people, than upon the rich.—Upon the question in the committee, for laying a duty on candles, ayes 77, noes 50. And upon the question to agree with the committee in the said resolution, ayes 123, noes 82.—Upon the question in the committee for laying a duty upon houses throughout Great-Britain, ayes 132, noes 111. And, upon the question in the committee, that the additional duty on every house having 20 windows, be 10 *s.* ayes 141, noes 92.

Chap. 13. *An act for continuing several impositions, additional impositions, and duties upon goods imported, to raise money by way of loan, for the service of the year* 1710; *and for taking off the over-sea duty on coals exported in British bottoms, &c.*

By this act, the impost on wines and vinegar, the impost on tobacco, the impost 1690, the impost 1692; and the duties on whalefins, continued by 7 Ann. chap. 8. to the 31st of July 1716, were further continued, until the 1st of August 1720; and upon this remote fund, her majesty was enabled to borrow the sum of 1,296,552 *l.* 9 *s.* 11 *d.* $\frac{3}{4}$ at 6 *l.* *per cent.* but, as this fund stood engaged for monies already borrowed upon it, to the said 1st of August 1716; therefore the duties on salt and rock-salt, (continued by 7 W. III, chap. 31, for ever) after satisfaction of the principal and interest charged on the fund mentioned in 1 Ann. sess. 1, chap. 13, until the said 1st of August 1716, were also appropriated to pay the interest upon this sum to grow due in the mean time, so far as the surplus would amount to; and, in case of no surplus, or not sufficient, the Treasury were empowered to borrow money quarterly at 6 *l.* *per cent.* to make good the said interest; so that, if this salt-duty produced no surplus, we were to pay a quarterly compound interest for this present sum of 1,296,552 *l.* a most frugal and easy way of procuring ready money! which shews how greatly the nation stands obliged to those *honest gentlemen* who lent their money upon such terms.

The loans to pay the interest on the above loans, till the said fund should take place, were as follow, *viz.* for and until the 25th of March 1711, computed, according to 9 Ann. chap. 11, at 74,875 *l.* 19 *s.* 1 *d.* ¼, for and until the 25th of December 1711, computed at, (as per the said 9 Ann. chap. 21, on the sum of 1,371,428 *l.* 9 *s.* 1 *d.* that is, 1,296,552 *l.* 9 *s.* 11 *d.* ¾, and 74,875 *l.* 19 s. 1 *d.* ¼.) 61,714 *l.* 5 *s.* 7 *d.*

The ways and means for raising the supplies granted in this session, (which began November the 25th, 1710,) were as follow: 9 Ann. 1710.

An act for granting an aid to her majesty by a land-tax, for the service of 1711. Chap. 1.

This land-tax was 4 *s.* in the pound, and the loan upon it was 1,880,000 *l.* at 6 *l. per cent.*

An act for charging and continuing the duties upon malt, &c. for 1711. Chap. 3.

The loan upon this act was 650,000 *l.* at 6 *l. per cent.*

An act for reviving, continuing, and appropriating certain duties upon several commodities to be exported; and certain duties upon coals to be water-borne, and carried coastwise; and for granting further duties upon candles, for 32 *years, to raise* 1,500,000 *l. by way of lottery, for the service of* 1711, *&c.* Chap. 6.

By this act the subsidy outwards, on several goods exported, (which had continuance until the 1st of August 1710, by 1 Ann. sess. 2, chap. 13, and by 5 Ann. chap. 18,) was revived, and further continued, from the 8th of March 1710, until March 9, 1742, except such duties as were formerly granted to be paid upon the exportation of sea coals for parts beyond the seas, instead of which other duties are hereby imposed. The following duties on coals exported, were granted for the same time, *viz.* coals of Wales, or the West of England and Scotland, exported to Ireland, or the Isle of Man, the chalder containing 36 bushels, Winchester measure, * twelve pence; the ton, containing twenty hundred weight, 8 *d.* coals of all sorts, exported to the British plantations, the chalder 2 *s.* the ton 1 *s.* 4 *d.* &c.—Question in the committee, that a duty be laid on all other coal, and collected at the pit, ayes 61, noes 157. The duty of 12 *d.* for every 112 *l.* upon leather exported, of all sorts, sheep-skins, and calve-skins, tanned, tawed, or dressed, first granted by 20 Char. II, chap. 5, and revived and continued by sundry acts, to the 25th of March 1710, &c. was revived and continued from the 8th of March 1710, until the 9th of March 1742. The duty of one *per cent.* outwards on goods exported in certain British ships to the Mediterranean, beyond Malaga (first granted by 14 Char. II, chap. 11, and continued by the several acts, which continued the old subsidy of tonnage and poundage,) was likewise continued until the time above mentioned. The duty of 5 *s.* upon every woollen cloth exported, granted by 6 Ann. chap. 8,

* Two shillings was the sum voted by the committee, but the same was lessened to twelve pence upon the report.

without limitation, was continued to the ſame time. All which duties were appropriated for eſtabliſhing a fund of 135,000*l. per annum*, on which was to be raiſed, for the public ſervice by way of lottery, at 10*l.* a ticket, the ſum of 1,500,000*l.* And, as in this lottery, the blanks were in 32 years to have their whole money repaid with 6*l. per cent.* intereſt till repayment, therefore a further ſum of 428,570*l.* was charged upon this fund, to be divided as directed among the fortunate tickets, and to be paid to them in 32 years, with the like intereſt till paid, ſo that the public were thus for ready money to pay, beſides intereſt, a premium of above 28*l.* 11*s.* 5*d. per cent*; and yet to get it even at this rate, we were obliged to make uſe of that bane of induſtry and frugality called a *lottery.*

An act for enabling and obliging the Bank of England, for the time therein-mentioned, to exchange all Exchequer bills for ready money upon demand, &c. Chap. 7.

By this act, the Bank were obliged to circulate all the Exchequer bills then out-ſtanding, that is to ſay, to pay the principal and intereſt due upon them when demanded, and alſo all the Exchequer bills that were to be iſſued quarterly, for the payment of intereſt upon ſums before borrowed on the ſecurity of anticipated funds; and that, whether theſe bills had before had a currency in the Exchequer or no; and for this ſervice they were, by this act, to have 45,000*l.* paid them annually, until ſo many of theſe bills ſhould be diſcharged and cancelled, as ſhould reduce them to 1,900,000*l.* which annual premium of 45,000*l.* they were to have, beſides the 3*l. per cent.* for circulating them, and this premium was secured to be paid them out of any of the unappropriated funds of this session, until July 31, 1714, and from that day out of the duties arising by the acts, 7 Ann. chap. 7, and 8 Ann. chap. 1. before any money could be reserved for cancelling any of the Exchequer bills, as provided by the former of these acts. This act therefore put money into the pockets of those who had bought up Exchequer bills at a discount, and made an addition to the annual expence of the public, but provided nothing for the current service.

Chap. 4. *An act for establishing a general post-office for all her majesty's dominions, and for settling a weekly sum out of the revenues thereof, for the service of the war, and other her majesty's occasions.*

By this act the Post-Office was put under a new regulation, and the postage of letters more heavily taxed; but a weekly sum of 700 *l.* was reserved for the public use for 32 years, from Michaelmas 1711; and a third part of the produce of the said office over and above 111,461 *l.* 17 *s.* 10 *d.* which was the produce of the same in the year, ending at Michaelmas 1710, and over and above the said 700 *l.* a-week, was also reserved for the public use.

Chap. 24. *An act for laying certain duties upon hides and skins, tanned, tawed, or dressed, and upon vellum and parchment for the term of 32 years, for prosecuting the war, and other her majesty's most necessary occasions.*

The duty upon leather, granted by 8 and 9 W. III, chap. 21, (see p. 72.) had been allowed to expire after the three years for which it was granted; as also the duty upon paper, vellum, and parchment, granted by 8 and 9

W. III, chap. 7, (see p. 65) after the two years for which it was granted; the first, because it was burthensome to the poor, and the second, because it was a discouragement to learning. But now our necessities were grown so great, that the first, with several improvements was revived, and also the second, so far as related to vellum and parchment; and both were now granted for 32 years, from June 24, 1711. But both were, in several respects, different from the former duties, and the home-duty, or rather excise, was by this act put under the management of commissioners, and officers, to be appointed for the purpose, who, by the act, were to have the same powers as the commissioners of excise. This act therefore not only increased our taxes, but the number of placemen, and the number of persons subject to the laws of excise.

An act for laying a duty upon hops. Chap. 12.

By this act a new duty of 3 *d.* per pound was laid on all hops imported, and an excise of 1 *d.* per pound on all hops growing in Great-Britain, to continue for four years after June 1, 1711; and upon this duty and excise her majesty was empowered to borrow 180,000 *l.* at 6 *l.* *per cent.* Thus, at last, many of our country farmers, and all dealers in hops, were brought under our laws of excise; but, as to the management, the duty was intrusted to the commissioners of the customs, and the excise to those of excise.

An act for taking, examining, and stating the public accounts of the kingdom. Chap. 13.

Whereas many great aids and provisions have been given, raised, and assigned for the necessary defence of your majesty and these kingdoms, in this great and important war, and for the support of the government; to the end therefore, that both your majesty, *and this whole kingdom* may be satisfied, and truly informed, that the same have been applied to the uses and purposes for which they were granted; may it please, *&c.*

Chap. 21. Origin of the South-Sea company. *An act for making good deficiencies, and satisfying the public debts; and for erecting a corporation to carry on a trade to the South Seas, and for the encouragement of the fishery, &c.*

The preamble to this act recites, that notwithstanding the many and great supplies granted to her majesty for carrying on the present war, the following debts and deficiencies are computed to remain still due and unprovided for, that is to say, the sum of 5,130,539 *l.* 5 *s.* 5 *d.* for the debt of the navy, to the 20th of September 1710, (exclusive of the debt for the register of the seamen;) the sum of 154,324 *l.* 15 *s.* 8 *d.* ¼ for the office of ordnance, to the 29th of September 1710; the sum of 425,721 *l.* 5 *s.* 4 *d.* ¼, for transport service, to the 29th of September 1710; the sum of 1,018,656 *l.* 17 *s.* 9 *d.* ¼, for the principal and interest-money, to the 29th of September 1710, on army and transport debentures; the sum of 12,025 *l.* 1 *s.* for the principal money and interest, to the 29th of September 1710, of deficient tallies, and orders for money lent on 8 W. III, chap. 3, and 1 Ann. sess. 2, chap. 4, the sum of 378,859 *l.* 5 *s.* 8 *d.* ¼, computed for debts incurred between the 29th of September, and the 25th of December 1710, in the Navy, Victualling, and Transport offices, and for interest in that time; the sum of 9375 *l.* to satisfy the money due upon account of subsidies to the Elector of Hanover and Duke of Zell: all which ſaid ſeveral ſums do amount in the whole to the ſum of 7,128,571 *l.* 10 *s.* 11 *d.* and the intereſt of ſuch part of the ſaid ſeveral debts as do carry intereſt from Chriſtmas 1710 to Chriſtmas 1711, are computed to amount to the ſum of 85,000 *l.* which, added to the principal, makes the total of the ſaid debts amount to 7,213,571 *l.* 10 *s.* 11 *d.* and that there was due for money lent purſuant to an act 8 Ann. chap. 13, the ſum of 1,296,552 *l.* 6 *s.* 11 *d.* ¾, and for intereſt due on the ſame on the 25th of March 1711, 74,875 *l.* 19 *s.* 1 *d.* ¼, which will make the deficiencies, and the principal and intereſt upon the ſaid act, 8 Ann. chap. 13, amount together to 8,585,000 *l.* the intereſt of which ſum, from the 25th of March, 1711, to the 25th of December 1711, doth amount unto 386,325 *l.* which, being added to the ſaid ſum, makes the ſum total to the 25th of December, 1711, amount to 8,971,325 *l.* To make a proviſion for the ſaid debts, deficiencies, and ſums of money, and for the raiſing the further ſum of 500,000 *l.* for the ſervice of the year, which makes the total amount to 9,471,325 *l.* and for paying an intereſt, or annuity of 6 *per cent.* until the principal be paid, as herein is mentioned, which doth amount unto the annual ſum of 568,279 *l.* 10 *s.* all the duties upon wines, vinegar, and tobacco, and upon India goods and wrought ſilks, and upon whale-fins, and upon any other goods, which, by the ſaid act, 8 Ann, chap. 13, were made payable to her majeſty, ſhall be further continued for ever; and the acts of parliament (which by the ſaid act were continued) as concerning the ſaid duties, ſhall be in force for ever.

§ 7. The duties upon candles, which by 8 Ann. chap. 9, were granted to her majeſty, ſhall be continued for ever; and alſo the ſeveral rates upon monies given with clerks, apprentices, and ſervants, which were granted by the laſt mentioned act, ſhall be continued for ever.

§ 8. After all the principal and intereſt, which, by the laſt mentioned act, are charged on the duties on candles, and rates on money given with clerks, apprentices, and ſervants ſhall be paid off; all the monies which ſhall ariſe by the ſaid impoſitions on candles, and monies given with clerks, *&c.* ſhall be paid into the receipt of the Exchequer, for the purpoſes in this act.

§ 20. Every year for ever, reckoning the year to begin from the 25th of December, the annual ſum of 568.279 *l.* 10 *s.* of the monies to ariſe by the ſaid duties, ſhall be the yearly fund for anſwering the annuities in this act expreſſed.

§ 22. In caſe the ſaid duties ſhall be ſo deficient, as that within any one year, the ſaid payment ſhall not be ſufficient to ſatisfy the ſaid yearly ſum of 568,279 *l.* 10 *s.* ſuch deficiency ſhall be made good out of the next aids to be granted by parliament.

§ 23. In caſe there ſhall be any ſurplus of the duties at the end of any year, ſuch ſurplus ſhall be applied towards diſcharging the principal of the capital ſtock of the intended company; and the yearly ſum of 568,279 *l.* 10 *s.* ſhall be abated in proportion.

§ 24. Upon one year's notice, upon repayment by parliament, of the principal ſum, of which the capital ſtock of the intended company ſhall conſiſt, and of all arrears of the ſaid annuities, the duties hereby appropriated, may be diſpoſed of by parliament, and the ſaid yearly fund charged thereupon, ſhall ceaſe.

§ 25. It ſhall be lawful for her majeſty, by letters-patent, to incorporate all perſons intitled to any of the public debts, deficiencies, or ſums of money, provided for by this act, with power to chooſe their governor, directors, and other officers; and the perſons ſo incorporated, ſhall be capable in law to purchaſe and retain, to them and their ſucceſſors, lands and hereditaments, not exceeding the yearly value of 1000 *l.*

§ 34. If it appear, that the joint ſtock of the company ſhall amount to more than 9,471,325 *l.* ſo that the annuity for the ſame, ſhall amount to more than 568,279 *l.* 10 *s.* then there ſhall be added to the ſaid annual ſum, ſo much more as ſhall make the ſame amount to 6 *per cent. per annum*, upon the whole capital ſtock, and ſuch additional annuity ſhall be chargeable upon the ſaid funds.

§ 35. Over and above the ſaid annual ſum, there ſhall be paid to the ſaid company, the further annual ſum of 8000 *l.* for charges of management out of the ſame funds.

Thus a very large debt was paid, and ſome of the current ſupplies provided for, without raiſing any money; but even this project, ingenious as it was, coſt the public a good deal more than the intereſt to be paid yearly; for, as many of the tallies and orders, eſpecially thoſe iſſued by virtue of the ſaid 8 Ann. chap. 13, were in the hands of the treaſurers, or paymaſters of ſome of the public offices; and, as they were empowered to ſubſcribe them into the ſtock of the ſaid company, which ſtock, or a great part of it, was afterwards ſold out at a great diſcount, that whole diſcount was a loſs to, and charge upon the public, as it ſtood engaged to pay off the capital at par, with an intereſt of 6 *l. per cent.* till paid; and, though it was called a paying off of the public creditors, yet it was so only to those who could wait for their money till the stock rose to par; for, as to our seamen, and other poor who had laboured hard, and perhaps ventured their lives in the service of their country, it was only giving them one unmerchantable commodity for another, by which means they were obliged to sell at 30 or 40 *per cent.* discount, which will always be the case, when our annual expence is made to exceed our annual revenue. This practice always has, and always will, grind the face of the poor, to fill the pockets of the rich.

Chap. 22. *An act for granting to her majesty several duties upon coals for building fifty new churches in and about the cities of London and Westminster, and suburbs thereof, and other purposes therein mentioned.*

By this act a new duty, over and above all other duties, was laid upon coals, brought into the river Thames, and appropriated to the building 50 new churches, in and about London and Westminster. This duty, was 2 *s.* per chalder or ton, from May 14, to September 29, 1716, and 3 *s.* per chalder or ton, from September 28, 1716, to September 29, 1724; on which fund the crown was enabled to borrow money, without limitation, at 6 *per cent.* and to pay the interest out of the money borrowed, till the commencement of this fund; so that we could not now even build churches without borrowing money for paying interest upon money borrowed. The supply voted for this purpose was 350,000 *l.*

Chap. 23. *An act for licensing and regulating Hackney coaches and chairs; and for charging certain new duties on stampt vellum, parchment, and paper, and on cards and dice, and on the exportation of rock-salt for Ireland; and for securing thereby, and by a weekly payment out of the Post-Office, and by several duties on hides and skins, a yearly fund of* 186,670*l. for* 32 *years, to be applied to the satisfaction of such orders as are therein mentioned, to the contributors of any sum not exceeding two millions, to be raised for carrying on the war, and other her majesty's occasions.*

By this act the crown was impowered to appoint commissioners, who after Midsummer, 1715, were to regulate and licence, for 32 * years, 800 hackney coaches, and 200 hackney chairs, within the bills of mortality, the former to pay monthly a tax of 5*s.* a week, and the latter quarterly 10*s.* a year each. By this act likewise a stamp duty was laid upon debentures for drawbacks, bills of lading, wine and alehouse licences, almanacks, cards, and dice, for 32 years, after Aug. 1, 1711; and a duty of 9*s.* per ton, on all rock-salt exported to Ireland, for 32 years †, after the 11th of June 1711. All which taxes, together with the weekly sum from the Post office, mentioned in chap. 10, of this session, and the duties imposed by chap. 11, of this session, were by this act appropriated for establishing a fund of 186,670*l. per annum*, the deficiency, if any, to be made good out of the next aids granted by parliament: on which fund was to be raised by way of lottery, at 100*l.* a ticket, the sum of 2,000,000*l.* for the public service; and out of the same fund was to be paid an additional sum of 602,200*l.* to be divided among the fortunate or benefit tickets, and to make a profit of

* Made perpetual by 3 Geo. I, chap. 7, sect, 1.
† Made perpetual by 3 Geo. I, chap. 7, sect, 1.

10 *l.* or more even upon every blank; so that this lottery might very properly be said to be all prizes and no blanks; and upon this entire sum of 2,602,200 *l.* the adventurers were to have an interest of 6 *l. per cent.* paid quarterly, until the principal should be paid off. Thus in the same session we were again reduced to the necessity of a lottery, and besides interest, to pay a premium of above 30 *l. per cent.* for ready money.

10 Ann. 1711. The ways and means for raising the supplies granted in this session, (which began the 7th of December 1711,) were as follow:

Chap. 1. *An act for granting an aid to her majesty, to be raised by a land tax, in Great-Britain, for the service of the year* 1712.

This land-tax was 4 *s.* in the pound, and the loan upon it was 1,880,000 *l.* at 6 *per cent.*

Chap. 3. *An act for charging and continuing the duties upon malt, mum, cyder, and perry, for the service of the year* 1712: *and for applying part of the coinage-duties to the deficiency of the value of plate coined; and to pay for the recoining the old money in Scotland.*

The loan upon this act was 650,000 *l.* at 6 *l. per cent.* And there are two clauses in it, one for applying 1915 *l.* 11 *s.* 6 *d.* part of the coinage-duty, to make good the loss upon the coinage of plate brought into the Mint to be coined; and the other for applying 2700 *l.* 5 *s.* 3 *d.* $\frac{1}{2}$, part of the same duty, to make good the loss upon the recoinage of the old money, current in Scotland before the union.

An act for laying several duties upon all soap and paper made in Great-Britain, or imported into the same; and upon chequer'd and striped linens imported; and upon certain silks, callicoes, linens, and stuffs, printed, painted, or stained; and upon several kinds of stampt vellum, parchment, and paper; and upon certain printed papers, pamphlets and advertisements, for raising the sum of 1,800,000 l. *by way of a lottery towards her majesty's supply; and for licensing an additional number of hackney chairs, and for charging certain stocks of cards and dice, &c.* Chap. 19.

By this act a duty of 2 *d.* per pound was imposed upon all soap imported into Great-Britain; and 1 *d.* per pound upon all soap made within the same, from June 10, 1712, until June 11, 1744.—Question to agree with the committee, that a duty be laid on all soap imported into, or made in Great-Britain; ayes 81, noes 52.—A petition being offered from Woolborough in Devonshire, relating to this duty; and several members acquainting the house, that they had petitions of the like nature; question, that it ought be brought up; negative. Question, that the petition of the soap-makers of London be brought up; negative.

By this act new duties were likewise imposed on paper, pasteboards, milboards, and scale-boards, imported into Great-Britain, or made within the same, granted from June 24, 1712, until June 25, 1744, a new duty on paper printed, painted, or stained, in Great Britain; to serve for hangings and other uses, for the same time; a duty of 30 *per cent.* ad valorem, upon all books, prints and maps, imported, bound or unbound, into Great-Britain, was granted for the same time, *&c. &c.* And by this act all our soap-boilers, paper-makers, and callicoe printers, were subjected to the laws of Excise, and the crown was impowered to appoint no less than three new sets of commissioners, one for the excise on home-made soap, one for that on home made paper, and one for that on home-made callicoes, with such subordinate officers as they might think necessary for each broad and each collection. All these duties, except a small duty upon cards and dice, made before June 12, 1711, and the duty upon 100 additional hackney chairs, were granted for establishing a fund of 168,003 *l. per annum*, for paying off in 32 years, the principal sum of 2,341,740 *l.* with interest at 6 *l. per cent.* and if ever any deficiency, the same to be made good out of the first aid, afterwards granted by parliament. And upon this fund was to be raised, by way of lottery, at 10 *l.* a ticket, no more than 1,800,000 *l.* for the public service, so that we were to pay 541,740 *l.* which is above 30 *l. per cent.* for this sum in ready money, besides interest upon the premium, as well as on the principal sum borrowed.

Chap. 26. *An act for laying additional duties on hides and skins, vellum and parchment; and new duties on starch, coffee, tea, drugs, gilt and silver wire, and policies of insurance, to secure a yearly fund for satisfaction of orders to the contributors of a further sum of* 1,800,000 *l. &c.*

By this act new and additional duties were laid upon the goods mentioned in the title; and a new body of people, namely, our starch-makers, for sale, or not for sale, and wire-drawers, were subjected to the laws of excise, and to two new sets of commissioners and officers to be appointed by the crown, one for levying this excise upon starch, and the other for that on wire. All these duties were granted for

32 years, from Auguſt 1, or June 16, or July 1, 1712, in order to eſtabliſh a fund of 168,003*l.* *per annum*, for paying off in 32 years the principal ſum of 2,341,990 *l.* with intereſt at 6 *l.* *per cent.* And here too it was provided, that if there ſhould ever be any deficiency, it ſhould be made good out of the firſt aid, to be afterwards granted by parliament; notwithſtanding which ſecurity, no more than 1,800,000 *l.* was upon this fund to be raiſed for the public ſervice, by a lottery at a 100 *l.* a ticket, conſequently for this ſum in ready money, we were to pay a premium of 541,990 *l.* which is above 30 *per cent.* with intereſt upon premium and principal, until the whole ſhould be repaid.

As a clauſe of appropriation was now become uſual at the end of every ſeſſion, a long clauſe was inſerted in this laſt act, by which the ſupplies granted in this ſeſſion were very particularly appropriated; but after that were two clauſes, one in favour of the South-Sea company, and another in favour of the annuitants, who had purchaſed upon the act of 6 Ann. chap. 5, by which it was provided, that no appropriation ſhould hinder the payment of the annuity due to the ſaid company, or making good the deficiencies of the quarterly payments to the ſaid annuitants, incurred before the 25th of December 1712.

It is remarkable, that the commiſſioners for taking, examining, and ſtating the public accounts, having reported ſeveral practices relating to the affairs of the army, and laid ſeveral diſpoſitions before the Houſe for proving thoſe practices, *Robert Walpole*, Eſq. (ſince Earl of Orford) was expell'd the Houſe, and committed to the Tower. for receiving 500 guineas, and a note for 500 *l.* more, on account of two contracts for forage for the troops quartered in Scotland, made by him when ſecretary at war;

and *Adam Cardonnel*, Esq. secretary to the Duke of Marlborough, was expelled the House, for taking a gratuity of 500 gold ducats annually, from the contractors for bread and bread waggons for the army on the Low Countries; and January 24, it was resolved, 1st, That the taking of several sums of money annually, by the Duke of Marlborough, from the contractors for furnishing the bread and bread-waggons for the army in the Low Countries, was unwarrantable and illegal. And 2d, That *the two and an half per cent.* deducted from the foreign troops in her majesty's pay, is public money, and ought to be accounted for. These, and such like proceedings, seemed to indicate a resolution to establish a new fund, by obliging numbers of people to refund; but they were carried no further; so that if there was any spoil, the spoilers have ever since continued in the quiet enjoyment of it, and the nation to this day without any redress; no parliament having since spirit enough to tell the king, as Richard the Second's did, "That he would find, in the confiscation of the mismanagers estates, wherewithal to answer the occasions of the state."

12 Ann. sess. 1. 1713. The ways and means for raising the supplies granted in this session, (which began the 9th of April 1713,) were as follow:

Chap. 1. *An act for an aid by a land-tax for the year* 1713.

This was 2 *s.* in the pound, and the sum borrowed upon it was 940,000 *l.* at 5 *per cent.*

Chap. 2. *An act for granting the duties upon malt, &c. for* 1713.

The loan upon this act was 700,000 *l.*

An act to raise 1,200,000 *l. for public uses, by circulating a further sum in Exchequer bills; and for enabling her majesty to raise* 500,000 *l. on the revenues appointed for the uses of her civil government, to be applied for or towards payment of such debts and arrears owing to her servants, tradesmen, and others, as are therein mentioned.* Chap. 11.

By this act the Treasury was impowered to issue new Exchequer bills to the amount of 1,200,000 *l.* which bills were to carry an interest of 2 *per cent.* per diem to the bearer, and the Band undertook and were obliged to circulate them, for which they were to have 3 *l. per cent. per annum*, payable weekly, and a further yearly sum of 8000 *l.* payable quarterly; which quarterly payments, together with 45,000 *l.* agreed to be paid them by 9 Ann. chap. 7, were to be continued without diminution, until no more than 1,900,000 *l.* of all these new and old bills, should be standing out, and uncancelled. With regard to the payment of this new debt, it was charged upon the general fund established by 7 Ann. chap. 7, and out of the same general fund, a yearly sinking fund of 270,999 *l.* 7 *s.* including the 200,000 *l.* established and appropriated to pay off and cancel the Exchequer bills charged upon it; with a proviso, that if this general fund should, in any one year be deficient for answering all these purposes, that deficiency should be made good out of the next aids granted by parliament. But, as most of the branches of this general fund were not yet free from the mortgage made of them before the said 7 Ann. chap. 7, therefore the same power was now again given to the Treasury, as was given by that act, namely, to compute quarterly what was grown due for interest and premium, for satisfaction of the same, until the said general fund should become free, and applicable to the uses by this and the said act of 7 Ann. chap. 7, intended and directed. Thus, for gaining a little popularity to our ministers, and a little ease to our land-holders, we were to pay a quarterly compound interest of above 6 *l. per cent.* for the money we were thereby obliged to borrow, which sort of interest always equals the principal in about ten years.

By sect. 27, of this act, her majesty was impowered to appoint, by letters-patent, the annual sum of 35,000 *l.* to be issued weekly, or quarterly out of the civil-list revenue for 32 years, from Michaelmas 1713, to be paid as she should direct, to such persons as should advance the sum of 500,000 *l.* for paying off the debts of the civil list; which annual sum was, during her life, to be issued out of the whole of the civil-list revenue established by 1 Ann. stat. 1, chap. 7, and, after her demise, it was to be issued out of the hereditary part of that revenue. And, to the disappointment of usurers, it was provided by sect. 34, of this act, that if any of the original creditors of the civil-list had sold and assigned the debt, or arrear due to them, they might, at any time, within six months after the end of that session, redeem the same, upon paying back the principal sum really advanced for such sale, with interest at 6 *per cent.* from the time it was advanced.

Upon report from the commissioners for stating the public accounts, it appeared to the House, that *William Churchill*, Esq; a member of the House, had, while he was a commissioner for sick and wounded seamen, reserved to himself half the profits to arise on some of the contracts made by that board; on which the following resolution was agreed to *nem. con.* *viz.*

That, for any commissioner, or other person, entrusted by her majesty in making contracts for public services, to be a partner in such contract, or to reserve a share for any other person, is an high breach of trust, and a notorious corruption. This was on May 7, and May 16, upon a report from the same commissioners, it appeared to the House, that *Thomas* Earl of *Wharton*, had received 1000 *l.* for procuring a place for a gentleman, both therein named, on which it was resolved, that the giving or taking money for procuring offices relating to the management of the public revenue, is a scandalous corruption, and highly detrimental to the public. But, as both those crimes were committed before the act of indemnity, 1708-9, and not excepted, as few such crimes ever are in any such act, the House could proceed no farther against the criminals.

The ways and means for raising the supplies granted this session, (which began the 16th of February 1713-14,) were as follow: 12 Ann. sess. 2. 1713.

An act for an aid to be raised by a land-tax, in Great-Britain for the year 1714. Chap. 1.

This was 2 *s.* in the pound, and the loan thereon was 940,000 *l.* at 5 *per cent. per annum.*

An act for charging and continuing the duties upon malt, &c. Chap. 13.

The loan upon this act was 700,000 *l.*

An act for laying additional duties on soap, and paper, and upon certain linens, silks, callicoes, and stuffs, and upon starch, and exported coals and upon stampt vellum, parchment, and paper, for raising 1,400,000 l. *by way of lottery, for* Chap. 9.

her majesty's supply; and for allowances on exporting made wares of leather, sheepskins, and lambskins, &c.

By this act the several following new duties, over and above all former duties, were imposed for 32 years, from the 2d of August 1714, *viz.* on all soap imported, 1 *d.* per pound; and on home-made soap an halfpenny. On paper, pasteboards, mill'd-boards, and scale-boards, imported, several different duties upon different sorts particularly named, and upon all other 10 *l. per cent. ad valorem.* Upon all home-made paper, &c. Several different duties upon the different sorts named, and upon all other sorts, 6 *l. per cent. ad valorem.* Upon chequer'd, striped, and printed linens, imported, except as therein excepted, and that may be worn here, 15 *l. per cent. ad valorem:* upon all silks printed at home, 6 *d.* per yard, reckoning half-yard wide; upon silk handkerchiefs so printed, 1 *d.* per yard square; upon all callicoes, yard wide, so printed, 3 *d.* per yard; and upon all linen and stuffs, except woollen, yard wide, so printed, three half-pence per yard: upon all starch imported, 2 *d.* per pound; and on home-made 1 *d.* per pound: upon all coals exported in foreign bottoms, 5 *s.* per chalder; and in British bottoms, 3 *s.* except to Ireland or the Isle of Man: and new stamp duties of different sizes upon several sorts of writings, and upon all deeds, not otherwise charged, 6 *d.* a sheet, or piece of paper; but this new duty did not extend to law proceedings.

All these duties were appropriated (with a clause as usual for making good the deficiency) towards establishing a yearly fund of 105,000 *l.* for paying off and discharging the principal sum of 1,876,400 *l.* with interest at 4 *l. per cent.* on which was to be raised by a lottery at

10 *l.* a ticket, only the ſum of 1,400,000 *l.* for the public ſervice; the additional ſum of 476,400 *l.* being to be paid by way of premium, and was diſtributed among the prizes, or furniture tickets; for the blanks were to have their whole money repaid with intereſt at 4 *l. per cent* ſo that this lottery too might properly enough be ſaid to be all prizes and no blanks, and the public was thus to pay a premium of above 34 *l. per cent*; for the money borrowed, with an intereſt at the rate of above 5 *l.* 7 *s. per cent.* for 4 *per cent.* upon 1,876,400 *l.* is above 5 *l.* 7 *s. per cent.* on 1,400,000 *l.* But, as the legal intereſt of money was, by an act of this ſeſſion, reduced to 5 *l. per cent.* it was neceſſary, it ſeems, to make the ignorant believe, that the public could borrow for *four*.

TAXES

SUBSISTING AT THE END OF

QUEEN ANNE's REIGN.

THESE may be properly divided into *customs*, *excises*, and *inland duties*. *Customs* we call those duties, that are paid by the importer, and are under the management of the commissioners of the *customs*; *excises* are those duties paid by the manufacturers, or retailers, and are under the management of the commissioners, and governed by the laws of excise, or under particular commissioners, armed with the powers of excise. And *inland duties* we call those which are paid by the retailers, but are under the management of particular boards of commissioners, with officers appointed for collecting them.

The *customs* consist of the following branches.

I. That properly called *customs*, which consist of five several parts, *viz.*

1. The *old subsidy*, or *subsidy inwards*, first granted by stat. 12 Char. II, chap. 4, and continued as to one half thereof, to August 1,

1808, by 6 Ann. chap. 11, and, as to the other half for ever, by 7 Ann. chap. 7. This is a tax of 6 *l.* per ton upon ſome wines, and 4 *l.* 10 *s.* upon others; and on perry, rape, cyder, and vinegar, imported into the port of London, by Britiſh ſubjects in Britiſh ſhips, navigated according to law; and upon all other goods ſo imported, it is a tax of 5 *l. per cent. ad valorem*; as to which it is obſervable, that when goods are to pay any tax according to the value, that value is to be aſcertained by the two books of rates, or, if not the rated, by the oath of the importer, or by the price at a public ſale; and when goods are valued by the oath of the importer, the officer may take the goods, paying the importer the price he puts upon them, with 10 *l. per cent.* profit, and the produce at a public ſale, after all diſburſements for duties, *&c.* is to be paid to the crown, for the uſe of the *ſinking fund.*

2. The *petty cuſtom*, or *alien's duty*, payable by alien or denizen importers, granted and continued by the ſame acts, and is a fourth more than the former.

3. The *additional duty*, granted and continued by the ſame acts, being an additional duty of 3 *l.* per ton on ſome wines, and 4 *l.* on all others; and a moiety of the neat old ſubſidy, by way of additional duty upon all wrought ſilks, except Eaſt-Indian; and upon all linens, except Iriſh and callicoes; and 1 *d.* per pound on tobacco of the Britiſh plantations.

4. The *one per cent. inwards*, granted by the act 14 Char. II, chap. 11, and continued by the ſaid two acts of Queen Anne, being a tax of 1 *l. per cent.* ad valorem, upon all goods imported from any place in the Mediterranean beyond Malaga, in any Britiſh ſhip that hath not two decks, and carries leſs than 16 guns

mounted, with two men for each gun, and ammunition proportionable. The design of this tax is to oblige our merchants to make use of defensible ships, in order to prevent our sea-men being made slaves by the Barbary pirates; but ships exporting British fish are excepted.

5. The *composition on petty seizures*; which is an indulgence allowed by custom to our Custom-house officers; for one moiety of all goods seized and condemn'd belongs to the crown, and must be paid, or secured before the officer can have the goods to sell; but, when the duty of the goods seized, does not exceed 40 *s.* the officer is allowed to compound with the collector.

II. The *subsidy outwards*, first granted by the said act, 12 Char. II, chap. 4, and continued to March 8, 1742, by 9 Ann. chap. 6, being a tax of 5 *l. per cent.* upon all goods exported, with several exceptions, and now most goods are exempted, except dying goods, and several others necessary in our manufactures, and except leather, white woollen cloths and coals, which pay particular duties after mentioned.

III. The *one per cent. outwards*, being the same, and first granted by the same act, with the *one per cent. outwards*; and continued by 9 Ann. chap. 6, to March 8, 1742.

IV. The duty on tanned leather exported, being a duty of 1 *s.* per hundred weight, first granted by 20 Char. II, chap. 5, and by 9 Ann. chap. 6, continued for 32 years, from March 8, 1710.

V. The *impost on wines and vinegar*, first granted by 1 James II, chap. 3, and by 9 Ann.

chap. 21, continued *for ever*; being an additional tax of 8 *l.* per ton on all vinegar and French wines, and 12 *l.* a ton on all other wines.

VI. The *impoſt on tobacco*, firſt granted by 1 James II, chap. 4, and by the laſt mentioned act of Queen Anne, continued for ever, being an additional tax of 3 *d.* per pound on tobacco of the Britiſh plantations, and 6 *d.* on all foreign tobacco.

VII. The *coinage-duty*, firſt granted by 18 Char. II, chap. 5, and by 7 Ann. chap. 24, continued to the end of the firſt ſeſſion of parliament, after March 1, 1715-16, being an additional tax of 10 *s.* per ton on all wines, vinegar, cyder, beer, brandy, and ſtrong waters, imported.

VIII. The *coal-duty*, firſt granted by 1 James II, chap. 15, and by 8 and 9 W. III, chap. 15, continued to September 29, 1716. It was at firſt 1 *s.* 6 *d.* per chalder on coals imported, or brought coaſt-ways into the port of London; but, by the act which continued it, was reduced to 1 *s.* and it was firſt appropriated to the building St. Paul's, London; and, by the ſaid 2d act, to the finiſhing that church, and repairing St. Peter's, Weſtminſter.

IX. The *impoſt* 1690, firſt granted by 2 W. and M. ſeſſ. 2, chap. 4, and made perpetual by 9 Ann. chap. 21. It is an additional tax of 55 different kinds, upon as many different ſorts of goods imported, many of which are neceſſary in our manufactures; ſuch as pot-aſhes, brimſtone, candles, cordage, drugs even for dyers uſe, unwrought iron, oil, hemp-ſeed, raw ſilk, ſtarch, ſteel, beaver wool, wood, *&c.* and the tax is generally at leaſt 5 *per cent. ad valorem.*

X. The *impoſt* 1692-3, firſt granted by 4 and 5 W. and M. chap. 5, and by 9 Ann. chap. 21, made perpetual. It is likewiſe an additional duty of 72 different kinds, upon as many different ſorts of goods particularly named; and upon all other ſorts of goods not particularly rated in the firſt book of Rates, except mum, and except goods particularly charged with this or the ſaid impoſt 1690; it is a general additional tax of 5 *l. per cent. ad valorem.* By this tax alſo many ſorts of goods that are neceſſary in our manufactures, are particularly charged; ſuch as rough amber, wood aſhes, lamp-black, dying woods, except thoſe particularly excepted, elephants teeth, rough flax, furs, goats hair, rough hemp, hides, incle, indico, iron, leather, roſin, ſalt not uſed in curing fiſh, tar, tow, *&c.* and all French goods in general, except wines, (hereby particularly charged with 8 *l.* per ton) brandies, vinegar, and ſalt, are charged with a duty of 25 *l. per cent. ad valorem.*

XI. The *ſalt duty*, firſt granted by 5 and 6 W. and M. chap. 7, and by 7 and 8 W. III, made perpetual. It is an additional tax of 3 *d.* a gallon upon all ſalt imported; and was put under the management of the commiſſioners of exciſe; but, as it is paid upon importation, and collected by the officers of the cuſtoms, it is here ſtated as a branch of our cuſtoms.

XII. The *new duty on ſpices and pictures*, firſt granted by 6 and 7 W. III, chap. 7, and by 7 Ann. chap. 7, made perpetual. It is an additional duty of 5 *l. per cent. ad valorem*, upon pictures, cinnamon, cloves, mace, nutmegs; and upon tea 1 *s.* coffee 6 *d.* cocoa 6 *d.* and chocolate 1 *s.* per pound.

XIII. The *second 25 per cent. on French goods*, first granted by 7 and 8 W. III, chap. 20, from February 28, 1696, to February 28, 1716-17; being an additional tax of 25 *l.* per ton on French wines; 30 *l.* on single, and 60 *l.* on double French brandies, 15 *l.* on French vinegar, and 25 *l. per cent. ad valorem* on all other French goods; so that by this and the said 9th branch, all French goods were subjected to a duty of 50 *l. per cent.* over and above all other duties.

XIV. The *new duty on coals, culm, and cinders.* This and the next branch were at first both granted together; but, as they were afterwards divided and appropriated to different purposes, it seems necessary to state them separately. Both these branches were first granted by 9 and 10 W. III, chap. 13, and extended to cinders by 10 and 11 W. III, chap. 21, being an additional duty of 7 *s.* 6 *d.* per chalder, and 5 *s.* per ton on coals imported, and 5 *s.* per chalder, and 3 *s.* 4 *d.* per ton, on coals carried coastways from one port of England to another, 1 *s.* per chalder on culm, and 5 *s.* per chalder on cinders. This duty having been continued to September 30, 1710, three-fifths of it was from thence continued to September 30, 1742, by 8 Ann. chap. 4.

XV. The *additional duty on coals, culm, and cinders*, first granted as mentioned in the foregoing branch; and, as to the other two fifths, continued to March 8, 1742-3, by 9 Ann. chap. 6.

XVI. The *new or further subsidy*, first granted by 8 and 9 W. III, chap. 23, and by 1 Ann. chap. 7, continued to the queen during her life; being an additional tax upon wines, and all goods imported equal to the old subsidy, with very few exceptions.

XVII. The *new duty on whale fins*, first granted by 9 and 10 W. III, chap. 45, and by 9 Ann. chap. 21, continued for ever, being an additional tax of 3 *d.* per pound weight on those imported by the Greenland company, and 6 *d.* per pound on those imported by others.

XVIII. The *further duty on salt*, first granted by 9 and 10 W. III, chap. 44, for ever, being an additional duty of 7 *d.* per gallon on all salt imported. This duty was likewise to be under the management of the commissioners of excise; but it is here stated as a branch of our customs for the reason assigned, with respect to the former duty on salt; see branch XI.

XIX. The *fifteen per cent. on muslins*, first granted by 11 and 12 W. III, chap. 3, and by 7 Ann. chap. 7, continued for ever, being an additional tax of 15 *l. per cent. ad valorem*, on muslins; under which general name are comprehended 25 different sorts of goods imported from the East-Indies. This tax was at first laid upon almost all other sorts of Indian manufactures; but they were soon after prohibited to be worn in Great-Britain, and freed from this tax.

XX. The excise on foreign liquors imported; as to which we need add nothing to what we have said in the former part of this history, page 92.

XXI. The duties called *prisage* and *butlerage*; the former of which was payable by all natives, importers of wines, except the merchants of London, Southampton, Chester, and the Cinque Ports, being *one* ton, if *ten* tons or more, and under 20, be imported, and *two* tons if 20 tons or more be imported by one ship; and the latter is payable by all foreigners, importers of wine, in lieu of prisage, being 2 *s.* per ton on the quantity imported; which duties belong by custom hereditarily to the crown. See p. 7.

XXII. A *new additional duty upon coals* imported into the port of London, first granted by 1 Ann. sess. 2, chap. 12, from May 15, 1708, to May 15, 1716, being an additional tax of 2 *s.* per chalder, or ton, and appropriated to the same purpose as the eighth branch of the customs before mentioned. This tax, together with the said 8th branch, were continued to the 28th of September 1724, and from the respective times of their expiration, appropriated to the building 50 new churches, by 9 Ann. chap. 22.

XXIII. The *one-third subsidy*, first granted by 2 and 3 Ann. chap. 9, and by 6 Ann. chap. 5, continued to March 8, 1806-7; being an additional tax upon all wines and merchandize, imported equal to one third of the old subsidy.

XXIV. The *additional duty on spice and pictures, and new duty on drugs*, first granted by 3 and 4 Ann. chap. 4, and by 7 Ann. chap. 7, continued for ever. By this branch an additional duty of 5 *l. per cent. ad valorem* is laid upon all spice, and 20 *l. per cent.* on all pictures (for sale or private use) imported; on drugs,

10 *l. per cent. ad valorem* on some, and 4 *l. per cent.* on others; on coffee, tea, and chocolate, an additional duty equal to that in the 11th branch; on china ware, 12 *l. per cent.* as sold at the public sale; and on white calicoes, not charged as muslins, on Indian dimities, and on all other manufactures of cotton, 15 *l. per cent.* as sold at the public sale.

XXV. The *two-thirds subsidy*, first granted by 3 and 4 Ann. chap. 5, and by 7 Ann. chap. 7, continued for ever; being an additional tax on all wines and merchandize imported, equal to two-thirds of the old subsidy; but several sorts of goods are exempted from this duty.

XXVI. The *new duty on pepper and raisins; and a further new duty on spice*, first granted by 8 Ann. chap. 7, to continue for 32 years, from Lady-day 1710, by which an additional duty of 1 *s.* 6 *d.* per pound, was laid on all pepper imported; (long pepper was afterwards excepted) 5 *s.* per hundred weight on raisins, 3 *s.* per pound on snuff, not of our plantations; and on spiceries, *viz.* nutmegs, cinnamon, cloves, and mace, a new duty equal to all the duties then payable upon them.

XXVII. The *new duty on candles imported*, first granted by 8 Ann. chap. 9, and by 9 Ann. chap. 21, continued for ever, begging an additional duty of 4 *d.* per pound on wax, and a halfpenny per pound on tallow candles imported.

XXVIII. The *duty on coals exported*, granted for 32 years, from March 8, 1710-11, in lieu of all former duties, by 9 Ann. chap. 6, being a duty of seven different kinds upon coals exported.

XXIX. The *additional duty on candles imported*, first granted by 9 Ann. chap. 12, to continue for 32 years, from March 25, 1711, being a new additional tax equal to the former.

XXX. The *new duty on hides, skins, parchment, vellum, cards and dice imported*, first granted by 9 Ann. chap. 11, to continue for 32 years from June 24, 1711, being an additional tax of 21 several particular kinds, upon 21 particular sorts of hides and skins named in the act, and upon others not named, or pieces of hides or skins, or manufactures consisting mostly of leather, 15 *l. per cent. ad valorem*; and upon parchment, 6 *d.* per dozen, and upon vellum, 1 *s.* per dozen.

XXXI. The *new duty on hops imported*, first granted by 9 Ann. chap. 12, for four years, from June 1, 1711, being an additional tax of 3 *d.* per pound on all hops imported.

XXXII. A *new duty upon rock-salt exported to Ireland*, after June 11, 1711, being a duty of 9 *s.* per ton; but the exporter is allowed the drawback for the former duty, upon shewing a certificate of its having been paid. It was first imposed for 32 years from the above day, by 9 Ann. chap. 23.

XXXIII. The *new duty on soap, paper, milboards, pasteboards, scaleboards, linen chequer'd, striped, &c. imported*, first granted by 10 Ann. chap. 19, to continue for 32 years; on soap, from the 10th of June 1712; on paper, from the 24th of June 1712; and on linens striped, printed, painted, stained, or dyed after the manufacture, from July 20, 1712. By this branch an additional duty of 2 *d.* per pound is laid upon all soap imported; additional duties of fifty several kinds are laid upon so many sorts of paper particularly named, and upon all sorts of paper not named, 20 *l. per cent. ad valorem*; and upon the linens above described, 15 *l. per cent. ad valorem*. Books, prints, and maps imported, were likewise by this act loaded with an additional duty of 30 *l. per cent. ad valorem*; but this tax was afterwards abolished.

XXXIV. The *additional duty on hides, skins, &c. imported*, was first granted by 10 Ann. chap. 26, to continue for 32 years, from August 1, 1712, on hides, &c. from July 1, 1712, on wire; and from June 16, 1712, on coffee, tea, and drugs, except drugs for dying, and turpentine from the plantations. By this branch new additional duties of 21 different kinds were laid upon 21 sorts of hides and skins particularly named; and on all others not named, on all pieces, and on all manufactures, mostly of leather, 15 *l. per cent. ad valorem*: And the following additional duties were laid upon the following goods imported, *viz.* on parchment, 2 *s.* per dozen; on vellum, 3 *s.* per dozen; on starch, 2 *d.* per pound; on coffee, 1 *s.* per pound; on tea, from the East-Indies, 2 *s.* per pound; and from any other place, 5 *s.* per pound; and on drugs, 20 *l. per cent. ad valorem.*

XXXV. The *new duty on coals exported*, first granted by 12 Ann. chap. 9, to continue for 32 years, from August 2, 1714, being an additional duty of 5 *s.* per chalder on coals exported in foreign bottoms, and 3 *s.* on those exported in British bottoms.

XXXVI. The *new duty on sail-cloth imported*, first imposed by 12 Ann. chap. 16, for seven years, from July 21, 1713, being an additional duty of 1 *d.* per ell.

XXXVII. The *additional duty on soap, paper, &c. imported*, first granted by 12 Ann. sess. 2, chap. 9, to continue for 32 years from August 2, 1714, being an additional duty upon soap and paper imported, of half the duty imposed by the 33d branch; upon the linens there described, an additional duty of 15 *l. per cent. ad valorem*, and a new additional duty of 2 *d.* per pound on starch.

These were our customs subsisting at the end of Queen Anne's reign; and from this short state of them we may see, what a labyrinth our merchants must be in; but, if we consider the many exceptions, and exceptions from exceptions, the many regulations, and regulations of regulations, for collecting those customs, and for paying the drawbacks upon goods re-exported, we must conclude it impossible for any merchant in this country to be master of his business, if he be what we call a General Merchant; consequently he must trust to those gentlemen called Custom-house officers, both for the duties he is to pay upon importation, and the drawbacks he is intitled to upon exportation. Can we wonder at the decay of our commerce under such circumstances? Should we not rather wonder that we have any left!

Now, with regard to our *excises* subsisting at the end of her reign, they were as follow, *viz.*

I. That called the *temporary excise*, first granted by 12 Char. II, chap. 23, and by 1 Ann. chap. 7, continued to her majesty during her life, being 15 *d.* per barrel upon every barrel of beer or ale, above 6 *s.* the barrel, and 3 *d.* per barrel, for every barrel of 6 *s.* or under, brewed for retail; 15 *d.* for every hogshead of cyder or perry sold by retail; 1 *d.* for every gallon of strong water, or *aqua vitæ*, &c.

II. The *hereditary excise*, granted *for ever*, by 12 Char. II, chap. 24, being the very same with the former. See. p. 29.

III. A *new excise*, granted at first to King William and Queen Mary, their heirs and successors for 99 years, from January 25, 1692-3, by 4 W. and M. chap. 3, and continued for 15 years longer, by 6 Ann. chap. 5, being for every barrel of beer or ale above 6 *s.* the barrel, 9 *d*; and for every barrel of 6 *s.* or under, 3 *d*; for every hogshead of cyder or perry, 1 *s.* 3 *d.* &c.

IV. A *second new excise*, first granted by 5 W. and M. chap. 7, until May 17, 1713, and by 4 Ann. chap. 6, continued from thence for 95 years, being for beer or ale the same with the last; and cyder or perry 1 *s.* per hogshead, &c.

V. A *third new excise*, at first granted for ever, by 3 W. and M. chap. 20. being the very same with the second new excise.

VI. *An excise upon salt*, first granted by 5 W. and M. chap. 7, and continued for ever, by 7 and 8 W. III, chap. 31, being three halfpence per gallon upon all home-made salt, or rock-salt.

VII. A *second excise upon salt*, granted at first for ever, by 9 and 10 W. III, chap. 44, being three pence halfpenny per gallon for all home-made salt, or rock salt.

VIII. *An excise upon malt*, first granted by 8 and 9 W. III, chap. 22, revived by 1 Ann. seff. 2, chap. 3, and continued annually, to the 24th of June 1715, being 6 *d*. per bushel on all malt made for sale or not for sale; for every barrel of mum made for sale, 10 *s*. for every barrel of sweets made for sale, 12 *s*. and for every hogshead of cyder and perry made for sale, 4 *s*; all these duties upon liquors being over and above the then present duties.

IX. *An excise on sweets*, over and above the excise imposed by the said malt act, or any former duty, was first granted by 10 and 11 W. III, and by 6 Ann. chap. 5, continued to March 25, 1808; being an additional duty of 36 *s*. per barrel upon all sweets made for sale.

X. *An excise on low wines or spirits*, first granted by 12 and 13 W. III, chap. 11, and by 6 Ann. chap. 5, continued to June 23, 1807, being then an additional excise, or duty of 6 *d*. a gallon upon spirits drawn from foreign materials; and on those drawn from English materials, 1 *d*.

XI. *A fourth new excise upon home-made liquors*, first granted from Lady-day, 1710, to Lady-day 1742, by 8 Ann. chap. 7, being an additional excise upon every barrel of beer or ale brewed for sale, above 6 *s*. the barrel, (exclusive of the duties) 3 *d*: and for every barrel at 6 *s*. or under, one penny; for every hogshead of cyder and perry, 5 *d*; for every gallon of strong waters, or *aqua vitæ*, one penny.

This excise was not laid upon any such liquors imported.

XII. *An excise on candles*, first granted by 8 Ann. chap. 9, and by 9 Ann. chap. 21, continued for ever; being a duty of 4 *d.* per pound on wax, and an half-penny per pound on tallow candles made in Great-Britain for sale, or not for sale; but makers for their own use, might compound at 1 *s.* a head for every person in their family.

XIII. *An additional excise on candles*, was at first granted for 32 years from Lady-day 1711, by 9 Ann. chap. 6, being the same with the former in every respect.

XIV. *An excise upon hides and skins, tanned, tawed, or dressed, &c.* in Great-Britain, first granted by 9 Ann. chap. 11, for 32 years from Midsummer 1711. This is an excise of 17 different kinds upon so many different sorts of hides and skins particularly named, and upon all others not named, 15 *l. per cent. ad valorem.*

XV. *An excise upon home-made vellum and parchment*, first granted by the same act, and for the same time being 1 *s.* per dozen on vellum, and 6 *d.* per dozen on parchment.

XVI. *An excise on hops of home-growth*, first granted by 9 Ann. chap. 12, for four years, from June 1, 1711, being 1 *d.* per pound.

XVII. *An excise on paper, pasteboards, mill'd-boards, and scaleboards*, was first granted for 32 years, from June 10, 1712, by 10 Ann. chap. 19, being a duty of 11 different kinds, on so many different sorts of paper, particularly named made in Great-Britain; on pasteboards, *&c.*

3 *s.* per hundred weight; and on all paper not named, 12 *l. per cent. ad valorem.*

XVIII. *An excise on soap*, first granted by the same act, for the same time; being a duty of 1 *d.* per pound on all soap made in Great-Britain.

XIX. *An excise upon printed silks, calicoes, linens, and stuffs, made in Great-Britain, and printed, painted, stained, or dyed here*, was first granted by the same act, and for the same time; being a duty of 3 *d.* on silks and calicoes, and three halfpence on linen and stuffs, per yard square; excepting silk handkerchiefs and calicoes, linens and fustians, dyed of one colour, and stuffs made of woollen, or the greatest part in value of woollen.

XX. *An additional excise on hides and skins, &c.* of Great-Britain, first granted for 32 years, from August 1, 1712, by 10 Ann. chap. 26, being an additional duty of 16 different kinds upon so many different sorts of hides and skins, particularly named, and on all others not named, 15 *l. per cent. ad valorem.*

XXI. *An additional excise on home-made vellum and parchment*, first granted by the same act, and for the same time; being an additional duty of 2 *s.* per dozen on vellum, and 1 *s.* per dozen on parchment.

XXII. *An excise on starch made in Britain*, first granted by the same act, and for the same time; being a duty of 1 *d.* per pound.

XXIII. *An excise on gilt and silver wire made in Britain*, first granted by the same act, for 32 years, from July 1, 1712; being a duty of 8 *d.* per ounce on gilt wire, and 6 d. per ounce on ſilver wire.

XXIV. *An additional exciſe on paper, paſte-boards, &c.* firſt granted by 12 Ann. ſeſſ. 2, chap. 9, for 32 years, from Auguſt 2, 1714; being an additional duty of 11 different kinds, on ſo many different ſorts of home-made paper particularly named; on paſteboards, *&c.* 1 *s.* 6 *d.* per hundred weight; and on all ſorts of paper not named, 6 *l.* *per cent. ad valorem*; and on painted paper for hangings, a halfpenny per yard ſquare.

XXV. *An additional exciſe on home-made ſoap*, firſt granted by the ſame act, and for the ſame time; being an additional duty of a halfpenny per pound.

XXVI. *An additional exciſe on home-made ſtarch*, firſt granted by the ſame act, and for the ſame time, being 1 *d.* per pound.

XXVII. *An additional exciſe on printed ſilks, callicoes, &c.* firſt granted by the ſame act, and for the ſame time; being an additional duty of 6 *d.* per yard of half-yard broad ſilks; 1 *d.* per yard ſquare of ſilk handkerchiefs; 3 *d.* per yard ſquare of callicoes, and three halfpence per yard ſquare of linens and ſtuffs; excepting as before callicoes, *&c.* dyed of one colour, and woollen ſtuffs.

And laſtly, with regard to the *inland duties* ſubſiſting at the end of Queen Anne's reign, they were as follow, *viz.*

I. *The Poſt-Office revenue*, or duty of letters by the poſt, firſt granted by 12 Char. II, chap.

35, for ever; but greatly increased, and again granted for ever, by 9 Ann. chap. 10. This is a duty of a great many kinds, according to the size of the letter, and the place it comes from, or is sent to; the lowest for a single letter being 2 *d.* and the highest for packets being 6 *s.* per ounce.

II. *The small branches and casual profits* arising to the crown by wine licences, seizures, *&c.* which have been immemorially possessed by the crown, or granted by several statutes.

III. *The first stamp duty*, first granted by 5 W. and M. chap. 21, and by 6 Ann. chap. 5, continued to August 1, 1807; being a duty of six different kinds upon every skin, sheet, or piece of vellum, parchment, or paper, on which shall be written any authentic document, or law proceeding, that was then thought on, except bills of exchange, and a few others.

IV. *The duty upon hackney coaches and chairs*, first granted as to coaches, by 5 W. and M. chap. 22, and by 9 Ann. chap. 23, continued for 32 years, from Midsummer 1715, being as it stood at the end of the queen's reign, a tax of 5 *s.* per week on each of 800 hackney coaches, and 10 *s.* a year on each of 300 hackney chairs within the bills of mortality.

N. B. The tax on marriages, *&c.* granted by 6 and 7 W. III, chap. 6, was allowed to expire after August 1, 1706.

V. *The duty on houses and windows*, first granted by 7 and 8 W. III, chap. 18, and continued *for ever*, by 5 Ann. chap. 13. This tax was 2 *s.* *per annum* on every inhabited house, except cottages, and on every such house having ten windows or more, and under 20, 6 *s* *per annum*, and on every house having 20 windows or more, 10 *s.* *per annum.*

VI. *An additional duty on houses*, granted by 8 Ann. chap. 4, being an additional 10 *s.* on every inhabited house having 20 windows or more, and under 30; and an additional 20 *s.* on every house having 30 windows or more; which addition was granted but for 32 years from Michaelmas 1710.

VII. *The duty on hawkers and pedlars*, first granted by 8 and 9 W. III, chap. 25, and by 6 Ann. chap. 5, continued to Midsummer 1807; being a tax of 4 *l.* *per annum* on every hawker or pedlar, and 4 *l.* *per annum* more for every horse or beast bearing or drawing burden, with which he travels.

VIII. *A second stamp duty*, at first granted for ever by 10 W. III, chap. 25, being an additional stamp duty, in most respects, the same with the former.

IX. *The apprentice duty*, first granted for 5 years from May 1, 1710, by 8 Ann. chap. 9, being a duty of 6 *d.* per pound for all sums paid, or agreed to be paid, with clerks or apprentices; and, if the sum to be paid, or agreed to be paid, exceed 50 *l.* the tax is then 1 *s.* per pound; but apprentices put out by the parish, or by any public charity, are excepted.

X. *A third stamp duty*, first granted for 32 years, from August 1, 1711, by 9 Ann. ch. 23, being a stamp duty on some things not before charged, *viz.* debentures, 8 *d.* bills of lading, 4 *d.* almanacks, on one sheet, 1 *d.* if on more,

2 *d. per annum*, wine licences, 4 *s.* alehouſe licences, 1 *s.*

XI. *The duty on cards and dice*, made or imported here, firſt granted by the ſame act for 32 years, from June 11, 1711, being a duty of 6 *d.* per pack of cards, and 5 *s.* per pair of dice.

XII. *A fourth ſtamp duty*, firſt granted for 32 years, from Auguſt 1, 1712, by 10 Ann. chap. 19, being a new duty of ſeveral kinds upon writings not before charged, and upon papers or pamphlets, and advertiſements; and an additional duty of 2 *s.* 3 *d.* on every transfer ſtock, in any company.

XIII. *A fifth ſtamp duty*, firſt granted for 32 years, from Auguſt 1, 1712, by 10 Ann. chap. 26, being an additional ſtamp duty of 2 *s.* 4 *d.* upon every policy of inſurance of any kind whatſoever.

XIV. *A ſixth ſtamp duty*, firſt granted for 32 years, from Auguſt 2, 1714, by 12 Ann. ſeſſ. 2, chap. 9, being an additional ſtamp duty of 5 different kinds, upon a great variety of deeds and writings therein mentioned.

XV. *The civil-liſt tax*, firſt granted for 32 years, from Michaelmas 1713, by 12 Ann. ſeſſ. 1, chap. 11, being a tax of 35,000 *l. per annum*, on the civil-liſt revenue. We ſhall afterwards aſſign the reaſon why we charge this as a tax upon the people.

XVI. To theſe we ſhall add *the land-tax*; for, though this tax was never granted for above a year at a time, yet as it was annually granted, and was subsisting at the death of Queen Anne, we may reckon it among our inland duties; and, it is almost certain, that we shall be subject to it as long as we are liable to any tax whatsoever. This tax, at least in its present form, was granted in the beginning of King William's reign, and continued for that time, at 1 *s.* 2 *s.* 3 *s.* or 4 *s.* in the pound, until the last year of Queen Anne, when, by 12 Ann, sess. 2, chap. 1, an aid was granted to her majesty to be raised by a land-tax of 2 *s.* in the pound for the year 1714, beginning as usual, March 25.

Thus we have at last made an end of our long list of taxes, which were subsisting at the end of Queen Anne's reign; but there were several others, that like noisome meteors, made their appearance for a year or more, and then vanished. These we have forborne to mention, because, we believe, the reader will be, by this time, as heartily tired of reading, as we are of collecting and writing such a disagreeable scroll as that we have now given. Let him consider then what the people must be who are to pay these taxes, and on account of these taxes made liable to an infinite number of pains, penalties, and hardships; besides being in many cases deprived of that which is the glory of Englishmen, *to be tried by God and their country*; and sure to suffer the utmost rigour of justice for an innocent act made criminal by law, if they have ever, upon any occasion, behaved like a *free-born Britain*, or disobliged a revenue commissioner, or a neighbouring justice of peace: whereas, if they have behaved like what place-men call *quiet and good subjects*, they may expect what mitigation they please, which these commissioners, or justices, are impowered to grant.

If the wars we engaged in were abſolutely neceſſary; and, if it was abſolutely neceſſary for us to carry them on in the manner we did, ſurely every man in England, had he foreſeen the conſequence, would have ſubmitted to a juſt and equal *pound-rate* upon his revenue, or annual income, whether from land, trade, or buſineſs, rather than ſubject the trade and people of his country, to ſo many dangers and difficulties, by obliging our rulers to raiſe money by taxes upon *conſumption*. This would have been for the particular intereſt of every man in the kingdom; for it may be demonſtrated, that from a pound-rate of 2 *s.* in the pound only, if juſtly and equally aſſeſſed, and effectually carried into execution, we ſhould, with moderate taxes upon luxury, ſo as not to occaſion ſmuggling, have raiſed more money annually, than the war coſt us, even in the laviſh manner it was carried on; whereas it is now generally admitted, that every man in the kingdom, one with another, pays 10 *s.* on account of our taxes upon conſumption, for every 20 *s.* he ſpends yearly for the ſupport of himſelf and family, ſo that every man is a great loſer by our method of raiſing money for the public ſervice, except miſers and hoarders of money.

But when that which we now call a *land-tax* was firſt thought of, there were many errors in the methods propoſed for carrying it into execution, particularly that of laying the whole upon the landlord, whereas one moiety only ſhould have been laid upon the landlord, and the other upon the tenant. We know it will be ſaid, that a tax upon the tenant is really a tax upon the landlord, becauſe it diſables the tenant from paying ſuch a high rent as he otherwiſe might; but does not a tax of equal amount upon conſumption produce the ſame effect? In this reſpect therefore they are equal;

what then muſt be the conſequence of a tax on conſumption *of quadruple the amount?* and, in general, we ought to conſider, that a tax, like every other burden, is the more eaſily borne, the more ſhoulders you put it on, unleſs you put it on ſuch ſhoulders as cannot bear any part of it; for then you are obliged to bear the bearer as well as his ſhare of the burden; which will always be the conſequence of laying taxes upon workmen, labourers, and ſervants, or upon any thing they muſt neceſſarily conſume; for ſuch taxes only ſerve to enhance the price of labour, and conſequently the price of every thing thereby produced, which of courſe leſſens our exportation, and injures every branch of our trade.

We could point out many other miſtakes; but ſhall now only add, that we believe they were deſigned. We believe ſome of the courtiers of thoſe days deſigned, that this method of raiſing money ſhould not prove effectual, in order to reduce us to the neceſſity of taxing conſumption: 1. Becauſe ſuch taxes muſt always be heavy upon trade, fiſheries, and manufactures, and conſequently prevent our being ſuch formidable rivals to the Dutch: and 2dly, Becauſe ſuch taxes increaſe the power of miniſters, and give them the abſolute diſpoſal of large ſums of money, as they have the power not only of naming the officers employed in the collection, but of appointing what number of officers, and what ſalaries they think fit. Theſe are our reaſons for being of ſuch an opinion; and *the then Marquis of Hallifax* ſeems to have been of the ſame opinion, as appears from a tract of his publiſhed in *the Hiſtory of England, by an impartial hand*, vol. 2, p. 467, which piece, as well as the hiſtory, we muſt recommend to the reader's peruſal.

The deſign of the court therefore being to render taxes upon conſumption neceſſary, they gave themſelves no trouble about the aſſeſſment that was to be made, in order to raiſe money by a *pound rate*; but, on the contrary, connived at moſt of the lands in the kingdom being aſſeſſed at leſs than half their yearly value, and at aſſeſſing ſtock in trade, inſtead of aſſeſſing the yearly profits made by trade, or any other ſort of employment: as to both which, indeed, they were warranted by the practice of former times; but the circumſtances of the nation were now very different. In former times, I mean before the reſtoration, or rather before the civil wars in King Charles the Firſt's reign, annual taxes were not neceſſary. Our aids and ſubſidies, tenths and fifteenths, were granted only upon particular occaſions, when war, or any other misfortune, required any extraordinary public expence; and, as war was then generally but of ſhort duration, theſe taxes did not often require to be annually renewed; but now, when we muſt have annual taxes, ſuch taxes ought to be impoſed either upon conſumption, or upon annual profits: it is therefore ridiculous to talk of ſtock in trade; becauſe ſome employments require a great ſtock, and yet may yield but very little profit, and others yield a great annual profit without any ſtock. As experience is the beſt inſtructor, we have now no occaſion to ſhew the miſchiefs that muſt be brought upon a free trading country by taxes upon conſumption, eſpecially when raiſed by exciſes, which are the only methods whereby they can be equally and effectually raiſed. Theſe miſchiefs every thinking man in the kingdom is now ſenſible of; but our landed gentlemen having once got their eſtates aſſeſſed at ſuch an undervalue, they would never think of effectual methods for taxing any other ſort of yearly income; becauſe if they had, they muſt have conſented to a new aſſeſſment, and indeed, to frequent aſſeſſments of their own eſtates; and, as taxes upon conſumption, give miniſters ſuch an addition of power, it is not to be expected, that they will ever think of raiſing money for the public ſervice by any other method.

This is the true cauſe of our having ſo long and ſo obſtinately perſiſted in this method of raiſing the neceſſary annual ſupplies. It is true, that by this method, the people are not ſo ſenſible of the public expence, or of what they pay towards it, eſpecially when every tax is mortgaged as ſoon as impoſed; but, for this very reaſon, every honeſt man ought to be againſt it; for the people ought always to be made ſenſible of both; becauſe they will then look more narrowly into the public accounts; they will be more cautious of involving themſelves in war: they will prevent our miniſters engaging in any wild and expenſive ſchemes, or perſiſting in them after experience has ſhewn them to be impracticable; and, we believe, every one will allow, that by this method alone, it was poſſible for our miniſters to bring the nation under ſuch a load of debts as that we groaned under at the end of Queen Anne's reign.

1 Geo. I, ſeſſ. 1. 1714. The ways and means for raiſing the ſupplies granted in this ſeſſion (which was properly a continuation of the former ſeſſion, and began Auguſt the 1ſt, and ended Auguſt the 25th, 1714,) were as follow;

Chap. 1. *An act for the better ſupport of all his majeſty's houſhold, and of the honour and dignity of the crown of Great-Britain.*

By this act the ſame revenue, and the ſame funds were ſettled during his majeſty's life, for the support of the civil list, as had been settled upon Queen * Anne; except the revenue of the dutchy of Cornwall, and of the first-fruits and tenths of the clergy, and of the 700 *l.* a week from the Post-Office, and the 35,000 *l.* a year settled for paying the debt of the civil-list revenue made by act of parliament. And, as a testimony of their loyalty to their new sovereign, a clause was added, authorizing and requiring the Treasury forthwith to issue and pay, out of any public money, the sum of 100,000 *l.* to any person, who should secure the person of the Pretender, whenever he should land, or attempt to land, in any of his majesty's dominions; which clause was, by an act of the next session improved, by inserting the words *dead or alive.*

An act for rectifying mistakes in the names of the commissioners for the land-tax for the year 1714; and for raising so much as is wanting to make up the sum of 1,400,000 l. intended to be raised by a lottery for the public service in the said year. Chap. 2.

In order to encourage people to subscribe to the lottery, established by 12 Ann. sess. 2, chap. 9, (see p. 161.) an annual addition was, by the present act, made to the fund settled by that act; the yearly sum of 116,573 *l.* 12 *s.* being granted in lieu of the yearly fund of 105,000 *l.* with a proviso to make good the deficiency, if any, out of any public money, or, in failure thereof, out of the next aids, to be granted by parliament.

This session began the 17th of March 1714, 1 Geo. I, and ended the 7th of August 1715, the ways sess. 2, and means for raising the supplies granted in it, 1714. were as follow:

* See p. 96, 97, 98.

Chap. 1. *An act for an aid by a land-tax for the service of the year* 1715.

This tax was 2 *s.* in the pound; and the loan upon it was 940,000 *l.*

Chap. 2. *An act for continuing the duties upon malt, &c. and for continuing certain duties on hops, for* 1715.

The loan upon this act was 700,000 *l.*

Chap. 12. General or Aggregate fund. *An act for enlarging the fund of the governor and company of the Bank of England, relating to Exchequer bills; and for settling an additional revenue of* 120,000 *l.* per annum *upon his majesty during his life, for the service of the civil government; and for establishing a certain fund of* 54,600 *l.* per annum, *to raise* 910,000 *l. for the public service, by sale of annuities, at* 6 *l.* per cent. per annum, *redeemable by parliament, &c.*

By this act a fund was named and established, which hath often since appeared in our statute books. For which purpose the following branches of the public revenue were by this act appropriated, *viz.* the moiety of the first branch of the *customs*, and the 12th, 13th, 19th, 24th, 25th, and 31st, branches of the * customs: and to the same fund were likewise appropriated the surplusses of the following branches, after payment of what was charged on them by former acts, *viz.* of the other moiety of the first branch of the *customs*; of the 23d branch of the *customs*; of the 3d, 4th, 5th, 9th, 10th, and 16th of † *excise*; and of the 3d and 7th of *inland duties.* And to all these was added the surplus of the civil-list revenue, in case it

* See p. 168, 169, 170, 171, 172, 173.
† See p. 176, 177, 178.

ſhould, with the addition by this act made to it, as under-mentioned, produce more than 700,000 *l.* *per annum*; and all other public monies, which, after Michaelmas 1715, ſhould be brought into the Exchequer, not appropriated to any uſe.

This hodge-podge of taxes and ſurpluſſes was by the act named *the general, or aggregate fund*; and, to render this fund perpetual, all the ſaid branches not before granted in perpetuity, were by this act granted *for ever*, that is to ſay, the 1ſt branch of the *cuſtoms* as to one moiety, and the 23d and 31ſt branches of the *cuſtoms*; the 3d, 4th, 9th, and 10th branches of exciſe; and the 3d and 7th of inland duties.

Then, with regard to the debts charged upon this fund, a yearly ſum of 120,000 *l.* was, by this act, added to the civil-liſt revenue, during his majeſty's life, upon condition, that if that whole revenue, with this addition, produced leſs than 700,000 *l.* the deficiency ſhould be made good by parliament; but, if it produced more, the ſurplus ſhould belong to this fund; ſo that the nation was, in the next reign, obliged to make good the 35,000 *l.* a year, part of the civil-liſt revenue, mortgaged by 12 Ann. ſeſſ. 1, chap. 11, which probably will be always ſo, when any part of that revenue is granted away from the next ſucceſſor.

It was by this act propoſed to raiſe 910,000 *l.* for the public ſervice by the ſale of annuities, at the rate of 6 *l.* *per cent. per annum*, and that for this purpoſe, the yearly ſum of 54,600 *l.* was to be ſet apart at the Exchequer, and paid into the Bank for anſwering the yearly payments to thoſe annuitants till redeemed. And this *general*, or *aggregate fund*, was charged with the payment of 2 *d.* *per cent. per diem* on all the Exchequer bills then iſſued, except during the time they ſhould be in the Exchequer, or in the hands of any receiver of the public revenue, and of 3 *l.* *per cent. per annum*, to the Bank for circulating them, as before. In the next place, it was charged with the payment of all monies that ſhould grow due to the Bank, on account of the 45,000 *l.* annuity due to them by 9 Ann. chap. 7, and the 8000 *l.* annuity due to them by 12 Ann. ſeſſ. 1, chap. 11. In the 3d place, it was charged with the ſaid 120,000 *l.* annually for the civil liſt. In the 4th, with the ſaid 54,600 *l.* annuity for the new annuities by this act to be ſold. In the 5th, with making good any deficiency that ſhould happen in the Bank's original fund of 100,000 *l.* *per annum*, ſecured to them by 5 W. and M. chap. 7, or in their other fund of 106,501 *l.* 13 *s.* 5 *d.* *per annum*, ſecured to them by 7 Ann. chap. 7. And, in the laſt place, with the yearly ſum of 270,999 *l.* 7 *s.* or ſo much thereof, as the reſidue ſhould amount to; which reſidue was appropriated to the paying off and cancelling the Exchequer bills then remaining uncancelled.

It was by ſect. 23, of this act, further provided, that if the ſaid fund ſhould, at the end of any one year, produce more than ſufficient for all theſe purpoſes, the ſurplus ſhould be diſpoſable by parliament; and, if leſs, the deficiency ſhould be made good out of the next aids to be granted in parliament; and that a part of the 180,000 *l.* remaining due of the money that had been borrowed on the duty on hops, ſhould be ſatisfied out of the ſaid 910,000 *l.* to be advanced by the purchaſe of annuities. But, what was moſt extraordinary, the ſum of 77,694 *l.* 1 *s.* 7 *d.* of unappropriated money brought into the Exchequer before the 12th of June 1714, was by this act applied towards diſcharging his majeſty's extraordinary expences from his acceſſion to the throne, till Michaelmas 1715; although no ſuch expence had been thought of, or any money granted for the ſame, as it ought to have been, in the committee of ſupply.

An act for raiſing 910,000 l. for public ſervices, by ſale of annuities, after the rate of 5 l. per cent. per annum, redeemable by parliament, &c. Chap. 19.

It had been found, that the ſaid ſum of 910,000 *l.* might be raiſed by the ſale of redeemable annuities at the rate of 5 *l. per cent. per annum*, and therefore this act appropriated only 45,500 *l.* yearly, part of the ſaid yearly ſum of 54,600 *l.* towards the payment of thoſe annuities with 250 *l.* yearly to the caſhier, and 200 *l.* yearly to the accomptant, to be appointed for this purpoſe by the Bank, and a reward of 500 *l.* to the former for his extraordinary trouble, to be allowed him out of the ſaid 910,000 *l.*

An act for enlarging the capital ſtock and yearly fund of the South-Sea company, and for ſupplying thereby 822,032 l. 4 s. 8 d. to public uſes; and for raiſing 169,000 l. for like uſes, by ſale of annuities, &c. Chap. 21.

By this act the ſum of 822,032 *l.* 4 *s.* 8 *d.* was raiſed for the current ſervice, by adding that ſum to the then capital of the South-Sea company, in order to make it compleat ten millions, and a further ſum of 169,000 *l.* was raiſed for the ſame purpoſe, by ſale of redeemable annuities at 5 *l. per cent. per annum*, for the payment of which 8450 *l. per annum*, other part of the ſaid 54,600 *l. per annum*, was appropriated; and the ſums allowed by the foregoing act to the caſhier and accomptant, were by this act lessened to 100 *l.* reward to the former, and 100 *l.* a year to each.

Chap. 23. *An act for making provision for the ministers of the 50 new churches, which are to be built in and about the cities of London and Westminster, &c.*

By this act the 22d branch of the * *customs* was continued to Michaelmas 1725, and the surplus appropriated as a fund for providing a maintenance for the ministers of the new churches, to be issued as should be afterwards directed by parliament. The grant for this purpose was 60,000 *l.*

Chap. 31. *An act for granting an aid to his majesty by a land-tax in Great-Britain, for the service of the year 1716.*

This tax was 4 *s.* in the pound, and the sum borrowed upon it was 1,880,000 *l.*

Chap. 36. *An act for charging and continuing the duties on malt, &c. for the year 1716, &c.*

The loan upon this act was 700,000 *l.*

Chap. 43. *An act to continue the coinage duties; and to charge the duties on senna, &c.*

By this act the † 7th branch of the *customs* was continued for seven years; but, as every branch of the public expence now began to be increased, the Treasury were, by this act, impowered to issue money yearly, by way of imprest, and upon account, out of the monies arising by this act, *or any other supplies*, for defraying the expence of the mints in England and Scotland; so as the same, with the coinage duties arising by this act, did not, in any one

* See p. 171. † See p. 167.

year, exceed 15,000 *l.* and, as *senna* had before been exempted from several duties as a drug for dyer's use, it was by this act subjected to all the duties upon drugs imported, and stock in hand bound to pay them, if exceeding 20 pounds weight.

By an act of the last session of Queen Anne the sum of 230,308 *l.* 9 *s.* 10 *d.* had been declared to be remaining due to the creditors of the public in Scotland, and for which the commissioners of Equivalent were thereby impowered to issue debentures bearing interest at 5 *l.* *per cent.* from June 24, 1714, payable out of the first money due to Scotland, by way of equivalent, in pursuance of the 15th article of the Union; and, in this session, upon report from a particular committee, an act was ordered in and passed, impowering the Treasury to issue 15,822 *l.* 8 *s.* 7 *d.* ¾, out of the customs, or excise in Scotland, for paying a year's interest on this sum, with the salaries and charges of the commissioners of Equivalent. And, by a private act passed in this session, upon report from a particular committee, the sum of 18,241 *l.* 10 *s.* 10 *d.* was declared to be due to *William Pateson*, Esq; with interest at 5 *l.* *per cent.* from March 25, 1713, and to be payable out of the equivalent due to Scotland.

This session began the 17th of February 1716-17, and the ways and means for raising the supplies granted in it were as follow: 3 Geo. I. 1716.

An act for granting an aid by a land-tax for 1717. Chap. 3.

This tax was 3 *s.* in the pound, and the loan upon it was 1,410,000 *l.*

Chap. 4. *An act for continuing the duties on malt, &c.*

The loan upon this act was 700,000 *l.*

Chap. 7. Origin of the Sinking Fund. *An act for redeeming the duties and revenues which were settled to pay off principal and interest on the orders made forth on four lottery acts, passed in the 9th and 10th year of her late majesty's reign; and for redeeming certain annuities payable on orders out of the hereditary excise, according to a former act in that behalf; and for establishing a general yearly fund, not only for the future payment of annuities at several rates, to be payable and trasferrable at the Bank of England, and redeemable by parliament; but also to raise monies for such proprietors of the said annuities as shall choose to be paid their principal and arrears of interest in ready money; and for making good such other deficiencies and payments as in this act are mentioned, &c.*

§ 1. For establishing a *general fund* for payment of annuities in lieu of lottery orders, on the four acts 9 and 10 Ann. and in lieu of the annuities given for the banker's debt, the funds of the four lottery acts, 9 and 10 Ann. *viz.* the customs of poundage upon export, granted by 12 Char. II, chap. 4, and not taken away by subsequent statutes, and which were revived by 9 Ann. chap. 6, [*the first lottery of* 9 Ann.] and the other duties granted and continued by 9 Ann. chap. 6, *viz.* the duty of 12 *d.* a hundred weight upon leather, sheep-skins, or calf-skins, tanned, tawed, or dressed, exported; and the duties upon coals exported, and the additional duties upon coals, culm, and cinders, shipped and water borne, and of coals imported, if any; the additional duty on candles, and the hereditary duty of 1 *per cent.* on goods exported from ports capable of a ship of 200 tons, to any place of the Mediterranean, beyond Malaga, in a ſhip not built, &c. according to the act, granted by 13 and 14 Char. II, chap. 11, and an hereditary duty of 5 s. for every white woollen broad cloth exported, granted by 9 Ann. chap. 8, and the yearly ſum of 135,000 *l.* appropriated out of the ſaid duties, by 9 Ann. chap. 6, and the ſurplus of the ſaid duties, and the weekly ſum of 700 *l.* payable out of the revenues of the Poſt-office, by 6 Ann. chap. 10, and the duties upon ſkins and hides, vellum and parchment, granted by 9 Ann. chap. 11, and the duties granted by 9 Ann. chap. 23, [*the ſecond lottery act*, 9 Ann.] *viz.* on hackney coaches and chairs, on ſtampt vellum, parchment, (*viz.* on bills of lading, almanacks, and licences for ſelling ale or wine) and paper, on cards and dice, and rock-ſalt exported to Ireland. And the yearly fund of 186,670 *l.* appropriated by 9 Ann. chap. 23, out of the duties granted by the ſaid three acts of 9 Ann. chap. 10, 9 Ann. chap. 11, and 9 Ann. chap. 23, and the duties on the additional hackney chairs thereunto added by 10 Ann. chap. 19, and the other duties granted by 10 Ann. chap. 19, [*the firſt lottery act*, 10 Ann.] *viz.* on ſoap, on paper, paſte-boards, milled-boards, and ſcale-boards, imported; on books, prints, and maps imported on paper, paſte-boards, milled-boards, and ſcale-boards, made in Great-Britain; on linens, printed, painted, ſtained, or dyed, imported; on ſilk, callicoes, linens, and ſtuffs, printed, ſtained, painted, or dyed in Great-Britain; on ſtamped vellum, parchment, and paper, *viz.* ſurrenders, transfers, &c. and on pamphlets and news-papers; and the yearly fund of 168,003 *l.* appropriated out of theſe duties by 10 Ann. chap. 19, and the duties granted by 10 Ann. chap. 26, [*the ſecond lottery act*, 10 Ann.] *viz.* on dressed skins, and hides imported; on skins and hides tanned, tawed, or dressed in Great-Britain; on vellum and parchment, on starch, on coffee and tea, [*repealed by* 10 Geo. I, chap. 10, *and in their place a moiety of the inland duties imposed by that act on coffee and tea, is substituted*] on gilt and silver wire; and stamp duties on policies of insurance, and the yearly fund of 168,003 *l.* appropriated out of these duties by 10 Ann. chap. 26, and also certain annual sums amounting to 39,855 *l.* 15 *s.* 7 *d.* one fifth charge upon the hereditary excise by stat. 12 W. III, chap. 12, and 2 Ann. chap. 3, in lieu of the *banker's debt*, shall continue for ever; but subject to such redemption as in this act is contained.—*The debts still remaining due upon the said acts of Queen Anne, are by this act computed to amount in the whole to* 8,762,625 *l.*

§ 4. The said yearly sums of 135,000 *l.* 186,670 *l.* 168,003 *l.* and 39,855 *l.* 15 *s.* 7 *d.* $\frac{1}{5}$; adding thereto, the above-mentioned surplus of the duties granted by 9 Ann. chap. 6, (which, *communibus annis*, hath amounted to 27,317 *l.* 11 *s.* 3 *d.*) amounting in the whole to 724,849 *l.* 6 *s.* 10 *d.* $\frac{1}{5}$, *per annum*, shall be a *general fund*; and, if all the monies, arising of the said customs, *&c.* shall not amount to the said sum of 724,849 *l.* 6 *s.* 10 *d.* $\frac{1}{5}$, then the monies so arising shall be part of the said *general fund*, for paying the annuities by this act chargeable thereon; and, in case any deficiency shall happen, so as within any one year, the said monies so arising, shall not amount to 724,849 *l.* 6 *s.* 10 *d.* $\frac{1}{5}$, then so much as shall be wanting, shall be supplied out of the first aid to be granted in parliament. [*The annuities charged on this general fund called Bank-annuities, were in great part subscribed into South-Sea Stock, pursuant to* 6 Geo. I, chap. 4, *and the rest were paid off pursuant to* 13 Geo. I, chap. 3.]

A yearly fund being thus eſtabliſhed, the Treaſury was empowered to open books for taking in ſubſcriptions for the purchaſe of annuities at 5*l.* *per cent. per annum*, redeemable upon repayment of their principal money, and all arrears of their ſaid annuities; and, in theſe books, the proprietors of the ſaid debts, who were willing to accept of ſuch annuities for what was due to them, were to ſubſcribe their names, and the Treaſury was to pay off thoſe who did not ſubſcribe, by ſelling to any other perſons who ſhould be willing to purchaſe ſuch annuities, or by calling for ſo much of the aforeſaid ſums from the Bank and South-Sea companies, as ſhould be wanted for that purpoſe, for which theſe two companies were each to have ſuch an annuity as before-mentioned, in proportion to the ſums called for; and the Treaſury was empowered to raiſe money by the ſame methods, for paying off the following ſums, *viz.*

	l.	*s.*	*d.*
Principal money remaining unſatisfied on the regiſter of loans, founded on the act for duties on low wines [3 and 4 Ann. chap. 4.] which expired June 24, 1714, carrying intereſt at 6 *per cent.*	61,707	3	2
Ditto, on the act for duties on candles, [9 Ann. chap. 6.] expired May 1, 1715, carrying like intereſt	314,219	11	$2\frac{1}{4}$
The deficiency of the laſt year's grants	577,014	16	$1\frac{1}{4}$
The bills of exchange for the *Canada* expedition	24,195	11	2
	977,137	1	$7\frac{1}{2}$

	l.	s.	d.
Brought over	977,137	1	7½
To this let us add the two sums before-mentioned, *viz.*			
The debts of Q. Anne	8,762,625	0	0
The *banker*'s debt	664,263	0	0
	10,404,025	1	7½

And to this we must add the annuities at 5 *l. per cent. per annum*, which should become due at Michaelmas 1717, when this fund was to commence, because they were to be added to the principal; for, as to the annuities of 6 *l. per cent.* that might be due at Midsummer 1717, they were all to be paid off by the produce of these taxes that might arise before Michaelmas 1717; consequently we may reckon that the whole charge upon this fund of 724,849 *l.* 6 *s.* 10 *d.* yearly, was under 10,600,000 *l.* at an interest of 5 *l. per cent.* except the said deficiency, and the *Canada* bills; for satisfying of which, redeemable annuities at 4 *per cent.* were to be sold by the Treasury, which interest, as to both, was to be paid quarterly till redeemed; but this fund was besides, by a clause in this act, charged with the payment of 4 *l. per cent.* interest on the debentures to be made forth by an act of the same session for stating the debts due to the army; for which purpose money was to be imprested to the paymaster of the army, that is to say, issued and paid to him, and for which he was afterwards to account. And it was enacted, that upon the repayment of the principal money, with all arrears of the annuities, the same should cease, and the fund be understood to be redeemed; but with a proviso, that not less than 500,000 *l.* of the principal money ſhould be repaid at a time; the whole of the annuities being for this purpoſe erected into a joint ſtock, and the annuities made payable at the Bank.

After all which was added the following clauſe, ſect. 37, *viz.*

"All the monies to ariſe, from time to time, "as well of the exceſs, or ſurplus of an act made "this ſeſſion for redeeming the funds of the "Bank of England, and of the exceſs or ſurplus "by virtue of one other act made likewiſe this "ſeſſion, for redeeming the funds of the South-"Sea company, as alſo of the exceſs or ſurplus "of the duties and revenues by this act appro-"priated as aforeſaid, and the overplus monies "of the ſaid general yearly fund by this act "eſtabliſhed, ſhall be appropriated to the diſ-"charging the principal and intereſt of ſuch "national debts as were incurred before the "25th of December 1716, and are declared "to be national debts, and are provided for "by parliament, in ſuch manner as ſhall be di-"rected by any future act, or acts of parlia-"ment, to be diſcharged therewith, or out of "the ſame, *and to or for none other uſe, intent,* "*or purpoſe whatſoever.*"

Theſe ſurpluſſes are, in ſubſequent acts of parliament, called the ſinking fund.

An act for redeeming ſeveral funds of the governor and company of the Bank of England, purſuant to former proviſoes of redemption; and for ſecuring to them ſeveral new funds and allowances redeemable by parliament; and for obliging them to advance further ſums, not exceeding 2,500,000*l.* *at* 5 *per cent. as ſhall be found neceſſary to be employed in leſſening the national debts and incumbrances; and for continuing certain proviſions formerly made for the expences of his majeſty's* Chap. 8.

civil government; and for payment of annuities formerly purchased at the rates of 5 l. per cent. and for other purposes in the act mentioned.

By this act it was recited, that the Bank had agreed, 1st, To accept of an annuity of 88,751 *l.* 7 *s.* 10 *d.* ½, in lieu of their annuity of 106,501 *l.* 14 *s.* 5 *d.* after Midsummer 1718, redeemable upon a year's notice, to be given at Michaelmas 1718, or any quarterly feast-day afterwards, on payment of their principal sum of 1,775,027 *l.* 17 *s.* 10 *d.* ¹, and all arrears of their said annuity *. 2dly, To discharge and deliver up to be cancelled Exchequer bills, to the amount of 2,000,000 *l.* principal, in consideration of an annuity of 100,000 *l.* to commence from Christmas 1717, redeemable upon one year's notice to be then given, or at any quarterly feast-day afterwards, on repayment of the said 2,000,000 *l.* and all arrears of the said annuity. 3dly, To continue to circulate the remainder (amounting to 2,561,025 *l.* principal money) of Exchequer bills, at the allowance of 3 *l. per cent. per annum*, amounting to 76,830 *l.* 15 *s. per annum*, the interest upon the said remainder to continue at 2 *d. per cent. per diem*, and their former allowances of 45,000 *l.* and 8000 *l.* for circulating the said bills to be continued to them †, until Christmas 1717; but after that day, the interest upon the bills to be reduced to 1 *d. per cent. per diem*, and their said allowances of 45,000 *l.* and 8000 *l. per annum* to cease; and from that day, the said allowances of 3 *l. per cent. per annum* only, and the said interest of 1 *d. per cent. per diem*; to be continued, redeemable however, upon a year's notice, to be given at Michaelmas 1717, or at any quarterly feast-day afterwards, on payment

* See 7 Ann. chap. 7. page 132.
† See 9 Ann. ch. 7. 12 Ann. sess. 1, ch. 11, p. 145, 149.

of all the principal and intereſt due on the ſaid bills, and all arrears of the ſaid allowances of 3 *l.* *per cent. per annum.* And 4thly, To advance the farther ſum of 2,500,000 *l.* or ſo much thereof as ſhould be required by the Treaſury, at any time before the 25th of March 1718, at an intereſt of 5 *l. per cent. per annum*, redeemable by parliament, but with a proviſo, that not above 500,000 *l.* part of the ſaid 2,500,000 *l.* ſhould be required of them at any one time.

This agreement was therefore, by this act eſtabliſhed; and to ſecure to the Bank the regular payment of the ſaid annuities, allowance, and the intereſt on the Exchequer bills, they were to circulate, and the money they were to advance, the *aggregate* fund before-mentioned, and the 5th branch of the *inland duties* * were appropriated to the purpoſes of this act, in the order after mentioned, together with all the other duties ſettled for payment of the former yearly ſums of 106,501 *l.* 13 *s.* 5 *d.* and the intereſt and allowances relating to former Exchequer bills; all which duties were granted to his majeſty and his ſucceſſors for ever. And this new fund was charged with the following yearly payments, and in the order following, *viz.* 1ſt, To pay off ſo much as at Midſummer 1718, ſhall grow due to the Bank on their ſaid annuity of 106,501 *l.* 13 *s.* 5 *d.* and ſo much as at Chriſtmas 1717, ſhall be due for the ſaid intereſt at 2 *d. per cent. per diem*, and ſo much as at the ſame feaſt-day ſhall be due for the allowance of 3 *l. per cent. per annum*, and upon the ſaid yearly ſums of 45,000 *l.* and 8000 *l.* 2dly, To pay ſo much as ſhall, from thenceforth grow due of the ſaid annuities of 88,751 *l.* 7 *s.* 10 *d.* ½, 100,000 *l.* and 76,830 *l.* 15 *s.* and the ſaid intereſt at the rate of 5 *l. per cent.* on ſo

* See page 181.

much of the ſaid 2,500,000 *l.* as ſhall be required to be advanced. 3dly, To pay the 120,000 *l. per annum*, in addition of the civil-liſt revenue, before charged on the *aggregate fund.* 4thly, To pay the 54,600 *l.* before charged on the ſame. 5thly, To make good the deficiencies on the Bank's original fund of 100,000 *l. per annum*, charged on five ſeventh parts of the 4th branch of *exciſe*. And, 6thly, To pay 4000 *l. per annum*, to the reſpective ſheriffs of England and Wales, for defraying the charges of taking forth their patents, paſſing their accounts, and obtaining their *quietus's*, which laſt was really a new grant to the civil-liſt revenue; for, as it is an expence of our civil government, either it ought not to be made good at all by the public, or it ought to be paid out of that revenue. And, as an additional ſecurity it was provided, that if, at the end of any quarter after Lady-day 1717, the produce of this fund ſhould not be ſufficient to anſwer all theſe purpoſes, the deficiency ſhould be made good out of the produce in any ſubſequent quarter, wherein there ſhould be an overplus; and if, at the end of any one year, to be reckoned at Michaelmas yearly, there ſhould be a deficiency, ſuch deficiency ſhould be made good out of the next aids to be granted in parliament; but if there ſhould be an overplus, ſuch overplus ſhould be at the diſpoſition of parliament.

And further, it was enacted, That after the redemption of all theſe annuities and intereſt, and after full payment of all arrearages of the ſaid yearly ſums of 120,000 *l.* for the civil liſt, and 54,600 *l.* for the annuities ſold in the preceding ſeſſion, and making good the deficiencies of the Bank's original fund of 100,000 *l. per annum*, the ſaid *aggregate fund*, and the duties appropriated thereto, ſhould be underſtood to be redeemed by parliament, and ſhould not be iſſued without the authority of parliament, except the 12th, 24th, and 25th branches of the *cuſtoms*, which ſhould continue to be iſſued for anſwering the ſaid 120,000 *l. per annum* to the civil liſt, the ſaid 4000 *l. per annum*, to the ſheriffs, and the ſaid 45,600 *l. per annum*, to the annuitants, until they ſhould be redeemed by parliament.

An act for redeeming the yearly fund of the South-Sea company (being after the rate of 6 l. per cent. per annum,) *and ſettling on the ſaid company a yearly fund after the rate of* 5 l. per cent. per annum *redeemable by parliament, and to raiſe for an annuity, or annuities, at* 5 l. per cent. per annum *any ſum, not exceeding two millions, to be employed in leſſening the national debts and incumbrances, and for making the ſaid new yearly fund and annuities to be hereafter redeemable in the time and manner thereby preſcribed.* Chap. 9.

This act recites, that in regard the rate of intereſt was very much leſſened, the South-Sea company had agreed to accept of an annuity of 500,000 *l.* with 8000 *l. per annum* for management as before, in lieu of 600,000 *l.* then due to them on their capital of 10,000,000 *l.* to commence from and after Midſummer 1718; and farther, that they had agreed to advance, at 5 *l. per cent.* intereſt, upon being required by the Treaſury, any ſum not exceeding 2,000,000 *l.* before Chriſtmas 1717, on condition, that not above 500,000 *l.* ſhould be required at any one time; and that they ſhould have a fortnight's notice each time. In conſideration of this, all the duties formerly appropriated to * them, were

* See 9 Ann. chap. 21. p. 148.

again appropriated and granted for ever; and the fund eſtabliſhed by chap. 7, of this ſeſſion, was made a collateral ſecurity, for the regular payment of their ſaid annuity, and the intereſt of the money they ſhould advance; with a proviſo, that if there ſhould be an overplus in their proper fund, it ſhould be at the diſpoſition of parliament; that, upon repayment of the ſaid 2,000,000 *l.* or ſuch part thereof as they ſhould be required to advance, the intereſt ſhould ceaſe; and that, upon one year's notice to be given by parliament at Midſummer 1723, or any quarterly feaſt-day afterwards, part of their ſaid capital might be paid off, and a proportionable part of their ſaid annuity to ceaſe; but, upon condition that not leſs than 1,000,000 *l.* ſhould be paid off at any one time. And, it was enacted, that after compleat payment of their capital, all the duties appropriated to them ſhould be underſtood to be redeemed by parliament, and ſhould not be iſſued without the authority of parliament. Thus the government had ſecured no leſs than 4,500,000 *l.* at 5 *l. per cent.* intereſt, towards paying off ſuch of the proprietors of the redeemable debts as ſhould not agree to accept of the ſame intereſt.

4 Geo. I, 1717. This ſeſſion began the 21ſt of November 1717, and ended the 17th of March 1717-18; the ways and means for raiſing the ſupplies granted in it, were as follow:

Chap. 1. *An act for an aid by a land-tax, for the ſervice of* 1718.

This tax was 3 *s.* in the pound, and the loan upon it was 1,410,000 *l.*

Chap. 3. *An act for continuing the duties on malt, &c.*

The loan upon this act was 700,000 *l.*

This session began the 11th of November 1718, and ended the 18th of April 1719; the ways and means for raising the supplies granted in it, were as follow: 5 Geo. I, 1718.

An act for an aid by a land-tax for 1719. Chap. 1.

This tax was 3 *s.* in the pound; and the loan upon it 1,410,000 *l.*—In this act there is a clause for charging the *general*, or *sinking fund*, with 110,312 *l.* 17 *s.* 4 *d.* ¾, to be raised by the sale of annuities, at 5 *l.* *per cent.* till redeemed, which sum had been paid by the treasurer of the navy to the South-Sea company, for making good the annuity due to them, over and above the 29,645 *l.* 8 *s.* 9 *d.* ¼, granted for this purpose by the preceding session, though no resolution had in this session been agreed to in the committee of supply, for making good this deficiency.

An act for continuing the duties on malt, &c. for 1719. Chap. 2.

The loan upon this act was 700,000 *l.*

An act for applying certain overplus monies, and further sums, to be raised, as well by way of a lottery, as by loans, towards paying off and cancelling Exchequer bills, and for lessening the present great charge in relation to those bills; and for circulating and exchanging for ready money the residue of the same bills for the future. Chap. 3.

This act recites 3 Geo I, chap. 7, 8, 9, and enacts, that the sum of 196,444 *l.* 18 *s.* 3 *d.* ½, which remained in the Exchequer at Michaelmas 1718, for the overplus-money of the *aggregate fund*; and all the overplus-monies of the civil-list fund for three years ended at Michaelmas 1718; and 19,577 *l.* 10 *s.* which remained in the Exchequer at the same time, for the overplus-money of the South-Sea fund; and 190,436 *l.* 15 *s.* 11 *d.* and $\frac{9}{25}$, being the surplus for the year ended at the said Michaelmas, upon the *general*, or *sinking fund*, over and above the sum of 130,000 *l.* reserved for paying the half-year's annuities charged on the said sinking fund, to grow due at Christmas 1718; and all the overplus monies of the said several funds, which should arise within the half year to end at Lady-day 1719, should be applied towards redeeming the annuity of 76,830 *l.* 15 *s.* granted to the Bank by 3 Geo. I, chap. 8, and for discharging the principal and interest due to the said Bank for circulating Exchequer bills.

For the same purpose there was likewise by this act, 500,000 *l.* to be raised at 4 *l.* *per cent.* interest, by way of lottery, at 3 *l.* a ticket; and 520,000 *l.* by way of loan at 5 *l.* *per cent.* interest: and as to the residue of the Exchequer bills that should remain uncancelled, the Treasury was empowered to contract with any person or persons, for circulating and exchanging them, at such an allowance as should be agreed on; therefore the said annuity to the Bank was to cease from and after Lady-day 1719; from which time the annuities, established by 3 Geo. I, chap. 7, were made payable half-yearly; and the *aggregate fund* was made a security for paying the interest of the said 500,000 *l.* to be raised by way of lottery, and for paying the interest and principal of the said 520,000 *l.* to be raised by way of loan, together with 5995 *l.* for the expence of drawing the lottery.

The reader may perhaps be surprized to see a sum granted in this session for making good the deficiency of the *general*, or *sinking fund*, and yet by this act a surplus of the same fund was appropriated; therefore we must desire him to recollect, that by the establishment of this fund, if the duties appropriated to it did not produce yearly 724,849 *l.* 6 *s.* 10 *d.* the deficiency was to be made good out of the next aids to be granted by parliament, and it was for making good this deficiency, that a ſum was granted in this ſeſſion; but, as the annuities charged upon it did not amount to above 520,000 *l.* or thereabouts, there was a ſurplus over and above what was charged upon it, which, with the ſum granted for making good the ſaid deficiency, amounted to the ſum appropriated by this act. What the reaſon was for being ſo very intent upon paying off the Exchequer bills, ſeems to be a myſtery; for ſurely there was no œconomy in borrowing money at 5 *l. per cent.* in order to pay off Exchequer bills, which then coſt the public but 4 *l.* 10 *s.* 5 *d. per cent.* as will appear from 3 Geo. I, chap. 8.

An act for continuing certain duties upon coals and culm, and for eſtabliſhing certain funds to raiſe money, as well to proceed in the building of new churches, as alſo to compleat the ſupply granted to his majeſty; and to reſerve the overplus monies of the ſaid duties for the diſpoſition of parliament, &c. Chap. 9.

By this act, the 7th and 22d branch of the cuſtoms, which had been continued by 1 Geo. I, ſeſſ. 2, chap. 23, to Michaelmas 1725, was further continued to Lady-day 1751. And, though a local duty, great part of it was now ſeized for the uſe of the public, notwithſtanding the city of London's petition againſt it, which was rejected. For, by this act, there was only 21,000 *l. per annum*, part of the produce of this duty eſtabliſhed as a fund for borrowing 360,000 *l.* at 4 *l. per cent.* to be applied to the uſes for which the duty was at firſt deſigned; and out of the reſidue the yearly ſum of 30,559 *l.* 14 *s.* was ſet apart as a fund for ſecuring the payment of the principal and intereſt at 4 *l.* *per cent.* of 505,995 *l.* for the ſervice of the enſuing year, which was to be raiſed by another lottery of 3 *l.* per ticket, the chance of which was to be determined by the drawing of the lottery juſt mentioned.

Chap. 19. *An act for redeeming the fund appropriated for payment of the lottery tickets which were made forth for the ſervice of the year* 1710, *by a voluntary ſubſcription of the proprietors into the capital ſtock of the South-Sea company*; *and for raiſing a ſum of money to pay off ſuch debts and incumbrances as are therein mentioned, &c.*

By this act, the lottery annuities eſtabliſhed by 8 Ann. chap. 4, were to be ſubſcribed into the South-Sea company's ſtock, as alſo the ſum of 168,748 *l.* 5 *s.* in arrear to the ſaid annuitants at Chriſtmas 1718; and farther, the company was to advance 778,750 *l.* or a proportional part thereof, in caſe all the ſaid annuities and arrears ſhould not be ſubſcribed into their ſtock, for diſcharging principal and intereſt of ſuch national debts as were incurred before Chriſtmas 1716. The annuities were to be taken in at 11 years purchaſe, and the arrear at *cent. per cent*; that is to ſay, for every 20 *s.* annuity, the annuitant was to have 11 *l.* 10 *s.* South-Sea ſtock, and for every 100 *l.* arrear, 100 *l.* ſtock. And the company's ſtock being, by this means, as well as by the money they were to advance, to be proportionally increaſed, they were to have 5 *l.* *per cent. per annum* in proportion to ſuch increaſe, added to their former annuity of 500,000 *l.* *per annum*, and 2000 *l.* *per annum*, or a proportional part thereof, in caſe all the annuities and arrears should not be subscribed, added to their former 8000 *l.* *per annum*, for expence of management. And no part of their said annuities was to be redeemed before Midsummer 1723, but upon a year's notice afterwards to be redeemable, upon paying not less than a million at a time. And for securing the payment of these additional annuities, the 14th branch of the * *customs*, and the 6th of † *inland annuities* were continued for ever, and appropriated to this use.

This session began the 23d of November 1719, and ended the 11th of June 1720; and the ways and means for raising the supplies granted in it, were as follow: 6 Geo. I, 1719.

An act for granting an aid by a land-tax for the year 1720. Chap. 3.

This tax was 3 *s.* in the pound, and the loan upon it was 1,410,000 *l.*

An act for continuing the duties on malt, &c. Chap. 2.

The loan upon this act was 700,000 *l.*

An act for enabling the South-Sea company to increase their present capital stock and fund, by redeeming such public debts and incumbrances as are therein mentioned; and for raising money to be applied for lessening several of the public debts and incumbrances; and for calling in the present Exchequer bills remaining uncancelled, &c. Chap. 4.

This act recites, that divers acts of parliament have been made and passed, whereby several public duties, revenues, and incomes have

* See p. 169. † See p. 182.

been granted, or continued in perpetuity, or for ſome eſtate, term, or intereſt then in being; and all, or moſt of the ſaid public duties, revenues, and incomes were, and ſtood clogged and incumbered by anthority of parliament, with ſundry annuities, yearly funds, debts, or payments charged thereupon reſpectively, and payable out of the ſame, either in perpetuity, or for term or terms of life, lives, or years, in ſome caſes abſolutely, or in other caſes ſubject to a power of redemption by parliament.

It then recites 4 and 5 W. and M. chap. 3, 5 and 6 W. and M. chap. 20, 12 and 13 W. III, chap. 12, 1 Ann. ſeſſ. 1, chap. 7, 2 and 3 Ann. chap. 3, 3 and 4 Ann. chap. 2, 4 Ann. chap. 6, 5 Ann. chap. 19, 6 Ann. chap. 5, 6 Ann. chap. 11, 8 Ann. chap. 7, 8 Ann. chap. 4, 5 Geo. I, chap. 19, 12 Ann. ſeſſ. 1, chap. 11, 12 Ann. ſeſſ. 2, chap. 9, 1 Geo. I, ſeſſ. 1, chap. 2, 3 Geo. I, chap. 7, 8 Ann. chap. 4, 8 Ann. chap. 7, 10 Ann. chap. 19, 10 Ann. chap. 26, 5 Geo. I, chap. 3, 5 Geo. I, chap. 9, and proceeds to ſtate the public debts, which the company were by this act to redeem or purchaſe, and were of two ſorts, *redeemable* or *irredeemable*.

The redeemable debts were ſuch as the parliament had a power to redeem, by paying off the principal and arrears of the annuity, or yearly intereſt due upon them, amounting in the whole to 16,546,482 *l.* 7 *s.* 1 *d.* ½. And theſe again were of two ſorts; that is, ſuch as had an annuity, or yearly intereſt of 5 *l. per cent.* attending them till redemption, amounting in the whole to 11,779,660 *l.* 11 *s.* 3 *d.* ¾; or ſuch as had an annuity of 4 *l. per cent.* only, attending them till redemption, amounting in the whole to 4,766,821 *l.* 15 *s.* 9 *d.* ½.

The irredeemable debts conſiſted of thoſe annuities which had been ſold for a certain term of years, without any power of redemption; and these likewise were of two sorts; for they consisted of annuities that had been sold for a long term of years, that is to say, for 99, 96, or 89 years, computed to amount in the whole to 666,821 *l.* 8 *s.* 3 *d.* ½ *per annum*, or they consisted of annuities that had been sold for a short term of years, that is to say, for 32 years, amounting in the whole to 127,260 *l.* 6 *s.* 1 *d.* *per annum.*

These were the public debts which the company were to redeem, and their proposals established by this act, were as follow, 1st, That before the 1st of March 1721, they would take in all the redeemable debts, either by purchase, subscriptions, or paying them off, provided they might have an addition to their then * capital of 100 *l.* for every 100 *l.* so taken in, and an addition to their then annuity of 5 *l.* *per annum* upon the first sort of redeemables, and 4 *l.* *per annum* upon the other sort of redeemables, for every 100 *l.* so taken in, until redemption. 2dly, That before the said day, they would, by purchase or subscription, take in all the irredeemables, at such prices as should voluntarily and mutually be agreed on between them and the several annuitants; provided they might have an addition to their then capital stock, after the rate of 20 years purchase of the long annuities, and 14 years purchase of the short annuities; and an annuity of 5 *l.* *per cent.* corresponding thereto, added to their then present annuity; that is to say, that for every 100 *l.* *per annum* of the long annuities so taken in by

* This capital was, by chap. 19, of the preceding session, increased to 11,746,844 *l.* 8 *s.* 10 *d.* for which they had an annuity of 587,342 *l.* 4 *s.* 5 *d.* together with 9397 *l.* 9 *s.* 6 *d.* *per annum* for charges of management.

them, they ſhould have 2000 *l.* added to their capital, and 100 *l.* *per annum* to their annuity; and for every 100 *l.* *per annum* of the ſhort annuities ſo taken in by them, they ſhould have 1400 *l.* added to their capital, and 70 *l.* *per annum* to their annuity, till redemption. 3dly, That their allowance for the charge of management ſhould be increaſed, in proportion to the increaſe of their capital, ſo as the ſame did not exceed the whole of one year's coſt the public was then at, for paying, aſſigning, and accounting for all the ſaid debts. 4thly, That their annuities upon their then preſent and their capital to be increaſed, ſhould continue at the rates then eſtabliſhed, until Midſummer 1727, incluſive; but after that day, the whole of their annuities ſhould be reduced to 4 *l.* *per cent. per annum.* 5thly, That for the liberty of taking in all the ſaid redeemable debts, they would pay into the Exchequer towards diſcharging ſuch national debts as were incurred before Chriſtmas 1716, the ſum of 4,156,306 *l.* 4 *s.* 11 *d.* 6thly, That for the liberty of purchaſing the irredeemables, they would pay into the Exchequer for the ſame purpoſe 450 *l.* and ſo proportionably, for every annuity of 100 *l.* *per annum* ſo purchaſed by them. 7thly, That they would pay into the Exchequer for the ſame purpoſe 100 *l.* for every 100 *l.* *per annum* of the long annuities, that ſhould not be purchaſed and taken in by them, before the ſaid 1ſt of March 1721. And 8thly, The company undertook to circulate and exchange for *ſeven* years, and to pay the intereſt of 2 *d.* *per cent. per diem* that ſhould from thenceforth grow due upon the new Exchequer bills, to be iſſued by the malt-act of this ſeſſion; and alſo to furniſh a proportional part of the ready money that ſhould be neceſſary for circulating any new bills that ſhould afterwards within the ſaid ſeven years, be issued by authority of parliament, and to pay a proportional part of the interest to grow due thereupon; the said proportional part to be, as the principal money in all the bills should be to a million; so the whole sum necessary to support the currency, or the whole interest to be paid, should be to what was to be furnished, or paid by the company; and for this purpose six trustees were to be appointed, three whereof to be named by the Treasury, and three by the company.

This was the agreement established by this act, and it was certainly a most beneficial agreement for the public, had it been possible to carry it into execution; but the recent fate of the Mississippi in France might have shewn our parliament men, if they had not been blind or worse, that it would be impossible to carry it into execution, without raising such a spirit of stock-jobbing, or gaming, as must necessarily end in the ruin of many thousands.

Now, as these redeemable, and irredeemable debts had several branches of the public revenue appropriated for securing the payment of their principal and interest, or their annuity, such of these branches, as had not before been granted in perpetuity, that is to say, the 26th, 35th, and 37th branches of the * *customs*; the 11th, 24th, 25th, 26th, and 27th branches of † *excise*; and the 14th branch of *inland-duties* were by this act continued *for ever*; and the 35,000*l.* *per annum* out of the civil-list fund granted by virtue of 12 Ann. sess. 1, chap. 11, was by this act to have continuance *for ever*. And it was enacted, that the said several duties, now granted for ever, and also all the duties before granted for ever, which had been charg-

* See p. 172, 174, 175. † See p. 177, 180.

ed in whole, or in part, with the payment of theſe annuities, or redeemable debts, ſhould be in whole or in part brought into the Exchequer, as alſo all the duties formerly appropriated to the South-Sea company, and an account kept of ſo much of the produce as ought to be applied towards payment of the company's then preſent annuity, and the additions to be made thereto; or of their yearly allowance for charges of management, and the additions to be made to the ſame, in order to be paid weekly to the ſaid company accordingly; and, as to the reſidue of the ſaid produce, it was to be applied to the payment of ſuch annuities, or debts, as ſhould not be taken into the ſaid company's capital ſtock, which were to continue to be paid, at the ſame offices, and out of the ſame duties, and at the ſame times, as formerly. Thus this famous and fatal ſcheme was eſtabliſhed, and the ſucceſs of it will appear from what follows in this hiſtory.

Chap. 10. *An act for making forth new Exchequer bills, not exceeding one million, at a certain intereſt; and for lending the ſame to the South-Sea company at an higher intereſt, upon ſecurity of repaying the ſame, and ſuch high intereſt into the Exchequer, for uſes to which the fund for leſſening the public debts, called* the ſinking fund *is applicable; and for circulating and exchanging upon demand the ſaid bills at or near the Excheq er.*

This act may be reckoned a part of the preceding ſcheme; for, as it was neceſſary for the company to have a large ſum of ready money at command, the Treaſury were impowered to iſſue a million in Exchequer bills, beſides thoſe iſſued by the malt-act of this ſeſſion, which bills were to carry an intereſt of 2 *d. per cent. per diem*, and to be lent to the company; for which they were, by this act, to pay the public 5 *l. per cent. per annum* (though the Treasury afterwards agreed to pay 4 *l. per cent.* interest) until repayment on or before March 1, 1721. And the sinking fund, together with the sum of 328,673 *l.* 4 *s.* 10 *d.* ½, advanced by the company upon 5 Ann. chap. 19, which was remaining in the Exchequer, were made a fund for the public's borrowing at 5 *l. per cent.* its proportional part of the money necessary for circulating these bills.

An act for laying a duty upon wrought plate; and for applying money arising for the clear produce by sale of the forfeited estates, towards answering his majesty's supply, &c. Chap. 11.

By this act a new tax was invented and imposed, *viz.* a tax of 6 *d.* per ounce troy, upon all silver plate that should be imported into, or made in this kingdom; and, because we had not before a sufficient number of lucrative places at the disposal of the crown, his majesty was impowered to appoint a new set of commissioners, who were to appoint officers under them, for levying and managing this duty, with such salaries as the Treasury should think fit to allow; and for due levying of the same, they were armed with all the powers of excise. This therefore may be called the 28th branch of *excise*, and was granted for ever after June 1, 1720; on which his majesty was enabled to borrow 312,000 *l.* at 4 *l. per cent.* with the sinking fund as a collateral security, to be applied to the supply of the ensuing year; and, for the same purpose, the sum of 200,737 *l.* 14 *s.* 9 *d.* ¼, was by this act to be taken out of the clear produce of the forfeitures for treason.

Chap. 18. Royal Exchange and London Assurance. *An act for the better securing certain powers and privileges intended to be granted by his majesty, by two charters for assurance of ships and merchandizes at sea, and for lending money upon bottomry, &c.*

By this act the Royal Exchange and London Assurance companies were established; each of which was to pay, in consideration of their charter, 300,000 *l.* for the use of his majesty, to discharge the debts and expences of his civil government; though no account of these debts had been laid before the House, nor any resolution of the committee of supply for paying them off: nay, when a motion was made, May 6, for an account of those debts, the same was rejected, and an address agreed to, for acknowledging his majesty's goodness in applying the advantages arising from the establishment of these companies, to the use of his civil government, without burthening his people with any new aid or supply; which seems something very extraordinary, as the House had no parliamentary knowledge of the existence of any such debts. This sum of 600,000 *l.* cannot therefore be reckoned among the grants or provisions made by this session.

7 Geo. I, 1720. This session began the 8th of December 1720; and soon after, the four following acts were passed concerning the South-Sea company.

Chap. 1. *An act for restraining the sub-governor, deputy-governor, directors, treasurer, or cashier, deputy-cashier and accomptant of the South-Sea company, from going out of this kingdom for the space of one year, and until the end of the then next session of parliament; and for discovering their estates and effects, and for preventing the transporting or alienating the same.*

Such a rage of ſtock-jobbing did this South-Sea ſcheme raiſe in the people of this kingdom, that, by the beginning of June, South-Sea ſtock ſold for near 900 *l. per cent.* but his majeſty having about that time declared his intention of going abroad, many of thoſe who were to attend him began to ſell out, which reduced the price to 640*l*; and from that to 750 *l.* it continued till the ſhutting of the company's books, June 22; after which time, as no ſtock could be transferred, or paid for till the opening, and conſequently ready money was not neceſſary for making bargains, there appeared ſuch a number of buyers, that the price roſe to 1000 *l. per cent.* for the opening. This of courſe produced a greater number of ſellers than of buyers at the opening, which gave a turn to the frenzy, and from that time the price continued ſinking, notwithſtanding all the arts that could be practiſed either by the directors or the miniſters, and was but about 200 *l. per cent.* when this ſeſſion was opened, December 8, 1720.

There was therefore a general ferment both within doors and without, when this ſeſſion opened; and the loſers were clamorous for the moſt ſevere puniſhments upon the guilty, without conſidering that they themſelves were almoſt as guilty as the contrivers; for, if they had not aſſiſted by ſubſcribing, or purchaſing at a much higher price than the ſtock could be worth, with no other view than that of taking advantage of the prevailing madneſs, it would have been impoſſible for the contrivers to have blown up the bubble; and no man, in either houſe of parliament, who conſented to the law that ſet the ſcheme on foot, could ſay that he was intirely innocent; the public was the only perſon, if we may be allowed the expreſſion, who was entirely innocent; and therefore the principal care of the parliament ſhould now have been, that the public ſhould not be a ſufferer by any redreſs that was to be given, or any new regulation that was to be made. Whether this rule was obſerved, we ſhall ſee in the ſequel; for, as it was neceſſary to puniſh ſome of the principal actors in this ſcene of authenticated villany; and, as ſome new regulations were neceſſary for reſtoring public credit, both houſes entered upon the affair in a very few days after their firſt meeting, the reſult whereof was the foregoing and the three following acts.

Chap. 2. *An act to diſable the preſent ſub-governor, deputy-governor, and directors of the South-Sea company to enjoy any office, place, or employment, after the next choice, in the ſaid company, or in the Eaſt-India company, or Bank of England, and from voting upon elections in the ſaid company.*

This act ſtands in no need of explanation.

Chap. 5. *An act to enable the South-Sea company to ingraſt part of their capital ſtock and fund, into the Bank, and another part thereof into the Eaſt-India company; and for giving further time for payments to be made by the ſaid company to the public.*

This act gave a power to the South-Sea company to aſſign and transfer to the Bank ſuch ſhare of that part of their capital, which carried an intereſt of 5 *l. per cent.* together with the fund attending the ſame, as ſhould be agreed on between the two companies, not exceeding in the whole *nine millions* capital ſtock; and a like power of aſſigning and transferring to the Eaſt-India company. The ſtock thus to be transferred was to be ſubject to the ſame reducement and redemption of intereſt or annuity, as it then was by law, but to be free from payment of any part of what the South-Sea company had agreed to pay by chap. 4, of the former session, and from the charge of circulating Exchequer bills, which that company had undertaken by chap. 10, of the same session, as also from all debts, *&c.* then incurred by the said company; and the Bank and East-India company were to have each a proportional share of allowance for charges of management. But, as the proprietors of the annuities and public debts, which had been subscribed into the South-Sea company, contended, that they were not bound by such their subscriptions, and were actually preparing to have the question decided by law; therefore it was provided, that if these proprietors should, by due course of law, be released from their subscriptions, any bargain, or assignment made by the said company, in pursuance of this act, should be void.

An act for raising money upon the estates of the late sub-governor, deputy-governor, directors, cashier, deputy-cashier, and accomptant of the South-Sea company, and of John Aislabie, *Esq; and likewise* James Craggs, *senior, Esq; deceased, towards making good the great loss and damage sustained by the said company; and for disabling such of the said persons as are living, to hold any office or place of trust under the crown, or to sit or vote in parliament for the future; and for other purposes in the said act expressed.* Chap. 28.

By this act, the estates of all the persons mentioned in the title were vested in trustees to be sold, and the produce thereof, over and above what was by the act allowed to each, was appropriated to the South-Sea company, for increasing their capital stock, and that of all the members thereof, in proportion to their respective shares therein.

These were the firſt regulations that were made; but, before this ſeſſion ended, it was thought neceſſary to determine the diſpute between the company and the ſubſcribing proprietors of the annuities and public debts, by act of parliament; and therefore an act paſſed, entitled, *An act for making ſeveral proviſions to reſtore the public credit, which ſuffers by the frauds and miſmanagements of the late directors of the South-Sea company and others.*

By this act it was enacted, 1ſt, That the company ſhould be free from what they had engaged to pay the public for liberty of increaſing their capital by the purchaſe of the public debts; and, in lieu thereof, *two millions* only of their capital ſtock ſhould be ſunk and annihilated from Midſummer 1722, together with the annuity attending the ſame. 2dly, That the company ſhould allow certain quantities of their ſtock as therein mentioned, to the proprietors of the ſaid annuities and public debts ſubſcribed, and the proprietors of the money-ſubſcriptions upon the money then advanced by them; and that the former ſhould accept of the ſame in full of all claims; and that the latter ſhould be free from all farther payments, notwithſtanding any doubt or queſtion concerning the validity of their ſubſcriptions. 3dly, That the increaſed capital ſtock, by means of this whole tranſaction, gained by the company, ſhould be divided among all the proprietors of the whole capital ſtock, in proportion to their ſeveral intereſts therein. And, 4thly, That ſuch perſons (brokers excepted) as had, ſince the 25th of March 1720, borrowed money of the company upon the pledge of ſtock, or ſubſcription-receipts, ſhould be free from any future demand upon that account, provided they paid to the company 10 *l.* *per cent.* of the money borrowed, before Midſummer 1722, and the pledges to belong to the company.

Thus the affairs relating to the company were ſettled; and it might have been expected, that after this, all contracts for ſtock at the high prices would have been declared void, which was abſolutely neceſſary for reſtoring credit between man and man, and it would have been but juſt in the legiſlature to have done ſo, as they had, by theſe regulations, rendered the ſtock not worth half the intrinſic value it was when thoſe contracts were made; but, perhaps ſome of the leading men in our legiſlature were ſellers in many of thoſe contracts, and therefore, all that was done in regard to them, was only to declare, that ſuch of them as ſhould be unperformed in whole or in part, and not compounded before September 29, 1721, ſhould be void, if not regiſtered before November 1, 1721, or, if the ſeller was not poſſeſſed of the ſtock at the time the contract was made, or within ſix days after; and farther, that no ſpecial bail ſhould be required upon any action brought on any ſuch contract. This, inſtead of being a relief to any buyer, not already a notorious bankrupt, was a forcing him to depart from any objection he might have in law againſt the contract he had made, and to compound, as ſoon as poſſible, in order to preſerve his credit, by preventing the regiſtering of the contract. We may therefore eaſily judge whether the contrivers of this ſham relief, were buyers or ſellers in ſuch contracts.

The ways and means for raiſing the ſupplies granted in this ſeſſion, were as follow:

Chap. 4. *An act for granting an aid to his majesty by a land-tax for the service of 1721.*

This tax was 3 *s.* in the pound, and the loan upon it was 1,410,000 *l.* at 6 *l. per cent.*

Chap. 20 *An act for continuing the duties on malt, &c. to raise money by way of a lottery, &c.*

By this act the usual malt-tax was continued for another year, and such a precarious situation had our public credit been reduced to by the South-Sea scheme, that, in order to borrow upon this fund, as we have for many years done upon all others as soon as granted, a 10 *l.* lottery was established; and, if the tax did not amount to 735,000 *l.* for paying the adventurers in this lottery, which was 35,000 *l.* more than advanced by them, the same was to be made good out of the next aids granted in parliament after September 29, 1722; and the tickets, both blanks and prizes, were to carry an interest of 4 *l. per cent.* from June 24, 1722, 'till paid off.

There was likewise a clause in this act for enabling the York-Buildings company to dispose of rent charges, or annuities by way of lottery, to the full value of such forfeited estates as they had purchased, or should purchase; and this without any limitation of time, or as to the sort or number of lotteries they were to set on foot.

Chap. 27. *An act for raising a sum not exceeding* 500,000 l. *by charging annuities at the rate of* 5 l. per cent. per annum, *upon the civil-list revenues till redeemed by the crown; and for enabling his majesty, his heirs or successors, (by causing such a deduction to be made as therein mentioned) to make good to the civil list, the payments which shall have been made upon the said annuities;*

and for borrowing money upon certain lottery tickets; and for diſcharging the corporation for aſſurances of part of the money which they were obliged to pay to his majeſty; and for making good a deficiency to the Eaſt-India company.

By this act his majeſty was enabled to borrow 500,000 *l.* at 5 *l. per cent.* intereſt, from September 11, 1721, until redeemed; and his majeſty, his heirs and ſucceſſors, were impowered to cauſe a deduction to be made of 6 *d.* in the pound, out of all monies, which, after Auguſt 1, 1721, ſhould be paid upon all penſions and annuities, charged on the hereditary, or temporary duties, and upon all ſalaries, fees, and wages, payable in reſpect of offices of profits, granted by, or derived from the crown, and upon all other payments from the crown whatſoever, or upon any arrears thereof, the pay of the army and navy excepted; which deductions were appropriated to the payment of the ſaid intereſt; and the debts then due upon the civil-liſt were, upon getting tallies, to be taken as ready money for the purchaſe of thoſe annuities, which were made payable at the Bank; but what was moſt extraordinary, the Bank, though all the other funds ſhould be redeemed, was to continue a corporation, till theſe annuities ſhould be redeemed by the crown.

As money was thus provided for paying off the debts of the civil-liſt, there was a clauſe in this act, from which it appears, that the two Aſſurance Companies had, by this time paid, or ſecured to be paid, 300,000 *l.* part of the 600,000 *l.* which they had engaged to pay by chap. 18, of the former ſeſſion, ſo that 300,000 *l.* ſtill remained to be paid; but this they were, by this act, releaſed and diſcharged from, after payment of all the ſeveral ſums of 38,750 *l.*

each, which they had secured to be paid; from whence we must compute, that his majesty had, in the whole 800,000 *l.* for paying off the debts contracted upon the civil-list in the first six or seven years of his reign.

And, by another clause in this act, a deficiency of 191,028 *l.* 16 *s.* 6 *d.* $\frac{1}{2}$, due to the East-India company at Michaelmas 1719, was ordered to be paid to them out of the Sinking Fund, and a small overplus of the duties on salt then remaining in the Exchequer; though no resolution for this purpose had been agreed to in the committee of supplies.

8 Geo. I, 1721. This session began the 19th of October 1721, and ended the 7th of March following; and the ways and means for raising the supplies granted in it, were as follow:

Chap. 1. *An act for granting an aid by a land-tax for the year 1722.*

This tax was 2 *s.* in the pound; and the sum of 940,000 *l.* was borrowed upon it at 5 *l. per cent.*

Chap. 2. *An act for continuing the duties on malt, &c.*

The loan upon this act was 700,000 *l.* at 5 *l. per cent.*

Chap. 20. *An act for paying off and cancelling one million of Exchequer bills, and to give ease to the South-Sea company, in respect of its present obligation to circulate or contribute towards circulating Exchequer bills; and to give further time to that company for repayment of one million which was lent to them; and for issuing a further sum in new Exchequer bills, and that the Exchequer bills which are to continue, may be circulated at easy and moderate rates, &c.*

By this act, the Exchequer bills then current were computed to amount to 1,919,912 *l.* 10 *s.* *viz.* a million lent to the South-Sea company, 896,662 *l.* 10 *s.* issued in lieu of old bills, by the malt-act of 6 Geo. I, and 23,250 *l.* issued by the said act for the interest on the old bills then cancelled. Of these current bills a *million* was by this act to be paid off and cancelled at Lady-day 1722, by the money then arisen, or afterwards to arise out of the Sinking Fund; and, in lieu of them, the Treasury were impowered to issue, after the said day, a like sum in new Exchequer bills, at 2 *d.* *per cent. per diem*; to be placed as so much cash in the hands of the tellers of the Exchequer for the service of the ensuing year; because the South-Sea company found themselves unable, and were afterwards, by this act, indulged with time, until June 7, 1723, to repay the million lent to them by 6 Geo I, chap. 10, (see p. 216.) And, as they were to pay 5 *l.* *per cent.* interest for the same, they were, by this act, acquitted of the obligation they lay under by the said act of 6 Geo. I, chap. 2, as to the circulation of Exchequer bills; and the Treasury were impowered to enter into a contract for circulating the same, with any persons who would agree to do so at a rate not exceeding 3 *l.* *per cent. per annum*, as well for paying the interest at their own costs, as in reward for their service, upon all such bills, so long as they should exceed *one million* in principal, and 20 *s.* *per cent. per annum* after their being reduced to a *million* or under. And, for securing such persons, the Sinking Fund, as well as the debt due by the South-Sea company, was charged with the payment of the principal and interest, or allowance for circulation, of all such bills.

Moreover, by a clause in this act, it was declared, that the civil-list revenues did produce, in clear money for one year, ended at Michaelmas 1720, 102,682 *l.* 7 *s.* 11 *d.* $\frac{3}{4}$, above the sum of 700,000 *l.* And, as this overplus-money belonged, and was to be replaced to the Sinking Fund, out of the 500,000 *l.* which his majesty was impowered to borrow by chap. 27, of last session; therefore, by proper clauses in this act, the method was prescribed, and the Treasury impowered to do so.

By this act likewise, a new tax was imposed, which we may call the 38th branch of the customs (see page 175.) and which was an additional duty of 2 *s.* per bushel, and proportionally over and above all former customs and duties, upon all apples imported after Lady-day 1722, during three years, or before the end of the session of parliament next following the said term. This new tax was appropriated for raising the supplies granted in this session; but there was no power granted by this act, for borrowing money upon, or mortgaging this new imposition.

Also, by some other clauses in this act, the duties then payable on pictures imported, were after Lady-day 1722 abolished, and, in lieu thereof, new duties imposed, according to their dimensions, *viz.* 3 *l.* per picture of four square feet or upwards; 40 *s.* per picture of two feet square, and under four; and 20 *s.* for every picture under that size. Those duties were appropriated to the same uses with the old, and to continue for the same time, that is to say, for ever.

9 Geo. I, 1722. This session began the 9th of October 1722, and ended the 27th of May 1723; the ways and means for raising the supplies granted in it, were as follow:

An act for granting an aid by a land-tax for the year 1723. Chap. 2.

By this act the sum of 18,243 *l.* 1 *s.* 2 *d.* ½, of former land-taxes then in the Exchequer, was appropriated to the supply, and a land-tax of 2 *s.* in the pound was continued for another year; on which a million was to be raised, either by loans, or by Exchequer bills, at 3 *l.* *per cent.*

An act for continuing the duties on malt, &c. Chap. 3.

By this act the sum of 750,000 *l.* was to be raised by a 10 *l.* lottery.

An act for redeeming certain annuities, now payable by the cashier of the Bank of England, at the rate of 5 l. per cent. per annum. Chap. 5.

In order to understand this act, which was founded upon the resolution of a committee of the whole House upon the state of public credit, agreed to December 18, we must observe, that the 5 *l.* *per cent.* annuities, which had been established by 3 Geo. I, chap. 7, (see page 196.) the capital sum of 1,204,786 *l.* 3 *s.* 4 *d.* ¾, remaining unsubscribed into the South-Sea company, and that notice had been given for paying off the same; therefore by this act, 204,786 *l.* 3 *s.* 4 *d.* ¾, part of the said sum was to be paid off by the produce of the Sinking Fund, and one million of Exchequer bills to be issued at 2 *d.* *per cent. per diem*, which bills were to be gradually paid off, and cancelled by the future produce of the same fund. We must likewise observe, that of the 5 *l.* *per cent.* annuities established 1 Geo. I, sess. 2, chap. 19, 21, (see page 193.) the capital sum of 235,297 *l.* 18 *s.* 4 *d.* remained unsubscribed into the South-Sea company; therefore by this act, and the resolution of the said committee, notice was given, that the said sum would be paid off at Lady-day 1724.

Chap. 6. *An act for reviving and adding two millions to the capital stock of the South-Sea company, and for reviving a proportional part of the yearly fund payable at the Exchequer, and for dividing their whole capital (after such division made) into two equal parts or moieties, and for converting one of the said moieties into certain annuities for the benefit of the members, and for settling the remaining moiety in the said company, &c.*

By this act, which had the same foundation with the preceding, the *two millions* capital stock of the South-Sea company, which had been sunk by virtue of 7 Geo. I, sess. 2, chap. 1, (see page 222.) was restored to them, together with the annuity attending the same. Thus every shilling advantage, which the public was to have reaped by this famous transaction was annihilated; and the proprietors, meaning the old proprietors, every one of whom ought to have been punished for consenting to the fraudulent management of their directors, were highly rewarded; for, by having the surplus-stock divided among all the proprietors, both old and new, in pursuance of the said act of 7 Geo. I, sess. 2, chap. 1, the old proprietors got near, if not above 40 *l. per cent.* added to their former capital; whereas, if justice had been done upon either of them, or to the public, the old proprietors ought to have been made to pay the whole of what the company engaged to pay to the public for leave to increase their capital, which might have been easily done by calling for the company's books, as they stood when that contract was approved of by the general court. This would for the future have made the proprietors of all public companies a little cautious of impowering their directors to set on foot any schemes for defrauding the public; but, by our thus allowing them to divide the spoil among them, without obliging them to pay one shilling of that which they had agreed to pay, we may be said to have sold them a legal licence to cheat mankind; and, after they had cheated as much as they could, we then released what they had promised to pay for it, which was a precedent of a most dangerous tendency.

By the same act, the capital of this company, which then amounted to 33,802,483 *l.* 14 *s.* 2 *d.* was divided into two parts, one moiety of which to remain as the South-Sea company's capital, and to have the advantage as well as risk of their trade, together with their allowances for expence of management, being 9397 *l.* 9 *s.* 6 *d.* *per annum*, and the other moiety was converted into annuities at 5 *l.* *per cent.* till Midsummer 1727, and 4 *l.* *per cent.* afterwards; the first moiety to be called the South-Sea company's trading-stock, and the other was to be called South-Sea annuities; and, as the whole of the annuity, payable to the company until Midsummer 1727, amounted to 1,651,730 *l.* 10 *s.* 10 *d.* ½, and afterwards to 1,352,099 *l.* 6 *s.* 11 *d.* ½ *per annum*, the annuitants were to have their annuities paid out of the same, and the residue to belong to the trading stock. If the produce of the duties should be deficient, the two moieties were to bear equal share of that deficiency, until it should be provided for by parliament; but the whole was again declared redeemable after Midsummer 1727, by payment of not less than 500,000 *l.* at a time, to be applied to the paying off so much of the *annuity*, or *trading-stock*, as the parliament should then direct.

Chap. 18. *An act for granting an aid to his majesty for laying a tax upon Papists, and for making such other persons, as, upon due summons, shall refuse, or neglect to take the oaths therein-mentioned, to contribute towards the said tax; for reimbursing to the public part of the great expences occasioned by the late conspiracies; and for discharging the estates of Papists from the two third parts of the rents and profits thereof for one year, and all arrears of the same, and from such forfeitures as are therein more particularly described.*

By this act the real and personal estates of Papists and Nonjurors were charged with 100,000 *l.* to be raised out of the same in 1723, over and above their double land-tax; and, for this purpose, the sum to be raised upon such estates was, by this act, particularly and distinctly assessed upon each county, and upon many of our cities; but the sum total of all these assessments amounted to no more than 95,989 *l.* 19 *s.* 9 *d.* so that we do not see how it could produce 100,000 *l.*; and yet upon this fund, the Treasury were impowered to borrow by loans, or Exchequer bills 100,000 *l.* at 3 *l. per cent.* although by the act there was above 6 *d.* in the pound to be allowed for collecting the same.

Chap. 19. *An act to continue the coinage duties, &c.*

By this act, the 7th branch of the customs (see page 167.) was continued for seven years longer, and to the end of the then next session; with an allowance to the Treasury as before, to make it good 15,000 *l.* a year. And, by the same act, the duties payable *ad valorem* on books, were abolished, and a duty of 14 *s. per hundred* weight imposed upon all bound books imported, after June 24, 1723.

This session began the 9th of January 1723, and ended the 24th of April 1724; the ways and means for raising the supplies granted in it, were as follow: 10 Geo. I. 1723.

An act for an aid by the land-tax for the year 1724. Chap. 1.

This tax was 2 *s.* in the pound, and the sum borrowed upon it 1,000,000 *l.* at 3 *l. per cent.* and the sum of 11,420 *l.* 1 *s.* 3 *d.* ¾, remaining in the Exchequer for arrears of several land-taxes, payable in 1721, or before, was applied as part of the supply for 1724.

An act for continuing the duties on malt, &c. Chap. 2.

By this act, the usual malt-tax was continued for another year, and the money to be raised, as before by that pernicious method called a *lottery.*

An act for redeeming certain annuities after the rate of 5 l. per cent. per annum, *and for payment of the principal and interest on the standing orders for the blank tickets in the lottery granted for the service of the year* 1714; *and for making good the loss which happened in the treasure of his majesty's Exchequer, by the reduction of guineas; and for granting relief to* Catherine Collingwood, *widow.* Chap. 20.

By this act, the produce of the Sinking Fund, on or before Lady-day 1724, (except what had before been appropriated) was applied towards paying off the principal and interest of such of the annuities, established by 1 Geo. I, sess. 2, chap. 19, 21 *, and such of the standing orders for the blank lottery tickets, established by 12 Ann. † sess. 2, chap. 9, as had not been subscribed into the capital stock of the South-Sea company; for which purpose the said produce, together with the monies applicable to the payment of the said standing orders, were to be issued by way of imprest, to the cashier of the Bank, and to the pay-master of the said orders. There was besides, in this act, a clause without any authority from the committee of supply, for allowing to the tellers of the Exchequer, 15,144 *l.* 19 *s.* to make good the loss by the reduction of guineas, from 21 *s.* 6 *d.* to 21 *s.* with respect to the guineas then in their office: and another clause for paying 6000 *l.* to Mrs. *Collingwood.*

Chap. 10. *An act for repealing certain duties therein mentioned, payable upon coffee, tea, cocoa nuts, chocolate, and cocoa paste imported; and for granting certain inland duties in lieu thereof.*

By this act, a considerable alteration was made as to the duties payable upon the importation of coffee, tea, cocoa nuts, chocolate, and cocoa paste; for the duties payable upon coffee and tea, by 6 and 7 W. III, chap. 7, by 3 Ann. chap. 4, and by 10 Ann. chap. 26, and the duties payable upon cocoa nuts, by the said acts of 6 and 7 W. III, chap. 7, and 3 Ann. chap. 4, were, from June 24, 1724, abolished, and, in lieu of these, the inland duties, or excises following, were imposed, *viz.* on all coffee to be sold, 2 *s.* per pound; on all tea to be sold, 4 *s.* per pound, and on all chocolate to be made or sold, 1 *s.* 6 *d.* per pound, over and above all customs and duties payable by other acts, upon

* See p. 193. † See p. 161.

the importation thereof; and chocolate ready made, or cocoa paste, were from that day prohibited to be imported. The reasons assigned for these alterations were, that the duties then subsisting upon coffee, tea, cocoa nuts, chocolate, and cocoa paste, were, or might be, very much lessened, not only by the clandestine importation thereof from parts beyond the seas, but also by fraudulent relanding of the same, after they have been exported from this kingdom for foreign parts, and the duties thereupon drawn back, without paying any duties for the same, to the detriment of the revenue, and the ruin of the said traders in the said commodities.

This session began the 12th of November 1724, and ended the 31st of May 1725; the ways and means for raising the supplies granted in it, were as follow: 11 Geo. I, 1724.

An act for an aid by a land-tax for 1725. Chap. 1.

By this act, a land-tax of 2 *s.* in the pound was imposed for 1725; and the sum of 13,010 *l.* 7 *s.* 2 *d.* ¾ remaining in the Exchequer for arrears of several land-taxes payable in 1721, or before, was applied as part of the supply for 1725.

An act for rating such unrated goods and merchandizes, as are usually imported into this kingdom, and pay duty ad valorem, *upon the oath of the importer; and for ascertaining the value of all goods and merchandizes, not inserted in the former, or present book of rates, &c.* Chap. 7.

By this act, a new book of rates was established, which was made part of the act, and printed therewith; so that from this time there were very few sorts of goods, but what had a certain rate fixed upon them, by which they were to pay the duties upon importation; but, if not rated in either of the books of rates, nor by any former act, they were, as before, to pay the duties, according to the value sworn to by the importer, and under the same condition, if undervalued, as before *. Several new rules and orders for regulating the payment of the duties were added: the additional duty upon apples granted by 8 Geo. I, chap. 20, was continued for seven years, from Lady-day 1725: the duty on drugs, imposed by 10 Ann. chap. 26, was abolished after Lady-day 1725: some new regulations were made as to the duties on paper imported; and rags, &c. fit for making paper, or pasteboard were, from the said day, freed from all duties upon importation; and lastly, a new regulation was made with respect to the duty or pictures imported.

Chap. 8. *An act for continuing the duties on malt, &c. in England, and for granting certain duties upon malt, &c. in Scotland, &c.*

By this act, the usual malt-tax was continued for another year in England; and was now, for the first time, extended to Scotland; but, as the malt in Scotland was not deemed so good as that in England, it was to pay but 3 *d.* per bushel, unless imported into England; in which case the duty was to be made good at the rate of 6 *d.* per bushel; and the duty upon mum, cyder, and perry, was made the same as in England. There was, however, a proviso, that in case the said duty in Scotland did not produce 20,000 *l.* the commissioners of excise should make such a surcharge upon all those who had made any malt in Scotland, as would make

* See before, p. 165.

the produce amount to that sum. By this act likewise the duty upon news-papers was increased, by making it a halfpenny for every half sheet of which they consisted.

An act for continuing the several annuities of 88,751 l. 7 s. 10 d. ½, *and* 100,000 l. *to the Bank of England, until Midsummer* 1727; *and from thence, for reducing the same to* 71,001 l. 2 s. 3 d. ¾, *and* 80,000 l. *redeemable by parliament, &c.* Chap. 9.

By this act, the annuities mentioned in the title of it were, with the consent of the Bank, to be reduced, as therein mentioned after Midsummer 1727; and redeemable upon payment of 1,775,027 *l.* 17 *s.* 10 *d.* ½, and 2,000,000 *l.* being the principal sums for which they were first granted, or proportionally upon payment of any part, not being less than 500,000 *l.* at a time.

An act for redeeming the annuities of 25,000 l. per annum, *charged on the civil-list revenues, by an act of the 7th year of his majesty's reign; and for discharging the debts and arrears due from his majesty to his servants, tradesmen, and others.* Chap. 17.

By this act, which was brought in, and passed in consequence of a message from his majesty, delivered April 8, his majesty was impowered to raise 1,000,000 *l.* either by issuing Exchequer bills at 2 *d. per cent per diem*, or by any other method at 3 *l. per cent. per annum*, one moiety of which was to be applied towards repaying the money borrowed, and redeeming the annuities established by 7 Geo. I, sess. 1, chap. 27, and the other moiety towards satisfying the debts and arrears, and other uses of his majesty's civil government; and, as a ſecurity for the repayment of this money, with the intereſt to grow due thereupon, his majeſty was to continue, during his life, the deduction of 6 *d.* per pound out of the payments by the ſaid act made liable thereto; and, after his demiſe, the ſaid ſum, or ſo much thereof, as ſhould remain unpaid, with all the intereſt due, was to remain a charge upon the hereditary revenue.

This ſeſſion became famous for the puniſhment of one noble lord, and the pardon of another, to wit, the Earl of *Macclesfield*, who was impeached by the Commons, and puniſhed by judgment of the Lords, for miſdemeanors in his office of lord high chancellor; and *Henry St. John*, late Lord Viſcount *Bolingbroke*, who having obtained his majeſty's pardon, got an act paſſed this ſeſſion for enabling him to take and enjoy lands, *&c.* notwithſtanding his attainder.

12 Geo. I, 1725. This ſeſſion began the 20th of January 1725, and ended the 24th of May 1726; the ways and means for raiſing the ſupplies granted in it, were as follow:

Chap. 1. *An act for granting an aid by a land-tax for the ſervice of* 1726.

By this act, a land-tax of 2 *s.* in the pound was continued for another year; and the money was to be raiſed by borrowing at 3 *l. per cent.* or by iſſuing a million of Exchequer bills, at 2 *d. per cent. per diem.*

Chap. 2. *An act for granting to his majeſty the ſum of one million to be raiſed by way of lottery.*

By this act, his majeſty, his heirs and ſucceſſors were enabled to continue the deductions of 6 *d.* per pound, upon all penſions and annuities charged upon the civil liſt, and upon all ſalaries, fees, and wages, payable in reſpect of any offices of profit, except as before in 7 Geo. I, ſeſſ. 1, * chap. 27, out of which 30,000 *l. per annum*, was eſtabliſhed as a fund for raiſing 1,000,000 *l.* at 3 *l. per cent.* by way of a lottery, at 10 *l.* a ticket, which money was to be applied towards diſcharging and cancelling the 990,000 *l.* value of Exchequer bills then remaining uncancelled, of thoſe that had been iſſued by 8 Geo. I, † chap. 20, for the uſe of the civil liſt. And, if theſe deductions amounted to more, the ſurplus was not to be iſſued without the authority of parliament; but if to leſs, the deficiency was to be made good out of the hereditary revenue.

An act for continuing the duties on malt, &c. Chap. 4.

This act continued the malt-tax for another year in England and Scotland; and there was to be raiſed upon it the ſum of 750,000 *l.* by borrowing at 3 *l. per cent.* or by Exchequer bills at 2 *d. per cent. per diem.* And, by this act, malt made for exportation was to pay no duty, nor to have any drawback.

An act for granting an aid to his majeſty, by laying a duty upon all victuallers and retailers of beer and ale, within the cities of London and Weſtminſter, and the weekly bills of mortality, &c. Chap. 12.

By this act, which was called *the pot-act*, ſuch a duty as the commiſſioners to be appointed by his majeſty ſhould direct, not under 1 *l.* nor above 6 *l. per annum*, was impoſed upon every victualler and retailer of beer and ale in the cities of London and Weſtminſter, and within the bills of mortality; for which purpoſe every ſuch retailer was to take out a permiſſion or licence from the commiſſioners yearly, and compound

* See p. 224. † See p. 226.

with them for the duty to be paid, under the penalty of 20 *l.* And all such retailers were prohibited to send any beer or ale out of their house, in any pot, cup, or other drinking vessel, belonging to themselves, that should contain less than one gallon, under the penalty of 40 *s.* which prohibition was designed as a favour; because they lost many of their pots by sending them out; but it was soon found to be impracticable, and therefore never carried into execution. Upon this tax, which was to commence at Midsummer 1726, and to continue *for ever*; and which may be called the 17th branch of inland-duties, the sum of 500,000 *l.* was to be raised by issuing Exchequer bills at 2 *d. per cent. per diem*; the surplus, if any, to be applied towards discharging the bills, and, if not sufficient to pay the interest yearly, the deficiency to be made good out of the Sinking Fund, to be replaced out of the first aids afterwards to be granted; according to a former precedent for making the Sinking Fund a collateral security, which precedent, we shall see, was often afterwards followed. Likewise, by clauses in this act, the commissioners were impowered to licence 100 more hackney chairs, at 10 *s.* each *per annum*, which was appropriated to the same use with the former tax on hackney coaches and chairs. And by another clause in this act, the sum of 7,046 *l.* 13 *s.* 8 *d.* ¾, for arrears of former land-taxes before 1723, was to be applied to the service of 1726.

Chap. 26. *An act for repealing the duty upon snuff, &c.*

By this act, the duty imposed upon snuff, by 8 Ann. * chap. 7, was, after the last day of May 1726, repealed; and snuff from the Bri-

* See p. 140.

tiſh and Spaniſh ſettlement in America was rated at 2 *s.* 6 *d.* per pound, and from all other parts, except France, at 5 *s.* per pound, according to which rates it was to pay the duties it remained liable to.

An act for veſting in his majeſty an impoſition of two pennies Scots upon all ale and beer, brewed and ſold in the city of Glaſgow, and privileges thereof for ſatisfying the damages and loſſes which Daniel Campbell, *Eſq; lately ſuffered in a riot there.* Chap. 27.

By this act, the ſum of 6080 *l.* was given to make ſatisfaction to Mr. *Campbell* (a member) for the damages by him ſuſtained in the late riot at Glaſgow, on account of the concern he had, or was ſuppoſed to have had, in promoting the act, for laying the duty upon malt, for the ſervice of the year 1725.

An act for relief of the ſuitors of the High Court of Chancery. Chap. 33.

By this act, a great many new ſtamp duties were impoſed upon law proceedings of almoſt all kinds, in order to make good the loſs which had been ſuſtained by many of the ſuitors in Chancery, by the inſolvency of ſome of the maſters; which was to commence from Auguſt 2, 1726, and to continue for ſixteen years; and is to be reckoned the 18th branch of our *inland-duties* *. Upon this fund the ſaid court was enabled to borrow 60,000 *l.* at 5 *l. per cent.* for anſwering, we preſume, ſuch ſuitors as had occaſion for their money; for ſurely, the court was not to borrow money at intereſt, in order to lodge it in the Bank, without any intereſt.

* See p. 183.

Whether the fine imposed upon the Earl of *Macclesfield* was applied towards making good the said loss, does not appear by the act.

13 Geo. I, 1726. This session began the 17th of January 1726, and ended the 15th of May 1727; and the ways and means for raising the supplies granted in it, were as follow:

Chap. 1. *An act for an aid by the land-tax for the year* 1727.

This tax was 4 *s.* in the pound, and the sum borrowed upon it 2,000,000 *l.* at 5 *l.* *per cent. per annum.*

Chap. 3. *An act for redeeming sundry annuities transferrable at the Bank of England, and the annuities payable on standing orders for army-debentures, by the produce of the* Sinking Fund, *for applying to the same fund, the money remaining in the Exchequer on the head of the banker's debt, and making provision for future claims on the same debt, and for applying the lottery tickets* 1726, *which were returned into the Exchequer, to the discharging the standing orders made out for the sufferers at Nevis and St. Christopher's, as far as the same will extend.*

By this act, such of the 4 *l.* annuities, established by 3 Geo. I, chap. 7, in lieu of army-debentures; and by the 5 Geo. I, chap. 3, in lieu of lottery tickets, as had not been subscribed into the South-Sea company, amounting in the whole to 650,453 *l.* 2 *s.* 8 *d.* ½ and also the 4 *l.* *per cent.* annuities since established in lieu of army debentures, in pursuance of several acts for stating the debts of the army, amounting to 548,939 *l.* 12 *s.* 6 *d.* ¼; these two sums amounting together to 1,199,392 *l.* 15 *s.* 2 *d.* ¾, were directed by this act to be paid off half-yearly, out of the growing produce of the Sinking Fund, and notice of redemption to be given accordingly; and if the Treasury should think proper, the same was to be paid off before discharging the Exchequer bills then charged upon the Sinking Fund. Also the sum of 10,725 *l.* 5 *s.* 3 *d.* ¼, then remaining in the Exchequer, on the head of the banker's debt, and never claimed, was appropriated to the Sinking Fund, in case no sufficient claim should afterwards be made thereto, or to any part thereof. And the sum of 103,272 *l.* 10 *s.* then remaining in the Exchequer for undisposed lottery tickets in the lottery of last year, was to be applied to such of the proprietors of St. Christopher's debentures as should be willing to accept of the 3 *l.* *per cent.* annuities, established by that lottery in lieu of their debentures.

An act for continuing the duties on malt, &c. Chap. 7.

The loan upon this act was 750,000 *l.* at 3 *l.* *per cent.*

An act for granting to his majesty the sum of 370,000 l. to be raised by loans, or Exchequer bills, to be charged on the surplus-monies of the duties on coals and culm, &c. Chap. 21.

By this act, his majesty was impowered to borrow 370,000 *l.* at 4 *l.* *per cent.* upon the surplus of the 22d branch of the customs, which had been continued for a long term by 5 Geo. I, chap. 9, and afterwards for ever by 6 Geo. I, chap. 4. And if this surplus should not be sufficient to pay the interest, the deficiency was to be made good out of the next aids, or out of the Sinking Fund.

Upon a report from the committee of the whole House, March 7, it was resolved, that in four years, from Midsummer 1719, to Mid summer 1723, no more than 1500 *l.* had been paid into the Exchequer on account of the duties on hawkers and pedlars; and that by this neglect, there was a deficiency of 36,693 *l.* 13 *s.* 5 *d.* And yet, though it thus appeared to the House, that the officers of the Exchequer had been negligent of their duty, not so much as a motion was made for enquiring into the conduct of any of them. Nay, the commissioners of hawkers and pedlars themselves were suffered to escape all manner of parliamentary punishment.

In the account laid before this session, how the money granted for last year had been disposed of, there was one article thus: *Item*, For securing the trade of this kingdom, and preserving the peace of Europe, 125,000 *l.*

And though any farther explanation of this gross article was, February 21, absolutely refused to the House; yet, upon the question, it was carried by a great majority, that no such explanation should be insisted on; which is a precedent that may make future ministers very indifferent how they squander the public money.

TAXES

SUBSISTING AT THE END OF

KING GEORGE THE FIRST'S REIGN.

ALL the taxes which ſubſiſted at the beginning of the former reign, were ſubſiſting at the beginning of the preſent, with ſome few alterations, which we have given an account of before in this hiſtory: and all except the land and malt-taxes, and a very few others, were now eſtabliſhed *for ever*; but the method of perpetuating our taxes, had been greatly altered in favour of the crown; for when taxes firſt began to be granted *for ever*, as a ſecurity for the money to be borrowed upon them, it was, as to many of them, provided by the act that granted them, that, as ſoon as the money borrowed upon them, with all arrears of intereſt, ſhould be fully paid and ſatisfied, the taxes ſhould ceaſe, and be no longer payable: but theſe, and all other taxes, have ſince been granted *for ever*, with a proviſion only, that after the money borrowed upon them, with all arrears of intereſt, ſhould be fully paid and ſatisfied, the produce ſhould not be iſſued without the authority of parliament, or ſhould be at the diſpoſal of parliament. Between theſe two methods of granting, the reader muſt ſee a very remarkable difference, with regard to the ſecurity of our conſtitution. By the firſt method the tax ceaſes of itſelf, as ſoon as the money borrowed upon it is paid off, and the people would no longer be bound by law to pay it. But, by the ſecond method, the people remain bound by law to pay the tax, even after the money borrowed upon it has been ſatisfied: nay, they muſt remain ſo bound until the crown has conſented to an act for repealing that by which the tax was granted:—And ſurely, a tyrannical ſovereign might more eaſily prevail with the officers of his Exchequer to iſſue the money in their hands *without authority of parliament*, than he could prevail with the people to pay any tax whatſoever without the authority of parliament. A *full* payment of all the national debt, which, indeed, is an event not much to be dreaded, would now therefore be one of the moſt dangerous things that could happen to our conſtitution, becauſe the king would then have a revenue of above *four millions* coming yearly into his Exchequer, *without any new grant from parliament*; and, after its being once there, it would be very eaſy for him to make himſelf maſter of it, which revenue would effectually enable him to render his proclamations of equal force with an act of parliament, eſpecially if our parliaments, *by a continued courſe of corruption and ſcreening*, ſhould render themſelves diſtaſteful to the people.

Now, as all the taxes ſubſiſting at the end of Queen Anne's reign, were ſubſiſting at the end of the laſt reign, and had all, except as before-mentioned, been made perpetual according to the new method, we need only refer the reader to the list of them in page 164, to page 184, of this history, and observe, that a 38th * branch had been added to the customs by 8 Geo. I, chap. 20, a 28th † branch to the *excise*, by 6 Geo. I, chap. 11, and the 17th and an 18th ‡ branch to our *inland-duties*, by 12 Geo. I, chap. 12, 33. The tax upon pensions, *&c.* granted by 7 Geo. I, seff. 1, chap. 27, may likewise be added to the number of *inland-duties*; because all those pensions are paid by the people, and might be diminished, if the possessors can spare to pay this tax upon them: and the alteration in the duties upon coffee, tea, and chocolate, made by 10 Geo. I, chap. 10, may properly enough be called the addition of a 29th branch to the excise. Thus we had subsisting, at the beginning of this reign 38 branches of || *customs*, 29 branches of *excise*, and 18 branches of *inland-duties*, in all 85 different kinds of taxes; many of which branches affect a great variety of sorts of goods; and the laws relating to them make

* See p. 175. † See p. 180.

‡ See p. 183.

|| In the account of the several branches of the customs in page 164, we have omitted the *duty on white woollen cloths exported*, being a duty of 5 *s.* per piece, granted without limitation in the 6th year of Queen Anne; as also, the Plantation and Barbadoes duties, the former was imposed by 25 Char. II, chap. 7, *for ever*; being duties of several kinds upon several goods, shipped in our Plantations, and not to be brought to England. The latter is a duty of 4 *l.* 10 *s.* *per cent.* payable in Barbadoes and the Leeward Islands, on goods exported from thence. To these we must add a duty of 5 *s.* per ton on all French ships, imposed by 12 Char. II, chap. 18, to continue as long as the duty of 50 sous per ton, or any part thereof, on British ships, is continued in France, and for three months after: so that, instead of 38, we may reckon 43 branches in our customs.

by far the greatest part of *the many large folio volumes of statutes* that have been enacted *since the revolution*; whereas all the statutes, from the beginning of our monarchy, to that *famous æra* are (including the original French and Latin, and the English translation) contained in two *folio volumes*; of which those that relate to taxes, make but a very inconsiderable part.

1 Geo. II, 1727. This session began the 27th of June 1727, and ended ———————; the ways and means for raising the supplies granted in it, were as follow:

Chap. 1. *An act for the better support of his majesty's houshold, and the honour and dignity of the crown of Great-Britain.*

By this act, the same revenues, which were payable to his late majesty during his life, for support of the civil list, were from his death granted and continued to his present majesty during his life; with a clause, that if the produce of those revenues (over and above all annual, weekly, and other payments and incumbrances, charged upon the same by any act of parliament, *and all grants made by his majesty's predecessors*) should, at any time, appear to be so deficient, that within one year, reckoning from Midsummer 1727, the same should not be sufficient to answer and satisfy the yearly sum of 800,000*l.* then, and as often as such deficiency should happen, it should be provided for, and made good out of the next aids to be granted by parliament. After which there was a clause, granting and continuing to his majesty, for his life, all the duties and revenues, which were payable to his late majesty in Scotland; so that his majesty was, by this act, to have 800,000 *l.* *per annum*, over and above the crown revenues of Scotland, with this farther advantage, which the late king had not, that if the revenues produced, in any one year, more than 800,000 *l.* the surplus was to belong to him; but if, in any one year, they produced less, the deficiency was to be made good to him by the next session of parliament.

An act for enabling his majesty to settle a revenue for supporting the royal dignity of the queen, in case she shall survive his majesty. Chap. 3.

By this act, his majesty was impowered to settle, by letters-patent, an annuity of 100,000 *l.* upon the queen during her life, to commence immediately after his majesty's demise, to be paid quarterly; the first quarterly payment to be made at such of the quarterly feasts as should next happen after his demise, and to be charged, not only upon the civil-list revenues, that should then be subsisting, but also upon the revenues of the *aggregate fund*; together with Somerset House and Richmond Lodge.

An act for continuing the duties on malt, &c. Chap. 1.

The loan upon this act was 750,000 *l.* at 3 *l. per cent.*

An act for granting an aid by a land-tax for the service of 1728. Chap. 5.

This tax was 3 *s.* in the pound, and the loan upon it 1,500,000 *l.* at 3 *l. per cent.*

An act for granting an aid to his majesty by sale of annuities to the Bank of England at 4 l. per cent. *redeemable by parliament, and charged upon the duties on coals and culm; and for further applying the produce of the Sinking Fund, &c.* Chap. 8.

We have before * shewn, that a great part of the 22d branch of the *customs*, including the 8th ditto, though a local tax, payable by the people in and about London only, and first granted for their sole use, was by 5 Geo. I, chap. 9, seized for the use of the public; but, by the preceding act of this session, a final end was put to the building of any more churches by the produce of this tax, and the whole of it seized for the use of the public; for, by this act, an annuity of 70,000 *l.* was established and charged upon this branch of the customs, which had been continued *for ever* by 6 Geo. I, chap. 4, upon which annuity the Bank undertook to lend 1,750,000 *l.* at 4 *l. per cent.* and out of this 1,750,000 *l.* so to be lent by the Bank, the following sums were directed to be paid, *viz.* 500,000 *l.* to the South-Sea company, and 193,140 *l.* for repaying and compleating the sum of 360,000 *l.* which, by the said act of 5 Geo. I, chap. 9, was to be raised for building churches.

It was likewise enacted by this act, that out of such monies of the Sinking Fund as should be in the Exchequer at Midsummer (1728, after payment of, or reserving sufficient to pay what was by this, or any other act, directed to be paid out of the same) there should be paid at the said day, and afterwards quarterly, as the same should arise, such sums of money as should, on such quarter-day, be in the Exchequer, towards redeeming the annuity of 71,001 *l.* 2 *s.* 3 *d.* $\frac{3}{4}$ granted to the Bank by 11 Geo. I, chap. 9, until the payments should amount to *one million*, and the said annuity to be diminished quarterly in proportion to such payments.

* See p. 209.

An act for granting an aid to his majesty of 500,000 l. towards discharging wages due to seamen, &c. Chap. 9.

By this act, the Treasury were impowered to raise 500,000 *l.* by loans, at 4 *l.* *per cent.* or by Exchequer bills, at 2 *d.* *per cent. per diem*, to be applied towards paying off so much of the seamen's wages then in arrear; which sum of 500,000 *l.* was charged upon the first aids, to be granted by parliament after Michaelmas 1728, or, in default thereof, upon the Sinking Fund, and to be replaced out of the next aids afterwards to be granted.

May 6. A message signed by his majesty, was presented to the House, signifying, that there was a sum, not very considerable, still wanting, for perfecting and fulfilling obligations entered into with the advice and concurrence of last parliament, for securing the trade and navigation of this kingdom, and for restoring and preserving the peace of Europe; and hoping the House would enable him to discharge the same. Upon this message the House, without any farther information, resolved upon, and presented an address to his majesty, assuring him that they would enable him to answer and defray the charges and expences of all such engagements.

This session began the 21st of January 1728, and ended the 14th of May 1729; the ways and means for raising the supplies granted in it, were as follow: 2 Geo. II, 1728.

An act for continuing the duties on malt, &c. for the year 1729. Chap. 1.

The loan upon this act was 750,000 *l.* at 3 *l.* *per cent.*

Chap. 4. *An act for granting an aid by a land-tax for the year* 1729.

This tax was 3 *s.* in the pound; and the sum borrowed upon it 1,500,000 *l.* at 3 *l. per cent.*

Chap. 3. *An act for raising the sum of* 1,250,000 *l. by sale of annuities to the Bank of England, after the rate of* 4 l. per cent. per annum, *redeemable by parliament; and for applying the produce of the Sinking Fund.*

On February the 3d, a motion was made, that the House would raise the supplies necessary for the current service of the year, without creating any new debt upon any fund whatsoever; but the question was carried in the negative, and this bill afterwards brought in and passed, by which an annuity of 50,000 *l.* was established, and charged upon the surplus of the 37th branch of the * *customs*; the 24th, 25th, 26th and 27th branches of † *excise*; and the 14th branch of ‡ *inland-duties*; with proper clauses for making good the deficiency, and disposing of the excess, if any should appear; upon which annuity the Bank engaged to advance 1,250,000 *l.* to be repaid at not less than 500,000 *l.* at a time. And, by the same act, a further direction was given for issuing the produce of the *Sinking Fund*, by paying 500,000 *l.* to the Bank, for redeeming a proportional part of their annuity of 80,000 *l.* established by 11 Geo. I, chap. 9. As the duties thus mortgaged to the Bank were first granted for paying off in 32 years, the principal as well as interest of the debts charged upon them, the surplus arising by the South-Sea company's paying off that debt, and getting a right to those

* See p. 175. † See p. 180.
‡ See p. 183.

duties, properly belonged to the *ſinking fund*; and therefore the re-mortgaging of that ſurplus was really, though not literally, an incroachment upon that *ſacred fund.*

An act for making good the lots occaſioned by a ſum of money being ſtolen out of his majeſty's Exchequer, in the year 1724. Chap. 6.

By this act, the treaſury were impowered to pay to Lord *William Powlet*, out of the monies of the *ſinking fund*, 4,191 *l.* 14 *s.* 6 *d.* to replace ſo much ſtolen out of his office as Teller of the Exchequer. This act was paſſed in purſuance of a petition from him, without being warranted by any reſolution of the committee of ſupply.

An act for laying a duty upon compound waters, or ſpirits, and for licenſing the retailers thereof. Chap. 17.

By this act, a duty of 5 *s.* per gallon was laid upon all compound ſpirits in hand at Chriſtmas 1729, or afterwards to be imported, or home-made, over and above all former duties; and an annual tax of 20 *l.* upon every retailer, in any quantity leſs then a gallon, to commence July 1, 1729; for which purpoſe every ſuch retailer was, before that day, to take out a licenſe, and to renew it annually. But this act was deſigned rather as a prohibition of the retail of ſuch liquors in ſmall quantities, than as the proviſion for raiſing money; and was to continue in force for five years only.

This ſeſſion began Nov. 9, and ended May 15, 1730. The ways and means for raiſing the ſupplies granted in it were as follow: 3 Geo. II. 1729.

Chap. 1. *An act for granting an aid to his majesty by a land-tax for the year* 1730.

This tax was 2 *s.* in the pound, and the sum borrowed upon it was 1,000,000 *l.* at 3 *l. per cent. per ann.*

Chap. 7. *An act for continuing the duties on malt*, &c.

The loan upon this act was 750,000 *l.* at 3 *l. per cent.*

Chap. 14. *An act for reducing the annuity, or fund of the United East-India company, and for ascertaining their right to trade to the East-Indies, and the continuance of their corporation for that purpose, upon the terms therein mentioned.*

By this act an agreement was established with the East-India company, by which that company was, on or before December 24, 1730, to advance, or rather to make a free gift to the government of 200,000 *l.* to be applied to the current service; and moreover they agreed, that from and after Michaelmas 1730, their annuity of 160,000 *l.* should be reduced to 128,000 *l.* in respect of their capital of 3,200,000 *l.* being at the rate of *four* instead of 5 per cent. interest; that, upon a year's notice after Lady-Day 1736, their said capital might be paid off by partial payments of not less than 500,000 *l.* at a time, and their said annuity of 128,000 *l.* to cease in proportion; and their exclusive privilege of trading to the East-Indies, should cease upon *three* years notice to be given to them after Lady-day 1766, and upon repayment of their said capital, and all arrears of their said annuity. How the company were induced to make all these concessions, does not appear by the act; for they seem to have been as generous to the government at the time this act was passed, as the government had been to them in the year 1712, when without any consideration, their *exclusive trade* was, by the act 10 Ann. ch. 28. continued to them *for ever*, and their annuity of 160,000 *l.* made irredeemable before Lady-day 1736. They took care, however, by this act, to have their corporation again established *for ever*; and that they might, after the ceasing of their *exclusive privilege*, continue to trade to the East-Indies as a corporation, in common with other of his majesty's subjects trading to those parts.

An act for raising 550,000 l. by Exchequer bills, towards the supply granted to his majesty; and for the further application of the produce of the sinking fund; for applying the arrears of former taxes, &c. Chap. 16.

As by the reduction of the East-India company's annuity, mentioned in chap. 14. preceding, a saving was gained of 32,000 *l.* per ann. therefore by this act the treasury were impowered to raise 550,000 *l.* by issuing Exchequer bills in the usual way at any time before Christmas 1730; to be repaid out of the first aid to be granted after Michaelmas 1730; and, in the mean time, to be charged on the surplus monies to arise after Lady-day 1730, from the duties then charged with the East-India company's annuity; after which this surplus was to attend the disposition of parliament; so that care was taken, that this saving should not be made part of the *sinking fund*, as in prudence, as well as justice, it ought to have been.

By the same act it was provided, that out of the surplusses of the *sinking fund* arisen at Midsummer 1730, or to arise afterwards, there should be issued to the South-Sea company, at the said feast-day, and afterwards, quarterly, such monies as ſhould then be in the Exchequer, for redeeming part of the annuities, and paying off part of the debt due to that company, until ſuch payments ſhould amount to *one million*; and, if the company ſhould deſire to have the whole million paid at once, the Treaſury were impowered to borrow at 4*l. per cent.* ſo much as ſhould be wanting to compleat the ſame at the ſaid feaſt of Midſummer upon the credit of the future produce of the ſaid fund. Then followed ſeveral clauſes for regulating the dividing of this payment among the proprietors of the South-Sea capital; for each proprietor was to receive a part of this million, in proportion to the ſhare of the company's capital which he was intitled to, and conſequently his ſhare was, from that time, to be proportionally reduced or leſſened. And there was likewiſe a clauſe for applying to the current ſervice 11,655 *l.* 11 *s.* 9 *d.* ½, arrears of land-taxes.

Chap. 20. *An act for taking off certain duties on ſalt, and for making good any deficiencies in the funds that may happen thereby; and for charging the reduced annuity, payable to the Eaſt-India company on the aggregate fund*, &c.

By this act, the 18th branch of the *cuſtoms*, and the 6th and 7th branches of *exciſe*, that is to ſay, the duties thereby impoſed upon ſalt, were from and after Chriſtmas 1730 aboliſhed; but the duties impoſed upon foreign ſalt, imported by the 10th and 11th branches of the cuſtoms, were kept ſtanding in the ſame ſtate they were before; and, as the ſaid 18th branch of the *cuſtoms*, together with the ſaid 7th branch of *exciſe*, had been appropriated with others, as a fund for paying the Eaſt-India company's annuity; therefore by this act, that annuity was, for the future, charged upon the *aggregate fund*, in case the remaining duties charged therewith, should, at the end of any quarter prove deficient; but, if the reduction, intended by chap. 14. of this session, should take place, then the said company's reduced annuity was to be, by this act, wholly charged upon the *aggregate fund*, in case the remaining duties charged therewith, should, at the end of any quarter, prove deficient; but, if the reduction intended by ch. 14. aforesaid, should take place, then the said company's reduced annuity was to be by this act wholly charged upon the *aggregate fund*, and the other duties charged therewith, was to be free from the same, and to be at the disposal of parliament. Moreover, as the said 6th branch of *excise* had been appropriated to the South-Sea company, therefore by this act it was provided, that if any deficiency should happen in that company's original fund, it should be quarterly made good out of the *aggregate fund*.

This was a most popular measure, not only as these duties on salt were very burthensome upon the poor, but as the collection was very expensive to the public; for they had been put under a particular commission, and large salaries allowed to the commissioners and officers, which the people hoped to be free from; but in this they were disappointed; for, by this act, the Treasury were impowered to continue the officers in pay for eighteen months, and before the expiration of that time, as we shall see, the duties were established; so that this abolition seems to have been a concerted scheme for nothing else but for obtaining a new fund of credit, for the purpose of running the nation further in debt.

4 Geo. II. 1730 This session began Jan. 21, 1730, and ended May 7, 1731. The ways and means for raising the supplies granted in it were as follow:

Chap. 1. *An act for continuing the duties on malt, &c.*

The loan upon this act was 750,000*l.* at 3*l.* *per cent.*

Chap. 4. *An act for granting an aid by a land-tax for* 1731.

This tax was 2 *s.* in the pound, and the loan upon it 1,000,000*l.* at 3*l.* *per cent.*

Chap. 5. *An act for the further application of the sinking fund, by paying off one million of South-Sea annuities.*

By this act a million was to be paid to the South-sea company out of the sinking fund at Michaelmas 1731. and afterwards quarterly, as the same should arise, which payment was directed to be divided amongst the South-sea annuitants, and money to be borrowed, as before, in case there should not be at Michaelmas sufficient in that fund to compleat the million.

Chap. 9. *An act for raising* 1,200,000*l.* *by annuities and a lottery*, &c.

The 8th branch of the * *inland duties*, originally appropriated to the East-India company, having, by chap. 14, 16, and 20, of the former session, been freed from that appropriation, and left to the disposal of parliament, it was now made a fund for running the nation into a new debt of 1,200,000*l.* which, by this act, was to be raised for the current service in the manner following; 400,000*l.* part thereof, was to be raised by sale of redeemable annuities, at 3*l.* 10*s.* per cent. to commence from Michaelmas 1731;

* See page. 182.

and 800,000 *l.* the remaining part thereof, was to be raiſed by a 10 *l.* lottery, at 3 *l.* per cent. intereſt, to commence at Chriſtmas 1731; and, as a fund for paying theſe annuities until redemption, the ſaid 8th branch of the *inland duties* was by this act appropriated. This was a ſort of legerdemain incroachment upon the ſinking fund; for, as the Eaſt-India company's annuity had, by chap. 20. of the laſt ſeſſion been charged upon the ſurpluſſes of the *aggregate fund*; and, as that fund conſiſted of taxes, all or moſt of which had been originally appropriated for paying off yearly a part of the principal, as well as the growing intereſt, of the debts before the time charged upon them, the ſurpluſſes of the ſame ought always to have been deemed a part of the ſinking fund, though not expreſly appropriated thereunto; therefore from the time the Eaſt-India company's annuity was charged upon this fund, the taxes formerly charged therewith, ought to have been deemed a part of the ſinking fund; and conſequently, the applying them to any other uſe, was, in effect, an incroachment upon that ſacred fund.—Beſides, the ſaid ſum of 1,200,000 *l.* there was, by this act, appropriated to the current ſervice the following ſums, viz. 32,516 *l.* 12 *s.* 11 *d.* ¾, arrears of former land taxes, payable in 1728, or before; 669 *l.* 9 *s.* 10 *d.* ½, arrears of former malt duties; and 9528 *l.* 3 *s.* 1 *d*, duty on compound liquors, &c. impoſed by 2 Geo. II. ch. 17.

An act to continue the duties for encouragement of the coinage of money. Chap. 12.

By this act the coinage duties, and the former power for making them up 15,000 *l.* *per annum*, for the uſe of the Mints, were continued from March 1, 1730, for ſeven years, and until the end of the session of parliament next following.

5 Geo. II, 1731. This session began the 13th of January 1731, and ended the 1st of June 1732; the ways and means for raising the supplies granted in it, were as follow:

Chap. 1. *An act for continuing the duties on malt, &c. for the year* 1732.

The loan upon this act was 750,000 *l.* at 3 *l.* *per cent.*

Chap. 5. *An act for granting an aid by a land-tax for the year* 1732.

This tax was 1 *s.* in the pound; and the loan upon it 500,000 *l.* at 3 *l.* *per cent.*

Chap. 6. *An act for reviving the duties on salt.*

By this act, all the duties upon salt, which had been abolished by 3 Geo. II, chap. 20, and the several regulations relating thereto, were revived from and after Lady-day 1732, for the space of * three years; and, upon this fund, 500,000 *l.* was to be raised by loans, or Exchequer bills, at 3 *l.* *per cent.* for the service of the ensuing year. The revival of these duties was violently opposed, and the several motions that were made, shew how pernicious these duties are to several sorts of manufactures, as well as our fisheries, navigation, and, indeed, our constitution. These motions were as follow, *viz.*

* These duties were, by 7 Geo. II, chap 6, continued for seven years; by 8 Geo. II, chap. 12, continued for four years; by 14 Geo. II, chap. 22, continued for seven years; by 18 Geo. II, chap. 5, continued for six years; and by 26 Geo. II, chap. 3, continued without limitation.

1. That the perfons employed in collecting and managing thefe duties fhould be reftrained from being a returning officer, or voting or influencing any elector, at any election of parliament men.

2. That home-made falt, ufed in victualling fhips, fhould be exempted from the duties.

3. That potters fhould be allowed a drawback of the duties upon all falt ufed in glazing their earthen ware.

4. That falt, ufed for manuring land, fhould be exempted from the duties.

5. That the affize of falt fold before thefe duties do take place, fhould be fixed.

6. That falt, ufed in dreffing and curing leather, fhould be exempted from the duties.

7. That falt, ufed in making glafs and glafs bottles, fhould be exempted from the duties.

But all thefe motions were rejected by a majority; and, it is almoft certain, that petitions would have been prefented againft the bill from moft parts of the kingdom; but this was prevented by the treatment of a petition from Briftol, which was offered to be prefented February 22, againft the revival of the falt-duties, and a motion made for bringing it up; but the queftion was carried in the negative by a great majority; fo that, upon the whole, we may, from the feveral fteps of this affair, form a pretty certain judgment of the complexion of this parliament; for, by the account of the falt-duty laid before the Houfe of Commons in the year 1731, it will appear, that in order to fave 1 *s.* in the pound, to the landed intereft, which is but a little more than 500,000 *l.* the nation was to pay 630,000 *l.* that is to fay, 185,000 *l.* yearly, being the neat produce; which for three years is 555,000 *l.* and 25,000 *l.* yearly for expences of management, which, for three years, is 75,000 *l.* besides the great trouble and expence which our salt-works and fisheries are exposed to, in order to intitle themselves to the drawbacks, and discounts mentioned in the said account.

Chap. 17. *An act for the further application of the Sinking Fund, by paying off one million of South-Sea stock, &c.*

By this act, it was enacted, that out of such monies as should be in the receipt of Exchequer, of the surplusses, called the Sinking Fund, at Lady-day 1732, there should be issued to the South-Sea company, 1,000,000 *l.* towards redeeming part of the annuities attending on their capital stock; and, that a proportionable part of the said stock should cease, for the benefit of the public. And, that the sum of 123,580 *l.* 2 *s.* 5 *d.* ½, granted for the service of the year 1731, and not applied, should be applied to the service of 1732.

6 Geo. II, 1732. This session was opened the 16th of January 1732, and ended the 13th of June 1733; and the ways and means for raising the supplies granted in it, were as follow:

Chap. 1. *An act for continuing the duties on malt, &c.*

The loan upon this act was 750,000 *l.* at 3 *l.* *per cent.*

Chap. 2. *An act for granting an aid by a land-tax for 1733.*

This tax was 1 *s.* in the pound, and the loan upon it 500,000 *l.* at 3 *l.* *per cent.* and by sect. 145 of this act, the sum of 33,143 *l.* 6 *s.* 1 *d.* ⅓, arrears of former land-taxes, was appropriated to the service of 1733.

An act for enabling his majesty to apply 500,000 l. *out of the Sinking Fund for the service of* 1733; *and for the farther disposition of the said Fund, by paying off one million of South-Sea annuities: and for enabling his majesty out of the monies arisen by sale of lands in the island of St. Christopher's, to pay* 80,000 l. *for the marriage portion of the Princess Royal, and* 10,000 l. *to the trustees for establishing the colony of Georgia in America, and for making good all deficiencies and charges, by taking of* broad pieces *into the Mint, out of the coinage duty, &c.* Chap. 25.

By this act, besides the *million* to be issued to the South-Sea company, in part of payment of that moiety of their capital, called South-Sea annuities *, the sum of 500,000*l.* was taken from the Sinking Fund, and applied to the current service; which misapplication was probably foreseen by some gentlemen in the House; for, in order to prevent it, a motion was made, February 7, that the House would raise the necessary supplies for 1733, without creating any new debt upon any fund whatsoever; but the question was carried in the negative.—The application of the 90,000*l.* arisen from the sale of the lands in St. Christopher's, as mentioned in the title of this act, was likewise an incroachment upon the Sinking Fund; for it ought certainly to have been applied towards payment of the debt contracted by St. Christopher's debentures, as fast as it came into the Exchequer. As to the clause relating to the coin; upon a petition from several merchants

* See 9 Geo. I, chap, 6, p. 230.

to the House it was resolved, that all the old broad pieces should be called in, at the rate of 4 *l.* 1 *s.* per ounce troy, in order to be recoined in guineas; and that the loss and charge thereof should be made good by the coinage duty, which resolution was established by this clause. By another clause in this act, the Treasury were impowered to pay out of the monies reserved for building fifty new churches, 4000 *l.* and 1200 *l.* for the church and dormitory of St. Peter, Westminster; and, by another clause, though nothing of it appears in the title of the act, a resolution of May 17th was established; which was, "That one seaman be allowed "upon the books of every ship of war in sea-"pay, in every hundred men that her comple-"ment shall consist of; and that the produce "of the wages of such seamen, and the value "of their victuals, be given and applied to-"wards the relief of poor widows of commission "and warrant officers of the royal navy, ac-"cording to such rules, orders and regulations, "as his majesty hath, or shall establish and "appoint for that purpose." This was, in effect, a new grant to the crown of 50 *s.* per month, or 32 *l.* 10 *s.* *per annum*, for every hundred seamen we should afterwards have in pay, which amounts to 13,000 *l.* *per annum*, when we have 40,000 seamen in pay, and but 2520 *l.* *per annum* when we have no more than 8000; so that this provision must generally be either too large or too small.

In this session we had no less than three select and secret committees chosen by ballot, one for enquiring into the frauds of the *charitable corporation*; one for enquiring into the frauds of the York-Buildings company, and one for enquiring into the frauds and abuses in the *customs*; but none of them produced any remarkable effect: and, in this session, the famous *excise-*

scheme was introduced; but ſuch a ſpirit was raiſed in the nation againſt it, that, though the queſtion was, upon every diviſion, carried in its favour, the miniſters at laſt were forced to drop this favourite project.

Some writers have obſerved, that ever ſince the revolution, that is to ſay, ever ſince we had any ſuch thing as a land-tax, there was almoſt every ſeſſion an application made for relief againſt the bankruptcies of the receivers of that tax, who are all appointed by the crown, and yet the people are obliged to make good their deficiencies, if the officers of the crown neglect to take ſufficient ſecurity, or to give proper notice of their being removed; and this year ſeveral of the hundreds of the county of Norfolk applied for being relieved againſt a loſs of this kind, amounting to 4412 *l.* 6 *s.* 11 *d.* $\frac{3}{4}$; therefore in this ſeſſion, when the Houſe was, April 2, to go into a committee on the land-tax bill, a motion was made for an inſtruction to the committee, to receive a clauſe to enable and direct the ſeveral commiſſioners to be appointed in the ſaid bill, to nominate and appoint a receiver, or receivers-general for each county, riding, *&c.* reſpectively, within England, and to make the ſaid reſpective counties, *&c.* anſwerable for any deficiency that might happen by ſuch receiver; but upon putting the queſtion, it paſſed in the negative, though the method propoſed has always been practiſed in Scotland, without any inconvenience, and with great ſafety to the people. But miniſters of ſtate muſt, by ſuch a method, part with the diſpoſal of many lucrative places and employments, and therefore——

Chap. 28. *An act for converting a further part of the capital stock of the South-Sea company into annuities redeemable by parliament, and for settling the remaining part of the said stock in the said company.*

By this act, a new division was made of the South-Sea * company's capital; for that which was then called South-Sea stock, amounting to 14,651,103 *l.* 8 *s.* 1 *d.* was, after Midsummer 1733, to be divided into four equal parts, three of which, amounting to 10,988,327 *l.* 11 *s.* 0 *d.* $\frac{3}{4}$, was to be called New South-Sea annuities, and to have no share of the profit or loss by trade, or management, but only the 4 *l. per cent.* annuity payable by the public; and the other fourth part, amounting to 3,662,775 *l.* 17 *s.* 0 *d.* $\frac{3}{4}$, was to remain as a trading stock, to run the risk of all loss by trade or management, and to have the whole profits, as well as the residue of the annuity paid yearly by government.

By an act of this session [chap. 17,] 2 Geo. II, † chap. 17, was repealed, from Midsummer 1733, and, from the same time, the duty on French brandy, imposed by 7 and 8 W. III, chap. 20, was to cease; in lieu of which, all brandies imported were subjected to an excise of 1 *s.* per gallon, if single, and 2 *s.* if double distilled, over and above the duties payable for the same by other former acts; so that, from henceforth, all foreign brandies, from whatever country, were made liable to higher duties than rum or spirits, of our plantations in America.

* See 9 Geo. I, chap. 6, p. 230.
† See p. 253.

This seffion began the 17th of January 1733, and ended the 16th of April 1734; and the ways and means for raifing the fupplies granted in it, were as follow: 7 Geo. II, 1733.

An act for continuing the duties on malt, &c. Chap. 1.

The loan upon this act was 750,000 *l.* at 3 *l.* 10 *s.* *per cent.*

An act for granting an aid by a land-tax for the year 1734. Chap. 7.

This tax was 2 *s.* in the pound, and the loan upon it 1,000,000 *l.* at 3 *l.* 10 *s.* *per cent.* and befides, the fum of 20,578 *l.* 11 *s.* 10 *d.* ½, arrears of former land-taxes were, by this act, applied to the current fervice.

An act for granting and continuing the duties upon falt, and upon red and white herrings for the further term of feven years, &c. Chap. 6.

By this act, the duties upon falt, and upon red and white herrings, were not only continued for feven years, from Lady-day 1735, but made a fund for borrowing *a million* at 4 *l.* *per cent.* fo that we were to pay at leaft five quarters intereft, which was 50,000 *l.* before one fhilling could be raifed from this fund, for payment either of principal or intereft. From hence, and from what we have faid upon the revival of thofe * duties, the reader may judge whether it would not have been better to have raifed the land-tax to 4 *s.* in the pound. But this was not the only difadvantage; for every new fund contributes towards preventing our being able to reduce the intereft payable upon the old.

* See 5 Geo. II, chap. 6, p. 260.

Chap. 12. *An act for enabling his majesty to apply the sum of* 1,200,000 l. *out of the Sinking Fund for the service of* 1734, *&c.*

By this act, the whole of the *Sinking Fund*, and probably more than the whole was diverted from the sacred use to which it was at first appropriated, and applied to the current service, at a time when we were at peace with the whole world, except *Angria* the East-Indian pirate. And, lest it should happen that there may be a want of money, before money sufficient may have arisen into the Exchequer from the Sinking Fund, there was a clause for impowering the Treasury to borrow what might be deficient, upon the credit of the growing produce of the said fund, at 4 *l. per cent.*

In this session was passed the famous law against that sort of gaming called *stock-jobbing*, which will remain upon our records as a proof, not only of the public spirit and humanity, but of the good sense and foresight of the honourable gentleman who contrived and promoted it. This act, however, wants amendment.

8 Geo. II, 1734. This session began the 23d of January 1734, and ended the 15th of May 1735; and the ways and means for raising the supplies granted in it, were as follow:

Chap. 1. *An act for continuing the malt-tax for* 1735.

The loan upon this act was 750,000 *l.* at 3 *l.* 10 *s. per cent.*

Chap. 2. *An act for granting an aid by a land-tax for* 1735.

This tax was 2 *s.* in the pound, and the loan upon it 1,000,000 *l.* at 3 *l.* 10 *s. per cent.*

An act for enabling his majesty to apply the sum of one million out of the Sinking Fund for the service of 1735. Chap. 11.

By this act, the *Sinking Fund* was not only diverted, but anticipated; for it was enacted, that before Lady-day 1736, a *million* should be issued out of the same for the current service, and the growing produce after that time, mortgaged for raising what should be wanting to compleat that sum by loans at 4 *l. per cent.*

An act for granting and continuing the duties on salt, &c. Chap. 12.

By this act, the duties on salt and red and white herrings, were continued for *four* years longer from Lady-day 1742; and a power given to borrow thereupon 500,000 *l.* at 4 *l. per cent.* Thus, in order to prevent raising the land-tax to 3 *s.* in the pound, we were to pay above 140,000 *l.* interest, before one shilling of this fund could be applied to pay off any part of the principal money borrowed upon it. A most surprising instance of parliamentary œconomy and public spirit!

This session opened the 15th of January 1735, and ended the 20th of May 1736; and the ways and means for raising the supplies, were as follow: 9 Geo. II. 1735.

An act for continuing the duties on malt, &c. for 1736. Chap. 1.

The loan upon this act was 750,000 *l.* at 3 *l. per cent.*

An act for granting an aid by a land-tax for 1736. Chap. 3.

This tax was 2 *s.* in the pound, and the loan upon it 1,000,000 *l.*

Chap. 32. *An act for continuing the additional duties upon stamped vellum, parchment and paper, laid by* 12 Geo. I, chap. 33.

By this act, the above statute of 12 Geo. I, chap. 33, was continued for *four* years, from August 2, 1742; and it was thereby provided, that when the deficiency of the suitors money shall have been paid, the surplus should be reserved for the public, and applied as directed by parliament. The deficiency provided for by this act was 11,485 *l.* 4 *s.* 5 *d.*

Chap. 23. *An act for laying a duty upon the retailers of spirituous liquors, and for licensing the retailers thereof.*

This was the famous act against distilled spirituous liquors, by which it was enacted, that no person should sell such liquors, *unmixed or mixed*, in a less quantity than two gallons, without a licence, for which they were to pay 50 *l.* yearly; and all such liquors were loaded with a duty of 20 *s.* per gallon, over and above all other duties. As this was designed for prohibiting the use of such liquors, and as it would be a loss to the *civil-list* revenue; for making good that loss, *the aggregate fund* was charged with 70,000 *l. per annum* to that revenue, which most people thought was really more than it could lose by the prohibition; and whatever deficiency might thereby happen in any other fund, was to be made good out of the *aggregate fund*. The reader may judge what confusion this would bring into our public accounts; and yet both these provisions were equally unnecessary, because the deficiency of the civil-list revenue, under 800,000 *l. per annum* must have been made good by parliament, and the other deficiencies would naturally have fallen upon the

Sinking Fund. The provision in favour of the civil-list was therefore a tacit confession, that the duties appropriated thereunto produced more than 800,000 *l.* *per annum*, and the other provision became necessary by way of a blind for this.

An act for enabling his majesty to borrow any sum or sums of money, not exceeding 600,000 l. *to be charged upon the surplusses, excesses, or overplus-monies, commonly called the* Sinking Fund, *redeemable by parliament; and for the further disposition of the said fund, by paying off one million of South-Sea annuities, &c.* Chap. 34.

By this act, the sacred *Sinking Fund* was mortgaged for 600,000 *l.* to be raised by loans at 3 *l. per cent.* A most dangerous precedent; and yet such a precedent was agreed to by parliament in a time of profound tranquillity! but, by way of sugar plumb, a million of the new South-Sea annuities was to be paid off by clauses in this act, founded on a resolution of a committee of the whole house, to consider of the application of the *Sinking Fund*, agreed to May 3, and, in case there should not then be so much money in that fund, the Treasury were impowered, as usual, to borrow what should be deficient, upon the credit of the growing produce.

This session began the 15th of January 1736, and ended the 21st of June 1737; and the ways and means for raising the supplies granted in it, were as follow: 10 Geo. II, 1736.

An act for continuing the duties on malt, &c. for the year 1737. Chap. 1.

The loan upon this act was 750,000 *l.*

Chap. 3. *An act for granting an aid by a land-tax for 1737.*

This tax was 2 *s.* in the pound: and the loan upon it 1,000,000 *l.* at 3 *l. per cent.*

Chap. 17. *An act for repealing the present duty on sweets, and for granting a less duty thereupon, &c. and for appropriating the supplies granted in this session, &c.*

By this act, a duty of 12 *s.* per barrel was imposed on all sweets made after Midsummer 1737, in lieu of the old duty of 36 *s.* per barrel, and a fund established thereby for borrowing 500,000 *l.* at 3 *l. per cent.* But this duty ought not to have been made a fund of credit; because the old duty had been appropriated to the South-Sea company, and the surplus of it to the * *aggregate fund*; and therefore this was an incroachment upon the *Sinking Fund*, to which both these funds had been appropriated. And, by a clause in this act, the sum of one million was to be issued for paying off so much of the South-Sea annuities.

11 Geo. II, 1737. This session was opened the 24th of January 1737, and ended the 20th of May 1738; and the ways and means for raising the supplies granted in it, were as follow:

Chap. 7. *An act for continuing the duties on malt, &c. for 1738.*

The loan upon this act was 750,000 *l.* at 3 *l. per cent.*

Chap. 14. *An act for granting an aid by a land-tax for 1738.*

This tax was 2 *s.* in the pound, and the loan upon it 1,000,000 *l.* at 3 *l. per cent.*

* See p. 190, 191, 200, 201.

An act for granting to his majesty the sum of two millions for the service of 1738; and for paying the governor and company of the Bank of England one million, for redeeming an annuity of 40,000 l. *payable to them; and for the further appropriating the supplies granted in this session of parliament.* Chap. 27.

By this act, it was enacted, that out of the money that had arisen, or should arise from the Sinking Fund, the sum of 1,500,000 *l.* should be applied towards the supply of 1738; and his majesty was impowered to raise, by loans, or Exchequer bills at 3 *l. per cent.* the further sum of 500,000 *l.* for the same use, upon the credit of the Sinking Fund; but then it was provided, that of this sum of 2,000,000 *l* *one million* should be paid to the Bank, for redeeming the annuity of 40,000 *l.* part of the 80,000 *l.* annuity, secured to them by 11 Geo. II, chap 9; so that, of this annuity, there would then remain due but an annuity of 20,000 *l.* the other 20,000 *l.* having been before redeemed, by virtue (as this act says) of 1 Geo. II, chap 8; but this seems to be a mistake, as appears by the said act; and therefore it is probable, the act intended to be here recited, was the 2d Geo. II, chap. 3.

This session began the 18th of January 1738, and ended the 29th of April 1738; and the ways and means for raising the supplies granted in it, were as follow: 12 Geo. I, 1738.

An act for continuing the duties on malt, &c. for 1739. Chap. 1.

The loan upon this act was 750,000 *l.* at 3 *l.* 10 *s. per cent. per annum.*

Chap. 3. *An act for granting an aid by a land-tax for 1737.*

This tax was 2 *s.* in the pound, and the loan upon it 1,000,000 *l.* at 3 *l. per cent. per annum.*

Chap. 5. *An act to continue the duties for encouragement of the coinage of money.*

By this act the coinage-duties were continued for *seven*-years, from March 1, 1738-9, and to the end of the then next session of parliament; during which time, all the acts concerning coinage, and the power of the Treasury, as to the issuing of 15,000 *l. per annum* for the coinage, were continued.

Chap. 19. *An act for granting to his majesty the sum of* 500.000 l. *out of the Sinking Fund, for the service of the year* 1739; *and for enabling his majesty to raise the further sum of* 500,000 l. *out of the growing produce of the said fund, &c.*

By this act, the Treasury were directed to issue before Midsummer-day 1739, 500,000 *l.* out of the Sinding Fund; and after that day to borrow 500,000 *l.* more, by loans or Exchequer bills, at 3 *l per cent.* upon the growing produce of the said fund, towards the supply of 1739 And the sum of 119,451 *l.* 17 *s.* 9 *d.* granted for 1738, and not applied, was directed to be applied to the supply of 1739. But, considering the circumstances of the nation at that time, it is surprising, that our ministers did not chuse to raise the land-tax to 4 *s. in the pound*, rather than seize upon the whole of the Sinking Fund for the current service; for the resentment of the nation then run so high against the insults and unjust treatment we had for so many years submitted to from Spain, that such a land-tax would have been readily agreed to.

One would from hence be apt to conclude, that our miniſters at that time were all of the ſame opinion with one of them, who ſome time before was ſo open as to ſay, that if it were not for our public funds, *and the jobs a miniſter might thereby make*, our government would not be worth ſerving. The truth is, our *public funds* are a ſort of falſe dice, which our ſtock-jobbers play with; and our miniſters may always know beſt and ſooneſt, whether the dice will run high or low; eſpecially if they take two or three Jews, Chriſtian or Hebrew, into their fraternity. Therefore it is to be feared, that we never ſhall have a miniſter ſo honeſt and diſintereſted, as to be ſincerely for putting a final end to our *public funds*, or to the *game* of *ſtock-jobbing*; and it is well known, that the famous law againſt *ſtock-jobbing* was crammed down their throats, by the weight and intereſt of one great and wiſe magiſtrate of the city of London; though even his weight, intereſt, and ſtrength of argument, were not afterwards ſufficient for carrying into execution a ſcheme, which would probably have put an end to moſt of our *public funds*, or at leaſt, to the transferring them from hand to hand, upon which the profitable *job-work* of our miniſters muſt always depend.

An act for providing a reward to Joanna Stephens, *upon a proper diſcovery to be made by her for the uſe of the public, of the medicine prepared by her for the cure of the ſtone.* Chap. 23.

This act directs how, and upon what condition the reward of 5000*l.* was to be paid to Mrs. *Stephens.*

13 Geo. II, 1739. This session began the 15th of November 1739, and ended the 29th of April 1740; the ways and means for raising the supplies granted in it, were as follow:

Chap. 2. *An act for continuing the duties on malt for the year* 1740.

The loan upon this act was 750,000 *l.* at 3 *l. per cent. per annum.*

Chap. 2. *An act for granting an aid to his majesty by a land-tax for* 1740.

This tax was 4 *s.* in the pound, and the loan upon it 2,000,000 *l.* at 3 *l. per cent.* (In the act not exceeding 3 *l.* 10 *s. per cent. per annum.*)

Chap. 23. *An act for granting to his majesty the sum of one million out of the* Sinking Fund, *for the service of the year* 1740; *and for enabling his majesty to raise the further sum of* 200,000 *l. out of the growing produce of the said fund; and for granting to his majesty the sum of* 21,000 *l.* 1 *s.* 8 *d.* ½, *remaining in the receipt of his majesty's Exchequer, arisen by sale of lands in the island of St. Christopher's, &c.*

By this act, the money above mentioned was to be raised by loans, or Exchequer bills, at 3 *l.* 10 *s. per cent.* interest; and the sum of 88,722 *l.* 7 *s.* 10 *d.* ¼, remaining in the Exchequer, and unapplied, of the money granted for 1739, was appropriated to 1740.

14 Geo. II, 1740. This session began the 18th of November 1740, and ended the 25th of April 1741; the ways and means for raising the supplies granted in it, were as follow:

An act for granting an aid by a land-tax for the year 1741. Chap. 1.

This tax was 4 *s.* in the pound, and the loan upon it 2,000,000 *l.* at 3 *l.* *per cent.* (In the act not exceeding 4 *l.* *per cent. per annum.*)

An act for continuing the duties on malt for the year 1741. Chap. 2.

The loan upon this act was 750,000 *l.* at 3 *l.* *per cent.* (In the act not exceeding 4 *l.* *per cent.*)

An act for granting and continuing the duties upon salt, and upon red and white herrings, for the further term of seven *years, &c.* Chap. 22.

By this act, the salt duties were continued from Lady-day 1746, for *seven* years, and upon this distant fund, the Treasury were impowered to raise the immediate sum of 1,200,000 *l.* by loans, or Exchequer bills, at 4 *l.* *per cent.* interest; so that for this sum in ready money, we were to pay five years interest, or 240,000 *l.* before the fund could be applied towards paying off *one shilling* of the principal or interest; and, as the duty, including expence of management, produces 210,000 *l.* yearly, (as appears from the account thereof laid before the House of Commons in the year 1731) which, in *seven* years, amounts to 1,470,000 *l.* we must reckon, that from this 1,200,000 *l.* in ready money, the nation was to pay 1,710,000 *l.* An admirably frugal method of raising the current supplies!

An act for granting to his majesty the sum of one million out of the Sinking Fund, and for applying other sums therein mentioned for the service of the year 1741, *&c.* Chap. 41.

By this act, besides the *million* taken from the *Sinking Fund*, the sum of 39,588 *l.* 10 *s.* 10 *d.* ¾, remaining in the Exchequer, unapplied, of last year's grants, and the sum of 11,434 *l.* 4 *s.* remaining in the Exchequer, and reserved for the disposal of parliament, were appropriated to the service of 1741. In this act likewise there was a power of borrowing the money upon the credit of the growing produce of the Sinking Fund, at 3 *d.* ½ *per cent.* interest, in case the monies of the said fund should not come in fast enough to answer the current service. But we need not wonder that such special care was taken to have ready money for answering *all* the services of the ensuing year, as *a new parliament* was *then* to be chosen.

15 Geo. II, 1741. This session opened the 1st of December 1741, and ended the 15th of July 1742; the ways and means for raising the supplies granted in it, were as follow:

Chap. 1. *An act for continuing the duties on malt, for the year* 1742.

The loan upon this act was 750,000 *l.* at 3 *l.* *per cent* (In the act not exceeding 3 *l.* 10 *s.* *per cent.*)

Chap. 11. *An act for granting an aid by a land-tax for* 1742.

This tax was 4 *s.* in the pound, and the loan upon it 2,000,000 *l.* at 3 *l.* *per cent.* (In the act not exceeding 3 *l.* 10 *s.* *per cent.*)

Chap. 3. *An act for granting to his majesty a certain sum out of the Sinking Fund, towards the supply of the year* 1742.

By this act, a *million* was to be raised by loans, or Exchequer bills, at 3 *l.* 10 *s.* *per cent.* interest, upon the credit of the *Sinking Fund.*

An act for establishing an agreement with the governor and company of the Bank of England, for advancing the sum of 1,600,000 *l.* *towards the supply for the service of the year* 1742. Chap. 13.

By this act, the corporation, and all the privileges of the Bank, were continued from 1742, to August 1, 1764, in consideration of which they engaged, and were, by this act, obliged to lend to the government the sum of 1,600,000 *l.* at several times, on or before December 25, 1742; for which they were to have an interest after the rate of 3 *l.* *per cent.* *per annum* out of the excise, and they were impowered to inlarge their capital with any further sum not exceeding 1,600,000 *l.* additional stock; but the whole made liable to redemption upon 12 months notice after the said 1st of August, and payment of all that should then be due to them.

An act for granting to his majesty the sum of 800,000 l. *to be raised by annuities transferrable at the Bank of England,* &c. Chap. 19.

By this act, the Treasury were impowered to raise 800,000 *l.* by sale of annuities, at the rate of 3 *l.* *per cent.* transferrable at the Bank, and payable half yearly, at Christmas and Midsummer; the first payment to be due at Christmas 1742. These annuities were made payable out of the *Sinking Fund* until redeemed by parliament, which they might be at any time, on a year's notice; and out of the same fund, the Treasury were to allow to the cashier and accomptant-general to be appointed by the Bank, 250 *l.* to the former, and 200 *l.* a-year to the latter; and, besides, they were to allow to the former out of the purchase-money, 500 *l.* for his trouble in receiving and accounting for it. And finally, the Bank was to continue a corporation, and enjoy all its privileges until these annuities should be redeemed.

Chap. 29. *An act for granting to his majesty an additional duty on foreign cambricks, imported into Great-Britain, &c.*

By this act, a duty of 1 *s.* 5 *d.* per half piece of 6 ½ ells, and 2 *s.* 10 *d.* per whole piece of 13 ells, was laid on all foreign cambricks for *seven* years, after August 1, 1742, over and above all former duties; and the same was made a fund for paying a bounty of *one penny* per yard, of all British and Irish linens from 6 *d.* to 12 *d.* per yard, price; and a half-penny per yard, for all under 6 *d.* that should be exported out of Great-Britain, to Africa, America, Spain, or Portugal, for seven years after Lady-day, 1743.

16 Geo. II, 1742. This session began the 16th of November 1742, and ended the 1st of April 1743; and the ways and means for raising the supplies granted in it, were as follow.

Chap. 1. *An act for granting an aid by a land tax for the year* 1743.

This tax was 4 *s.* in the pound, and the loan upon it 2,000,000 *l.* at 3 *l.* *per cent. per annum.*

Chap. 2. *An act for continuing the malt-tax for* 1743.

The loan upon this act was 750,000 *l.* at 3 *l.* *per cent.*

An act for repealing certain duties on spirituous liquors, and on licences for retailing the same, and for laying other duties on spirituous liquors, and on licences to retail the said liquors. Chap. 8.

By this act, the high prohibitory duties upon spirituous liquors, and upon licences for retailing the same, were all abolished; and such moderate duties imposed, after Lady-day 1743, as might raise a considerable revenue, without lessening the consumption, or even the immoderate use of such liquors; for which reason the bill was strenuously opposed by our bishops, as it was plainly an incroachment upon the church; for it shewed, that our ministers had resolved to raise money for the public service upon the sins, as well as upon the luxuries and necessities of the people; whereas, before this time, none but the clergy ever attempted to sell indulgences, or to raise money upon the sins of the people. In times of popery, when public stews and common prostitutes were to be rated, our histories well inform us, that all those about London were under the jurisdiction of the bishop of Winchester, and obliged to keep within his liberty in Southwark, called the Clink, from a little bell they had for regulating the time when those shops of lewdness were to be opened and shut. However, as the king is now head of our church, he has a right to raise money upon the sins of the people; and, as it was foreseen, that a plentiful revenue would from hence arise, therefore notwithstanding the opposition of all our lords spiritual, the bill passed into a law. See the following act:

An act for repealing the several rates and duties upon victuallers and retailers of beer and ale, within the cities of London and Westminster, and Chap. 17.

the weekly bills of mortality; and for transferring the Exchequer bills unsatisfied thereupon, to the duties for licences to sell spirituous liquors and strong waters by retail; and also for enabling his majesty to raise a certain sum of money for the service of the year 1743, *to be further charged on the said duties for licences.*

As licences were, by chap. 8, aforesaid, to be granted and annually paid for, by all victuallers and alehouse-keepers who sold any spirituous liquors, and as a double duty upon licences might be a hurt to the revenue; therefore what was called *the pot-act*, that is to say, the 12th of Geo. I, chap. 12, was repealed after Midsummer 1743, by the foregoing act; and, as there was the sum of 481,400 *l.* part of the 500,000 *l.* that had been borrowed upon the said pot-act, still standing out in Exchequer bills, this sum, together with 518,600 *l.* now to be borrowed at 3 *l. per cent.* making in the whole, 1,000,000 *l.* was, by this act, charged upon the licence-duty granted by chap. 8, of this session.

Chap. 13. *An act for raising by annuities, and a lottery in manner therein mentioned, the sum of* 1,800,000 *l. at* 3 l. per cent. per annum *for the service of* 1743.

By this act, the sum of 1,800,000 *l.* was to be borrowed at 3 *l. per cent.* by sale of redeemable annuities, or by Exchequer bills, and by a lottery; that is to say, 1,000,000 *l.* by annuities, or Exchequer bills, and 800,000 *l.* by a lottery at 10 *l.* per ticket, both of which were charged upon the duties on spirituous liquors granted by chap. 8, aforesaid,

An act for granting to his majesty the sum of one million out of the Sinking Fund, and for applying a further sum therein mentioned, for the service of 1743, *&c.* Chap. 25.

By this act, besides the *million* to be issued out of the *Sinking Fund*, the sum of 12,492 *l.* 2 *s.* 5 *d.* remaining in the Exchequer unapplied, of the supplies for the former year 1742, was applied to the service of 1743, with a clause of loan for borrowing the said *million* at 3 *l. per cent.* by loans or Exchequer bills.

This session began the 1st of December 1743, and ended the 12th of May 1744; and the ways and means for raising the supplies granted in it, were as follow: 17 Geo. II, 1743.

An act for granting an aid by a land-tax for 1744. Chap. 1.

This tax was 4 *s.* in the pound, and the loan upon it 2,000,000 *l.* at 3 *l. per cent.*

An act for continuing the duties on malt, &c. Chap. 2.

The loan upon this act was 750,000 *l.* at 3 *l. per cent.*

An act for granting to his majesty the surplus, or remainder of the monies arisen, or to arise, by the duties on spirituous liquors, granted by an act of the last session of parliament, &c. and for establishing an agreement with the united company of merchants of England trading to the East-Indies. Chap. 17.

As the tax upon spirituous liquors, imposed by the last session had been found to produce a great deal more than would answer the first charge upon it, a case that very seldom happens; and, as this surplus was reserved for the disposition of parliament, that surplus was, by this act, vested in his majesty, and made a fund for borrowing a *million* from the East-India company; for the lending of which, their former annuity of 128,000 *l.* together with this annuity of 30,000 *l.* were made irredeemable before a year's notice, to be given after Lady-day 1745, and their exclusive trade to the East-Indies was continued from Lady-day 1766, to Lady-day 1780; and even then not to cease but upon *three* years notice to be given after that day.

Chap. 18. *An act for raising by annuities and a lottery, in manner therein mentioned, the sum of* 1,800,000 l. *at* 3 l. per cent. per annum *for the year* 1744.

By this act, the surplus mentioned in the foregoing act [chap. 17,] was made a fund for borrowing 1,800,000 *l.*; part thereof, *viz.* 1,200,000 *l.* to be raised by sale of annuities, and 600,000 *l.* by a 10 *l.* lottery; the annuities upon both to be at the rate of 3 *l. per cent.* but then the purchasers of the annuities for the 1,200,000 *l.* were to have a premium of 3 *l.* upon every *hundred pounds* they contributed, to be paid out of the purchase-money; so that, at the very beginning of the war we were now engaged in, we returned to that destructive method of paying premiums for the advance of money, so much practised at the end of the war in Queen Anne's time. There was now no less a sum than 5,600,000 *l.* charged upon these new duties on spirituous liquors, and the licences for retailing the same, and they were soon found to be more than sufficient for answering the *growing interest*; for this is all that is now thought of, the payment of the principal being always left to the care of future generations. As this first instance of the government's raising money upon the sins of the people, has succeeded so well, we may perhaps see the precedent followed in more cafes than one; confequently we may expect to fee money raifed upon whoring, gaming, ufury, *&c.*

An act for granting to his majefty one million out of the Sinking Fund, and for applying a fum remaining in the Exchequer arifen by the coinage-duty, for the fervice of 1744, *&c.* Chap. 23.

By this act, befides the million to be taken from the *Sinking Fund*, the fum of 36,000 *l.* remaining in the Exchequer, arifen from the coinage-duty, more than had been found neceffary for anfwering that fervice, was applied to the fervice of the enfuing year. And, as every money act has generally a borrowing claufe, the Treafury were impowered to borrow a *million* upon this act at 3 *l. per cent.* by loans, or Exchequer bills. In all which cafes it is to be hoped, the Treafury chofe to borrow by Exchequer bills, as being lefs expenfive to the public; becaufe it is not neceffary to iffue the bills but by degrees, as the money comes to be wanted, and the intereft ceafes as foon as money comes into the Exchequer to pay them off, or, as foon as they are paid into the hands of any of the revenue collectors. But this is a fact which our parliaments have never thought fit to inquire into.

This feffion began the 27th of November 1744, and ended the 2d of May 1745; and the ways and means for raifing the fupplies granted in it, were as follow: 18 Geo. II, 1744.

An act for granting an aid by the land-tax for the year 1745. Chap. 1.

This tax was 4 *s.* in the pound, and the loan upon it 2,000,000 *l.* at 3 *l.* 10 *s. per cent. per annum.*

Chap. 2. *An act for continuing the duties on malt, &c.*

The loan upon this act was 750,000 *l.* at 3 *l.* 10 *s. per cent.*

Chap. 5. *An act for granting and continuing the duties upon salt, and upon red and white herrings, for the further term of six years, &c.*

This act continued the duties on salt, *&c.* from Lady-day, 1753, (when, by 14 Geo. II, chap. 22, they were to expire) to Lady-day, 1759; and, upon this fund, the Treasury were impowered to borrow *a million*, at 3 *l.* 10 *s. per cent.* payable at the Exchequer, and to commence at Lady-day, 1745, though the last payment of the principal was not to be advanced, and paid into the Exchequer until November 21, 1745.

Chap. 9. *An act for granting to his majesty several additional duties upon all wines imported into Great-Britain; and for raising a certain sum of money by annuities, and a lottery in manner therein mentioned, to be charged on the said additional duties.*

By this act, a new duty of 8 *l.* per ton on French wine or vinegar, and 4 *l.* per ton on all other wines or vinegar, over and above all other duties, was imposed from Lady-day 1745; and upon this fund, the Treasury were impowered to raise 2,000,000 *l.* at 3 *l. per cent.* payable at the Bank; that is to say, 1,500,000 *l.* by sale of annuities, and 500,000 *l.* by a 10 *l.* lottery; and, as an encouragement to subscribe, every subscriber for ten tickets in the lottery, was to have an additional annuity of 4 *l.* 10 *s. per annum* for his own, or the life of any person he should name.

An act for granting to his majesty the sum of 800,000 l. out of the Sinking Fund; and for granting a sum remaining in the Exchequer, arisen by the surplus of the duties upon malt, &c. for the service of the year 1745, &c. Chap. 22.

By this act, besides the 800,000 *l.* to be taken from the Sinking Fund, with a clause for borrowing the money at 3 *l.* 10 *s.* *per cent.* the sum of 21,244 *l.* 13 *s.* 8 *d.* ¾, being the surplus of the duties on malt for 1743, was appropriated to the service of the year 1745, *&c.*

An act for repealing the present inland duty of 4 s. per pound upon all tea sold in Great-Britain, and for granting to his majesty certain other inland-duties in lieu thereof, &c. Chap. 26.

By this act, the inland-duties, then payable on tea, were abolished; and, from Midsummer 1745, all the tea sold in Great-Britain, was subjected to a duty of 1 *s.* per pound weight, and 25 *l.* *per cent.* of the gross price, for which it should be sold at the East-India sales, over and above all customs on importation, to be paid in ready money before taking it out of the warehouse.

This session began the 17th of October 1745, and ended the 12th of August 1746; and the ways and means for raising the supplies granted in it, were as follow: 19 Geo. II, 1745.

An act for granting an aid by a land-tax for the year 1746. Chap. 3.

An act for continuing the duties on malt, &c. for the year 1746. Chap. 4.

With respect to these two acts, we must recollect, that, upon the success of the young

Chevalier, or Pretender, in Scotland, and his entering England, though his little army never amounted to 5000 effective men, such a pannic seized the people of this country, that it was found impracticable to borrow money as usual from private hands, either upon the land, or malt-tax acts; therefore application was made, and both mortgaged to the Bank, for *one million* (see the following act) only at 4 *l. per cent.* from which it is evident, that notwithstanding the many addresses, offering lives and fortunes, there were very few who would venture any considerable part of their fortune for the preservation of our present happy establishment. And yet, at the same time, there were many voluntary subscriptions for money set on foot, to which multitudes subscribed a *guinea* or more, as they thought they could spare it, out of their annual income, by which, we suppose, they imagined, that they intitled themselves to some post or place in the government, as soon as it was resettled. But, whatever their views were, we must observe, that this method of raising money for the public service, was both illegal, and of the most dangerous consequence to our constitution; for it is expresly against law for any person to lend or give money for the support of the government without the authority of parliament; and therefore, in all our money-acts in which there is a clause of credit, that clause impowers the king to borrow, only by impowering the subject to lend. In order to prevent the danger that might ensue from such a precedent, we are surprized, that the parliament, as it was then sitting, did not pass a short act for authorizing these voluntary contributions; but we are still more surprized, that a parliament consisting mostly of those who called themselves *Whigs*, has never since passed an act for preventing this practice being ever hereafter made a precedent, nor has ever called for any account of the money raised by these voluntary contributions. How different are Whigs *in* place from Whigs *out* of place!

An act for establishing an agreement with the governor and company of the Bank of England, for cancelling certain Exchequer bills upon the terms therein mentioned; and for obliging them to advance the sum of one million upon the credit of the land-tax, and malt-duties granted to his majesty for the service of the year 1746. Chap. 6.

By this act, the Bank agreed, and was obliged to advance a *million* upon the above-mentioned two acts, at such time as the Treasury should direct, but not above 250,000 *l.* at a time, and each time to have 14 days notice; the whole at 4 *l. per cent.* And further, the Bank agreed, and were by this act obliged, to pay off and deliver up to the Treasury to be cancelled, all the Exchequer bills then standing out, which had been charged upon the duties for licences to sell spirituous liquors, by 16 Geo. II, chap. 8, amounting to 986,800 *l.* for which they had settled upon them an annuity of 39,472 *l.* charged upon the said duties, and a power to add the said sum of 986,800 *l.* to their then capital stock, if they thought fit, and in what method they thought most proper.

An act for granting to his majesty several rates and duties upon glass, and upon spirituous liquors; and for raising a certain sum of money by annuities, and a lottery, to be charged on the said duties, &c. Chap. 12.

By this act, several new duties of different kinds, over and above all former duties, were laid upon all sorts of glass to be imported into, or made within this kingdom after Lady-day 1746, by which all our glaſs-makers were ſubjected to the laws of exciſe, and a great diſcouragement laid upon the manufacturing of any glaſs for exportation; for, as a great deal is waſted in the manufacturing of fine glaſs, the exporter could never intitle himſelf to draw back the whole of the duty, both being to be computed by the weight of the glaſs; and this beſides the danger of weighing: but no matter what becomes of our trade or manufactures, if money can but be raiſed for the ſervice of our foreign projects!

By the ſame act, new duties of different kinds were impoſed upon all ſorts of ſpirituous liquors, to be made, extracted, or manufactured in Great-Britain after Lady-day 1746; but great care was taken not to make theſe additional duties ſo high as to prevent poor people's getting drunk as often as they pleaſed; for our view now was to raiſe money, not to prohibit the conſumption.

Upon theſe two new duties, the government was impowered to raiſe 3,000,000 *l.*; that is to ſay, 2,500,000 *l.* by the ſale of annuities at 4 *l.* *per cent. per annum*, to commence from Lady-day 1746, though the laſt of the ſubſcription-money was not to be paid till December 20, 1746; and 500,000 *l.* by a 10 *l.* lottery, upon which likewiſe there were to be annuities at the ſame rate, and to commence from Chriſtmas, 1746; but then every ſubſcriber for *ten* tickets of this lottery was to be intitled to an annuity of 9 *l.* *per annum*, and ſo in proportion for any greater number, during his life, or the life of ſuch perſon as he ſhould name, over and above the redeemable annuity of 4 *l.* *per cent. per annum.* This may perhaps be thought a very extravagant premium; but then we muſt obſerve, that upon this, as well as the two former lotteries, every ſubſcriber to the lottery was obliged to ſubſcribe for a proportional value of the annuities to be ſold by virtue of the act; that is to ſay, if he deſired to ſubſcribe for ten tickets in this lottery, he muſt, at the ſame time, ſubſcribe for 500 *l.* value of the annuities; conſequently every ſubſcriber for 600 *l.* was to have 24 *l. per annum* 'till redeemed; and 9 *l. per annum* during life; which life-annuities, amounted in the whole to 45,000 *l. per annum*; and, ſuppoſing this to be worth ſixteen years purchaſe, we muſt reckon, that in this, which was but the ſecond year of the French war, we paid 720,000 *l.* or 24 *l. per cent.* premium for the advance of this 3,000,000 *l.* beſides the expence of drawing the lottery.

An act to continue the duties for encouragement of the coinage of money. Chap. 14.

This act was only to continue the coinage-duties with the ſame power to the Treaſury as before, for *ſeven* years from March 1, 1745, and to the end of the then next ſeſſion of parliament.

An act for ſettling an additional revenue of 25,000 l. *upon his Royal Highneſs* William *Duke of Cumberland, and the heirs-male of his body, for the ſignal ſervices done by his Royal Highneſs to his country.* Chap. 29.

This act ſettled the above revenue on his Royal Highneſs, payable out of the *aggregate fund*, to commence at Lady-day 1746.

An act for granting to his majeſty a certain ſum of money out of the Sinking Fund, for the ſervice of 1746; *and alſo for enabling his majeſty to* Chap. 31.

raise a further sum of money for the uses and purposes therein mentioned, &c.

By this act, besides a *million* to be taken from, or borrowed at 4 *l. per cent.* upon the Sinking Fund, his majesty was impowered, by sign-manuel to the Treasury, to raise 500,000 *l.* at 4 *l. per cent.* to be paid out of the next supplies before Midsummer 1747, out of the Sinking Fund.

20 Geo. II, 1746. This session opened the 18th of November 1746, and ended the 17th of June 1747; and the ways and means for raising the supplies granted in it, were as follow:

Chap. 2. *An act for granting an aid by a land-tax for the year 1747.*

This tax was 4 *s.* in the pound, and the loan upon it 2,000,000 *l.* at 4 *l. per cent.*

Chap. 5. *An act for continuing the duties on malt, &c.*

The loan upon this act was 750,000 *l.* at 4 *l. per cent.*

Chap. 3. *An act for repealing the several rates and duties upon houses, windows, and lights; and for granting to his majesty other rates and duties upon houses, windows, or lights, and for raising* 4,400,000 l. *to be charged on the said rates and duties.*

By this act, the new duties imposed were, for every dwelling-house inhabited within England, 2 *s.*; and over and above the said 2 *s.* for every window, or light in every such house in Great-Britain, containing from 10 to 14 windows, both inclusive, 6 *d.*; from 15 to 19 windows, both inclusive, 9 *d.*; and from 20 inclusive and upwards, 1 *s.*; which duties were to commence from Lady-day, 1747, and were to be paid by the inhabitants of the houses, and the act to be carried into execution by the commissioners of the land-tax. And upon this fund, was to be borrowed the sum of 4,000,000 *l.* at 4 *l.* *per cent.* with a premium of 10 *l.* *per cent.* from the time of lending, so that every lender was to have a yearly interest of 4 *s.* 8 *d.* and to be paid 110 *l.* for every 100 *l.* he advanced; yet this must be allowed to be a better bargain for the public than that which had been made the preceding session; and every one may now see, that it would have been still better for the public to have given 5 *l.* *per cent.* interest without any premium.

An act for granting to his majesty several rates and duties upon coaches, and other carriages therein mentioned; and for raising the sum of one million by way of lottery, to be charged upon the said rates and duties. Chap. 10.

By this act, a duty of 4 *l.* *per annum* was laid from Lady-day 1747, upon all four-wheel coaches, *&c.* except hackney-coaches, either for one's own use, or to be let out to hire; and 40 *s.* *per annum* on all two-wheel calashes, *&c.* Thus our rich people, at last, who can keep coaches of their own, submitted themselves to a tax which had been long paid by those who could not, and were therefore obliged to make use of hackney-coaches; but still they took special care of themselves; for a gentleman, who hires a hackney coach, must pay at the rate of 13 *l.* a-year, but those who are rich enough to keep coaches of their own, are to pay but 4 *l.* *per annum.*—The levying of this duty was committed to the commissioners of excise, and all the penalties and forfeitures inflicted by the act, made determinable and recoverable as our other excise-penalties are; so that even our quality may now be said to be subjected to the laws of excise. But stage-coaches, and post-chaises, kept for hire, by any post-master, are exempted from this duty; and the produce was charged with the payment of annuities at 4 *l.* *per cent.* upon a *million* to be raised by a lottery of 10 *l.* per ticket.

Chap. 36. *An act for granting to his majesty a certain sum of money out of the Sinking Fund, for the service of the year* 1747; *and also for enabling his majesty to raise a further sum of money for the uses and purposes therein mentioned, &c.*

By this act, besides a *million* to be taken from the Sinking Fund, and to be raised at 4 *l.* *per cent.* by loans or Exchequer bills, his majesty was impowered to raise by Exchequer bills, the further sum of 500,000 *l.* at 4 *l.* *per cent.* for the service of 1747, to be repaid out of the first supplies granted after Michaelmas 1747, or, in failure thereof, out of the Sinking fund.

21 Geo. II, 1747. This session began the 10th of November 1747, and ended the 13th of May 1748; and the ways and means for raising the supplies, were as follow:

Chap. 1. *An act for continuing the duties on malt, &c.*

The loan upon this act was 750,000 *l.* at 4 *l.* *per cent.*

Chap. 7. *An act for granting an aid to his majesty by a land-tax for the year* 1748.

The loan upon this act was 2,000,000 *l.* at 4 *l.* *per cent.*

An act for granting to his majesty a subsidy of poundage upon all goods and merchandizes to be imported into this kingdom; and for raising a certain sum of money by annuities and a lottery, to be charged on the said subsidy, &c. Chap. 2.

By this act, a new burden was laid upon our trade by imposing a new duty, over and above all former duties, of 5 *l. per cent. ad valorem*, upon all goods and merchandizes imported into this kingdom, after March 1, 1747, and to be levied in the same manner as the old subsidy. The whole of this duty is indeed to be drawn back, if the goods be exported in *three* years; but this does not prevent all the inconveniencies merchants are exposed to by such duties, or all the prejudices our trade is thereby exposed to. Upon this new subsidy a larger sum was to be borrowed than was ever before attempted to be borrowed upon any one of the many taxes in this kingdom; for no less than 6,300,000 *l.* was to be borrowed upon it at 4 *l. per cent.*; and besides this annuity, the lenders were to have a 10 *l.* lottery ticket, by way of additional capital for every hundred pound they advanced; which additional capital was likewise to be attended with an annuity of 4 *l. per cent.* till repaid; so that, for this 6,300,000 *l.* the nation was to pay 6,930,000 *l.* with 4 *l. per cent.* interest, till the same should be repaid; which interest, it was supposed, the produce of this new subsidy would answer yearly; or, if it did not, the deficiency, as in every other case, was to be made good out of the next supplies; but, as to the principal, the payment of it was, as usual, left to some very distant future generation; for, without a breach of parliamentary faith, the *Sinking Fund* cannot be applied to the payment of any new debt, till the whole of that due in 1716 hath been paid off *.

As the subscriptions to all the loans hitherto made, had soon sold at an advanced price, by which the subscribers got considerable advantage; therefore, upon this loan, the courtiers resolved to reserve the subscription to themselves and their particular friends, by which some of the chief Jews in the city, both Hebrew and Christian, were excluded; but these last had such an interest among their friends, both at home and abroad, that they prevented their buying from, or lending money to the courtiers, to make their future payments; so that the subscriptions fell to a great discount, which obliged the parliament to suspend the two payments that should have been made April 22, and May 24, to October 22, and November 24. This was done by two resolutions agreed to April 1, and by clauses in the † *act for permitting tea to be exported to Ireland and the plantations, without paying the inland-duties*, &c. That this discount upon the subscriptions was owing to some such management as we have mentioned, and not to any want of money, is evident; because, as soon as the peace was concluded, the subscriptions rose to a premium; but we hope, it did not oblige our courtiers to accept of any conditions they would not otherwise have agreed to. For indeed, it seems, that soon after Christmas, they were resolved to have a peace at any rate; otherwise they would never have consented to that resolution which was agreed to *nem. con.* Jan. declaring that it was the opinion of that house, that the exportation of corn to foreign parts, was very beneficial to this kingdom, *and ought not to be prohibited at that time.* As there was then a perfect famine

* See p. 201. † See chap. 14, of this session.

all over the kingdom of France, one would think, that it was then a very proper time to do as the parliament and government did in the 8th year of Queen Anne, by prohibiting for a year the exportation of corn, and taking all poſſible care that the enemy ſhould not be ſupplied with it from Dantzick, Barbary, or any other place.

An act for granting to his majeſty the ſum of one million out of the Sinking Fund, for the ſervice of the year 1748; *and for applying a ſum of money remaining in the Exchequer, ariſen by the rates and duties on houſes, which determined at Lady-day*, 1747, *&c.* Chap. 23.

This act was only for applying a *million* out of the *Sinking Fund* to the current ſervice, and enabling the government to borrow the money at 4 *l. per cent.*

This ſeſſion began the 29th of November 1748, and ended the 13th of June 1749; and the ways and means for raiſing the ſupplies granted in it, were as follow: 22 Geo. II. 1748.

An act for continuing the duties on malt, &c. Chap. 1.

The loan upon this act was 750,000 *l.* at 4 *l. per cent.*

An act for granting an aid by a land-tax, &c. Chap. 2.

This tax was 4 *s.* in the pound, and the loan upon it 2,000,000 *l.* at 4 *l. per cent.*

An act to charge the Sinking Fund with the payment of annuities in diſcharge of navy, victualling, Chap. 23.

and transport bills, and ordnance debentures, to the amount therein mentioned.

By this act, the Sinking Fund was charged with the payment of annuities at 4 *l. per cent.* upon the principal sum of 3,230,382 *l.* 5 *s.* 1 *d.* for paying off the debts mentioned in the title of the act.

Chap. 42. *An act for granting to his majesty the sum of one million out of the Sinking Fund, for the service of* 1749; *and for enabling his majesty to raise the further sum of one million for the uses and purposes therein mentioned, &c.*

By this act, besides the million to be taken from the Sinking Fund, or raised upon the credit thereof at 4 *l. per cent.* his majesty was enabled to raise another *million* by loans, or Exchequer bills, at 4 *l. per cent.* from Lady-day, 1749, to be repaid out of the first supplies granted after Michaelmas 1749; or, if no sufficient supplies be granted before Midsummer 1750, to be charged upon the Sinking Fund, and replaced out of the first supplies afterwards granted. And both these sums were to be applied towards answering the supplies granted by this session.

23 Geo. II, 1749. This session began the 16th of November 1749, and ended the 12th of April 1750; and the ways and means for raising the supplies granted in it, were as follow:

Chap. 1. *An act for reducing the several annuities, which now carry an interest after the rate of* 4 l. per cent. per annum *to the several rates of interest therein mentioned.*

As there was now great plenty of money, it encouraged our ministers to form a scheme for reducing the intereſt upon all our funds to 3 *l. per cent.* for which purpoſe it was by this act enacted, that all the public creditors, at 4 *l. per cent. per annum*, amounting in the whole to 57,703,475 *l.* 6 *s.* 4 *d.* ½, who ſhould, on or before February 28, 1749, ſubſcribe their names, or ſignify their conſent, to accept of an intereſt of 3 *l. per cent. per annum* to commence December 25, 1749, ſhould have 4 *l. per cent.* until December 25, 1750, and from thence 3 *l.* 10 *l. per cent.* until December, 1757, without being liable to be redeemed.

This ſcheme was not, it ſeems, at firſt concerted with the proper perſons; for the three great companies, and moſt of our rich Hebrew, as well as Chriſtian Jews, at firſt refuſed to come into it; but the chief leaders of theſe great bodies of men being ſoon after, we ſuppoſe, properly talked to, they were all brought into the ſcheme, and moſt of theſe public creditors had ſubſcribed before the day appointed; and, as to thoſe who had not ſubſcribed, they were by a reſolution of the committee of ways and means, and a new act paſſed in purſuance of it, allowed to ſubſcribe on or before May 30, 1750; but then, by way of puniſhment for their obſtinacy, their yearly intereſt was to be reduced to 3 *l. per cent.* at Chriſtmas 1755; which moſt of them ſubmitted to before the ſaid 30th of May; and thus was carried into execution one of the moſt beneficial ſchemes, that has, for a long time, been ſet on foot in this country.

An act for granting an aid by a land-tax for the year 1750. Chap. 2.

This tax was 3 *s.* in the pound, and the loan upon it 1,500,000 *l.* at 3 *l. per cent. per annum.*

Chap. 3. *An act for continuing the duties on malt, &c.*

The loan upon this act was 750,000 *l.* at 3 *l.* *per cent.*

Chap. 16. *An act for granting to his majesty the sum of one million, to be raised by annuities at* 3 l. per cent. per annum, *and charged on the Sinking Fund, transferrable at the Bank of England.*

As this nation, by the punctual payment of the interest growing due upon our public debts for so many years, is now become the common repository or sink for the money of almost all those idle drones throughout Europe, who resolve to live upon the interest of their money, without employing it, either in trade, manufactures, or land, by which the poor are employed, and get a living, it became so plenty here, that the government found they could already borrow all they wanted at 3 *l. per cent.*; therefore neither the land, nor the malt-tax acts of this year, allowed of a higher than that interest; and the subscription for the purchase of annuities at 3 *l. per cent.* was filled as soon as opened; as the first payment of the purchase-money was only 10 *l. per cent.* to be made April 20, and the last payment of 25 *l. per cent.* not till December 18, 1750, whereas the annuity was to commence from Lady-day 1750.

Chap. 21. *An act for granting to his majesty the sum of* 900,000 l. *out of the Sinking Fund, for the service of* 1750; *and for applying certain surplus-monies, remaining in the Exchequer, as part of the supply of the said year, &c.*

Besides the 900,000 *l.* to be issued out of the Sinking Fund, or raised at 3 *l. per cent.* upon the credit of this act, for the current service, the following ſurpluſſes, remaining in the Exchequer, after ſatisfying all payments and annuities due thereon, were applied to the ſame uſe, *viz.*

	l.	*s.*	*d.*
Surplus of the additional duties at Chriſtmas laſt, upon all wines imported,	17,553	10	10
Ditto at Michaelmas laſt, of the duties upon houſes, windows, and lights, and on coaches and other carriages,	29,856	1	11½
Ditto at Michaelmas laſt, of the ſubſidy of tonnage and poundage, on goods and merchandizes imported,	71,116	17	6
	118,526	10	3½

This act likewiſe directed, that the ſum of 65,674 *l.* 8 *s.* 6 *d.* ſavings on forage, *&c.* for the troops of Ruſſia, and the ſubſidies to the landgrave of Heſſe-Caſſel, elector of Bavaria, and duke of Wolfenbuttle, and the ſum of 46,849 *l.* 11 *s.* 10 *d.* ſavings from the pay of the land forces, ſhould be applied towards the expences of t' e land forces in 1749. But, as theſe ſums were to be taken out of the ſavings upon other articles, then in the hands of the paymaſter-general, we have not ſtated them, as they were not to be provided for by this ſeſſion in any other way than by directing how thoſe ſavings ſhould be applied.

An act for making good a deficiency upon the revenue of the office of keeper or clerk of the hanaper, *and for preventing any future deficiency therein, to anſwer the public ſervices provided for out of* Chap. 25.

the same; and for augmenting the income of the office of master or keeper of the Rolls.

By this act, the new stamp-duty first imposed by 12 Geo. I, chap. 33, which had been allowed to expire in 1746, as the deficiencies charged upon it were all then satisfied, with a surplus of 13,698 *l.* 1 *s.* 11 *d.* over, was revived, and continued from the 24th of June 1750, *for ever.* Out of the surplus then in the Bank, the debt of the *hanaper* office was by this act directed to be paid; and the residue, together with the yearly produce, was made a fund for the 3000 *l. per ann.* granted to that office and the *Master of the Rolls.* The following recital in this act will explain the nature of the abovementioned debt due to the *hanaper*, viz. "And "whereas the office of keeper, or clerk of "the *hanaper* in Chancery, is a very ancient "office, held and enjoyed by grant from his "majesty's royal predecessors, kings and queens "of this realm; and the yearly revenue thereof, "consisting of several certain yearly rents or "sums, reserved upon grants made by the "crown of the several offices, commonly called "the Seal, or Green-wax office, the Alienation "Office, and the Six-penny Writ Office, in "Chancery the (grant of which last-mentioned "office is now expired and determined) and "also of fees paid upon grants, commissions, "and other patents, passing under the great "seal, which are uncertain and contingent, "hath constantly been issued and applied in and "for the payment of several ancient fees, salaries, and allowances belonging to the lord-"chancellor, or lord-keeper of the Great Seal, "the master of the Rolls, the masters in Chan-"cery, clerk of the parliaments, and other "officers attending the parliament and Great "Seal, and of several bills and disbursements,

" always paid and allowed out of the revenues " of the Hanaper office: and whereas the office " of maſter or keeper of the Rolls, is an office " of great truſt and conſequence to the public, " and the revenue belonging thereto is not " adequate to the trouble, dignity, and impor- " tance of the ſaid office; and whereas the in- " come or revenue of the ſaid office of the " *hanaper*, hath not for ſeveral years laſt paſt, " been ſufficient to anſwer and pay the ſeveral " fees, ſalaries, allowances, and diſburſements, " iſſuing and payable out of the ſame; and " and there remained due, and in arrear, at " Michaelmas 1749, to the ſeveral perſons " claiming and intitled to ſuch fees, ſalaries, " allowances, and diſburſements reſpectively, " ſeveral ſums of money, amounting together " to the ſum of 10,590*l.* 12*s.* 11*d.* and, as the " revenue of the *hanaper* office will, in all pro- " bability, ſtill continue to be deficient, not " only the preſent debt upon the ſaid office " will be loſt, but the ſervices to which the " ſame for the future are to be applied, will " remain unprovided for," *&c.*

This ſeſſion began the 17th of January 1750, and ended the 25th of June 1751; and the ways and means for raiſing the ſupplies granted in it, were as follow: 24 G. II. 1750.

An act for continuing the duties on malt, &c. Chap. 1.

The loan upon this act was 750,000*l.* at 3*l.* *per cent.*

An act for granting to his majeſty the ſum of 2,100,000*l.* *to be raiſed by annuities and a lot-* Chap. 2.

tery, and charged on the Sinking Fund, redeemable by parliament.

This act directed that the sum of 1,400,000*l.* should be raised by annuities at 3l. *per cent. per annum*, payable at the South-Sea house half yearly; and the sum of 700,000*l.* by a lottery at 10*l.* per ticket.

N. B. *The charges of management allowed the company on these annuities are* 1,181*l.* 5*s.* per annum.

Chap. 7. *An act for granting an aid by a land-tax for* 1751.

This tax was 3*s.* in the pound, and the loan upon it 1,500,000*l.* at 3*l.* *per cent.*

Chap. 4. *An act for enabling his majesty to raise the several sums of money therein mentioned, by Exchequer bills to be charged on the sinking fund; and for impowering the commissioners of the Treasury to pay off the old and new unsubscribed South-Sea annuities out of the supply granted to his majesty for the service of* 1751, &c.

By this act the Treasury were impowered to agree with the Bank for raising the several sums of 1,013,148*l.* 4*s.* 6*d.* and 176,893*l.* 11*s.* 7*d.* by Exchequer bills at 3*l.* *per cent. per ann.* to be charged on the sinking fund.

Chap. 11. *An act for reducing the interest of the capital stock of the South-sea company, from the time and upon the terms therein mentioned*, &c.

By this act, the South-sea company were to receive 4*l.* per cent. on their capital stock, until the 25th of December 1757; and from thence only 3 *l.* per cent.

An act for granting to his majesty an additional duty upon spirituous liquors, and upon licences for retailing the same; and for repealing the act of 20 Geo. II. ch. 39, *&c.* Chap. 46.

The reason of making this act, appears in the preamble to it, which is as follows: "Whereas the immoderate drinking of distilled "spirituous liquors, by persons of the meanest "and lowest sort, hath of late years increased, "to the great detriment of the health and mo-"rals of the common people; and the same "hath, in a great measure, been owing to the "number of persons who have obtained licen-"ces to retail the same, under pretence of being "distillers, and of those who have presumed to "retail the same without licence, more espe-"cially in the cities of London and Westmin-"ster, the borough of Southwark, and other "places within the weekly bills of mortality, "contrary to the good and wholesome laws "heretofore made for preventing thereof: and "whereas we your majesty's dutiful and loyal "subjects the Commons of Great Britain in "parliament assembled, ever attentive to the "preservation and health of your majesty's "subjects, have taken this great evil into our "serious consideration, and proposed such laws "and provisions, as appear to us to be most "likely to put a stop to the same; but it may so "happen, that in consequence of the necessary "regulations for that purpose, there may "accrue a failure or deficiency in the respective "funds to which the duties charged upon "spirituous liquors and distiller's licences, "were appropriated and applicable: now for "the more effectual restraining such abuses, "and to the end that such failure, or defi-"ciency, may be made good; and that the "public faith, so essential to the well-being of "this kingdom, may be supported, *&c.*"

The following duties of excise are hereby granted, from and after the 1st of July 1751, (over and above all duties, charges, and impositions, by any former acts respectively set, rated, and imposed) viz.

For every gallon of low wines, or spirits of the first extraction, made or drawn from any sort of drink, or wash, brewed, or made from any sort of malt, or corn, or from brewers wash, or tilts, or any mixture with such brewers wash, or tilts, to be paid by the distillers, or makers thereof, 3 half-pence.

For every gallon of low-wines, or spirits of the first extraction, made or drawn from cyder, or any sort or kind of British materials, except those before mentioned, or any mixture therewith, to be paid by the distillers or makers thereof, 1 *d.* three farthings.

For every gallon of strong water, or aquavitæ, made for sale, of the materials aforesaid, or any of them, to be paid by the distillers, or makers thereof, 4 *d.* halfpenny.

For every gallon of spirits made for sale, from cyder, or any sort or kind of British materials, except those before mentioned, to b paid by the distillers, or makers thereof, 3 *d.* ½.

The duty of 5 *l.* payable by every distiller for a licence to sell spirituous liquors by retail, granted by the 20th of Geo. II. ch. 39. is hereby repealed, from and after the 24th of June 1751; and no distiller is permitted to sell any spirituous liquors, mixed or unmixed, with any ingredients by retail, after the said time; the act setting forth, that the permitting distillers to take out licences for the retailing spirituous liquors, has greatly tended to increase the drinking of spirituous liquors; many of them suffering the same to be drank in their shops contrary to the directions of the said act of 20 Geo. II. ch. 39.

An act for granting to his majesty the sum of 600,000 l. out of the sinking fund, for the service of 1751, &c. Chap. 47.

By this act the treasury were impowered to make new Exchequer bills for raising the said sum of 600,000 l. at 3 l. *per cent.* to be charged on the sinking fund.

This session began the 14th of November 1751, and ended the 26th of March 1752; and the ways and means for raising the supplies granted in it, were as follow: 25 Geo. II, 1751.

An act for continuing the duties on malt, &c. Chap. 1.

The loan upon this act was 750,000*l.* at 3*l.* *per cent. per annum.*

An act for granting an aid to his majesty by a land-tax for 1752. Chap. 3.

This tax was 3*s.* in the pound, and the loan upon it 1,500,000*l.* at 3*l.* *per cent. per annum.*

An act for granting to his majesty a certain sum of money therein mentioned, out of the Sinking Fund, and for enabling his majesty to raise a further sum of money therein also mentioned, by Exchequer bills, to be charged on the said Sinking Fund, for the service of 1752, &c. Chap. 25.

By this act the sum of 500,000*l.* was to be issued out of the Sinking Fund for the current service; and the Bank was obliged to advance the further sum of 1,400,000*l.* at 3*l.* *per cent.* interest to be charged on the Sinking Fund.

Chap. 27. *An act for converting the several annuities therein mentioned into several joint stocks of annuities, transferrable at the Bank of England, to be charged on the Sinking Fund; and also for consolidating the several other annuities therein mentioned, into several joint stock of annuities, transferrable at the South-Sea house.*

This act recites that in pursuance of 4 Geo. II. chap. 9. for raising 1,200,000 *l.* by annuities and a lottery, several persons did advanced and lend 800,000 *l.* part of the said 1,200,000 *l.* upon the credit of the duties in the said act mentioned for the purchase of annuities, after the rate of 3 *l. per cent.* transferrable at the Bank of England, and redeemable by parliament; and, that in pursuance of an act of 15 Geo. II. chap 19. for raising 800,000 *l.* to be raised by annuities transferrable at the Bank of England, several persons did advance and lend the said sum of 800,000 *l.* upon the credit of the surplusses, excesses or overplus-monies, commonly called the *Sinking Fund*, by the said act granted and appropriated in that behalf, for the purchase of annuities after the rate of 3 *l. per cent.* transferrable at the Bank of England, and redeemable by parliament; that, in pursuance of another act of 16 Geo. II. chap. 13. for raising by annuities and a lottery, the sum of 1,800,000 *l.* at 3 *l.* per *per cent. per annum*, for the service of 1743, several persons did advance and lend the said sum of 1,800,000 *l.* upon the credit of the duties therein mentioned, for the purchase of annuities after the rate of 3 *l. per cent.* transferrable at the Bank of England, and redeemable by parliament; that, by 17 Geo. II. chap. 18. for raising the sum of 1,800,000 *l.* at 3 *l. per cent. per ann.* for the service of the year 1744, several persons did advance and lend the sum of 1,800,000 *l.* upon the credit therein mentioned, for the purchase of annuities after the rate of 3 *l.* *per cent.* transferrable at the Bank of England, and redeemable by parliament; that, by 18 Geo. II. ch. 9. several persons did advance and lend the sum of 2,000,000 *l.* for the purchase of annuities, after the rate of 3 *l.* *per cent. per ann.* transferrable at the Bank of England, and redeemable by parliament; that by 23 Geo. II. ch. 18. several persons did advance and lend the sum of 1,000,000 *l.* upon the credit therein mentioned, for the purchase of annuities after the rate of 3 *l.* *per cent. per ann.* transferrable at the Bank of England, and redeemable by parliament; that the said principal sums, for which the said several annuities, now carrying an interest of 3 *l.* *per cent. per ann.* transferrable at the Bank, are payable, do amount in the whole, to the sum of 8,200,000 *l.* and it is thought necessary, that the said principal sum be (with the consent of the proprietors thereof, to be signified within the time herein after mentioned;) converted into one joint stock of annuities, and that the interest, or annuities, shall be paid out of the produce of the sinking fund, until redemption thereof by parliament, in manner herein after mentioned; and that the several duties and revenues, which were given and granted for payment of the said annuities, and on which the same were charged, shall be carried into, and made part of the said sinking fund: and the commons being of opinion, that it will be of advantage to the public, and also a great convenience to the proprietors of the said annuities, if the same were consolidated into one joint stock of annuities, *&c.* be it therefore enacted, *&c.* that after the 24th of June, 1752, and before the 5th of January, 1753, the several sums afore mentioned, amounting to 8,200,000 *l.* carrying an intereſt after the rate of 3 *l. per. cent. per ann.* ſhall be converted into one joint ſtock of annuities, transferrable at the Bank of England, in the ſame manner and form as the ſaid ſeveral and reſpective annuities are now transferred, until redemption thereof by parliament, in manner herein after mentioned.

And §. 11. of this act recites, that in purſuance of 19 Geo. II. chap. 12. ſeveral perſons did advance and lend upon the credit of the rates and duties therein mentioned, the principal ſum of 3,000,000 *l.* for the purchaſe of annuities transferrable at the Bank of England, and redeemable by parliament; which ſum of 3,000,000 *l.* is now reduced to the principal ſum of 2,824,428 *l.* 13 *s.* 11 *d.* attended with annuities after the rate of 3 *l. per cent.* purſuant to certain acts of parliament in that behalf; that, by another act, 20 Geo. II. chap. 3. ſeveral perſons did advance and lend upon the credit of the duties therein mentioned, the principal ſum of 4,000,000 *l.* for the purchaſe of annuities transferrable at the Bank of England, upon which (for the encouragement of perſons who ſhould advance and lend the ſame) there was an allowance of 10 *l. per cent.* ſo that the capital ſum amounted to the ſum of 4,400,000 *l.* redeemable by parliament; which ſum of 4,400,000 *l.* is now reduced to the principal ſum of 4,189,365 *l.* 5 *s.* attended with annuities at 3 *l.* 10 *s.* purſuant to certain acts of parliament in that behalf, that by another act of 20 Geo. II. chap. 10. ſeveral perſons did advance and lend upon the credit of the duties therein mentioned, the principal ſum of 1,000,000 *l.* for the purchaſe of annuities. transferrable at the Bank of England, and redeemable by parliament; which ſum of 1,000,000 *l.* is now reduced to the principal ſum of 921,276 *l.* 10 *s.* 6 *d.* attended with annuities after the rate of 3 *l.* 10 *s. per cent.*

pursuant to certain acts of parliament in that behalf; that by an act of 21 Geo. II. c. 2. several persons did advance and lend the principal sum of 6,300,000 *l.* for the purchase of annuities transferrable at the bank of England; and for the encouragement of all persons who should advance and lend the same, there was an advance of 630,000 *l.* being 10 *l. per cent.* on the said sum contributed; so that the whole capital sum amounted to the sum of 6,930,000*l.* redeemable by parliament; which said sum of 6,930,000 *l.* is now reduced to the principal sum of 6,660,006 *l.* 18 *s.* 3 *d.* attended with annuities, after the rate of 3 *l.* 10 *s.* *per cent.* pursuant to certain acts of parliament in that behalf; that, by an act of 22 Geo. II. chap. 23. certain persons who were possessed of navy, victualling, and transport bills, and ordnance debentures, to the amount of 3,072,472*l.* 10*d.* for annuities transferrable there, and redeemable by parliament; which said sum of 3,072,472 *l.* 10*d.* is now reduced to the principal sum of 2,968,496 *l.* 8 *s.* 8 *d.* attended with annuities after the rate of 3 *l.* 10 *s.* *per cent.* pursuant to certain acts of parliament in that behalf; that the principal sums before mentioned, now carrying an interest of 3 *l.* 10 *s.* *per cent. per ann.* transferrable at the Bank of England, as aforesaid, do amount, in the whole, to the sum of 17,571,573*l.* 16 *s.* 4 *d.* whereof the sum of 14,857,955*l.* 18 *s.* 4 *d.* was first subscribed, in pursuance of 23 Geo. II. chap. 1. for an annuity of 3 *l.* 10 *s.* *per cent.* until the 25th of December, 1757, which will be the 5th of December, 1758; and from and after the said 25th of December, 1757, for annuities of 3 *l. per cent.* and the residue thereof, amounting to the sum of 2.713,617 *l.* 18 *s.* was last subscribed, in pursuance of another act of the ſame ſeſſion of parliament, for an annuity of 3*l.* 10*s.* *per cent.* until the 25th of December, 1755, which will be the 5th of January, 1756, and from and after the 25th of December, 1755, for annuities of 3 *l.* *per cent.*; and, whereas it is likewiſe thought neceſſary, that the ſeveral principal ſums, amounting to the ſum of 14,857,955 *l.* 18 *s.* 4 *d.* ſhall be converted into one joint ſtock of annuities, the intereſt or annuity to be charged, and chargeable upon the ſinking fund; and that the ſaid ſeveral principal ſums, amounting to the ſum of 2,713,617 *l.* 18 *s.* be, with the conſent of the proprietors thereof, converted into one other joint ſtock of annuities; the intereſt, or annuity, to be charged upon the ſaid ſinking fund; and that, from and after the fifth of April, 1758, the ſaid intended joint ſtock of 14,857,955 *l.* 18 *s.* 4 *d.* together with the intended joint ſtock of 2,713,617*l.* 18*s.* or ſo much thereof as ſhall be then unſatisfied, ſhall be one joint ſtock of annuities; and that the ſeveral duties and revenues, which were given and granted for the payment of the ſaid annuities, and on which the ſame were charged, ſhall be carried into, and made part of the ſaid ſinking fund: it is therefore enacted, *&c.* that, after the 10th of October, 1752, and before the 5th of April, 1753, the ſaid ſeveral annuities, amounting to 14,857,955*l.* 18*s.* 4*d.* may be conſolidated and made one joint ſtock of annuities, transferrable at the Bank of England; and that the ſaid ſeveral annuities, amounting to 2,713,617*l.* 18 *s.* may, after the ſaid 10th of October, 1752, and before the ſaid 5th of April, 1753, be conſolidated and made one other joint ſtock annuities, transferrable at the Bank of England, in the ſame manner as the ſaid ſeveral and reſpective annuities are now transferrable, until the redemption thereof by parliament in manner after mentioned.

And this act provides, that from and after the said 5th day of April, 1758, the joint stock of the first subscribed Old South-Sea annuities, with as much of the joint stock of the second subscribed Old South-Sea annuities as shall be then unsatisfied, shall be made one joint stock of Old South-Sea annuities; and, from the said 5th of January 1758, the joint stock of the first subscribed New South-Sea annuities, with so much of the joint stock of the second subscribed New South-Sea annuities as shall be then unsatisfied, shall be made into one new joint stock of South-Sea annuities.

This session began the 11th of January 1752, and ended the 7th of June 1753; and the ways and means for raising the supplies granted in it, were as follow: 26 Geo. II. 1752.

An act for continuing the duties, on malt, &c. Chap. 1.

An act for granting an aid by a land-tax, &c. Chap. 4.

This tax was 2 *s.* in the pound.

An act for granting to his majesty a certain sum of money therein mentioned, out of the Sinking Fund; and for applying certain surplus-monies remaining in the Exchequer for the service of the year 1753; *and for the further appropriating the supplies,* &c. Chap. 23.

By this act the sum of 420,000*l.* was granted out of the Sinking Fund, together with the following sums remaining in the Exchequer, *viz.*

	l.	s.	d.
On the two seventh parts of the additional excise granted in the 5th year of Will. and Mary,	100,482	14	3 ½
Surplus of the funds for the lottery of 1714,	79,812	16	0
Surplus of the additional duties on low wines, &c. granted by 16 and 24 Geo. II.	54,580	9	0
Overplus of the grants unappropriated, for the year 1752,	18,035	9	0 ¾
	252,911	8	4 ¼

27 Geo. II, 1753. This session began the 15th of November 1753, and ended the 6th of April 1754; and the ways and means for raising the supplies granted in it, were as follow:

Chap. 2. *An act for continuing the duties on malt,* &c.

Chap. 4. *An act for granting an aid by a land-tax for the year* 1754.

This tax was 2*s.* in the pound.

Chap. 10. *An act for granting to his majesty a certain sum of money therein mentioned, out of the Sinking Fund; and applying certain surplus-monies remaining in the Exchequer for the service of* 1754; *and for the further disposition of the said Sinking Fund, by paying thereout the remainder of the sum advanced on the credit of the duty on sweets, and the interest thereof,* &c.

By this act the sum of 700,000 *l.* was granted out of the Sinking Fund; together with the following sums remaining in the Exchequer, *viz.*

	l.	s.	d.
Overplus of the laſt year's grants,	7,937	14	2½
Surplus of the duty on coals,	23,562	7	9½
Surplus of the duties for retailing ſpirituous liquors,	32,652	15	7
Surplus of the funds of the lottery 1714,	30,159	3	6½
	94,312	1	1½

And this act further provided, that the ſum of 499,600 *l.* ſhould be iſſued out of the Sinking Fund to the Bank, to cancel and diſcharge Exchequer bills, made out in purſuance of 10 Geo. II, chap. 17, and charged upon the duty on ſweets; as alſo ſuch ſum, or ſums of money, as ſhall, from time to time, become due, and payable for intereſt upon the ſaid Exchequer bills, until the ſame ſhould be paid off, or money ſufficient ſhould be reſerved for that purpoſe.

This ſeſſion began the 14th of November 1754, and ended the 25th of April 1755; and the ways and means for raiſing the ſupplies granted in it, were as follow: 28 Geo. II, 1754.

An act for continuing the duties on malt, &c. Chap. 2.

An act for granting an aid by a land-tax for 1755. Chap. 5.

This tax was 2 *s.* in the pound.

An act for granting to his majeſty the ſum of 1,000,000 l. to be raiſed by a lottery. Chap. 15.

The annuities granted by this act, in reſpect of the principal ſum of 900,000 *l.* part of the said principal sum of one million, were charged upon, and payable out of the Sinking Fund, and to carry interest at 3 *l. per cent.* to commence from January 5, 1756, and payable half-yearly.

Chap. 22. *An act for granting to his majesty a certain sum of money therein mentioned, out of the Sinking Fund, and for applying certain monies remaining in the Exchequer, for the service of the year 1755; and for carrying the surplus of certain duties to the Sinking Fund; and for the further appropriating the supplies granted in this session of parliament.*

By this act, the sum of 1,420,000 *l.* was to be raised at 3 *l. per cent. per annum* upon the credit of the Sinking Fund; and the following sums remaining in the Exchequer were directed to be issued in aid of the supply, *viz.*

	l.	*s.*	*d.*
Overplus of the last year's grants,	3,341	19	2¼
Surplus of the duties on coals,	16,494	17	10½
Surplus of duties for retailing spirituous liquors,	19,923	12	9
Surplus of the funds of the lottery 1714,	28,201	19	8
	67,962	9	5¾

This act further directed, that from and after the 5th day of July 1755, the surplus, or over-plus monies of the duties on coals and culm, granted by 1 Geo. II, chap 8, and also the surplus, or overplus-monies, of the duties and revenues on soap, paper, linens, silks, callicoes, and stuffs, and upon starch and exported coals, and upon ſtampt vellum, parchment, and paper, firſt granted by 12 Ann. chap. 9, (after payment of the annuity charged upon them by 2 Geo. II, chap. 3.) ſhould be carried to, and made part of the Sinking Fund.

This ſeſſion began the 13th of November 1755, and ended the 15th of July 1756; and the ways and means for raiſing the ſupplies granted in it, were as follow: 29 Geo. II, 1755.

An act for continuing the duties on malt, &c. Chap. 1.

An act for granting an aid by a land-tax for the year 1756. Chap. 2.

This tax was 4 *s.* in the pound.

An act for granting to his majeſty the ſum of two millions, to be raiſed by way of annuities and a lottery, and charged on the Sinking Fund, redeemable by parliament, &c. Chap. 7.

By this act, the ſum of 1,500,000 *l.* was to be raiſed by annuities, at 3 *l.* 10 *s. per cent.* intereſt; and 500,000 *l.* by a lottery, at 3 *l. per cent.* The annuities were to commence from February 11, 1756; and the intereſt on the tickets from January 5, 1757, payable half-yearly.

An act for granting to his majeſty a duty upon licences for retailing beer, ale, and other exciſeable liquors, &c. Chap. 12.

By this act, an additional ſtamp duty of 20 *s.* was laid on licences for retailing beer, and other exciſeable liquors, and the produce of ſuch duty was to be carried into the Sinking Fund, towards making good the intereſt of two millions, charged on the ſaid fund by chap. 7, of this ſeſſion.

Chap. 13. *An act for granting to his majesty an additional duty on cards and dice.*

This act recites the 9th of Ann. chap. 23, 10 Ann. chap. 19, 5 Geo. I, chap. 19, 6 Geo. I, chap. 25, and 3 Geo. I, chap. 7; and enacts, that there shall be paid for every pack of cards, the sum of 6 *d.* over and above the duty of 6 *d.* payable for the same; and for every pair of dice, the sum of 5 *s.* over and above the duty of 5 *s.* payable thereupon. The duties granted shall be carried to, and made part of the Sinking Fund, towards making good the interest of the sum of two millions charged thereupon by chap. 7, before mentioned.

Chap. 14. *An act for granting to his majesty several rates and duties payable by all persons, and bodies politic or corporate, having certain quantities of silver plate.*

By this act it is enacted, that after July 5, 1756, shall be paid by all persons, and bodies politic or corporate, for all silver plate which they shall own, use, have, or keep, these several annual duties, *viz.* for every hundred ounces troy weight, and not amounting to 200, 5 *s.* for 200, 10 *s.* and so 5 *s.* more for every hundred ounces to the number of 4000; and for 4000 ounces and upwards, shall be paid the sum of 10 *l.* the same to be under the management of the commissioners of excise. But plate belonging to places of religious worship, and only used there shall not be charged. The neat produce of this duty, for the years 1757, 1758, and 1759, as appears from the books at the Excise office, was as follows:

	l.	s.	d.
For the year 1757 - -	21,923	10	4
———— 1758 - -	20,732	7	4
———— 1759 - -	18,844	19	1¾
	61,500	16	9¾

An act for granting to his majesty certain sums of money out of the Sinking Fund, and applying certain monies remaining in the Exchequer for the service of the year 1756. Chap. 24.

By this act, the following sums were directed to be applied to the current service, *viz.*

	l.	s.	d.
Surplus of the Sinking Fund, remaining in the Exchequer, for the quarter, ending April 5, 1756	255,955	11	11½
Out of the growing produce of the said fund,	1,300,000	0	0
Remaining in the Exchequer unappropriated,	83,412	2	5½
	1,639,367	14	5

An act for enabling his majesty to raise one million for the purpose therein mentioned; and for further appropriating the supplies, &c. Chap. 29.

By this act, the sum of one million was to be raised by Exchequer bills, in the same manner as in the malt-act of this session is directed to be repaid out of the next supplies; and, if none sufficient be granted before July 5, 1757, they are to be charged upon, and paid out of the Sinking Fund; and the monies issued thereout, to be replaced out of the first supplies.

30. Geo. II, 1756. This session began the 2d of December 1756, and ended the 4th of July 1757; and the ways and means for raising the supplies granted in it, were as follow:

Chap. 3. *An act for granting an aid by a land-tax, for 1757.*

This tax was 4 *s.* in the pound.

Chap. 4. *An act for continuing the duties on malt,* &c.

Chap. 5. *An act for granting to his majesty a sum not exceeding* 1,050,005 *l.* 5 *s. to be raised by way of lottery.*

The tickets in this lottery were 1 *l.* 1 *s.* each.

Chap. 19. *An act for granting to his majesty several rates and duties upon indentures, leases, bonds, and other deeds; and upon news-papers, advertisements and almanacks; and upon licences for retailing wine; and upon coals exported to foreign parts; and for applying, from a certain time, the sums of money arising from the surplus of the duties on licences for retailing spirituous liquors; and for raising the sum of three millions, by annuities, to be charged on the said rates, duties, and sums of money,* &c.

By this act, every subscriber of 100 *l.* was intitled to an annuity after the rate of 3 *l. per cent. per annum,* transferrable at the Bank of England, and redeemable by parliament; and also to an annuity for life, after the rate of 1 *l.* 2 *s.* 6 *d. per cent. per annum.* The 3 *l. per cent.* annuities to commence from July 5, 1757, and to be paid half yearly.

An act for enabling his majesty to raise the sum of one million, for the uses and purposes therein mentioned. Chap. 23.

By this act, the sum of one million was granted to his majesty, to defray any extraordinary expences of the war, incurred, or to be incurred; and his majesty, by warrant under his sign-manual, may authorize the Treasury to take in loans, or issue Exchequer bills, for the said sum, in the same manner, as loans, or Exchequer bills, are to be taken, or made by the land-tax act of this session: and the Bank was impowered to lend his majesty the said sum, on the credit of this act; such loans, with the interest, to be paid out of the first supplies; and, if none shall be granted before July 5, 1758, out of the Sinking Fund; and the monies issued to be replaced out of the first supplies.

An act for granting to his majesty a certain sum of money out of the Sinking Fund, and applying certain monies remaining in the Exchequer, and the savings out of the monies graneted in this session of parliament for the pay of the troops of Hanover, *for the service of the year* 1757, *and for further appropriating the supplies*, &c. Chap. 26.

By this act, the following sums were directed to be issued for the current service, *viz.*

	l.	*s.*	*d.*
Out of the Sinking Fund	300,000	0	0
Surplus remaining in the Exchequer of the said fund, on April 5, 1757,	50,491	17	8
Out of the said fund, as the same shall arise into the Exchequer,	849,508	2	3½
	1,199,999	19	11½

	l.	s.	d.
Brought forward	1,199,999	19	11½
Surplus remaining in the Exchequer of the duties on licences for retailing ſpirituous liquors,	16,190	5	3
Overplus remaining in the Exchequer of the grants,	140,568	5	2½
Savings in the pay of the troops of Hanover,	19,416	14	9½
	1,376,175	5	2½

31 Geo. II, 1757. This ſeſſion began the 1ſt of December 1757, and ended the 3d of Auguſt 1758; and the ways and means for raiſing the ſupplies granted in it, were as follow:

Chap. 2. *An act for continuing the duties on malt*, &c.

Chap. 4. *An act for granting an aid by a land-tax for* 1758.

This tax was 4 *s.* in the pound.

Chap. 22. *An act for granting to his majeſty ſeveral rates and duties upon offices and penſions; and upon houſes; and upon windows or lights; and for raiſing the ſum of five millions by annuities, and a lottery, to be charged on the ſaid rates and duties.*

By this act, employments of profit, penſions, and gratuities, exceeding 100 *l. per annum*, were to pay 1 *s.* per pound; and the following rates were charged upon houſes, windows. or lights, *viz.* 1 *s.* additional duty upon every dwelling-houſe in England, and 1 *s.* upon every dwelling-houſe in Scotland; and 6 *d.* additional duty for every window, or light in every dwelling-houſe containing 15 windows, or more. And the ſum of 4,500,000 *l.* was to be raised by annuities, at 3 *l.* 10 *s. per cent.* and 500,000 *l.* by a lottery at 3 *l. per cent.* payable out of, and to be charged upon the said additional and new duties. The 3 and a half *per cent.* annuities, were to be deemed one capital or joint stock, and made transferrable; and are not redeemable, till after the expiration of 24 years, from the 5th of July, 1758; and the 3 *l. per cent.* annuities were to be made a joint stock, with annuities of like value incorporated by * 25 Geo. II, chap. 27.

An act for granting to his majesty a certain sum of money out of the Sinking Fund for the service of 1758, &c. *and for obliging the retailers of wines, commonly called* sweets, *or* made wines, *to take out a wine licence.* Chap. 31.

This act directed that the following sums should be issued out of the Exchequer towards the supply for 1758, *viz.*

	l.	*s.*	*d.*
Out of the surplusses of the Sinking Fund,	300,000	0	0
Surplus-monies remaining in the Exchequer of the said fund for the quarter ending Oct. 10, 1757,	93,371	11	7¾
Like surplus remaining in the Exchequer, for the quarter ending April 5, 1758,	492,400	8	3
Out of the growing produce of the Sinking Fund	1,606,076	5	1¼
	2,491,848	5	0

* See p. 308.

And by this act it is enacted, that after July 5, 1758, no person whatsoever, unless he be authorized, and enabled by having taken out a licence, as by * 30 Geo. II, chap. 19, is directed, subject to the payment of such duties as are, in the said act, charged upon licences to sell wine by retail, shall sell, or utter by any retail-measure, or in bottles, in any quantity less than 25 gallons, any kind of liquor made in Great-Britain, by infusion, fermentation, or otherwise, from foreign fruit or sugar, or from British fruit or sugar, mixed with any other ingredients, commonly called *sweets*, or *made wines*; or any kind of liquor made in Great-Britain, and known by the name of *sweets*, or, *made wines*, of whatsoever materials, or in whatsoever manner, the same may be made, upon pain to forfeit for every such offence, 100 *l.*

Chap. 32. *An act for repealing the duty granted by* 6 Geo. I, chap. 11, *on silver-plate, made, wrought, touched, assayed, or marked, in* Great-Britain; *and for granting a duty on licences, to be taken out by all persons dealing in gold or silver plate*, &c.

By this act, the duty laid upon plate by 6 † Geo. I, chap. 11, was repealed, and all traders in, and venders of plate, were to take out licences, which were to be granted upon paying 40 *s.* for each licence.

Chap. 33. *An act for enabling his majesty to raise the sum of* 800,000 l. *for the uses and purposes therein mentioned; and for further appropriating the supplies*, &c.

By this act, his majesty, by warrant under his sign-manual, was enabled, at any time before

* See p. 320. † See p. 217.

January 5, 1759, to authorize the commissioners of the Treasury to raise the said sum, either by loans, or Exchequer bills; the money so raised, to be repaid out of the first supplies; and, if none be granted before July 5, 1759, then to be paid out of the Sinking Fund.

This session began the 23d of November 1758, and ended the 2d of June 1759; and the ways and means for raising the supplies granted in it, were as follow: 32 Geo. II, 1758.

An act for granting an aid by a land-tax for 1759. Chap. 3.

This tax was 4 *s.* in the pound.

An act for continuing the duties on malt, &c. Chap. 4.

An act for granting to his majesty a subsidy of poundage upon certain goods and merchandizes to be imported into this kingdom; and an additional inland-duty on coffee and chocolate; and for raising the sum of 6,600,000 l. *by way of annuities and a lottery; to be charged on the said subsidy and inland-duty.* Chap. 10.

By this act, an additional subsidy of 12 *d.* in the pound was granted upon all tobacco, foreign linens, sugar, and other grocery, as the same is understood in the the Book of rates, except currants; East India goods, except coffee and raw silks; foreign brandy and spirits, except rum of the produce of the British sugar plantations; and paper, which shall be imported or brought into Great-Britain, according to the value or rate respectively set upon each of the said commodities by the several books of rates, or any act, or acts of parliament relating thereunto. And an additional duty of 1 *s.* per pound was laid upon coffee, and 9 *d.* per pound on chocolate; which subsidies, rates, and duties, were to be charged with annuities, which, by this act, are directed to attend, as well the principal sum of 6,600,000 *l.* and the additional capital of 5 *l.* to be added to every 100 *l.* thereof, as additional capital which will arise by 10 *l.* to be given in and by a lottery ticket, upon every 100 *l.* advanced and paid towards the said sum of 6,600,000 *l.* The annuities were to bear 3 *l.* *per cent.* interest, and to commence from January 5, 1759; and subscribers for every 100 *l.* subscribed, were intitled to a lottery-ticket to carry interest, and to commence from January 5, 1760.

Chap. 22. *An act for adding certain annuities granted in* 1757, *to the joint stock of* 3 l. per cent. *annuities, consolidated by the acts of the* 25*th*, 28*th*, *and* 29*th of* Geo. II, *and for carrying the several duties therein mentioned to the Sinking Fund; and for charging the annuities on single lives, granted in* 1757, *on the produce of the said fund.*

This act directed that the sum of 3,000,000 *l.* borrowed by virtue of * 30 Geo. II, chap. 19, should be added to the joint stock of 3 *l.* *per cent.* consolidated annuities, transferrable at the † Bank, and to be paid out of the Sinking Fund; and that the produce of the duties, granted by the said act of 30 Geo. II, chap. 19, should be made part of the Sinking Fund, and applied accordingly; and likewise, that the life-annuities granted by the said act, should be paid out of the Sinking Fund.

* See p. 320. † See 25 Geo. II, chap. 27, p. 308.

An act for granting to his majesty certain sums of money out of the Sinking Fund; and for applying certain monies remaining in the Exchequer, for the service of the year 1759, &c. Chap. 31.

By this act the following sums were to be issued out of the Exchequer for the current service, *viz.*

	l.	*s.*	*d.*
Surplus remaining in the Exchequer, of the produce of the Sinking Fund, for the quarter ending April 5, 1759,	18,076	17	0¾
A further sum not exceeding 2,250,000 *l.* to be issued and applied out of the growing produce of the said fund,	2,250,000	0	0
Surplus remaining of the sum of 100,000 *l.* granted in the last session, towards defraying the charge of pay and cloathing of the militia. [It does not appear in the act what this sum is.]			
Overplus of the grants for the year 1758,	73,308	3	10¼
Sum voted to the Empress of Russia in 1755, repaid into the Exchequer,	100,000	0	0
	2,441,385	0	11

An act for augmenting the salaries of the puisne judges in the court of King's-Bench, the judges of the court of Common-Pleas, the barons of the Coif in the court of Exchequer at Westminster, Chap. 35.

the judges in the courts of Session, and Exchequer in Scotland, and justices of Chester, and the great sessions for the counties in Wales.

By this act, additional stamp-duties were imposed upon the proceedings in the courts at Westminster, for paying the following sums to the judges, in augmentation of their salaries, *viz.* 500 *l.* to each of the puisne judges of the court of King's-Bench; 500 *l.* to each of the judges in the court of Common-Pleas; 1000 *l.* to the chief baron of the Exchequer; 500 *l.* to each of the other barons of the Coif; 200 *l.* to the chief justice of Chester; 150 *l.* to the second justice of Chester; 150 *l.* to each of the Welch judges, to be paid yearly, as the salaries have accustomarily been paid; and, if the duties should be deficient, the Treasury may apply any unappropriated monies in the Exchequer in aid thereof. And, when any deficiency should happen, the payments to the judges were to be in proportion to the salaries respectively allowed them; and the surplus-monies of the duties were to be reserved for the future disposition of parliament.—The salaries of the judges in Scotland were to be augmented out of the duties appropriated for that purpose by 10 Ann. chap. 26, *viz.* 300 *l.* to the president of the court of Session; 300 *l.* to the chief baron of the court of Exchequer; and 200 *l.* to each of the other judges in the said courts.

Here we cannot forbear taking notice of a remarkable petition 18 Hen. VI, [*A. D.* 1430.] Rot. 27, of the judges of the King's-Bench and Common-Pleas, the justices of Assize, the king's serjeants and attorney, (there was no sollicitor-general, till Edward the Fourth's time) complaining of the lord-treasurer *Kenwoldmershe*, that he had not paid them their salaries, and given them their robes and usual fees; upon which they desired that the clerk of the Hanaper might pay them out of the first money that came into his hands, and that the collectors and receivers of the great and petty customs, in the ports of London, Bristol, and Kingston upon Hull, may have like power, and be obliged to pay them, without any delay or respite, twice a year at Easter and Michaelmas, their respective salaries; and that they may have money for their robes, twice a-year at Christmas and Whitsuntide, according to custom. But the collectors were not to be charged with the payment of these wages, till the clerk of the Hanaper had been examined by the lord-chancellor, whether he had money to pay the several sums charged on his receipt. This petition was confirmed in parliament, and accordingly writs issued to the treasurer and chamberlains of the Exchequer, to know what were the judges salaries; who returned, that they had usually paid the two chief justices *forty pounds* a-year each, and the other judges *forty marks*; that the justices of assize and king's serjeants had twenty pounds a-year, and the attorney-general ten pounds. And these several sums were accordingly paid them.

An act for enabling his majesty to raise the sum of one million for the uses and purposes therein mentioned; and for further appropriating the supplies, &c. Chap. 36.

By this act, his majesty was enabled, by warrant under his royal sign-manual, to authorize the Treasury to raise the sum of one million by loans, or Exchequer bills; to be paid out of the next supplies; and if none sufficient should be granted before July 5, 1760, then they are to be paid out of the Sinking Fund; and the monies ſo iſſued, to be replaced out of the firſt ſupplies.

33 Geo. II, 1759. This ſeſſion began the 13th of November 1759, and ended the 22d of May 1760; and the ways and means for raiſing the ſupplies granted in it, were as follow:

Chap. 1. *An act for granting an aid by a land-tax for 1760.*

This tax was 4 *s.* in the pound.

Chap. 3. *An act for continuing the duties on malt*, &c.

Chap. 7. *An act for granting to his majeſty ſeveral duties upon malt; and for raiſing the ſum of eight millions by way of annuities and a lottery to be charged on the ſaid duties*, &c.

By this act, all malt made in England was to pay 3 *d.* per buſhel, over and above all other duties payable thereon; and all malt made in Scotland was to pay three halfpence over and above all other duties; which duties were appropriated for the payment of annuities to carry 4 *l. per cent. per annum* for 21 years; and, after the expiration of that term, 3 *l. per cent.*; the 4 *l. per cent.* annuities, to take place January 5, 1760, and every ſubſcriber for 100 *l.* was intitled to a lottery-ticket, to carry 4 *l. per cent.* for 20 years, and to commence January 5, 1761.

Chap. 9. *An act for preventing the exceſſive uſe of ſpirituous liquors, by laying additional duties thereon*, &c.

This act recites, that the high price of ſpirituous liquors hath been a principal cauſe of the diminution of the home-conſumption thereof, and hath thereby greatly contributed to the health, ſobriety, and induſtry of the common people; and that therefore it is of the utmoſt importance to the public welfare, that ſome timely proviſion ſhould be made for preventing the return of all thoſe miſchiefs which muſt unavoidably enſue, in caſe ſuch ſpirituous liquors ſhould again be ſuffered to be ſold at as low a rate as formerly; and foraſmuch, as the moſt effectual and expedient method of continuing the high price of ſpirituous liquors, will be by laying a large additional duty on ſuch ſpirituous liquors; it is therefore enacted, *&c.* that the following additional duties ſhall be laid on ſpirituous liquors, *viz.*

For every gallon of low wines, or ſpirits of the firſt extraction, made or drawn from any ſort of drink or waſh, brewed or made from any ſort of malt, or corn, or from brewers waſh or tilts, or any mixture with ſuch brewers waſh or tilts, to be paid by the diſtillers, or makers thereof, 5 *d.*

For every gallon of ſtrong waters, or aqua vitæ, made for ſale of the materials aforeſaid, or any of them, to be paid by the diſtillers, or makers thereof, 1 *s.* 3 *d.*

For every gallon of low wines, or ſpirits of the firſt extraction, made, or drawn from any foreign or imported materials, or any mixture therewith, to be paid by the diſtillers, or makers thereof, 1 *s.* 3 *d.*

For every gallon of ſpirits, made or drawn from any foreign or imported materials, or any mixture therewith, to be paid by the diſtillers, or makers thereof, 8 *d.*

For every gallon of low wines, or ſpirits of the firſt extraction, made or drawn from cyder, or any ſort or kind of Britiſh materials, except thoſe before mentioned, or any mixture therewith, to be paid by the diſtillers, or makers thereof, ſixpence three farthings.

For every gallon of ſpirits made for ſale from cyder, or any ſort or kind of Britiſh materials, except thoſe before mentioned, to be paid by the diſtillers or makers thereof, 1 *s.* 1 *d.* ¾.

For every gallon of ſingle brandy ſpirits, or aqua vitæ, imported into Great-Britain from beyond the ſeas, to be paid by the importer before landing, 1 *s.*

For every gallon of brandy ſpirits, or aqua vitæ, above proof, commonly called *double brandy*, imported into Great-Britain from beyond the ſeas, to be paid by the importer before landing, 2 *s.*

Chap. 12. *An act for adding certain annuities granted in the year* 1759, *to the joint ſtock of* 3 l. per cent. *annuities, conſolidated by the acts of* 25, 28, 29, *and* 32 *years of* Geo. II, *and for carrying the duties therein mentioned to the Sinking Fund; and for cancelling ſuch lottery tickets as were made forth in purſuance of* 30 Geo. II, chap. 5, *and were not diſpoſed of.*

By this act, the principal ſum of 6,600,000 *l.* borrowed on the credit of 32 Geo. II, chap. 10, together with the additional capital of 990,000 *l.* added thereto, ſhall be made part of the joint ſtock of 3 *l. per cent.* annuities, conſolidated by acts 25, 28, 29, and 32 Geo. II, chap. 22, and the charges to be paid out of the Sinking Fund; and the duties appropriated for payment of the annuities chargeable on the ſaid principal ſums, ſhall be carried to the Sinking Fund, and made part thereof, and applied accordingly.

Chap. 18. *An act for enabling his majeſty to raiſe the ſum of one million, for the uſes and purpoſes therein mentioned, and for further appropriating the supplies granted in this session of parliament.*

By this act, his majesty was enabled to authorize the Treasury, by warrant under his sign-manual, to raise the said sum, by loans or Exchequer bills; the principal and interest, with the charges attending, to be paid out of the next supplies, and, if none sufficient be granted before July 5, 1761, then they are to be paid out of the Sinking Fund; and the monies so issued, to be replaced out of the first supplies.

An act for granting to his majesty a certain sum of money out of the Sinking Fund for the service of 1760. Chap. 21.

By this act, the sum of 2,602,706 *l.* 9 *s.* 9 *d.* was granted to his majesty out of the Sinking Fund; and the Treasury impowered to raise the same by loans, or Exchequer bills.

An act for enabling his majesty to raise a certain sum of money towards paying off and discharging the debt of the navy; and towards naval services for the year 1760. Chap. 23.

By this act, his majesty was enabled to authorize the Treasury, by warrant under his sign-manual, to raise the sum of 1,500,000 *l.* by loans, or Exchequer bills; the principal and interest, with the charges attending, to be paid out of the next supplies; and, if none sufficient be granted before July 5, 1761, they are then to be paid out of the Sinking Fund; and the monies so issued, to be replaced out of the first supplies.

This session began the 18th of November 1760, and ended the 19th of March 1761; and the ways and means for raising the supplies granted in it, were as follow: 1 Geo. III, 1760.

Chap. 1. *An act for the support of his majesty's household, and the honour and dignity of the crown of* Great-Britain.

By this act, the same funds were settled during his majesty's life, as had been settled upon * King George II, for paying the clear yearly sum of 723,000 *l.* out of the *aggregate* fund, for the support of his majesty's household, and of the honour and dignity of the crown, during the continuance of the several annuities of 50,000 *l.* to the Princess Dowager of Wales; 15,000 *l.* to the Duke of Cumberland, and 12,000 *l.* to the Princess Amelia; with the addition of the said annuities, as they shall severally determine; and, upon their determination, the yearly sum of 800,000 *l.* to be then paid him during his life.

Chap. 2. *An act for granting an aid by a land-tax for* 1761.

This tax was 4 *s.* in the pound.

Chap. 3. *An act for continuing the duties on malt*, &c.

Chap. 7. *An act for granting to his majesty an additional duty upon strong beer and ale; and for raising the sum of twelve millions, by way of annuities and a lottery, to be charged on the said duty; and further encouraging the exportation of strong beer and ale.*

By this act, an additional duty of 3 *s.* per barrel, was granted on all beer or ale, above 6 *s.* the barrel, brewed for sale in England, and a † proportional duty for every barrel of two-penny ale, brewed for sale in Scotland, to commence January 24, 1761; which duty is appropriated for the payment of the annuities directed

* See p. 248.

† This proportion, by the 7th article of the Treaty of Union, is as 2 *s.* is to 4 *s.* 9 *d.*

to attend the principal sum of twelve millions borrowed on the credit of this act; which sum of twelve millions was to be raised in manner following: *viz.* the sum of 11,400,000 *l.* by annuities after the rate of 3 *l. per cent. per annum* transferrable at the Bank of England, and redeemable by parliament; and every contributer to the said 11,400,000 *l.* should also be intitled to an annuity of 1 *l.* 2 *s.* 6 *d.* for every 100 *l.* contributed, to continue for a certain term of 99 years irredeemable, and to be transferrable at the Bank of England; and the sum of 600,000 *l.* was to be raised by a lottery, attendant on the said annuities, the blanks and prizes whereof to be converted into like 3 *l. per cent.* transferrable annuities, with the above-mentioned 3 *l. per cent.* annuities, to be payable in respect of the said 11,400,000 *l.* and all the said 3 *l. per cent.* annuities to be added to, and made part of, the joint stock of 3 *l. per cent.* annuities, consolidated at the Bank of England. The 3 *l. per cent.* and long annuities were to commence from January 5, 1761, and the annuities on the lottery, from January 5, 1762.

An act for granting to his majesty a certain sum of money out of the Sinking Fund, and for applying certain monies remaining in the Exchequer for the service of the year 1761. Chap. 18.

By this act, the following sums were granted for the current service, *viz.*

	l.	*s.*	*d.*
Out of the Sinking Fund	1,762,400	0	0
Part of 90,000 *l.* granted to his late majesty on account of the militia, remaining in the Exchequer	88,667	10	0
	1,851,067	10	0

Chap. 19. *An act for enabling his majesty to raise the sum of one million for the uses and purposes therein mentioned; and for further appropriating the supplies granted in this session of parliament; and for exempting any annuities, or sums of money, granted, or to be granted to the royal family, from payment of taxes.*

By this act, his majesty was enabled, by warrant under his sign-manual, to authorize the Treasury to raise one million, by loans or Exchequer bills; the principal and interest, with the charges attending, to be paid out of the next supplies, and if none sufficient be granted before July 5, 1762, then they are to be paid out of the Sinking Fund; and the monies so issued, to be replaced out of the first supplies.

Chap. 20. *An act for enabling his majesty to raise a certain sum of money towards paying off and discharging the debt of the navy, and towards naval services, for the year* 1761, &c.

By this act, his majesty was enabled, by warrant under his sign-manual, to authorize the Treasury to raise 1,500,000 *l.* by loans, or Exchequer bills; the principal and interest, with the charges attending, to be paid out of the next supplies; and, if none sufficient be granted before July 5, 1762, then they are to be paid out of the Sinking Fund.

2 Geo. III, 1761. This session began the 3d of November 1761, and ended the 2d of June 1762; and the ways and means for raising the supplies granted in it, were as follow:

Chap. 3. *An act for granting an aid by a land-tax for* 1762.

This tax was 4 *s.* in the pound.

An act for continuing the duties on malt, &c. Chap. 4.

An act for enabling his majesty to raise a certain sum of money towards paying off and discharging the debt of the Navy, and towards naval services for the year 1762. Chap. 7.

By this act, his majesty was enabled, by warrant under his sign-manual, to authorize the Treasury to raise 1,500,000 *l.* by loans on Exchequer bills; the principal and interest, with the charges attending, to be paid out of the next supplies; and if none sufficient be granted before July 5, 1763, then they are to be paid out of the Sinking Fund; and the monies so issued, to be replaced out of the first supplies.

An act for granting to his majesty several rates and duties upon windows, or lights. Chap. 8.

The new duties imposed by this act were, 1 *s.* upon every window, or light, in houses containing 8 or 9 windows, and no more; 6 *d.* additional on all containing 10 or 11, and not more; 1 *s.* additional on all containing 12, 13, or 14, and not more; 3 *d.* additional on all containing 15, 16, 17, 18, or 19, and not more. These duties were to commence from April 5, 1762, and to be raised and paid as the like duties granted by 20th, 21 and 31st * Geo. II, are directed. And the monies arising by these duties were to be paid into the Exchequer, separate and apart from all other branches of the public revenue; and to be carried into the Sinking Fund.

An act for charging certain annuities granted in the year 1760, on the Sinking Fund; and for car- Chap. 9.

* See p. 292, 294, 322.

rying the duties therein mentioned to the said fund, &c.

By this act, the principal sum of 8,000,000 *l.* borrowed on the credit of the statute 33 Geo. II, * chap. 7, and the additional capital of 240,000 *l.* directed to be added thereto, are to be charged upon, and payable out of the Sinking Fund.

Chap. 10. *An act for raising by annuities, in manner therein mentioned, the sum of twelve millions, to be charged on the Sinking Fund*, &c.

By this act, every contributor to the said twelve millions was, for every hundred pounds contributed, intitled to an annuity, transferrable at the Bank of England, after the rate of 4 *l. per cent. per annum*, for 19 years, and then to stand reduced to 3 *l. per cent. per annum*, redeemable by parliament; and also an annuity, transferrable at the Bank of England, of 1 *l. per cent. per annum*, to continue irredeemable for a certain term of 98 years, and then to cease; and that every such contributor should, for every sum of 80 *l. per cent.* paid in to the cashiers of the Bank of England, upon account of his share in the said annuities, after the rate of 4 *l. per cent. per annum*, be intitled to 100 *l.* capital in the said stock of 4 *l. per cent.* annuities; and for every sum of 20 *l.* paid in like manner, upon account of his share in the said annuities of 1 *l. per cent.* should be intitled to an annuity of 1 *l.* to continue for a certain term of 98 years, to commence on January 5, 1762.

Chap. 33. *An act for granting to his majesty a certain sum of money out of the Sinking Fund; and for applying certain monies remaining in the Exchequer for*

* See p. 330.

the service of the year 1762; and for settling and securing a certain annuity for the use of the right honourable Arthur Onslow, Speaker of the House of Commons in the last five parliaments.

By this act, the following sums were granted for the current service, &c.

	l.	s.	d.
Out of the Sinking Fund	1,009,217	2	8½
Granted by an act in the 2d year of his late majesty, upon account of his late majesty's Civil List revenues, and now, by his majesty's direction, replaced and refunded out of the arrears of the said revenues, which were standing out at the time of his late majesty's demise,	115,000	0	0
Remaining unapplied of the money granted in the year 1758, towards the charge of pay and cloathing for the militia,	20,000	0	0
Remaining unapplied of the money granted in the year 1760, towards pay and cloathing of the unembodied militia,	80,000	0	0
Remaining also unapplied of the money granted in the year 1761, for the like purposes,	70,000	0	0
Surplus in the Exchequer of the duties on malt, to January 5, 1762,	73,678	0	0
	1,367,895	2	8½

Chap. 34. *An act for enabling his majesty to raise the sum of one million, for the uses and purposes therein mentioned; and for further appropriating the supplies granted in this session of parliament, &c.*

By this act, his majesty was enabled, by warrant under his royal sign-manual, to authorize the Treasury to raise the sum of one million by loans, or Exchequer billls; to be paid out of the next supplies; and if none sufficient should be granted before July 5, 1763, then they are to be paid out of the Sinking Fund; and the monies so issued, to be replaced out of the first supplies.

3 Geo. III, 1762. This session began the 25th of November 1762, and ended the 18th of April 1763; and the ways and means for raising the supplies granted in it, were as follow:

Chap. 1. *An act for continuing the duties on malt, &c.*

Chap. 2. *An act for granting an aid by a land-tax for 1763.*

This tax was 4*s.* in the pound.

Chap. 9. *An act for granting annuities to satisfy certain navy, victualling, and transport bills, and ordnance debentures; and for charging the payment of such annuities on the Sinking Fund; and making good the same to the said fund, in manner therein mentioned.*

This act recites, that, notwithstanding the great supplies which had been granted for carrying on the war, several debts and deficiencies remained unprovided for, particularly upon account of the bills payable in the course of the the Navy and Victualling-offices, and for transports, made out on or before the 31st of December 1762, to the amount of 3,075,316*l.* 0*s.* 3*d.* and upon account of debentures payable out of the office of ordnance, which were dated on or before the 31ſt of December 1762, amounting to 595,423 *l.* 2 *s.* 5 *d.* In order therefore to make proviſion for diſcharging thoſe debts, and ſupplying thoſe deficiencies, it was enacted, that the proprietors of the ſaid bills and debentures ſhould be intitled to an annuity for the principal and intereſt due thereon, after the rate of 4 *l. per cent. per annum*, to commence the 25th of March 1763, and to be paid half yearly, on the 29th of September, and the 25th of March.

An act for granting to his majeſty ſeveral additional duties upon wines imported into this kingdom, and certain duties upon all cyder and perry; and for raiſing the ſum of three millions five hundred thouſand pounds, by way of annuities and lotteries, to be charged on the ſaid duties. Chap. 12.

By this act, were impoſed the following duties, *viz.*

For every ton of *French* wine, and *French* vinegar, which ſhall be imported into this kingdom, the ſum of 8 *l.* and ſo after that rate for any greater or leſs quantity.

And for every ton of all other wines and vinegar imported into this kingdom, the ſum of 4 *l.* and after that rate for a greater or leſs quantity; to take place from and after the 31ſt of March 1763.

For every ton of cyder or perry imported into Great-Britain from beyond the ſeas, 40 *s.* and ſo proportionately for a greater or leſs quantity, over and above all other duties payable for the ſame; and to take place from and after the 5th of July 1763.

For all cyder and perry which ſhall be made in Great-Britain, from and after the 5th of July

1763, 4 *s.* upon every hogshead, to be paid by the maker thereof; and so proportionably for a greater or less quantity, over and above all other duties now payable for cyder or perry.

The said duties are appropriated for the payment of the annuities chargeable on the principal sum of 3,500,000 *l.* borrowed on the credit of this act, in manner following, *viz.* the sum of 2,800,000 *l.* by annuities, after the rate of 4 *l. per cent. per annum*, transferrable at the Bank of England, and redeemable by parliament; and the sum of 700,000 *l.* by two lotteries, to be drawn at different times, in the year 1763, each lottery to consist of 35,000 tickets, and every blank to be of the value of 5 *l.* The subscribers to be intitled to 4 *l. per cent.* interest on the said sum of 2,800,000 *l*, and to a ticket in each lottery, for every 80 *l.* subscribed, upon payment of 10 *l.* for such ticket; and the 700,000 *l.* raised by the lotteries to carry an interest of 4 *l. per cent.* All the said annuities to take place on the 5th of April 1763, and to be paid half-yearly, *viz.* on the 10th of October, and the 5th of April; and the deficiency of the fund established for payment of the said annuities, to be made good, from time to time, out of the Sinking Fund; which are to be replaced out of the first supplies.

Chap. 14. *An act for the encouraging of* John Harrison, *to publish and make known the invention of a machine, or watch, for the discovery of the longitude at sea.*

Upon a full and clear discovery, by John Harrison, his executors or administrators, of the principles of his watch, and the method of constructing the same, to the committee in the act mentioned, and their publishing the same, and certifying such discovery to the commissioners of the Navy, the commissioners are to make out bills for 5000*l.* payable to him by the treasurer of the Navy.

An act for raising a certain sum of money, by loans, or Exchequer bills, for the service of the year 1763; *and for further appropriating the supplies granted in this session of parliament,* &c. Chap. 17.

By this act, the commissioners of the Treasury are impowered to raise 1,800,000*l.* by loans or Exchequer bills, the principal and interest, with the charges attending, to be paid out of the next supplies; and, if none sufficient be granted before July 5, 1764, then they are to be paid out of the Sinking Fund; and the monies so issued, to be replaced out of the first supplies.

An act for granting to his majesty a certain sum of money out of the Sinking Fund; and for applying certain monies, remaining in the Exchequer, for the service of the year 1763. Chap. 18.

By this act, the following sums were granted for the current service, *viz.*

	l.	*s.*	*d.*
Out of the Sinking Fund, with a clause of loan for raising it by Exchequer bills,	2,000,000	0	0
Surplus remaining in the Exchequer, of the duties on beer and ale,	47,120	9	6
And such part of the sum of 20,000*l.* granted in the last session, towards pay of the unembodied militia, as shall be unapplied,			
	2,047,120	9	6

4 Geo. III, 1763. This ſeſſion began the 15th of November 1763, and ended the 19th of April 1764; and the ways and means for raiſing the ſupplies granted in it, were as follow:

Chap. 1. *An act for continuing the duties on malt*, &c.

Chap. 2. *An act for granting an aid by a land-tax for* 1764.

This tax was 4 *s.* in the pound.

Chap. 7. An act to explain and amend ſuch part of an act made in the laſt ſeſſion of parliament (Intitled, *An act for granting to his majeſty ſeveral additional duties upon wines imported into this kingdom, and certain duties upon all cyder and perry, and for raiſing the ſum of three millions five hundred thouſand pounds, by way of annuities and lotteries, to be charged on the ſaid duties*) as relates to cyder and perry made in this kingdom.

The preamble recites clauſes in the cyder-act of laſt ſeſſion, and extends the time limited by the former act for payment of the duties, to ſix months; after the expiration of which, they may be recovered and levied as thereby directed.

In lieu of the former compoſition, officers of exciſe are authorized to compound with private families, at the rate of 2 *s.* per head *per annum*, for each perſon of eight years old and upwards, in the liſts delivered in to them, *&c.*

Chap. 9. *An act for repealing the duties now payable upon beaver ſkins imported, and for granting other duties in lieu thereof; and for granting certain duties upon the exportation of beaver ſkins and beaver wool; and for taking off the drawback allowed on the exportation of such skins.*

By this act, the former duties payable upon beaver skins imported, are to cease after the 7th of April 1764, and other duties to be paid in lieu thereof, *viz.* for every beaver skin imported into Great-Britain from any of his majesty's dominions in America, the sum of one penny; and for every beaver skin, or piece of beaver skin, exported from Great-Britain, the sum of seven pence; and for every pound weight averdupoise of beaver wool or wombs exported from Great-Britain, the sum of one shilling and sixpence. The new duties to be paid, and applied as the former; and the provisions in former acts respecting the same, to be in force, and extended to the duties of this act; and no drawback to be allowed on the exportation of beaver skins.

An act for granting to his majesty a certain sum of money out of the Sinking Fund, for the service of the year 1764; and for preventing in certain cases, the obtaining of allowances in respect of the leakage of wines imported into this kingdom; and for making forth duplicates of Exchequer bills, tickets, certificates, receipts, annuity orders, and other orders, lost, burnt, or otherwise destroyed. Chap. 13.

By this act it is enacted, that towards raising the supplies granted, there may be issued out of the Sinking Fund, a sum not exceeding 2,000,000 *l.*—Clause of loan for raising this sum.

An act for charging on the Sinking Fund certain annuities granted by an act passed in the first year of the reign of his present majesty; and for carrying the duties therein mentioned, to the said fund; and also for consolidating such of Chap. 18.

the said annuities as are granted for a certain term of years, irredeemable, with other annuities granted by an act passed in the second year of his present majesty's reign.

This act recites 1 Geo. III, chap. 7, and 2 Geo. III, chap. 10, and enacts, that the long annuities granted by the recited act of 1 Geo. III, with the consent of the proprietors shall be added to and made a joint stock with those granted by act 2 Geo. III, and shall be charged upon, and payable out of the Sinking Fund.

Chap. 23. *An act for raising a certain sum of money by loans or Exchequer bills; and for applying certain monies remaining in the Exchequer, for the service of the year 1764; and for application of certain savings of public monies, and of monies arisen by the sale of military stores; and for further appropriating the supplies granted in this session of parliament; and for relief,* &c.

By this act, the Treasury are impowered to take in loans, or issue Exchequer bills, for any sum not exceeding 800,000 *l.* in like manner as is prescribed by the malt-act of this session, concerning loans or Exchequer bills, thereby authorized to be taken and made. And the Bank are impowered to advance on the credit of the said loan, any sum or sums not exceeding 800,000 *l.* And towards making good the said supply, the Treasury are further impowered to issue the sum of 3497 *l.* 9 *s.* 9 *d.* surplus of the duties upon beer, *&c.* granted by act 1 Geo. III, to the 5th of January 1764; and surplus of 150,000 *l.* granted the last session, for pay and cloathing of the militia, remaining in the Exchequer; also the sum of 102,469 *l.* 19 *s.* 3 *d.* ¼, savings of the grant of the last session, for pay of the Brunswick troops, subsidies, and former grants, *&c.* and 61,088 *l.* 4 *s.* other savings; and by ſale of ſtores in Germany and Portugal, to be applied towards the extraordinary expences of the land forces, &c. incurred to the 5th of December 1763, not provided for; alſo 170,906*l.* 2*s.* 8*d.* ſavings upon the non-effective accounts of ſeveral regiments; to be applied towards the unſatisfied claims in Germany, reported to be due.

The monies ariſing by the malt-act, land-tax, with the ſum of 2,000,000*l.* charged on the Sinking Fund, and alſo the ſum of 1,110,000*l.* to be raiſed by the Bank; and alſo the aforeſaid ſum of 3497*l.* 9*s.* 9*d.* alſo the ſavings on ſaid 150,000*l.* granted the laſt ſeſſion for pay and cloathing of the milita; and 800,000*l.* granted by this act, together with the money ariſing by ſale of French prizes taken before the war, are appropriated, *viz.*

For the marriage portion of the Princeſs Auguſta, 80,000*l.*

Towards naval ſervices in general, 1,430,568*l.* 11*s.* 9*d.*

For building four houſes for the officers of the hoſpital at Plymouth, 3000*l.*

To the Commiſſioners of Greenwich hoſpital, for out-penſioners, upon account, 10,000*l.*

Towards paying off the debt of the Navy, 650,000*l.*

For paying a bounty for the year 1764, to the oldeſt chaplains in the Navy, who have ſerved four years on board in the late war, and have not preferment of 50*l.* *per annum* value, *viz.* to 15 ſuch 2*s.* 6*d.* *per diem*, and to 15 others 2*s.* *per diem*.

Charge of the office of ordnance for land ſervice, 173,080*l.* 8*s.* 6*d.*

Charge of the office of ordnance for land ſervice not provided for in 1763, 52,359*l.* 8*s.* 1*d.*

For pay, &c. of the land forces in general, 2,610,745 *l.* 10 *s.* 7 *d.* whereof 617,704 *l.* 17 *s.* 10 *d.* ¾ for charge of 17,532 *l.* effective men, including invalids, for guards and garrisons, &c.; 372,774 *l.* 6 *s.* 4 *d.* ¾ for the forces and garrisons in the Plantations, and in Minorca and Gibraltar, and for provisions for them; 11,322 *l.* 7 *s.* 3 *d.* for pay of the general and general staff officers; 80,000 *l.* on account, for pay and cloathing of the militia; 30,188 *l.* 18 *s.* to the reduced officers of the land forces and marines, for the year 1764; 125,455 *l.* 13 *s.* to the reduced officers of the land forces disbanded in 1763, and such as are to be reduced for the year 1764; 2605 *l.* 15 *s.* to the officers and private gentlemen of the two troops of Horse-guards, Regiment of Horse reduced, and superannuated gentlemen of the four troops of Horse-guards; 1696 *l.* for pensions to officers widows; 103,794 *l.* 2 *s.* for out-pensioners of Chelsea hospital; 18,331 *l.* 17 *s.* 11 *d.* deficiency in the grant of the last year for out-pensioners of the said hospital in 1763; 43,901 *l.* 3 *s.* 7 *d.* ¾ subsidy to the Duke of Brunswick, pursuant to treaty; 50,000 *l.* on account, to the Landgrave of Hesse-Cassel, pursuant to treaty; 823,876 *l.* 12 *s.* 2 *d.* ¾ for extraordinary expences of land forces, &c. incurred in 1763, not provided for; 329,093 *l.* 17 *s.* 4 *d.* upon account, towards satisfying the claims in Germany, reported to be due.

For paying off Exchequer bills made out by virtue of an act of the last session, 1,800,000 *l.*

For supporting the civil establishment in Nova Scotia, 5703 *l.* 14 *s.* 11 *d.*

For charges of the civil establishment in Georgia, 4031 *l.* 8 *s.* 8 *d.*

For charges of the civil establishment of East Florida, 5700 *l.*

For charges of the civil eſtabliſhment of Weſt Florida, 5700.

For charges of general ſurveys in North America, 1818 *l.* 9 *s.*

For ſupporting the forts and ſettlements on the coaſt of Africa, 20,000 *l.*

To the Foundling Hoſpital; to be iſſued without fee, 38,347 *l.* 10 *s.*

To make good to his majeſty the like ſum, iſſued by him, purſuant to the addreſſes of the Commons, 7350 *l.*

To enable the Commiſſioners for paving, &c. the ſtreets of Weſtminſter, to perform the truſts repoſed in them, 10,000 *l.*

To the Truſtees of the Britiſh Muſeum, 2000 *l.*

To J. Blake, Eſq; for carrying on his fiſh ſcheme, 2500 *l.*

Compenſation for lands purchaſed, &c. under act 2 Geo. III, for erecting forts on the Sea Coaſts, 545 *l.* 15 *s.*

For intereſt of principal money for lands purchaſed under the ſaid act of 2 Geo. III.

To Samuel Touchet, merchant, expences incurred in fitting out veſſels in the expedition againſt Senegal, &c.

To replace to the Sinking Fund the like ſum iſſued thereout, for the half year's payment due the 29th of September 1763, on the annuities granted on the Navy and Victualling bills, 69,671 *l.* 1 *s.* 2 *d.*

To make good the deficiency on the 5th of July 1763, of the duties on offices and penſions, and upon houſes and lights, 41,223 *l.* 1 *s.* 6 *d.*

To make good the deficiency on the 10th of October 1763, of the additional duties upon wines imported, and duties upon cyder and perry, 36,699 *l.* 15 *s.* 4 *d.* halfpenny.

To make good the deficiency of the grants for the year 1763, 129,489 *l.* 0 *s.* 3 *d.*

Chap. 25. *An act for establishing an agreement with the governor and company of the Bank of England, for raising certain sums of money towards the supply for the service of the year* 1764; *and for more effectually*, &c.

This act recites 7 Ann. chap. 7, 12 Ann. stat. 1, chap. 11, 15 Geo. II, chap. 13, and that the governor and company of the Bank of England are willing and contented to advance, towards the supply for 1764, the sum of one million, on Exchequer Bills, bearing interest at the rate of 3 *l. per cent. per annum*, the said interest to be paid quarterly, and the said Exchequer Bills to be charged upon, and repaid out of, the first aids or supplies which shall be granted by parliament for the service of the year 1766; and also to pay into the Exchequer, towards the said supply, the sum of 110,000 *l.* without any repayment of the principal, or allowance of interest for the same, provided that the privilege of exclusive banking, and all other the abilities, capacities, powers, authorities, *&c.* in this or any former act contained, be granted to the said governor and company, in manner therein mentioned. And then the act enacts, that the Treasury may direct Exchequer Bills, to be made out for any sum not exceeding 1,000,000 *l. &c.*

5 Geo. III, 1765. This session began the 10th of January, and ended the 25th of May 1765; and the ways and means for raising the supplies granted in it, were as follow:

Chap. 2. *An act for continuing and granting to his majesty certain duties upon malt*, &c.

An act for granting an aid to his majesty by a land-tax, to be raised in Great-Britain for the service of the year 1765. Chap. 5.

This tax was 4 *s.* in the pound.

An act for granting to his majesty a certain sum of money out of the Sinking Fund; for applying certain monies therein mentioned for the service of the year 1765; *for further appropriating the supplies granted in this session of parliament; for allowing*, &c. Chap. 40.

By this act, the sum of 2,100,000 *l.* granted out of the Sinking Fund, for the service of the current year, may be accordingly issued by the Treasury, who are impowered to raise the said sum, or any part thereof, by loans or Exchequer Bills, on the credit of the Sinking Fund.

And for and towards making good the supply, the Treasury are impowered to issue and apply the sum of 135,213 *l.* 5 *s.* remaining in the Exchequer on the 10th of October 1764, unapplied of the Sinking Fund; 308,000 *l.* agreed to be paid by the French king on the 27th of February 1765; 80,000 *l.* remaining in the Exchequer, granted the last session for pay and cloathing of the militia; 12,000 *l.* produce of the duties granted this session on gum senega and gum arabic.

The sum of 251,740 *l.* 2 *s.* 7 *d.* $\frac{3}{4}$ out of the exceedings of the several sums granted for sundry services, and of the monies, paid in to the paymaster-general by contractors and others, may be issued and applied towards discharging the unsatisfied claims for expences incurred in Germany during the late war.

The sum of 60,000 *l.* out of the monies granted the last session, and reserved for the disposition of parliament, shall be applied towards maintaining the forces and garrisons in America.

The monies arising by the malt-tax, 5 Geo. III, chap. 2, land tax, 5 Geo. III, chap. 5, loans, &c. and other sums remaining in the Exchequer, &c. duties on gum senega and gum arabic, and 2,000,000 *l.* granted out of the Sinking Fund; together with the residue of the money arising by the sale of French prizes, shall be applied to the following uses and purposes:

Towards naval services 1,439,734 *l.* 11 *s.* 3 *d.*

Towards the support of Greenwich hospital 5000 *l.*

Bounty to certain chaplains who served in the Navy the last war, 1231 *l.* 17 *s.* 6 *d.*

For charge of the office of ordnance, for the year 1765, 174,673 *l.* 15 *s.* 10 *d.*

To the said office, for services performed in 1764, not provided for, 55,519 *l.* 10 *s.* 7 *d.*

Towards the land forces and other services in general, 2,001,602 *l.* 10 *s.* 6 *d.*; of which 608,130 *l.* 10 *s.* 7 *d.* for guards and garrisons in Great-Britain, Guernsey, and Jersey; 327,502 *l.* 3 *s.* 11 *d.* ½ for guards and garrisons in the Plantations, Minorca, and Gibraltar, and provisions for the forces abroad; 6346 *l.* 3 *s.* 5 *d.* to make good difference of pay between the British and Irish Establishment of five regiments of foot at Gibraltar, Minorca and ceded Islands; 11,291 *l.* 8 *s.* 6 *d.* ½, for general and general staff officers; 80,000 *l.* towards pay and cloathing of the militia; 135,606 *l.* 12 *s.* 6 *d.* to the reduced officers of the land forces, and marines; 2361 *l.* 14 *s.* 2 *d.* to the officers and gentlemen of Horse Guards, &c. reduced; 1664 *l.* to the pensions of officers widows; 109,107 *l.* 18 *s.* 4 *d.* to the out-pensioners of Chelsea hospital; 10,343 *l.* 16 *s.* 9 *d.* subsidy to the Duke of Brunswick; 50,000 *l.* succour to the Landgrave of Hesse-Cassel; 404,496 *l.* 7 *s.* 6 *d.* extraordinary expences of the land forces, and other services incurred in 1764, not provided for; 248,259 *l.*

17 *s.* 4 *d.* ¼ towards the unſatisfied claims in Germany; 6491 *l.* 17 *s.* 4 *d.* charge of three independent companies in Africa.

Towards paying off Exchequer Bills iſſued purſuant to an act of the laſt ſeſſion, (4 Geo. III, chap. 23,) 800,000 *l.*

For defraying the civil eſtabliſhment of Nova Scotia, 4911 *l.* 14 *s.* 11 *d.*; and for ſundry expences incurred there in former years not provided for, 7000 *l.*

For the civil eſtabliſhment of Georgia, 3966 *l.*

For the civil eſtabliſhment of Eaſt India, 5200 *l.*

For the civil eſtabliſhment of Weſt Florida, 5200 *l.*

Towards expence of general ſurveys in America, 1601 *l.* 14 *s.*

Towards building a lazaret, 5000 *l.*

To the Foundling hoſpital, 38,000 *l.*

For maintaining the Britiſh forts and ſettlements in Africa, 13,000 *l.*; and 7000 *l.* for a Block-houſe at Cape Appolonia; and 5500 *l.* for defraying the charges of a civil eſtabliſhment upon the coaſt of Africa.

To make good to his majeſty the like ſum iſſued in purſuance of addreſſes of the Houſe of Commons, 2400 *l.*

Compenſation to the government of the iſland of Barbadoes, 10,000 *l.*

Towards repairing London bridge, 7000 *l.*

To replace to the Sinking Fund the deficiency of the duties on offices and penſions, and windows, 48,176 *l.* 1 *s.* 11 *d.* halfpenny.

To replace to the Sinking Fund, the deficiency of the additional duties upon wines imported, and upon cyder and perry, 49,742 *l.* 1 *s.* 2 *d.* halfpenny.

To replace to the Sinking Fund the annuities granted in respect of Naval and Victualling bills, *&c.* cancelled, 139,342 *l.* 2 *s.* 4 *d.*

To make good the deficiency of the grants for the last year, 249,660 *l.* 4 *s.* 10 *d.*

6 Geo. III, 1765 and 1766. This session began the 17th of December 1765, and ended the 6th of June 1766; and the ways and means for raising the supplies granted in it, were as follow:

Chap. 2. *An act for continuing and granting to his majesty certain duties upon malt*, &c.

Chap. 9. *An act for granting an aid to his majesty by a land-tax to be raised in* Great-Britain *for the service of the year* 1766.

This tax was 4 *s.* in the pound.

Chap. 14. *An act for repealing the duties granted upon cyder and perry, by an act made in the third year of his present majesty's reign, and for granting other duties on cyder and perry in lieu thereof; and for more effectually securing the duties on cyder and perry imposed by several former acts.*

This act recites 3 Geo. III, chap. 12, and 4 Geo. III, chap. 7, and enacts, that after the 5th of July 1766, the duties granted by the recited act of 3 Geo. III, are to cease; as also the powers and regulations, *&c.* established by the said act, together with the recited act of 4 Geo. III, except as to arrears, or penalties incurred before that time.

In lieu of the duties so repealed, the following new or additional duties are to take place, *viz.* on all foreign cyder and perry imported, 3 *l.* per ton, and on all cyder and perry made in Great-Britain, and sold by retail, 6 *s.* per hogshead, to be paid by the retailer; and on all cyder and perry made in Great-Britain, and consigned to any factor for sale, 16 *s.* 8 *d.* per hogshead, to be paid by the factor.

An act for raising a certain sum of money by loans or Exchequer Bills, for the service of the year 1766. Chap. 15.

By this act, the sum of 1,800,000 *l.* was to be raised by loans or Exchequer Bills, to be charged upon the first aids to be granted in the next session.

An act for redeeming one third part of the remainder of the joint stock of annuities, established by an act made in the third year of his present majesty's reign, in respect of several navy, victualling, and transport bills, and ordnance debentures. Chap. 21.

By this act, a sum not exceeding 870,888 *l.* 5 *s.* 5 *d.* ½ was granted to his majesty, to enable him to redeem and pay off one third part of the capital stock of annuities, after the rate of 4 *l.* *per cent. per annum*, granted in respect of certain navy, victualling, and transport bills, and ordnance debentures, delivered in and cancelled, pursuant to an act of 3 Geo. III.

An act for repealing the several duties upon houses, windows, and lights; and for granting to his majesty other duties upon houses, windows, and lights. Chap. 38.

This act recites the acts of 20 Geo. II, chap. 3, 31 Geo. II, chap. 22, and 2 Geo. III, chap. 8, and enacts, that after the 10th of October 1766, the rates granted by these acts are to cease, (all arrears thereof excepted) and in lieu thereof the following yearly rates are to be paid, *viz.* 3 *s. per annum* for every dwelling-house inhabited within England; and 1 *s. per annum* for all ſuch in Scotland. For all dwelling-houſes throughout Great-Britain, with ſeven windows only, 2 *d.* each; with eight windows, 6 *d.* each; with nine, 8 *d.*; with ten, 10 *d.*; with eleven, 1 *s.*; with twelve, 1 *s.* 2 *d.*; with thirteen, 1 *s.* 4 *d.*; with fourteen to nineteen, 1 *s.* 6 *d.*; with twenty 1 *s.* 7 *d.*; with twenty-one 1 *s.* 8 *d.*; with twenty-two, 1 *s.* 9 *d.*; with twenty-three, 1 *s.* 10 *d.*; with twenty four, 1 *s.* 11 *d.*; with twenty-five, or upwards 2 *s.*—Window-tax to be paid over and above the duties on houſes. Houſes in Scotland, with not more than five windows, exempted from the duty on houſes.

Chap. 39. *An act for raiſing the ſum of one million five hundred thouſand pounds, by way of annuities and a lottery, to be charged on the Sinking Fund.*

By this act, the ſum of 900,000 *l.* was to be raiſed by annuities after the rate of 3 *l. per cent.* to commence from the 5th of January 1766; and the ſum of 600,000 *l.* by a lottery, to conſiſt of 60,000 tickets, every blank to be of the value of 6 *l.*; blanks and prizes to be attended with the like 3 *l. per cent.* annuities, to commence from the 5th of January 1767.

Chap. 41. *An act for granting to his majeſty a certain ſum of money out of the Sinking Fund; and for applying certain monies therein mentioned for the ſervice of the year* 1766, *and for further appropriating the ſupplies granted in this ſeſſion of parliament.*

By this act, the ſum of 2,150,000 *l.* may be iſſued out of the Sinking Fund, towards raiſing the ſupply. The ſum of 80,000 *l.* remaining in the Exchequer for pay and cloathing of the militia, for the year 1765; the ſum of 181,000 *l.* payable for maintenance of the French priſoners; and produce of the duties on gum ſenega and gum arabic may be iſſued towards making good the ſupply. The ſum of 2321 *l.* 14 *s.* 10 *d.* ſavings on the charge of three independent companies of foot, on the African coaſt, *&c.* ſhall be alſo iſſued towards the ſaid ſupply. The ſum of 60,000 *l.* monies unappropriated in the Exchequer, and ſuch as ſhall be paid in before the 5th of April 1767, of the duties granted by act 4 Geo. III, towards the charge of defending the Colonies in America, ſhall be applied in like manner. The ſum of 74,777 *l.* 14 *s.* ſavings of pay of the land forces, ſhall be applied in like manner.

The monies ariſing by the malt-tax, land-tax, loans, lottery, *&c.* and other ſums remaining in the Exchequer, *&c.* together with the ſeveral ſums before granted and ſpecified, with the reſidue of the monies ariſing from the ſale of French prizes taken before the declaration of war, and ſuch ſums as ſhall ariſe by ſale of lands in the ceded Iſlands, ſhall be appropriated and applied to the uſes following, *viz.*

Out of the aids in general, the ſum of 1,522,283 *l.* 6 *s.* 3 *d.* towards naval ſervices.

Towards paying off the debt of the Navy, 1,000,000 *l.*

For the office of ordnance, 180,445 *l.* 19 *s.* 3 *d.* To the ſaid office for ſervices performed in 1765, not provided for.

Towards the land forces, and other ſervices in general, 1,923,313 *l.* 19 *s.* 8 *d.*; of which 605,608 *l.* 19 *s.* 9 *d.* for guards and garriſons in Great-Britain, Guernſey, and Jerſey; 332,183 *l.* 6 *s.* 5 *d.* for guards and garriſons in the Plantations, and Africa, Minorça, and Gibraltar, *&c.* and proviſions for forces abroad; 7993 *l.* 11 *s.* 4 *d.* to make good the difference of pay between the Britiſh eſtabliſhment, of troops in the Iſle of Man, Gibraltar, Minorca, and ceded Iſlands; 11,291 *l.* 8 *s.* 6 *d.* ½, for general and general ſtaff officers; 150,000 *l.* towards paying and cloathing the militia; 138,674 *l.* to the reduced officers of the land forces and marines; 5718 *l.* 6 *s.* 8 *d.* for reduced officers within the 10th company of ſeveral battalions; 1614 *l.* to the penſions of officers widows; 109,875 *l.* to the out-penſioners of Chelſea hoſpital; 50,000 *l.* to the Landgrave of Heſſe-Caſſel, in extinction of all demands; 404,310 *l.* 16 *s.* 6 *d.* extraordinary expences of the land forces, and other ſervices not provided for; 106,043 *l.* 13 *s.* 8 *d.* towards diſcharging the unſatisfied claims in Germany.

Towards paying off Exchequer Bills iſſued purſuant to an act of 4 Geo. III, 1,000,000 *l.*; and 800,000 *l.* towards paying off Exchequer Bills iſſued purſuant to an act of the laſt ſeſſion.

For ſupporting the civil eſtabliſhment of Nova Scotia 4866 *l.* 3 *s.* 5 *d.*; and 8008 *l.* 12 *s.* 7 *d.* for ſundry expences incurred there in former years, not provided for.

For the civil eſtabliſhment of Georgia, 2986 *l.*

For the civil eſtabliſhment of Eaſt Florida, 5250 *l.*; and for the eſtabliſhment of Weſt Florida, 5300 *l.*

Towards expence of general ſurveys in America, 1784 *l.*

For the forts and ſettlements in Africa, under direction of the African company, 13,000 *l.*; and 5550 *l.* charges of the civil eſtabliſhment of Senegambia.

To the Foundling hoſpital, 32,725 *l.*

To the Britiſh Muſeum, 2000 *l.*

To replace to the Sinking Fund the deficiency of the duties on offices, and penſions, and windows, 45,561 *l.* 7 *s.* 10 *d.*

To replace to the Sinking Fund the deficiency of the additional duties upon wines imported, and upon cyder and perry, 29,211 *l.* 12 *s.* 6 *d.*

To replace to the Sinking Fund annuities granted in respect of navy and victualling bills, &c. cancelled, 139,342 *l.* 2 *s.* 4 *d.*

To replace to the Sinking Fund charges of management, &c. 4898 *l.* 14 *s.* 9 *d.*

To replace to the Sinking Fund the monies issued thereout to discharge certain annuities, &c. 8708 *l.* 17 *s.* 7 *d.*

To make good the deficiency of the grants for the last year, 292,828 *l.* 0 *s.* 4 *d.*

This session began the 11th of November 1766, and ended the 2d of June 1767; the ways and means for raising the supplies granted in it, were as follow: 7 Geo. III, 1766 and 1767.

An act for continuing and granting to his majesty certain duties upon malt, mum, cyder, and perry, for the service of the year 1767. Chap. 6.

An act for granting an aid to his majesty by a land-tax to be raised in Great-Britain, *for the service of the year* 1767. Chap. 14.

This tax was 3 *s.* in the pound.

An act for raising a certain sum of money by loans or Exchequer Bills, for the service of the year 1767. Chap. 16.

By this act, the Treasury are impowered to raise any sum not exceeding 1,800,000 *l.* by loans or Exchequer Bills, in the same manner as by the malt-act of this session is prescribed with respect to loans or Exchequer bills, thereby authorized to be taken or made.

Chap. 19. *An act to enable his majesty to settle certain annuities on their Royal Highnesses the Dukes of* York, Gloucester, *and* Cumberland.

This act recites 1 Geo. III, chap. 1, 1 Ann. stat. 1, chap. 7, 9 Ann. chap. 10, and 5 Geo. III, chap. 25, and impowers his majesty by letters-patent, or indentures under the great seal, to grant an annuity of 8000 *l.* to the Duke of York, and a like annuity to the Duke of Gloucester, and a like annuity to the Duke of Cumberland, to commence from the 5th of January 1767, and to be paid quarterly, and to be payable out of the aggregate fund, during the continuance of 1 Geo. III; and after the expiration thereof, then out of such of the hereditary duties, *&c.* as were made part of the said fund by the said acts, out of such of the rates of postage, granted by 5 Geo. III, as shall then belong to the Crown.

Chap. 20. *An act for granting to his majesty additional duties upon bast or straw, chip, cane, and horse-hair hats and bonnets, and upon certain materials for making the same, imported into this kingdom.*

This act was repealed by 10 Geo. III, chap. 43.

Chap. 24. *An act for raising the sum of one million five hundred thousand pounds, by way of annuities, and a lottery attended with annuities, to be charged on the Sinking Fund.*

By this act, the sum of 1,500,000 *l.* was to be raised, *viz.* 900,000 *l.* by annuities, after the rate of 3 *l. per cent.* and 600,000 *l.* by a lottery.

An act for redeeming one fourth part of the joint stock of annuities established by an act made in the third year of his present majesty's reign, intitled, An act for granting to his majesty several additional duties upon wines imported into this kingdom; and certain duties upon all cyder and perry; and for raising the sum of three millions five hundred thousand pounds by way of annuities and lotteries, to to be charged on the said duties. Chap. 25.

By this act, the sum of 875,000 *l.* was to be paid to the governor and company of the Bank, out of the supplies granted this session, for paying off one fourth part of the joint stock of annuities established by 3 Geo. III, and so much money as shall be necessary for discharge of the annuities attending the same, to be paid them out of the Sinking Fund, which they are to apply accordingly.

An act for redeeming the remainder of the joint stock of annuities established by an act made in the third year of his present majesty's reign, in respect of several navy, victualling, and transport bills, and ordnance debentures. Chap. 26.

By this act, the sum of 1,741,776 *l.* 10 *s.* 11 *d.* was to be paid to the governor and company of the Bank, out of the supplies granted this session for redeeming the joint stock of annuities established by act 3 Geo. III, and so much money as shall be necessary for discharge of the annuities attending the same, to be paid them out of the Sinking Fund, which they are to apply accordingly.

An act for granting to his majesty additional duties upon certain linen cloth imported; and for carrying such duties, together with the additional duties granted in this session of parliament upon Chap. 28.

the importation of bast or straw, chip, cane, and horse hair hats and bonnets, and certain materials for making the same, to the Sinking Fund.

By this act, the following additional duties upon certain linen cloth imported, were to take place on the 25th of May 1767, *viz.* for every ell of linen cloth or sheeting above one yard *English* in width (except *Flanders* Holland cloth) which shall be imported into Great-Britain, 3 *d.*; for every ell of linen cloth called drilling, which shall be imported into Great-Britain, 3 *d.* And after those rates, for any greater or less quantity respectively, over and above all other duties imposed thereon by any former act of parliament.

Chap. 32. *An act for applying the money granted in this session of parliament, for carrying on an additional building for a more commodious passage to the House of Commons, from* Saint Margaret's-lane, *and* Old Palace-yard.

This act recites 29 Geo. II, chap. 38, and enacts that three or more commissioners for Westminster-bridge are authorized to agree for the purchase of any freeholds, &c. necessary for the purpose of carrying on an additional building for a more commodious passage to the House of Commons; and for that purpose a sum not exceeding 2000 *l.* may be issued and applied, out of the aids granted in this session, towards the said building.

Chap. 33. *An act to inforce, in that part of* Great-Britain *called* Scotland, *the execution of an act of the last session of parliament, intitled,* An act for repealing the several duties upon houses, windows, and lights; and for granting to his majesty other duties upon houses, windows, and lights; and for explaining the ſaid act.

This act recites 6 Geo III, chap. 38, and 26 Geo. II, chap. 17, and enacts, that the powers and directions, *&c.* in act 26 Geo. II, where not altered by the recited act of laſt ſeſſion, ſhall be carried into execution in Scotland, with reſpect to the duties on houſes, windows, and lights there, granted by the ſaid act of 6 Geo. III, from the 10th of October 1766.

An act for granting to his majeſty a certain ſum of money out of the Sinking Fund, and for applying certain monies therein mentioned for the ſervice of the year 1767; and for further appropriating the ſupplies granted in this ſeſſion of parliament; for carrying to the aggregate fund a ſum of money which hath ariſen by the two ſevenths exciſe, for impowering his majeſty, &c. Chap. 54.

By this act, the ſum of 2,010,121 *l.* 10 *s.* 3 *d.* was granted out of the Sinking Fund for the ſervice of the current year, to be iſſued by the Treaſury accordingly, who are impowered to raiſe the ſaid ſum, or any part thereof by loans or Exchequer Bills, on the credit of the Sinking Fund.—The following ſums remaining in the Exchequer for the diſpoſition of parliament, *viz.* 469,147 *l.* 14 *s.* ſurplus of the Sinking Fund; and 35,202 *l.* 9 *s.* 2 *d.*; 181,000 *l.* payable for maintenance of the French priſoners; alſo 150,000 *l.* granted in the laſt ſeſſion for paying and cloathing of the militia; and produce of the duties on gum ſenega and gum arabic, ſhall be iſſued towards making good the ſupply.

The ſum of 261,571 *l.* 13 *s.* 3 *d.* ſavings ariſing upon former grants, *&c.* received of the Earl of Chatham, shall be applied towards defraying the extraordinary expences of the land forces, *&c.* incurred and not provided for; together with the sum of 7844 *l.* 17 *s.* 9 *d.* remaining in the hands of E. Sainthill, Esq;

The sum of 110,000 *l.* out of such monies as shall be paid into the Exchequer between the 5th of April 1767, and the 5th of April 1768, produce of the revenues reserved for the disposition of parliament, shall be applied towards the charge of defending the colonies in America.

The monies arising by the malt-tax, land-tax, loans, lottery, *&c.* and other sums remaining in the Exchequer, *&c.* together with the several sums before granted and specified, with the residue of the monies arising from the sale of French prizes taken before the declaration of war; and such sums as shall arise by sale of lands in the ceded islands, shall be applied to the following uses, *viz.*

For the marriage portion of the Queen of Denmark, 40,000 *l.*

Towards naval services specified, 1,539,321 *l.* 4 *s.* 8 *d.*

For hemp to replenish the king's magazines, 30,000 *l.*

Towards paying off the debt of the Navy, 300,000 *l.*

For the office of ordnance, 169,600 *l.*

To the said office, for services performed in 1766, not provided for.

Towards the land forces and other services in general, 1,206,156 *l.* 2 *s.* 10 *d.*; of which 593,986 *l.* 15 *s.* 7 *d.* for guards and garrisons in Great Britain, Guernsey, and Jersey; 295,607 *l.* 2 *s.* 11 *d.* for guards and garrisons in the Plantations, and Africa, Minorca, and Gibraltar, *&c.* and provisions for the forces abroad; 7201 *l.* 14 *s.* 7 *d.* to make good the difference of pay between the British and Irish establishment, of troops in the Isle of Man, Gibraltar, Minorca, and ceded islands; 12,203 *l.* 18 *s.* 6 *d.* for general and general staff officers; 135,299 *l.* 8 *s.* 4 *d.* to the reduced officers of the land forces and marines; 2103 *l.* 11 *s.* 8 *d.* to the troops of Horse Guards, and regiment of horse reduced, and to the superannuated gentlemen of the four troops of Horse Guards; 5633 *l.* 3 *s.* 4 *d.* for reduced officers, with the 10th company of battalions reduced; 1536 *l.* to the pensions of officers widows; 106,083 *l.* 2 *s.* 6 *d.* to the out-pensioners of Chelsea hospital; and 46,501 *l.* 5 *s.* 4 *d.* extraordinary expences of the land forces incurred, and not provided for.

Towards paying off Exchequer Bills issued pursuant to the act of the last session, 1,800,000 *l.*

To make good to his majesty the like sum issued pursuant to the addresses of the House of Commons, 12,951 *l.* 2 *s.* 2 *d.*

For supporting the civil establishment of Nova Scotia, 4855 *l.* 3 *s.* 5 *d.*; and 691 *l.* 8 *s.* for sundry expences incurred there in 1767, and not provided for.

For the civil establishment of Georgia, 3986 *l.*

For the civil establishment of East Florida, 4750 *l.*; and for the civil establishment of West Florida, 4,800 *l.*

Towards expence of general surveys in America, 1601 *l.* 14 *s.*; and 2000 *l.* contingent expences of the forces in North America.

For the forts and settlements in Africa, under the direction of the African company, 13,000 *l.*; and 5550 *l.* charges of the establishment of Senegambia; and 3500 *l.* on account of the establishment of Senegal and its dependencies.

To the Foundling hospital, 28,000 *l.*; and 1500 *l.* towards apprenticeing children from thence; but not more than 7 *l.* to be given with any child; and both sums to be issued without fee.

To Dr. Swinton, as a compensation for damage done to his estate at the time of the late rebellion, 700 *l.*

To replace to the Sinking Fund the deficiency of the duties on offices and pensions, and windows, 49,660 *l.* 9 *s.* 2 *d.*

To replace to the Sinking Fund the deficiency of the additional duties upon wines imported, and upon cyder and perry, 12,758 *l.* 13 *s.* 7 *d.*

To replace to the Sinking Fund the annuities granted in respect of certain navy and victualling bills, *&c.* unredeemed, 104,506 *l.* 11 *s.* 10 *d.*; and 1592 *l.* 1 *s.* 9 *d.* to replace to the Sinking Fund the charges of management of the said annuities.

To replace to the Sinking Fund, 8708 *l.* 17 *s.* 7 *d.* to discharge certain annuities, *&c.*

To make good the deficiency of the grants for the last year, 129,144 *l.* 2 *s.* 8 *d.*

The sum of 84,604 *l.* 3 *s.* 3 *d.* remaining in the Exchequer, of the additional rates and duties of excise, shall be carried to the Sinking Fund.

8 Geo. III, 1767. and 1768. This session began the 24th of November 1767, and ended the 10th of March 1768; and on the 11th of March the parliament was dissolved by proclamation. The ways and means for raising the supplies, were as follow:

Chap. 4. *An act for continuing and granting to his majesty certain duties upon malt, mum, cyder, and perry, for the service of the year* 1768.

Chap. 8. *An act for granting an aid to his majesty by a land-tax to be raised in* Great-Britain, *for the service of the year* 1768.

This tax was 3 *s.* in the pound.

An act for raising a certain sum of money, by loans or Exchequer bills, for the service of the year 1768. Chap. 18.

By this act, the sum of 1,800,000 *l.* was to be raised by loans or Exchequer bills.

An act for redeeming the remainder of the joint stock of annuities established by an act made in the third year of his majesty's reign, intitled, An act for granting to his majesty several additional duties upon wines imported into this kingdom, and certain duties upon all cyder and perry; and for raising the sum of three millions five hundred thousand pounds, by way of annuities and lotteries, to be charged on the said duties. Chap. 29.

This act recites act 3 Geo. III, chap. 12, and enacts, that the following sums may be issued to the Bank, out of the supplies granted this session, *viz.* on or before the 5th of July 1768, the sum of 875,000 *l.*; by the 10th act 875,000 *l.* and by the 5th of January 1769, the sum of 875,000 *l.* which money shall be applied by the Bank in payment of the said several sums, for the redemption, and in full satisfaction of the said respective parts of the said capital and joint stock.

An act for granting to his majesty a certain sum of money out of the Sinking Fund; and for applying certain monies therein mentioned, for the service of the year 1768; *and for further appropriating the supplies granted in this session of parliament.* Chap. 30.

By this act, the sum of 2,250,000 *l.* was granted out of the Sinking Fund, for the service of the current year, and the Treasury was impowered to raise the same by loans or Exchequer bills, on the credit of that fund.

The sum of 400,000 *l.* payable into the Exchequer by the East India company, and produce of the duties on gum senega and gum arabic shall be issued towards making good the supply.

The sum of 70,000 *l.* out of such monies as shall be paid into the Exchequer between the 2d of February 1768, and the 5th of April 1769; produce of the revenues reserved for the disposition of parliament, towards the charge of defending the colonies in America, shall be applied accordingly.

The sum of 106,358 *l.* 17 *s.* 8 *d.* out of the several sums, *&c.* herein particularized, shall be applied in making good the supply granted towards defraying the extraordinary expences of the land forces, *&c.* incurred, to the 25th of December, not provided for.

The monies arising by the malt-tax, land-tax, loans, lottery, and the sum of 400,000 *l.* which was to be paid into the Exchequer by the East India company in pursuance of an act of last session, and other sums remaining in the Exchequer, *&c.* together with the several sums before granted and specified, and such sums as shall arise by sale of lands in the ceded islands, shall be applied to the following purposes, *viz.*

Towards naval services specified, 1,526,357 *l.* 0 *s.* 11 *d.*

For charge of the office of ordnance, 159,328 *l.* 11 *s.* 6 *d.*

To the said office, for services performed in 1766, not provided for, 68,944 *l.* 12 *s.* 11 *d.*

Towards the land forces and other services in general, 1,296,125 *l.* 13 *s.* 2 *d.*; of which 606,221 *l.* 12 *s.* 10 *d.* for guards and garrisons in Great-Britain, Guernsey, and Jersey; 326,950 *l.*

4 *s.* 9 *d.* for guards and garrisons in the Plantations, and Africa, Minorca, and Gibraltar, *&c.* and provisions for the forces abroad; 7226 *l.* 17 *s.* 2 *d.* to make good difference of pay between British and Irish establishment of troops in the Isle of Man, Gibraltar, Minorca and ceded islands; 12,237 *l.* 7 *s.* 3 *d.* for general and general staff officers; 132,431 *l.* to the reduced officers of the land forces, and marines; 1713 *l.* 13 *s.* to the two troops of Horse Guards, and Regiment of Horse reduced, and to the superannuated gentlemen of the four troops of Horse Guards; 5227 *l.* 14 *s.* for reduced officers, with the 10th company of battalions reduced; 1536 *l.* to the pensions of officers widows; 108,949 *l.* 17 *s.* 6 *d.* to the out-pensioners of Chelsea hospital; 93,629 *l.* 6 *s.* 6 *d.* extraordinary expences of the land forces, and other services incurred, and not provided for.

Towards paying off Exchequer bills issued pursuant to an act of the last session, 1,800,000 *l.*

To make good to his majesty the like sum, issued pursuant to the addresses of the House of Commons, 10,500 *l.*; and 5000 *l.* towards building a passage to the House of Commons.

For supporting the civil establishment of Nova Scotia, 3895 *l.*; and 3986 *l.* for the establishment of Georgia.

For the civil establishment of East Florida, 4750 *l.*; and for the establishment of West Florida, 4400 *l.*

Towards expence of general surveys in America, 2036 *l.*

For the forts and settlements in Africa, under direction of the African company 13,000 *l.*; and 5550 *l.* charges of the civil establishment of Senegambia.

To the Foundling Hospital 29,000 *l.*; and 2000 *l.* towards apprenticeing children from thence; but not more than 7 *l.* to be given with any one child; both ſums to be iſſued without fee.

To the Truſtees of the Britiſh Muſeum, 2000 *l.*

To replace to the Sinking Fund the like ſum iſſued thereout, to make good the deficiency of the fund for paying annuities eſtabliſhed by act 31 Geo. II, 53,480 *l.* 17 *s.* 8 *d.*

To replace to the ſaid fund the like ſum paid thereout, for deficiency in annuities on the act of 3 Geo. III, 59,322 *l.* 16 *s.* 10 *d.*

To replace to the Sinking Fund the annuities granted in reſpect of certain navy and victualling bills, *&c.* unredeemed, 88,435 *l.* 19 *s.* 6 *d.*

To replace to the Sinking Fund the like ſum iſſued thereout, to diſcharge the annuities attending ſuch part of the joint ſtock eſtabliſhed by act 3 Geo. III, as was redeemed in purſuance of an act of the laſt ſeſſion, 8750 *l.*

To make good the deficiency of the grants for the laſt year, 392,484 *l.* 4 *s.* 5 *d.*

Chap. 31. *An act for raiſing a certain ſum of money by way of annuities, and a lottery attended with annuities, to be charged on the Sinking Fund; and for carrying certain duties on wines, and on cyder and perry, granted by two acts of the third and ſixth years of his preſent majeſty, to the ſaid fund.*

By this act, the ſum of 1,900,000 *l.* was to be raiſed, *viz.* 1,300,000 *l.* thereof by annuities, and 600,000 *l.* by a lottery.

8 Geo. III, 1768. The firſt ſeſſion of this new parliament began the 10th of May 1768, and ended the 11th of Auguſt 1769.

This second session began the 8th of November 1768, and ended the 9th of May 1769; the ways and means for raising the supplies granted in it, were as follow: 9 Geo. III, 1768. and 1769.

An act for granting to his majesty certain duties upon malt, mum, cyder and perry, for the service of the year 1769. Chap. 2.

An act for granting an aid to his majesty by a land-tax, to be raised in Great-Britain, *for the service of the year* 1769. Chap. 5.

This tax was 3 *s.* in the pound.

An act for raising a certain sum of money, by loans, or Exchequer bills, for the service of the year 1769. Chap. 15.

By this act, the sum of 1,800,000 *l.* was to be raised by loans or Exchequer bills.

An act for granting to his majesty a sum of money to be raised by a lottery. Chap. 33.

By this act, the sum of 780,000 *l.* was granted to his majesty to defray his public expences, to be raised by a lottery.

An act for granting to his majesty a certain sum of money out of the Sinking Fund; and for applying a certain sum of money therein mentioned, for the service of the year 1769; *and for further appropriating the supplies granted in this session of parliament.* Chap. 34.

By this act, the sum of 1,664,882 *l.* 4 *s.* 5 *d.* was granted out of the Sinking Fund, for the service of the current year, and the Treasury was impowered to raise the said sum by loans or Exchequer bills, on the credit of the said fund.

The sum of 135,177 *l.* 15 *s.* 6 *d.* surplus of the Sinking Fund in the Exchequer, on the 5th of April 1769, to be applied to the service of the current year.

The monies arising by the malt-tax, land-tax, loans, lottery, East-India agreement, and such other sums as shall be paid into the Exchequer by the 5th of April 1770; duties upon gum senega and gum arabic, and 59,879 *l.* 8 *s.* 5 *d.* remaining in the Exchequer on the 5th of April 1769, with the residue of the monies arising by sale of the French prizes, and by sale of lands in the ceded islands, shall be applied to the following purposes, *viz.*

Towards naval services specified, 1,524,668 *l.* 8 *s.* 1 *d.*

Towards paying off the debt of the Navy, 400,000 *l.*

For charge of the office of ordnance, 177,947 *l.* 18 *s.*

To the said office, for services performed in 1768, not provided for, 43,812 *l.* 19 *s.*

Towards the land forces and other services in general, 1,358,056 *l.* 8 *s.* 11 *d.*; of which 602,673 *l.* 15 *s.* 7 *d.* for guards and garrisons in Great-Britain, Jersey, and Guernsey; 567,835 *l.* 18 *s.* 7 *d.* for guards and garrisons in the Plantations, and Africa, Minorca, and Gibraltar, *&c.* and provisions for the forces abroad; 4661 *l.* 12 *s.* 7 *d.* to make good the difference of pay between the British and Irish establishment, of troops in the Isle of Man, Gibraltar, Minorca, and ceded Islands; 12,200 *l.* 18 *s.* 6 *d.* ½ for general and general staff officers; 127,020 *l.* to the reduced officers of the land forces and marines; 1351 *l.* 13 *s.* to the two troops of Horse Guards, and regiment of Horse reduced; and to the superannuated gentlemen of the four troops of Horse Guards; 4763 *l.* 5 *s.* to reduced officers, with the 10th company of battalions reduced; 1480 *l.* to the pensions of officers widows; 167,394 *l.* 15 *s.* 10 *d.* to the out-pensioners of Chelsea hospital; 128,692 *l.* 2 *s.* 9 *d.* extraordinary expences of the land forces, and other services incurred, and not provided for.

To discharge the civil list debt, 513,511 *l.*

Towards paying off Exchequer bills issued pursuant to an act of the last session, 1,800,000 *l.*

To make good to his majesty, issued pursuant to the address of the House of Commons, 16,500 *l.*

For a passage to the house of Commons, 3000 *l.*

For supporting the civil establishment of Nova Scotia, 4375 *l.* 17 *s.* 11 *d.*

For the civil establishment of Georgia, 3086 *l.*

For the civil establishment of East Florida, 4750 *l.*

For the civil establishment of West Florida, 4800 *l.*

Towards expence of general surveys in America, 1785 *l.* 4 *s.*

For the forts and settlements in Africa, under the direction of the African company, 13,000 *l.*

Charges of the civil establishment of Senegambia, 5550 *l.*

To the Foundling Hospital, 19,967 *l.* 10 *s.*; and towards apprenticeing children from thence, 5600 *l.*

To repay money advanced by the governors in apprenticeing children out, 3231 *l.* 16 *s.*

Toward erecting a magazine for gun-powder in Portsmouth harbour, 4000 *l.*

To the Levant Company, 5000 *l.*

For repairing and widening roads in Carnarvonshire, 2000 *l.*

To Charles Dingley for erecting a wind saw-mill, &c. 2000 *l.*

To replace to the Sinking Fund the like sum paid thereout, for deficiency in annuities on the act of 31 Geo. II, 47,531 *l.* 18 *s.* 6 *d.*

To replace to the said fund deficiencies paid thereout on annuities granted by act 3 Geo. III, 18,930 *l.* 3 *s.* 4 *d.* $\frac{3}{4}$.

To make good the deficiency of the grants for 1768, 186,043 *l.* 1 *s.* 7 *d.*

Chap. 36. *An act for applying certain monies therein mentioned, for the service of the year* 1769.

By this act, the sum of 400,000 *l.* payable into the Exchequer by the East India Company, and produce of the duties on gum senega and gum arabic, and 59,879 *l.* 8 *s.* 5 *d.* reserved in the Exchequer for the disposition of parliament, shall be issued towards making good the supplies granted this session.

The sum of 30,000 *l.* out of such monies as shall be paid into the Exchequer between the 4th of April 1769, and the 5th of April 1770, of the duties appropriated for the defence, &c. of the British American colonies, shall be applied in paying the troops there.

The sum of 109,864 *l.* 19 *s.* 4 *d.* winter stoppages unapplied, of the cavalry serving in Germany in the last war, and balance of stock-purse, with the balance of Lord Chatham's account as paymaster-general of the army, and of Thomas Calcraft as paymaster of the widows pensions, and money reserved in the office of the paymaster-general of the army, &c. not provided for, shall be applied towards making good the supply granted towards defraying the extraordinary expences of his majesty's land forces, &c.

This session began the 9th of January, and ended the 19th of May 1770; the ways and means for raising the supplies granted in it, were as follow: 10 Geo. III, 1770.

An act for continuing and granting to his majesty certain duties upon malt, mum, cyder, and perry, for the service of the year 1770. Chap. 5.

An act for granting an aid to his majesty by a land-tax, to be raised in Great-Britain *for the service of the year* 1770. Chap. 6.

This tax was 3 *s.* in the pound.

An act for raising a certain sum of money, by loans or Exchequer bills, for the service of the year 1770. Chap. 11.

By this act, the sum of 1,800,000 *l.* was to be raised by loans or Exchequer bills.

An act for repealing the duties upon bast or straw, chip, cane, and horse-hair hats and bonnets, and upon certain materials for making the same, imported into this kingdom; and for granting other duties in lieu thereof; and for the more effectual preventing the fraudulent importation of such goods. Chap. 43.

By this act, the following duties are to be paid, *viz.* for hats or bonnets not exceeding twenty-two inches diameter, 12 *s.* 6 *d.* per dozen; and, exceeding that diameter, 1 *l.* 5 *s.* per dozen, and for platting, &c. 6 *s.* 8 *d.* per pound averdupois.

An act for establishing a lottery, and for other purposes therein mentioned. Chap. 46.

By this act, persons possessed of annuities in the joint stock of 4 *l. per cent.* and who should signify their consent in books opened at the Bank, to accept of an annuity of 3 *l.* *per cent.* were intitled for every 100 *l.* to 100 *l.* in the joint stock of 3 *l.* *per cent.* and two lottery tickets; and to have a receipt for 4 *l.* in part of 14 *l.* for each ticket, *&c.*

Chap. 52. *An act for granting to his majesty a certain sum of money out of the Sinking Fund, and for applying certain monies therein mentioned for the service of the year* 1770; *and for further appropriating the supplies granted in this session of parliament.*

By this act, the sum of 1,700,000 *l.* was granted out of the Sinking Fund, for the service of the current year, and the Treasury impowered to raise it by loans or Exchequer bills, on the credit of the said fund.

The sum of 299,375 *l.* 6 *s.* 6 *d.* surplus of the Sinking Fund in the Exchequer on the 5th of January 1770; 773,240 *l.* 16 *s.* surplus of the produce of said fund for the quarter ended, the 5th of April 1770; and 13,596 *l.* 5 *s.* 10 *d.* surplusses remaining in the Exchequer on the 5th of April 1770; the sum of 400,000 *l.* (East India agreement) directed by an act of last session, and such monies as shall be paid into the Exchequer between the 6th of April 1770, and the 5th of April 1771, of the duties on gum senega and gum arabic, charged by 5 Geo. III, to be applied to the service of the current year.

The sum of 20,000 *l.* out of monies paid into the Exchequer between the 6th of April 1770, and the 5th of April 1771, being the produce of duties reserved towards expence of defending, *&c.* the British colonies in America, *&c.* towards making good the sum granted for maintaining the garrisons in the Plantations, and for provisions for the forces in North America,

Nova Scotia, Newfoundland, and the ceded islands; and 55,495 *l.* 15 *s.* 8 *d.* ¼, remaining in the office of the paymaster-general of his majesty's forces, and 3948 *l.* 3 *s.* 7 *d.* final balance of account of Thomas Earl of Kinnoul, to be applied towards defraying the extraordinary expences of the land forces, *&c.* incurred to the 26th of December 1769, and not provided for, shall be issued towards making good the supply.

The monies arising by the malt-tax, land-tax, loans, lottery, and 299,375 *l.* 6 *s.* 6 *d.* ¼ remaining in the Exchequer on the 5th of January 1770, surplus of the Sinking Fund; and 77,340 *l.* 16 *s.* ½, and 13,596 *l.* 5 *s.* 10 *d.* ½, surplusses remaining on the 5th of April 1770; and 400,000 *l.* payable by an act of last session; and such monies as shall be paid into the Exchequer between the 6th of April 1770, and the 5th of April 1771, of the produce of the duties on gum senega and gum arabic; and 1,700,000 *l.* granted by this act out of the Sinking Fund, together with the residue of the monies arising from the sale of French prizes taken before the declaration of war; and also also such monies as his majesty shall direct, out of the monies arising by sale of ceded lands in the West Indies, shall be applied to the following purposes, *viz.*

Towards naval services specified, 1,522,067 *l.* 1 *s.* 11 *d.*

Towards paying off the debt of the Navy, 100,200 *l.*

For charge of the office of ordnance, 166,984 *l.* 11 *s.* 5 *d.*

To the said office for services performed in 1760, not provided for, 40,533 *l.* 10 *s.* 8 *d.*

Towards the land forces, and other services in general, 1,468,487 *l.* 1 *s.* 10 *d.*; of which 624,992 *l.* 0 *s.* 2 *d.* for defraying the charge of 17,666 effective men, *&c.* and 1522 invalids, for guards and garrisons, *&c.* in Great-Britain, Jersey and Guernsey; 363,248 *l.* 1 *s.* 11 *d.* and one eighth of a penny, for guards and garrisons in the Plantations, and Africa, Minorca and Gibraltar, *&c.* and provisions for the forces abroad; 4533 *l.* 12 *s.* 8 *d.* to make good the difference of pay between the British and Irish establishment, of troops in the Isle of Man, Gibraltar, Minorca and ceded Islands; 12,203 *l.* 18 *s.* 6 *d.* for general and general staff officers; 123,133 *l.* 2 *s.* 6 *d.* to the reduced officers of the land forces and marines; 1289 *l.* 1 *s.* 3 *d.* to the troops of Horse Guards, and regiments of Horse reduced, and to the superannuated gentlemen of the four troops of Horse Guards; 4513 *l.* 16 *s.* 8 *d.* to reduced officers, with the 10th company of battalions reduced; 664 *l.* to the pensions of officers widows; 112,425 *l.* 4 *s.* 7 *d.* to the out-pensioners of Chelsea hospital; 175,820 *l.* 11 *s.* 6 *d.* ½, towards extraordinary expences of the land forces, and other services incurred, and not provided for; 45,565 *l.* 12 *s.* to the Landgrave of Hesse-Cassel.

Towards paying off Exchequer bills issued pursuant to an act of last session, 1,800,000 *l.*

To make good to his majesty the like sum issued pursuant to the addresses of the House of Commons, 13,100 *l.*

For a passage to the House of Commons, 2000 *l.*

For supporting the civil establishment of Nova Scotia, 4239 *l.* 5 *d.*

For the civil establishment of Georgia, 3086 *l.*

For the civil establishment of East Florida, 4750 *l.*

For the civil establishment of West Florida, 4800 *l.*

Towards expence of general surveys in America, 3885 *l.* 4 *s.*

For the forts and ſettlements in Africa, under the direction of the committee of the African company, 13,500 *l.*

Charges of the civil eſtabliſhment of Senegambia, 5550 *l.*

To the Foundling Hoſpital, 9640 *l.*

Towards apprenticeing children from thence, 3500 *l.*

To inhabitants of Barbadoes, to defray expences of cleanſing the channel, *&c.* 5000 *l.*

To Levant Company, 5000 *l.*

To the truſtees of the Britiſh Muſeum, 2000 *l.*

For diſcharging debts claimed upon forfeited eſtates, 71,000 *l.*

And the annuity claimed by Mary Mackenzie, widow.

And for purchaſe of ſuperiories, *&c.*

Towards roads of communication and bridges in the Highlands of North-Britain, 6998 *l.* 10 *s.* 2 *d.*

To make good to his majeſty the like ſum paid to ſeveral perſons in the county of Southampton, in full ſatisfaction for the loſſes they have incurred, purſuant to orders of council, for the preventing the ſpreading of the diſtemper amongſt the horned cattle, 796 *l.* 7 *s.* 6 *d.*

To enable his majeſty to make compenſation to Francis Dalby, merchant, for the loſs of his ſhip the Britannia, *&c.* 6195 *l.* 8 *s.* 11 *d.*

To replace to the Sinking Fund, the like ſum paid out of the ſame, to make good the deficiency of the fund for paying annuities eſtabliſhed by act 31 Geo. II, 46,463 *l.* 12 *s.* 8 *d.*

To make good the deficiency of the grants for the year 1769, 55,011 *l.* 7 *s.* 5 *d.*

11 Geo. III, 1770 and 1771. This seſſion began the 13th of November 1770, and ended the 8th of April 1771; and the ways and means for raiſing the ſupplies granted in it, were the following:

Chap. 2. *An act for continuing and granting to his majeſty certain duties upon malt, mum, cyder, and perry, for the ſervice of the year* 1771.

Chap. 5. *An act for granting an aid to his majeſty by a land-tax, to be raiſed in* Great-Britain, *for the ſervice of the year* 1771.

This tax was 4 *s.* in the pound.

Chap. 25. *An act for raiſing a certain ſum of money, by loans or Exchequer bills, for the ſervice of the year* 1771.

By this act, the ſum of 1,800,000 *l.* was to be raiſed by loans or Exchequer bills.

Chap. 47. *An act for granting to his majeſty a certain ſum of money, to be raiſed by a lottery.*

By this act, the ſum of 650,000 *l.* was to be raiſed by a lottery, to conſiſt of 50,000 tickets, at 13 *l.* each.

Chap. 48. *An act for granting to his majeſty a certain ſum of money out of the Sinking Fund; and for applying certain monies therein mentioned, for the ſervice of the year* 1771; *and for further appropriating the ſupplies granted in this ſeſſion of parliament, for carrying to the aggregate fund a ſum of money which hath ariſen by the two-ſevenths exciſe, and for enabling the commiſſioners for executing the office of treaſurer of his majeſty's Exchequer, or the Lord High Treaſurer for the time being, to pay to* John Dobſon, *owner of the Greenland ship* Lord Molyneux, *the bounty due for the said ship on the last year's fishery.*

By this act, the sum of 1,650,000 *l.* was granted out of the Sinking Fund for the service of the current year, and the Treasury impowered to raise the said sum by loans or Exchequer bills.

The sum of 691,977 *l.* 7 *s.* 9 *d.* surplus of the Sinking Fund in the Exchequer on the 5th of April 1771, and 20,000 *l.* 1 *s.* 6 *d.* remaining in the Exchequer on the 5th of April 1771, and 89,658 *l.* 10 *s.* 9 *d.* directed by the act of last session; 400,000 *l.* by act 9 Geo. III, to be paid by the East India Company, and such monies as shall be paid into the Exchequer between the 4th of April 1771, and the 5th of April 1772, of the duties on gum senega and gum arabic, charged by act 5 Geo. III, are directed to be applied for the service of the current year.

The sum of 20,000 *l.* out of the monies paid into the Exchequer, on the 5th of April 1772, being the produce of duties reserved towards expence of defending, *&c.* the British colonies in America, *&c.* is directed to be applied towards making good the sum granted for maintaining the garrisons in the Plantations, and for provisions for the forces in North America, Nova Scotia, Newfoundland, and the ceded Islands.

The monies arising by the malt-tax, land-tax, loans, lottery, and 691,977 *l.* 7 *s.* 9 *d.* remaining in the Exchequer on the 5th of April 1771, surplus of the Sinking Fund; and 20,000 *l.* 1 *s.* 6 *d.* surplusses remaining on the 5th of April 1771; and 89,658 *l.* 16 *s.* 9 *d.* remaining in the Exchequer; and 400,000 *l.* (East India agreement,) and such monies as shall be paid into the Exchequer between the 4th of April 1771, and the 5th of April 1772, of the produce of the duties on gum senega and gum arabic, and 1,650,000 *l.* granted by this act out of the Sinking Fund, together with the residue of the monies arising from the sale of French prizes taken before the declaration of war, and also such monies as his majesty shall direct, out of monies arising by sale of ceded lands in the West Indies, are directed to be applied to the following purposes, *viz.*

Towards naval services specified, 2,882,499 *l.* 18 *s.* 7 *d.*

Towards paying off the debt of the Navy, 200,000 *l.*

For charges of the office of ordnance, 259,074 *l.* 16 *s.* 11 *d.*

To the said office, for services performed in 1770, not provided for, 35,443 *l.* 7 *s.*

Towards the land forces and other services in general, 1,790,319 *l.* 13 *s.* 1 *d.*; of which 720,629 *l.* 12 *s.* 3 *d.* for defraying the charges of 23,432 effective men, *&c.* and 2102 invalids, for guards and garrisons, *&c.* in Great-Britain, Jersey, and Guernsey; and 459,170 *l.* 1 *s.* 11 *d.* for guards and garrisons in the Plantations, and Africa, Minorca, and Gibraltar, *&c.* and provisions for the forces abroad; 4533 *l.* 12 *s.* 8 *d.* to make good the difference of pay between the British and Irish establishment, of troops in the Isle of Man, Gibraltar, Minorca, and ceded Islands; 11,291 *l.* 8 *s.* 6 *d.* for general and general staff officers; 117,858 *l.* 10 *s.* to the reduced officers of the land forces and marines; 1277 *l.* 15 *s.* 5 *d.* to the two troops of Horse Guards, and regiment of Horse reduced, and to the superannuated gentlemen of the four troops of Horse Guards; 2962 *l.* 11 *s.* 8 *d.* to reduced officers, with the 10th company of battalions reduced; 664 *l.* to the pensions of officers widows; 112,005 *l.* to the out-pensioners of Chelsea hospital; 359,927 *l.* 0 *s.* 7 *d.* towards extraordinary expences of the land forces, and other services incurred, and not provided for.

For discharging Exchequer bills of last session, 1,800,000 *l.*

To make good to his majesty the like sum issued pursuant to the addresses of the House of Commons, 14,700 *l.*

For supporting the civil establishment of Nova Scotia, 5796 *l.* 10 *s.* 5 *d.*

For the civil establishment of Georgia, 3086 *l.*

For the civil establishment of East Florida, 4350 *l.*

For the civil establishment of West Florida, 6100 *l.*

For defraying expences attending surveys in North America, 1885 *l.* 4 *s.*

Not exceeding 13,000 *l.* for repairing and maintaining the forts in Africa.

Not exceeding 6336 *l.* 0 *s.* 9 *d.* ½, for supporting the civil establishment of Senegambia.

Not exceeding 2000 *l.* for repairing the fort of Cape Coast Castle.

Not exceeding 2970 *l.* for the maintenance, *&c.* of deserted young children, from the 31st of December 1770, to the 31st of December 1771.

Not exceeding 27,030 *l.* for defraying expences of children admitted into the Foundling Hospital before the 25th of March 1760.

Towards building a bridge across the Thames, 2000 *l.*

To merchants trading to the Levant, 5000 *l.*

Incurred by the East India Company, antecedent to the surrender of Manilla, 28,365 *l.* 5 *s.* 8 *d.*

To the Province of New Hampshire for provisions, *&c.* to the troops in 1756, 6009 *l.* 13 *s.* 3 *d.*

For defraying expence of new roads, *&c.* in the Highlands of Scotland in 1771, 6928 *l.* 2 *s.*

(To be made good to his majesty) paid to persons in preventing the distemper amongst horned cattle, 799 *l.* 12 *s.* 2 *d.*

To make good deficiencies in 1771, 35,085 *l.* 2 *s.*

12 Geo. III, 1772. This session began the 21st of January, and ended the 9th of June 1772; the ways and means for raising the supplies, were the following:

Chap. 3. *An act for granting an aid to his majesty by a land-tax to be raised in* Great-Britain, *for the service of the year* 1772.

This tax was 3 *s.* in the pound.

Chap. 6. *An act for continuing and granting to his majesty certain duties upon malt, mum, cyder, and perry, for the service of the year* 1772.

Chap. 39. *An act for raising a certain sum of money by loans or Exchequer Bills, for the service of the year* 1772.

By this act, the sum of 1,800,000 *l.* was to be raised by loans or Exchequer bills, in the usual manner.

Chap. 63. *An act for redeeming* 1,500,000 l. *capital stock of* 3 l. per cent. *annuities, in the manner, and on the terms therein mentioned; and for establishing a lottery.*

By this act, subscribers shall, for every 100 *l.* capital stock, be intitled to four tickets in a lottery, to consist of 60,000 tickets at 12 *l.* 10 *s.* each.

Chap. 70. *An act for granting to his majesty a certain sum of money out of the Sinking Fund; and for applying certain monies therein mentioned for the service of the year* 1772, *and for further appropriating the supplies granted in this session of parliament, and*, &c.

By this act, the sum of 1,856,723 *l.* 1 *s.* 2 *d.* was granted out of the Sinking Fund for the service of the current year, and the Treasury impowered to raise the said sum by loans or Exchequer bills.

The sum of 136,416 *l.* 0 *s.* 8 *d.* surplus of the Sinking Fund in the Exchequer on the 10th of October 1772; 55,192 *l.* 6 *s.* 11 *d.* remaining in the Exchequer on the 5th of January 1772; and 805,398 *l.* 13 *s.* 2 *d.* remaining in the Exchequer on the 5th of April 1772; and 10,426 *l.* 9 *s.* 3 *d.* remaining in the Exchequer; and 21,710 *l.* remaining in the Exchequer on the 5th of April 1772; also 400,000 *l.* directed to be paid by the East India company, by act 9 Geo. III, and such monies as shall be paid into the Exchequer between the 5th of April 1772, and the 5th of April 1773, of the duties of gum senega and gum arabic, charged by act 5 Geo. III, are directed to be applied to the service of the current year.

The sum of 138,090 *l.* 5 *s.* 10 *d.* out of saving arising upon an augmentation to the land forces for 1771, and 36,772 *l.* 10 *s.* from the sum voted for extra-ordinances in 1770, 1863 *l.* 13 *s.* 10 *d.* upon grants for difference between British and Irish pay of the 64th and 65th regiments in 1768; and 40,000 *l.* out of savings upon grants for pay of reduced officers in 1757, to 1772, to be applied as aforesaid.

The sum of 20,000 *l.* out of the monies paid into the Exchequer, on the 5th of April 1770, being the produce of duties reserved towards expence of defending, *&c.* the British colonies in America, *&c.* to be applied towards making good the sum granted for maintaining the garrisons in the Plantations, and for provisions for the forces in North America, &c.

The monies arising by the malt-tax, land-tax, loans, lottery, and 136,416 *l.* 0 *s.* 8 *d.* $\frac{1}{2}$, remaining in the Exchequer on the 10th of October 1771; and 55,192 *l.* 6 *s.* 11 *d.* $\frac{3}{4}$, surplusses remaining on the 5th of January 1772; and 805,798 *l.* 13 *s.* 2 *s.* remaining in the Exchequer on the 5th of April 1772; and 10,426 *l.* 9 *s.* 5 *d.* and 21,710 *l.* so remaining in the Exchequer; and 400,000 *l.* by act 9 Geo. III, and such monies as shall be paid into the Exchequer between the 5th of April 1770, and the 5th of April 1773, of the produce of the duties on gum senega and gum arabic; and 1,856,723 *l.* 1 *s.* 2 *d.* granted by this act out of the Sinking Fund, together with the prize-money taken before the declaration of war; and also such monies as his majesty shall direct out of monies arising by sale of ceded lands in the West Indies.

Towards naval services herein expressed, 2,270,664 *l.* 17 *s.* 6 *d.*

Towards paying off the debt of the Navy, 215,883 *l.* 17 *s.* 4 *d.*

For charge of the office of ordnance, 32,458 *l.* 6 *s.* 3 *d.*

Towards the land forces, 1,314,701 *l.* 12 *s.* 5 *d.*; of which 629,491 *l.* 12 *s.* 4 *d.* for defraying the charges of 17,547 effective men, &c. and 1522 invalids, for guards, &c. in Great-Britain, &c.; not exceeding 368,953 *l.* 12 *s.* 7 *d.* for guards and garrisons in the Plantations, and Africa, &c. and provisions for forces abroad; 4723 *l.* 16 *s.* 2 *d.* to make good the difference of pay between the British and Irish establishment of troops in the Isle of Man, &c.; 11,322 *l.* 7 *s.* 3 *d.* for general and general staff officers; 115,765 *l.* 16 *s.* to the reduced officers of the land forces and marines; 1281 *l.* 0 *s.* 6 *d.* to the two troops of Horse Guards reduced; and to the superannuated gentlemen of the four troops of Horse Guards; 644 *l.* to the pensions of officers widows; not exceeding 124,813 *l.* 12 *s.* 6 *d.* to the out-pensioners of Chelsea hospital; 57,705 *l.* 14 *s.* 11 *d.* towards extraordinary expences of the land forces, and other services incurred, and not provided for.

For discharging Exchequer bills of last session, 1,800,000 *l.*

To make good to his majesty the like sum issued pursuant to the addresses of the House of Commons; 5346 *l.* 10 *s.* 5 *d.* for supporting the civil establishment of Nova Scotia.

For the civil establishment of Georgia, 3186 *l.*

For the civil establishment of East Florida, 4950 *l.*; and for the civil establishment of West Florida, 5650 *l.*

For defraying expences attending surveys in North America, 1885 *l.* 4 *s.*

For repairing and maintaining the forts in Africa, 13,000 *l.*

For supporting the civil establishment of Senegambia, 6336 *l.* 0 *s.* 9 *d.*

For repairing the fort of Cape Coast Castle, 2400 *l.*; and for prosecuting discoveries towards the South Pole, 4000 *l.*

To merchants trading to the Levant, 5000 *l.*

To the trustees of the British Museum, to carry on the trust reposed in them by parliament, 2000 *l.*

To enable his majesty to purchase a collection of Etruscan, Grecian, and Roman antiquities, 8410; and for a repository for the said collection, 840 *l.*

For defraying the expence of new roads, *&c.* in the Highlands of Scotland in 1772, 6998 *l.* 14 *s.* 5 *d.*

Not exceeding 794 *l.* 3 *s.* 11 *d.* (to be made good to his majeſty) paid to perſons in preventing the diſtemper among horned cattle.

To Charles Irving for a late diſcovery of a method of making ſea water freſh and wholeſome; and the ſum of 1500 *l.* as a compenſation to Edmund Hill, for diſcontinuing the uſe of his peſtles in making gunpowder upon Hounſlow Heath.

To make good ſums payable to perſons who have ſubſcribed their capital ſtock of 3 *l. per cent.* annuities, 1,350,000 *l.*

To make good deficiencies in 1771, 42,445 *l.* 5 *s.* 5 *d.*; and not exceeding 39,456 *l.* 0 *s.* 10 *d.* to make good deficiencies of grants for 1771.

SUMS TOTAL
OF THE
SUPPLIES,
AND
WAYS AND MEANS, YEARLY,
FROM THE
REVOLUTION
TO THE
PRESENT SESSION.

		Supplies.			Ways and Means.		
		l.	*s.*	*d.*	*l.*	*s.*	*d.*
W. & M.	1688	2,908,680	—	—	2,743,142	6	2
	1689	3,668,191	10	—	3,768,191	10	—
	1690	3,656,255	—	—	2,651,702	18	—
	1691	3,676,677	16	3	1,816,702	18	—
	1692	4,017,080	9	6	2,000,000	—	—
	1693	5,549,087	15	7	5,588,506	5	10
	1694	4,882,712	—	—	5,413,709	11	1
1*st* W. III.	1695	5,537,853	19	11	8,161,469	—	—
	1696	5,520,078	19	11	5,600,000	—	—
	1697	8,237,210	18	1½	5,184,015	1	11¾
	1698	2,350,000	—	—	1,484,015	—	—
	1699	981,342	—	—	1,000,000	—	—
	1700	2,886,536	14	6	2,620,000	—	—
	1701	4,380,045	11	—	6,913,628	15	5¾

		Supplies.			Ways and Means.		
		l.	*s.*	*d.*	*l.*	*s.*	*d.*
1st Anne.	1702	3,535,457	7	2	3,887,630	—	—
	1703	4,005,369	8	6	4,200,000	—	—
	1704	4,717,488	3	4	4,914,888	3	3½
	1705	5,075,761	16	2	5,282,223	17	2
	1706	5,041,841	14	10¼	6,142,381	15	6¼
	1707	5,926,849	18	6¾	6,189,067	15	6¾
	1708	6,563,138	10	10½	6,868,839	—	—
	1709	6,425,268	10	2¼	6,896,552	9	11¾
	1710	14,370,744	5	4¾	16,246,325	—	—
	1711	6,671,386	1	10½	6,304,615	16	9½
	1712	3,520,072	10	5½	3,400,000	—	—
	1713	3,062,079	3	11	3,100,000	—	—
Geo. I.	1714	3,282,223	16	6½			
	1715	3,053,363	5	11½	7,317,751	15	6½
	1716	3,697,767	13	6¾	3,211,313	1	—
	1717	2,644,437	4	8¾	2,229,514	3	2½
	1718	2,989,109	11	10 19/20	2,735,509	3	2½
	1719	2,623,537	14	9 7/10	2,742,000	17	10¾
	1720	2,738,156	3	2 7/10	2,920,264	13	8
	1721	2,923,108	18	— 19/20	2,719,412	10	9
	1722	2,666,295	9	1½	2,600,872	13	3 4/5
	1723	1,926,551	16	11¼	1,869,220	5	2½
	1724	1,918,092	18	4	1,778,859	2	7¼
	1725	2,094,132	8	11¼	1,748,543	6	3¼
	1726	3,409,696	1	2	3,257,046	13	8¾
	1727	3,444,818	13	8½	3,139,068	15	5¾
Geo. II.	1728	4,618,947	6	7¼	4,515,757	15	—
	1729	3,634,798	7	1½	3,519,352	6	10½
	1730	2,565,462	8	6½	2,521,149	14	—½
	1731	2,902,985	15	11¼	3,007,815	18	4¾
	1732	2,002,242	11	9½	1,880,847	8	5½
	1733	2,075,307	—	11½	1,787,963	15	10½
	1734	4,014,768	6	2¾	3,978,362	10	10½
	1735	3,280,262	2	8	3,259,165	13	—
	1736	2,417,908	11	5¼	2,355,507	7	11
	1737	3,283,882	11	2¾	3,255,561	6	3
	1738	3,432,717	19	7	3,552,169	17	4
	1739	2,787,729	9	10¾	2,876,451	17	9
	1740	4,024,560	17	9	4,064,149	8	7¾
	1741	5,267,030	7	5¼	5,003,298	9	10¼
	1742	6,137,507	17	6¼	6,150,000	—	—
	1743	6,181,826	6	10¼	6,061,092	2	5¾
	1744	6,763,421	18	3½	6,586,000	—	—
	1745	6,583,194	16	6	6,571,244	13	8¾
	1746	7,385,378	4	7	7,250,000	—	—
	1747	9,954,336	17	9	9,362,508	19	2
	1748	10,620,180	9	6½	10,050,000	—	—

		SUPPLIES.			WAYS *and* MEANS.		
		l.	*s.*	*d.*	*l.*	*s.*	*d.*
	1749	5,125,736	5	3	4,750,000	—	—
	1750	4,334,323	11	3½	4,268,526	10	3½
	1751	6,194,793	1	6½	6,140,041	16	1
	1752	4,131,964	10	11¼	4,150,000	—	—
	1753	2,414,973	14	1¾	2,422,911	8	4¼
	1754	2,541,006	1	11¼	2,544,348	1	1½
	1755	4,241,004	16	4¼	4,237,966	9	5¾
	1756	6,936,496	18	11½	7,077,065	4	2
	1757	8,410,822	8	6¼	8,126,020	7	5½
	1758	10,068,540	1	1¾	11,041,848	5	—
	1759	13,108,555	1	2¼	13,033,385	—	11
	1760	15,942,217	2	8	15,852,706	9	9
Geo. III.	1761	19,213,680	15	5¼	19,101,067	10	—
	1762	18,625,046	11	9¾	18,617,825	2	8½
	1763	10,346,609	9	9	10,117,120	9	6
	1764	7,722,657	14	7	7,472,997	9	9
	1765	7,969,337	12	1	7,745,213	5	0¼
	1766	8,729,334	19	3⅝	8,632,720	—	8⅛
	1767	9,108,240	2	8⅛	8,801,725	11	3¾
	1768	8,923,185	17	4¼	8,779,614	11	1
	1769	7,317,757	3	3½	7,264,649	19	9½
	1770	7,856,929	16	10¾	7,946,588	13	8
	1771	8,111,276	13	2⅝	8,081,912	12	11¾

THE END.

INDEX.

E R R A T A.

In the margin of page 31, for chap. 1. read chap 3. In the margin of page 50, for 3 Will. and Mary 1691, read 4 Will. and Mary 1692. In the margin of page 51, for chap. 14. read chap. 5; and for chap. 1. read chap. 14. In page 57, for 51, in the third line from the bottom, read 49; and in the ſame page, for 56 in the firſt line from the bottom, read 54. In page 58, for 56 in the ſecond line, read 52. In page 63, for 53 and 58 in the ſeventh line from the bottom, read 54 and 59. In the margin of page 95, for 9 Will. read 13 Will. In the margin of page 161, for chap. 13. read chap. 3.